CONTENTS

WHY LIBERALS
WIN THE
CULTURE WARS
(Even When They Lose Elections)

WHY LIBERALS WIN THE CULTURE WARS
(Even When They Lose Elections)

The Battles That Define America
from Jefferson's Heresies to Gay Marriage

STEPHEN PROTHERO

HarperOne
An Imprint of HarperCollinsPublishers

HarperOne

HarperCollins books may be purchased for educational, business, or sales promotional use. For information, please e-mail the Special Markets Department at SPsales@harpercollins.com.

HarperCollins website: http://www.harpercollins.com

FIRST EDITION

Designed by Joseph Rutt

Library of Congress Cataloging-in-Publication Data

Names: Prothero, Stephen R. author.
Title: Why liberals win the culture wars (even when they lose elections) : the battles that define America from Jefferson's heresies to gay marriage / Stephen Prothero.
Description: First edition. | San Francisco : HarperOne, 2016. | Includes bibliographical references and index.
Identifiers: LCCN 2015024207 | ISBN 9780061571299 (hardback)
Subjects: LCSH: Politics and culture—United States—History. | Christianity and politics—United States—History. | Culture conflict—United States—History. | Liberalism—United States—History. | BISAC: RELIGION / History. | POLITICAL SCIENCE / Political Ideologies / Conservatism & Liberalism. | HISTORY / Social History.
Classification: LCC E169.1 .P924 2016 | DDC 306.20973—dc23 LC record available at http://lccn.loc.gov/2015024207

ISBN 978-0-06-157129-9

16 17 18 19 20   RRD(H)   10 9 8 7 6 5 4 3 2 1

INTRODUCTION

The Culture Wars Cycle

T HIS BOOK BEGAN A few years ago as conservative activists were turning a local zoning question about the construction of an Islamic community center in Lower Manhattan into a national furor. The proposed building wasn't exactly at Ground Zero; it was two blocks north, in an abandoned Burlington Coat Factory on Park Place. And it wasn't exactly a mosque. It was a thirteen-story Islamic community center meant to include an auditorium, swimming pool, art studio, fitness center, performing arts center, and prayer space. But when protesters dubbed it the "Ground Zero Mosque" the name stuck.

I knew there was hay to be made in conservative circles by stoking anxieties about Islam, so I was not surprised by the protests or by an incendiary ad calling the proposed project "a monument" to 9/11 terrorism and "an invitation for more."[1] But I did not expect this issue to become a centerpiece of the 2012 Republican primaries. And I was shocked to see leading figures in the Grand Old Party, including its most recent presidential and vice-presidential nominees, John McCain and Sarah Palin, enlist in the battle. Two bedrock principles of American life are religious liberty and private property, and both of these principles argued for the right of Sharif El-Gamail to develop his Park51 building. Why all the fuss?

In an effort to make sense of this controversy, I started investigating the culture wars that have preoccupied American politics for my entire adult life. As I was digging into these fights over sex and art and family and education, I quickly realized that in order to understand them I would need to explore earlier moments when Americans clashed over moral and religious questions. I would need to make sense of efforts to excommunicate "infidels," Catholics, and Mormons from the American family. I would need to explore the culture wars before "the culture wars."[2]

This book is the result of my investigations. It provides a new lens on the contemporary culture wars—a lens that views our current battles over abortion and homosexuality and Islam as part of a long story of cultural conflict dating back to the withdrawal of George Washington from political life. All too frequently, U.S. citizens have forgotten, disregarded, and twisted beyond recognition some of our highest ideals. Despite the First Amendment promise of "the free exercise of religion," many Americans have used the coercive powers of the federal government to mandate their way of life and enforce the prerogatives of their religion. Protestants have claimed that Catholics, Mormons, and Muslims do not have religious liberty rights because their alleged "religions" are actually insidious financial schemes or nefarious political enterprises. To investigate today's "Islam wars" is to wade hip deep into a sad history of bigotry and violence in which one group of Americans has repeatedly described its political opponents as enemies of the state and of God Almighty. Among the toxic by-products of the production and distribution of our culture wars is the poisonous partisanship we see today online, on television, and in Washington, DC.

Perhaps the Internet is at fault, for seducing us into spending less time with our rivals, whether on Facebook or on hyperlinked blogs that lead us from one hall of mirrors to the next. The partisan re-drawing of congressional districts may also be to blame. Either way, Republicans and Democrats are more deeply divided than ever, with roughly a third of rank-and-file party members viewing the oppos-ing party as "a threat to the well-being of the country."[3] In 2015, Rep. Randy Weber of Texas likened President Barack Obama to Hitler, and Sen. Ted Cruz, also of Texas, labeled him an "apologist for radical Islamic terrorists."[4] Meanwhile, Capitol Hill Democrats were calling their Republican colleagues "terrorists," and Repub-licans were declaiming Democrats as "radicals," "socialists," and card-carrying members of the Communist Party. No wonder the approval rating for Congress dropped to just 7 percent—lower than the popularity of root canals, head lice, and brussels sprouts.[5]

This hyperpartisanship has gotten so bad that it now infects art, sports, and even foreign policy. Companies such as Chick-fil-A and Hobby Lobby wear their conservative politics on their sleeves. And a smartphone app called BuyPartisan will help you spend your money on companies that mirror your political ideology. (Ap-parently, Dawn dish soap is Republican, and Celestial Seasonings tea is Democratic.)[6] "This is a civil war without violence," writes conservative blogger Andrew Sullivan. "And we are the two coun-tries now."[7]

This book is a historian's explanation of how this division came to be. Its purpose is not to reopen old wounds or to lay bare a sordid past. Its purpose is to make sense of contemporary American cul-ture by making sense of America's *longue durée* of culture wars. How do culture wars begin? How do they end? What can they tell us about America and Americans?

America's culture wars are not all sound and fury. They are battles over symbolic worlds. As such, they call out for cultural analysis. And though they often reveal us at our worst, their effects are not all bad. Through culture wars, from Jefferson to Obama and beyond, Americans have defined and redefined themselves.

One side has fought for a more restrictive understanding of the American family. The other has fought for a more expansive understanding. To examine their disagreements is to discover the fault lines in American society. It is also to discover how we have come to agree on many "American values"—to see what we hold dear. In the culture wars of the nineteenth century, we decided that you do not have to be a Protestant to be a real American. And in the contemporary culture wars we are coming to agree, far more quickly than most expected, that membership in the American family should not be restricted to heterosexuals. Virtually all of us will be embarrassed, ashamed even, by the arguments of some of the culture warriors in this book. Who today will defend the proposition that Thomas Jefferson's odd theology made him a traitor? Or that Catholics or Mormons cannot be patriotic Americans? But in the end the arc of our culture wars bends toward more liberty, not less. As each of our cultural battles comes to an end, we are left with a more inclusive country, with an understanding of "we the people" that reflects more of "us."

To my liberal friends, it often feels as if conservatives are winning the culture wars, in part because conservatives have been so adept at controlling the conversation—at transforming an Islamic community center into the "Ground Zero Mosque," and at turning "liberalism" and even "government" into dirty words. From this perspective, New York City mayor Michael Bloomberg was spitting into the wind when he stood in front of the Statue of Liberty in August 2010 and proclaimed that "Muslims . . . are as welcome to worship in Lower Manhattan as any other group."[8] But are conservatives really winning the nation's battles over cultural questions? Is that an accurate understanding of even our recent past?

In this book I push back against the widespread view that culture wars are nip-and-tuck contests between liberals and conservatives, with relatively equal win/loss records on each side. That is not what I discovered. In almost every case since the founding of the republic, conservatives have fired the first shots in our culture wars. Equally often, liberals have won.

Why have our political pundits so regularly missed how lopsided the culture wars have been? Because we have short memories. Because we move on. When liberals win—when anti-Mormon violence becomes a scandal or when a gin and tonic ceases to be one—both sides come to accept the new normal and conservatives move on to the next fight. A liberal win becomes part of the new status quo and eventually fades from our collective memory. No conservative today wants to disenfranchise Mormons or outlaw five o'clock cocktails. So these victories no longer even appear to be "liberal." They are simply part of what it means to be an American.

Many Culture Wars

IT IS COMMON to see the contemporary culture wars as an aberration—a time when American politics took a sharp turn down an odd road and suggestible citizens, under the hypnotic powers of President Ronald Reagan, perhaps, started to worry more about obscure religious matters than bread-and-butter economic ones. The United States is supposed to be a nation of immigrants and a nation of religions; the Statue of Liberty opens her arms to newcomers from every land, and the First Amendment guarantees every citizen religious liberty. So where there are Quran burners or mosque arsonists, the reflex is to see them as exceptional, departures from American norms of tolerance, laissez-faire, and fair play. But is cultural conflict really as un-American as pomegranate pie?

With compromises meant to smooth over differences between the states, the founders created a union that left unsettled key questions that would foment discord and even rebellion in decades to come. One concerned slavery. Another concerned religion. So American politics has always been a staging ground for moral and religious conflicts. The culture wars did not begin in the 1960s or

1970s, when most books on this topic open. They did not begin in the 1920s, as some dissenters claim. They began in the birth pangs of the republic itself. More than two centuries before Barack Obama was accused of being a covert Muslim, Thomas Jefferson was said to be a secret "believer in the alcoran [Quran]."[9]

Philosopher Horace Kallen once described the United States as an "orchestration of mankind" in which people of many different races and religions contribute to a "symphony of civilization."[10] And there *is* a strong tradition in American life of coming to the defense of religious minorities and conducting our public debates with some measure of civility (and a modicum of blood). But the United States has also been a babel of civilizations in which people of different races and religions turned the nation into something akin to Tennyson's vision of the state of nature: "red in tooth and claw." In fact, it is difficult to find moments when U.S. politics were not roiled in clashes of religious identities and moral commitments. Because Americans have not inherited an ancient culture, they have had to invent one (or many). But Americans have always disagreed about which of these inventions they should hold most dear. Even their core texts—from the Constitution to the Gettysburg Address to the Pledge of Allegiance—contradict one another. So culture here has always been hotly contested.

In fact, Americans have been engaging in the cultural equivalent of war at least since the early republic. Colonial Puritans likely played a role, by twisting God and governance tight and transforming their New World into a land of tight-jawed moralists ever on the lookout for demons in their ranks. During the American Revolution and in the first years of the republic, patriots were united in their hatred of British rule and their love of George Washington.[11] As Washington was retiring to Mount Vernon, however, Americans turned on one another in a series of culture battles about the propriety of the French Revolution and the meanings and ends of their new nation. On questions as varied as polygamy, free thought, abortion, the papacy, and the saloon (to name just a few), they denounced their fellow Americans as ungodly and immoral. In the process, they divulged competing visions of the American Dream and the American Nightmare.

Given this long history of cultural warfare, it is surprising that the contemporary culture wars took so long to settle on a name. By the time James Davison Hunter popularized the term in his 1991 bestseller *Culture Wars: The Struggle to Define America* and presidential hopeful Pat Buchanan warned delegates at the 1992 Republican National Convention that a "cultural war" was being waged "for the soul of America," American conservatives had been redirecting their energies for well over a decade from the obvious stuff of politics to bedroom ethics and school prayer.[12] The Moral Majority, founded in 1979 in an effort to inoculate American society from the immorality and ungodliness that had infected it in the 1960s, had already disbanded. And President Reagan—the George Washington of the contemporary culture wars—had begun his journey from the White House into what he would later describe as "the sunset of my life."[13]

But the culture wars are much older than the Moral Majority or the Reagan Revolution. In fact, they are nearly as old as the country itself. Many of the attacks in recent years on the narcissism and libertinism of the Swinging Sixties reprised conservative attacks on the Roaring Twenties. And many of the anti-Catholic tropes of the 1928 presidential campaign, in which Protestants claimed that a vote for Democratic candidate (and devout Catholic) Al Smith was a vote for the Antichrist, were recycled from nineteenth-century attacks on Catholics as traitors to God and country. The 2012 presidential election pitting Romney against Obama was a bare-knuckles bout, but the election of 1800 was bloodier. It, too, featured a candidate who was accused of being insufficiently Christian. In 1800, however, state militias were marshalling to march on the capital if their candidate was not declared the winner.

This book tells the story of America's culture wars in the plural. Instead of viewing U.S. history in light of military battles or political upheavals, social movements or financial cycles, it interprets that history in light of a series of cultural conflicts—moments when disagreements over God and the Good turned nasty or bloody or both.[14] These battles were in part about politics and economics. At the beginning of the republic, Jefferson and John Adams fought fiercely about the proper balance of power between the federal government and the states, just as politicians today clash over the size of government and the burden of taxation. But the election of 1800 was also (and more viscerally) about Jefferson's views of God, and one current flashpoint is Islam. Today's culture wars, this book argues, are part of a recurring pattern in U.S. history—episodes in the story of one not-so-indivisible nation forever at war with itself.

Five Episodes

THE APPROACH OF this book is episodic rather than exhaustive. It begins with America's "second revolution": the election of 1800, which pitted Congregationalist ministers and Federalist politicians against "infidels" and Jeffersonians. It understands the culture war that swirled around this election—and the rise of modern American conservatism itself—as responses to the French Revolution, which at the time served as a cultural Rorschach test. Was the nation going to include in its ranks heretics like Jefferson? And if it did, what was to prevent it from going the way of the guillotine and France's Reign of Terror? Subsequent chapters examine four additional overlapping episodes: the anti-Catholic crusade in antebellum America; anti-Mormonism before and after the Civil War; prohibition in the 1920s and 1930s; and the culture wars of the 1970s and beyond.

Neither the Civil War nor the civil rights movement commands a chapter of its own. Both *were* cultural events, rooted in moral and religious concerns. The battle between the Union and the

Confederacy grew out of a fight over the Bible and slavery, and was prompted in part by Harriet Beecher Stowe's popular 1852 novel *Uncle Tom's Cabin*, which tugged at Christian heartstrings in the years leading up to Fort Sumter. The civil rights movement was also a matter of heart and soul, as well as law and order. But race and culture, while inseparable, are nonetheless distinct, and this book focuses on the latter rather than the former. The struggles over slavery, Reconstruction, Jim Crow segregation, and mass incarceration today are first and foremost racial conflicts. And the questions that emerge out of the history of race in America differ from the questions that animate this history of the culture wars. At issue in the Civil War was whether one race of humans was to purchase, bind, transport, and sell humans of another race and, in the process, build on the scarred backs of slaves the world's largest economy. At issue in this book are such cultural matters as tolerance, inclusion, and pluralism.

Nonetheless, the trope of slavery played a key role in virtually all of the nation's culture wars, with conservatives referring to polygamy as "white slavery," Catholicism as a "slave creed," and alcohol as a slave master. Closer to our time, members of the Moral Majority described themselves as slaves suffering under the yoke of federal slave masters, and pro-lifers fancied themselves the "new abolitionists." The specter of the Civil War has also hovered over America's many culture wars, prompting South Carolina and other states to remove the Confederate battle flag from their state capitols in 2015.

Defining "Culture Wars"

SO, WHAT *IS* a culture war? In this book, the term "culture wars" refers to angry public disputes that are simultaneously moral and religious and address the meaning of America.[15] As such, they exhibit four key features:

- First, they are public disputes recorded in such sources as presidential speeches; the Congressional Record; and popular books, magazines, and newspapers.

- Second, they extend beyond economic questions of taxing and spending to moral, religious, and cultural concerns, which are typically less amenable to negotiation and compromise.

- Third, they give rise to normative questions about the meaning of *America* and who is and who is not a true *American*.

- Fourth, they are heated, fueled by a rhetoric of war and driven by the conviction that one's enemies are also enemies of the nation.

No democracy is absent of conflict. In fact, one sign of a healthy democracy is a vibrant public square where people disagree, and disagree sharply. In a country like the United States, where moral and religious differences run deep, these disagreements are naturally going to extend beyond economic or political debates. But cultural conflicts are one thing and culture wars are another. There is nothing wrong with the rowdy, little-bit-of-revolution cultural contests that made the United States a vibrant, pluralistic democracy. But, as we will see throughout this book, culture wars amplify and contort these contests, turning citizens against one another and transforming moral and religious debates into pitched battles between the forces of light and the forces of darkness.

In an effort to distinguish fundamentalists from their evangelical kin, church historian George Marsden famously defined a fundamentalist as "an evangelical who is angry about something."[16] Culture warriors are citizens who are angry about something. What sets them off is the decline of American culture and the evildoers who in their view are responsible for it. Repeatedly they resort to martial metaphors, accusations of sedition, and threats of civil war. With the defiant Reformation icon Martin Luther, they say, "Here I stand. I can do no other." And then they get about the business of another Reformation.

Given the central role played by the Religious Right in recent culture wars, it is tempting to see America's many culture wars as battles between the godless and the godly—between Jefferson and Jesus, or, to be more precise, between a vision of a largely secular public sphere in which church and state keep to themselves and a vision of an unapologetically religious public sphere in which the wall between church and state is permeable. According to free-thinker Susan Jacoby, at the "heart of the culture wars" lies this question: Is America "founded 'for man, and for man alone,'" or is it "a society singularly blessed by and answerable to God"?[17] And many conservative culture warriors see themselves as struggling for survival in a post-Christian society. The contemporary culture wars fit this bill to some extent, at least through the 2004 election, when President George W. Bush proclaimed his born-again faith from the mountaintops while Massachusetts senator and Democratic chal-lenger John Kerry seemed to be choking on a Communion wafer whenever he was asked about his Catholicism. But the United States is by no means "post-Christian," and our culture wars typically have been intrareligious affairs, pitting religious folks against religious folks: Protestants against Catholics, for example, in both the "Bible wars" of the 1840s and the alcohol wars of the 1920s and 1930s.

The real combatants in America's culture wars are conservatives and liberals. Of course, the meanings of these terms are not stable over time. Liberalism has cycled through many incarnations in American life: a laissez-faire Enlightenment liberalism wary of state power and zealous for individual liberty (see Thomas Jefferson); a progressive liberalism intent on using state power to tame the ill effects of industrial capitalism (see Franklin Delano Roosevelt); and a postwar liberalism focused on individual rights and equality (see Barack Obama).[18] Conservatism, too, has shape-shifted, taking its stand both for and against the national parks, the Equal Rights Amendment, and Romneycare/Obamacare, depending on which conservative principles were being emphasized (or overlooked) at the time. Compounding this problem is the fact that liberals and conservatives have traditionally defined themselves in contrast to each other, so when liberals shift on a particular policy (or principle), conservatives often adjust in turn.

Given these shifting sands, left–right battle lines in the culture wars can be hard to draw and harder to find. Those who argued for prohibition, for example, seem liberal in their commitment to social reform. Yet they seem conservative in their emphasis on social order over individual liberty. Still, conservatism and liberalism have been around in one incarnation or another at least since news of the French Revolution alit on American shores, and most modern readers can recognize both when they see them without undue difficulty.

In this book, my focus is on cultural conservatism and cultural liberalism. I understand cultural conservatism to be characterized by (a) anxiety over beloved forms of life that are passing away, (b) a commitment to restore what has been lost, and (c) an effort to exclude from full cultural citizenship those who are responsible for this loss. I understand cultural liberalism to be characterized by (a) an eagerness to embrace new forms of culture, (b) a belief in progress, and (c) a determination to include more and more groups in the public life of the nation. Cultural conservatism, in short, is centripetal. It posits a shared center in American culture and carefully enforces its boundaries. Cultural liberalism is centrifugal, forever spinning off new forms of culture and including them in the mix. Assuming William Butler Yeats was right—that "things fall apart; the centre cannot hold"—the key question is what you make of the rupture. Liberals find the "turning and turning in the widening gyre" (Yeats again) thrilling—a portent of something new (and better) to come. Conservatives find it dangerous—a threat to social order and intellectual coherence. Here Jefferson's famous confession to Abigail Adams ("I like a little rebellion now and then. It is like a storm in the Atmosphere."[19]) is liberal. John Adams's fear of democracy as a threat to social order ("Democracy never lasts long. It soon wastes, exhausts, and murders itself."[20]) is conservative.

Conservative Instigators and Liberal Winners

AS I RESEARCHED pivotal moments in American history—from the exploits of Federalists and Jeffersonians to evangelicals and Catholics, "wets" and "drys," and "pro-choice" and "pro-life" advocates—I made two main discoveries. Both surprised me.

The first is that America's culture wars are conservative projects, instigated and waged disproportionately by conservatives anxious about the loss of old orders and the emergence of new ones. What liberals see as progress, they see as loss. And they are willing to fight to defend what is already passing away. Culture wars *are* battles between conservatives and liberals over conflicting cultural, moral, and religious goods. But at a deeper level, they are conservative dramas in which liberals are merely props. If liberals weren't there, conservatives would have to invent them (and, truth be told, they often do).

There is much debate over whether America's recent culture wars began on the left or the right—almost as much debate as there is over what the terms "liberal" and "conservative" mean. Many liberals argue that "the sixties liberation movements—the New Left, broadly construed—lobbed the first shots in the culture wars."[21] This argument is also a staple among conservatives who blame the Left for starting the culture wars by banning prayer from the public schools, pushing for multiculturalism in the universities, or agitating for feminism or black power. Conservatives are merely defending their turf. "I object to the suggestion, which I see everywhere, that conservative Christians started the culture wars," writes fantasy author Lars Walker. "Say what you like. We're the Indians. You're the settlers."[22]

There *were* 1960s radicals who saw "the man" as a mortal enemy and talked about a revolution. So there is some sense to seeing Reagan-era cultural conservatives as "counterrevolutionaries" in a cultural war started by 1960s protesters.[23] But this narrative owes much to liberal nostalgia and even more to right-sided spin. In the imaginations of today's cultural conservatives, feminists in the 1960s were bra burners: angry activists who hated not only men but also the traditional family (and probably America itself). And some feminists were radicals. But many were not. In fact, many were moderate Republicans who voted for Richard Nixon in 1968 and 1972. Every four years from 1940 to 1976 the GOP platform endorsed the Equal Rights Amendment, which was ratified by Texas, Tennessee, and Kentucky—states rarely associated with liberal elites.

A longer view reveals that conservatives typically fire the first shots in our culture wars. Anti-Catholicism and anti-Mormonism were not backlash movements against revolutions from the left. They were right-wing reactions to Catholic immigration and Mormon migration, and to the moral, theological, social, and economic threats those communities posed to Protestant power. Similarly, the culture wars of the 1920s and 1930s were conservative responses to the rise of the saloon and the speakeasy—to mixed drinks and interracial mixing—and to the cultural pluralism brought on by rapid urbanization and immigration waves. Many now view the culture of victimhood so visible on the right—in Bill O'Reilly's war on the so-called War on Christmas, for example—as a pale imitation of the victimhood culture of left-wing identity politics. But this tradition goes back much further—to Protestants who saw themselves as victims of Deism in 1800, of Catholicism in the 1830s and 1840s, and of Mormonism before and after the Civil War.

Those who insist that the contemporary culture wars started on the left can point to angry radicals—black power advocates are one example—who wanted to fundamentally transform American society and, in so doing, resorted to a discourse of war. But they miss this crucial fact: cultural conservatives do not need a revolution to go to war. All they need is enough change to activate the anxiety that their world is passing away. This anxiety *can* be activated by a cultural revolution. But immigration can also do the trick. Or a Supreme Court opinion. Or a talk show host. In the call-and-response of the culture wars, conservatives almost always issue the call. Liberals do the responding.

As conservative projects, culture wars are not just instigated by the Right, however. They are also waged disproportionately by the Right. The metaphor of war conjures up two relatively equal sides—blue coats and red coats, perhaps, advancing on each other in relatively equal numbers. But most of the shots in the Concords and Lexingtons of our culture wars were fired by those who had the most to lose as the nation opened its borders to Irish and Italian Catholics and its arms to gays and lesbians. To be sure, the Left responded in each case and provoked skirmishes of its own. But if you are looking for the "infatuation with violence" (both real and imagined) that characterizes the culture wars, you are going to find it more often and more floridly on the right.[24] It is the Right that is enamored of the rhetoric of war. Culture war is its invention, and its signature mode of politics. From the French Revolution forward, the rhetoric of cultural decline is *the* most characteristic (and consistent) way American conservatives have expressed their conservatism. So it should not be surprising that the annals of anxiety that give voice to America's culture wars are weighted heavily toward thinkers on the right—to Federalists and fundamentalists worried about God withdrawing his blessing from America if its voters elect the "infidel" Jefferson or continue to aid and abet the "holocaust" of the unborn.

Many have attempted to reduce modern conservatism to anti-intellectualism, but modern conservatism has at its heart an idea.

That idea is not states' rights or individual liberty or free markets or limited government or federalism, however. Over the course of U.S. history, conservatives have argued for and against all these principles. The "big idea" behind modern conservatism is this: a form of culture is passing away and it is worth fighting to revive it. What activates this idea, transforming it into action, is a feeling. This feeling is akin to nostalgia, but it runs deeper and is more fierce. As America's first conservatives looked across the Atlantic to Paris, they saw the French Revolution not as a victory of equality over hierarchy but as a victory of chaos over order. They feared their own Reign of Terror. So as they fought to restore their beloved past (real or imagined), they turned fellow citizens who supported the French into enemies, and they labored to banish those enemies from the American family, sometimes via argument but also via force.[25]

Animated by this narrative of loss and restoration, modern American conservatism has elective affinities with modern evangelicalism, which also offers meaning amid uncertainty via narratives of loss and restoration—of lost souls at revivals and of a "Christian America" stolen away by secularists. Modern conservatism has elective affinities with biblical narratives, too. As Adam and Eve look over their shoulders on their expulsion from Eden—as they mourn their loss and plot its reversal—they become the first conservatives.

My second discovery was that America's culture wars are won by liberals. If culture wars are conservative dramas produced and directed by conservatives, then we should expect liberals to be assigned the bit parts. What is unexpected is how these carefully orchestrated dramas end. Gays and lesbians get marriage. An "infidel" (Jefferson) and then a "papist" (Kennedy) get the White House. Nearly as predictably as night follows day, those who declare war on "infidels" or Catholics or the sins of the 1920s or the abominations of the 1960s go down in defeat.

Liberals win because they typically have the force of American traditions on their side, not least the force of the Bill of Rights itself, which on any fair reading protects the rights of minorities against the impositions of majorities. Liberals also win because the causes conservatives pick to rev up their supporters are, surprisingly, lost from the start. Culture wars begin with an anxiety.[26] This anxiety—about the demise of the patriarchal family or Anglo-American dominance or "Christian America"—is then expressed in two forms: first, as a narrower complaint about a specific public policy; second, as a broader lament about how badly the nation has fallen from its founding glory and how desperately it is in need of deliverance.

But this is what is most surprising: the fight is fiercest when the cause at hand is already well on its way to being lost. For example, conservatives mobilize against Catholics only when it is becoming clear that the Catholic population is growing too quickly to remain on the margins; they attack same-sex marriage only when attitudes toward homosexuality have gravitated toward acceptance. In other words, conservatives typically choose for their rallying cries causes that are already on the verge of being lost.

This dynamic is easy to miss if you are looking merely at winners and losers on Election Day. U.S. electoral politics have toggled back and forth in recent generations between Democratic and Republican control, so one might assume that our culture wars play out in the same way, with relatively evenly distributed victories and losses. But that is not the case. If we focus on the fate of particular cultural battles—over Catholics or Mormons or abortion or alcohol or same-sex marriage—then we see that, over time, cultural politics have tilted to the left.

This does not mean that the United States is more progressive on moral and religious questions than European countries. In fact, polls show that Americans are typically more culturally conservative than Europeans. When asked in a 2013 survey "Should society accept homosexuality?" 88 percent of respondents in Spain said yes as did 77 percent in France, compared with just 60 percent in the United States.[27] So the argument of this book is not comparative. It is simply that when any given cultural battle comes to an end, liberals almost always come out the winners. "All conservatism begins with loss," writes Andrew Sullivan.[28] At least when it comes to America's culture wars, conservatism *ends* with loss, too.

The Culture Wars Cycle

AS I INVESTIGATED the story of America's culture wars from Jefferson to Obama, I discovered a "culture wars cycle" that propels the nation from one cultural conflict to the next. Again and again, our religious and cultural battles follow this same pattern. The culture wars cycle begins on the right, with conservatives anxious about some cultural change they are experiencing as loss. This catalyst is different in each case. During the election of 1800, which was held amid the aftershocks of the French Revolution, Federalists were worried about their country falling into chaos. During the anti-Catholic and anti-Mormon culture wars, Protestants were worried about the emerging public power of immigrants and non-Protestants. The drama of prohibition and repeal was about alcohol, of course, but it was activated by an anxiety about the "blooming, buzzing confusion" of modern life, including the greatest immigration wave in U.S. history and a massive population shift from mono-cultural towns to multicultural cities.[29] In the contemporary culture wars, conservatives give voice to their anxieties about the multiplicity of families, religions, and ethnicities. In the face of these anxieties, conservatives launch an attack, blaming their political opponents for the losses they are experiencing and for threatening the health and welfare of the nation. The result is a long primal scream against the rise of "them" in the name of "us."

After the Right strikes out, the Left strikes back. In this second stage in the culture wars cycle, liberals launch a counterattack, either by defending the contested change as a positive good or (more often) by appealing to the American principle of liberty to insist that U.S. citizens have every right to secure an abortion or to drink beer after work or to run for office without pledging their allegiance to Jesus.

Next comes some sort of accommodation. Culture wars *are* characterized by a rhetoric of "no compromise"—by appeals to moral absolutes and unchanging divine commandments. They are rarely resolved without some sort of negotiation, however. Catholicism came to be accepted as a legitimate American religion only after Catholics accepted the separation of church and state. Mormons became exemplary Americans only after they had renounced polygamy.

In the fourth stage, liberals win. Culture wars may be conservative dramas, but at the curtain call liberals take the big bows. Conservative efforts to exclude Catholics or Mormons or gays and lesbians from the American family fail, and the United States becomes as a result a more inclusive nation. But this is why liberals today do not feel so victorious. Causes once labeled "liberal" become "American values," embraced by liberals and conservatives alike. And the arc of American history bends a little more toward inclusion and toleration.

How can this be? In a nation that seems so evenly divided between left and right, and in recent years so politically polarized, how can liberals win these cultural battles so consistently? Liberals may win for constitutional reasons (because the American principle of liberty is on their side or because the Bill of Rights protects minorities) or for practical reasons (because a "majority minority" nation is around the corner). But the most important reason they win is because their opponents attach themselves to lost causes. In culture wars from 1800 to today, conservatives picked fights they were already losing. This strategy makes no sense if the goal is to win a particular cultural battle. But that is not the goal of culture warriors. Their goal is to stand erect in the pulpit, to preach a gospel of the fallen and the lost, and, in so doing, to demonstrate just how far

America has descended from the glory of its founding, and just how urgently it requires revival, recovery, and restoration.

There are always culture warriors who want to retire after losing a big fight. Writing after the Supreme Court's landmark decision supporting gay marriage in 2015, columnist David Brooks called on his fellow conservatives to "put aside a culture war that has alienated large parts of three generations from any consideration of religion or belief."[30] But for many conservatives any given loss simply energizes them for the next conflict, not least because it confirms their sacred status as martyrs. Having lost one culture war, they become even more convinced that American society is going to hell. So they cast about for another grievance. They hang on fiercely to something else that is precious and passing away. And the culture wars cycle begins anew.

As the fight over the "Ground Zero Mosque" escalated, local planning authorities voted 29 to 1 to allow the project to go forward and New York City's Landmarks Preservation Commission supported the developers in a 9 to 0 vote. After the 2012 Republican primaries, however, this controversy largely faded from view. In 2014, the owners of the property announced their intention to turn the site into an Islamic museum, and today they are free to develop it largely unmolested. The broader Islam wars are still being fought, however. In fact, they have intensified, with Republicans vying for the 2016 presidential nomination stirring up the specter of creeping Shariah law in the United States and Islamophobia becoming, according to some, the new "acceptable racism."[31]

If we look at this battle over Islam through the lens of the culture wars cycle, it is fair to predict that this, too, shall pass. Cultural conservatives will likely continue to rage over the threats posed by Islam to the American way of life, but eventually the Muslim population will become large enough, the American principle of liberty will resound loudly enough, and Muslims will be included in the American family alongside Protestants, Catholics, and Mormons.

How can we be confident this is how the Islam wars will likely play out? Because we have been here before. Because Catholics and Mormons ran a similar gantlet. Because even Thomas Jefferson, one of the nation's preeminent founding fathers, found himself banished from the American family by conservatives anxious about the terrors of unfaithful France storming American shores.

1

The Jefferson Wars

M OST OF US LIVE in our own world rather than the world that brought it into being, so we tend to assume that our problems are unprecedented. The rage on the right that descended over the United States upon Barack Obama's 2009 inauguration—the analogies to Nazism and socialism, the questioning of the president's citizenship, the insistence that he was a Muslim ("Islamapologist-in-Chief")—seemed to many on the left to be wholly new.[1] But American politics has always been infused with the animal spirits of morality and religion, which when mixed have created a volatile cocktail: an absolutist politics of good and evil in which anxiety is palpable, compromise is elusive, and the metaphors are martial—culture as war. For this sort of politics, nothing tops the presidential elections of 1796 and 1800, when political feuds led to fisticuffs and founding fathers denounced one another as enemies of the state.

Here, just years after the founding, we see the culture wars cycle start to spin. Conservatives in John Adams's Federalist Party attacked Thomas Jefferson's religion. Jeffersonians in the Democratic-Republican Party—the liberals in this fight—counterattacked. According to the Constitution, there can be no religious test for the presidency. But can voters impose one? Is the United States a religiously plural nation with a godless Constitution? Or is it a Christian nation under the watchful eye of the Endower of unalienable rights? But the questions in this culture war were not confined to theology (or theocracy). They concerned as well the passing away of a society of white, Protestant, New England men—a hierarchical society rooted in colonial Puritanism, held together by a culture of deference, supported by clerical and business elites, and governed by the wise, the virtuous, and the wealthy. The cultural commitments of this society, in which free citizens turned out to vote on Election Day only to agree to be governed by their betters, included "pride of race, distrust of money-getting men, fears of 'leveling,' and suspicion of aliens."[2] Preserving these values was the Federalists' lost cause.

The American Revolution had let loose a torrent of egalitarianism and diversity. The Jeffersonians tapped into that centrifugal force, directing its expansive energies into party politics. The Federalists, defenders of a waning centripetal order (an ancien régime of their own), were determined to hold this torrent back—to stanch rule by "the worthless, the dishonest, the rapacious, the vile, the merciless and the ungodly."[3] Jefferson they saw as a Jacobin from the South, the standard-bearer of a foreign culture of impiety, vice, and guttersnipe party politics.

As they fought over competing visions of their new republic—as they struggled to determine what America was to become—Federalists and Jeffersonians debated not only who should be included in the American family but also who should lead it. Those who cast their ballots in the elections of 1796 and 1800 would not settle these questions for all time, but they would decide that even heretics like Jefferson could be patriots. In fact, they could be president.

Patriot King

DURING THE AMERICAN Revolution, colonists had come together to oppose England's King George III, whom they accused in their Declaration of Independence of "a long train of abuses . . . scarcely paralleled in the most barbarous ages." When that war was over— after Paul Revere had concluded his midnight ride, and the minute- men were done firing on the redcoats at Lexington and Concord, and town criers had read every word of the Declaration aloud, and the ink on the Treaty of Paris had dried, and the tea floating in Boston Harbor had been eaten by fish who were then eaten by free citizens—Americans united under a different man. The general who had crossed the Delaware and endured that horrible winter at Valley Forge was revered as president when representatives of "we the people" gathered in Philadelphia in the summer of 1787 to craft a Constitution in order to form "a more perfect union."

This union would never be perfect, of course, and the vexed com- promises that attended the drafting of the Constitution—between federal and state power, between a more aristocratic Senate and a more democratic House, between slaveholding and antislavery states, and between proponents and opponents of established religion—by no means buried the differences. In fact, they were the seeds of bitter partisan fruit to come. Nonetheless, in its early years the United States largely lived up to its motto: e pluribus unum ("out of many, one"). And the magician behind that sleight of hand was the Great Unifier, George Washington.

This "Patriot King" won the presidency by acclamation in 1788 and 1792, but long before and after his eight-year reign, he was *the* father among the founders, a symbol of the unity of the states and the unifying icon of the nation that would come to grace its capital city with his name.[4] America's patriarch did more than symbol- ize national unity, however. He labored to foster moderation and civility in his own cabinet and beyond. Jefferson and Alexander

Hamilton—the two great thinkers serving under Washington—were, according to Jefferson, "daily pitted in the cabinet like two cocks."[5] They fought about such matters as a national bank and the French Revolution, and about the ideas—liberty, equality, republicanism—that were coming to define America. In an August 23, 1792, letter to Jefferson, Washington begged for "charity for the opinions and acts of one another in governmental matters."[6] Three days later, in a letter to Hamilton, he pleaded for a "middle course"—for "mutual forbearances and temporising yieldings on all sides." "Without these," Washington wrote, "I do not see how the Reins of Government are to be managed, or how the Union of the States can be much longer preserved."[7]

Washington did manage to hold the union together, but his vision of a politics of civility and moderation, free of "party animosities,"[8] proved to be quixotic as the nation split for the first time into a political Left (the Jeffersonians) and a political Right (the Federalists). Historians disagree on the temperature of the partisanship that flared up during Washington's second term, but nearly all resort to metaphors of combustion to describe, as one put it, "the partisan fires that blazed like a raging inferno" through much of the 1790s.[9]

The French Revolution, which saw the storming of the Bastille in 1789 and the guillotining of Louis XVI and Marie Antoinette in 1793, stoked that inferno, as partisans of British-loving Federalists, on the one hand, and French-loving Jeffersonians, on the other, worked the bellows from both sides. But domestic crises also roiled the nation. Washington's decision to meet the antitax resistance movement known as the Whiskey Rebellion with force—he led a militia of nearly thirteen thousand men (larger than the army he commanded in the Revolution) into western Pennsylvania in 1794—and then to denounce the rebels as "incendiaries of public peace and order,"[10] cheered Federalists keen on a strong federal government. But this show of force angered Democratic-Republicans ever wary of centralized military and economic power.

After deciding not to seek a third presidential term, Washington published a farewell address on September 19, 1796. Solemnly warning "against the baneful effects of the spirit of party," he described the emergent party system as the "worst enemy" of government and factionalism as a sort of hell: a "fire not to be quenched," in his paraphrase of the Gospel of Mark (9:44-48). Of the spirit of party, he wrote:

It serves always to distract the public councils and enfeeble the public administration. It agitates the community with ill-founded jealousies and false alarms, kindles the animosity of one part against another, foments occasionally riot and insurrection. It opens the door to foreign influence and corruption, which finds a facilitated access to the government itself through the channels of party passions.

Long before Washington had retired to Mount Vernon, however, efforts to "discourage and restrain" the "mischiefs of the spirit of party" had failed.[11] As the refined Deism of the founding period gave way to evangelical enthusiasm, the unquenchable fire of partisan politics burst into flames during the election of 1796, and during the election of 1800 those flames threatened to consume the nation. The political battle between Federalists on the right and Democratic-Republicans on the left turned into a cosmic battle between God and the devil, and America's first culture war was on.

Election of 1796

IN BOTH OF these pivotal elections—1796 and 1800—the principals were John Adams, who had served as vice president under Washington, and Thomas Jefferson, who had been Washington's secretary of state. The parties were Adams's Federalists, who had run the country from the start, and Jefferson's Democratic-

Republicans, who drew their strength from an odd combination of religious minorities (Baptists and Methodists) and nascent Democratic-Republican societies committed to citizen liberty. The elephant in the room was the French Revolution, which had produced, first, a Reign of Terror that had left tens of thousands dead and, later, a dechristianization campaign that sought to break the chain of memory between the French people and their Roman Catholic past by seizing church lands, forcing priests and nuns to marry, and rechristening the Notre-Dame Cathedral the Temple of Reason. The French Revolution also produced modern Anglo-American conservatism, classically articulated in Edmund Burke's *Reflections on the Revolution in France* (1790). In the United States, events in France alarmed Federalists and inspired a Gothic literature that would resurface in later fights over Catholicism, Mormonism, and slavery. In this case, conservatives prophesied streets of blood, fields of corpses, and guillotined heads if their ordered culture of deference were displaced by the Jeffersonians' anarchic culture of radical egalitarianism. Jefferson was according to the Federalists the gateway drug to this "terrorism," and to the unbelief that had made it all possible. According to many Democratic-Republicans, however, it was Adams who was opening the "sluices of terrorism"—by supplanting liberty and democracy with aristocracy and monarchy.[12]

America's first culture war would eventually extend to a battle on the House floor (instigated by a shot of tobacco spit to the eye) between a Connecticut Federalist brandishing a hickory cane and a Vermont Democratic-Republican wielding fireplace tongs; a deadly pistol duel between a former secretary of the treasury and a sitting vice president; and all manner of rumors, lies, and conspiracy theories. It would be aided and abetted by increased political activity and an expanding public square, which saw the nation's newspapers swell from under one hundred to well over two hundred during the 1790s.

Virtually all of these newspapers were unapologetically partisan, "delighting and indulging in all manner of abusive, extravagant, witty, hyperbolic, outrageous, obscene, and *ad hominem* attacks."[13] The discourse that energized this expanding public square sounded more like Bill O'Reilly on FOX News in the 2010s than Edward Murrow on CBS in the 1950s. (The Federalist *Gazette of the United States* called Jeffersonians "the very *refuse* and *filth* of society" while the Democratic-Republican *Philadelphia Aurora* judged Adams "blind, bald, crippled, toothless."[14]) It spread via its own sort of web, which extended in this case to popular pamphlets and not-so-private letters (the blogs of the day), all circulating through close to one thousand post offices (up from only seventy-five at the start of the 1790s).[15] In these media, everyone was spinning for one cause or another. "Public discussions" in this era, Jefferson later observed, "were conducted by the parties with animosity, a bitterness, and an indecency, which had never been exceeded."[16] Or as *Niles' Weekly Register* put it, "They called us 'jacobins'—we called them 'tories'—they called us 'Frenchmen' and we called them 'Englishmen'; and, with the use of these repulsive terms, we could not come together, in peace, on any public occasion."[17]

Even Washington came under not-so-friendly fire. "If ever a nation was debauched by a man, the American nation has been debauched by Washington; if ever a nation was deceived by a man, the American nation has been deceived by Washington," editor Benjamin Franklin Bache wrote in his *Aurora* shortly before Washington's retirement.[18] After Washington stepped down, Bache added that "every heart in unison with the freedom and happiness of the people, ought to beat high with exultation that the name of Washington from this day ceases to give a currency to political iniquity, and to legalize corruption."[19] Such invective earned Bache a beating, both literally and otherwise. Federalist journalist William Cobbett called him "a liar; a fallen wretch; a vessel formed for reprobation" before concluding that "therefore we should always treat him as we would a TURK, a JEW, a JACOBIN or a DOG."[20] Bache was also physically attacked, both in his offices and in the Philadelphia streets. He was later arrested for "libeling the President & the Executive Government, in a manner tending to excite sedition."[21] He died of yellow fever while awaiting trial.

The election of 1796, America's first real presidential race, pitted Adams and Thomas Pinckney of the Federalists against Jefferson and Aaron Burr of the Democratic-Republicans. Adams and Jefferson were once close friends, and as was customary at the time, neither campaigned. Jefferson sequestered himself at his Monticello estate in Virginia; Adams stayed close to home near Boston, Massachusetts. So neither delivered any stump speeches or kissed any babies. Their partisans pulled no punches, however, and thought nothing of hitting below the belt. The future of America was at stake, and the two parties had opposing visions.

Led by Hamilton, who would later find his way onto the ten-dollar bill, the Federalists backed a strong national bank, a strong executive branch, a strong judiciary, and a strong Senate. Though they agreed not to use federal power to support any Protestant denomination, they supported state religious establishments, such as Episcopalianism in South Carolina and Congregationalism in Connecticut. In disputes between England and France, they sided with England, and they mistrusted all who trusted godless France. Elitists at heart, they feared mob rule and believed in government by the best and the brightest. Their key words were "security," "order," and "stability," and they believed that deference to the well born, well bred, well read, and well wed was essential to each. Federalists blasted their opponents as France-loving anarchists willing and eager to sacrifice social order on the altar of liberty. So they recoiled when Jefferson responded to an antitax revolt in Massachusetts called Shays's Rebellion by writing (to John Adams's wife, Abigail), "I like a little revolution now and then."[22] The Federalists also presented themselves as the anti-party party, anxious, like Washington, about "the mischiefs of the spirit of party." But that was just their way of playing partisan politics—an effort to disqualify Jeffersonians on procedural grounds before the fighting began.

Unlike the Federalists, who were popular with New England merchants, the Jeffersonians were popular with Southern farmers. They favored agriculture over industry and commerce. They preached low taxes, limited government, and popular sovereignty. They opposed a national bank. If the Federalists feared the tyranny of the people, Jeffersonians feared the tyranny of government (though, it should be noted, their emphasis on majority rule extended only to white males with property). Jeffersonians read the controversial Jay Treaty, negotiated in 1794 with England by Supreme Court Chief Justice John Jay, as a betrayal of the Declaration of Independence—proof positive of the Federalists' secret passion for monarchy and aristocracy. Their key word was "liberty," which in their view could be secured only by representative government, states' rights, and separation of the federal government from church life. According to Jefferson, Federalists were Tories in disguise—"an Anglican, monarchical and aristocratical party" consisting of "timid men who prefer the calm of despotism to the boisterous sea of liberty."[23]

In retrospect, the gap between these two parties seems to have been bridgeable. Yes, they called on different strains of American identity, with Federalists tapping into Massachusetts Bay Colony governor John Winthrop's call in his *Arbella* sermon for organic order and Jeffersonians stressing "the sacred cause of liberty."[24] They disagreed on foreign policy, religion's role in political life, the right size of the federal government, and the proper burden of taxation. Still, they might have found room for compromise. They might have seen in the election of 1796 different interpretations of shared ideals rather than a black-and-white battle between good and evil. The individual liberty so prized by Jeffersonians and the social order coveted by Federalists are plainly needs of all modern societies. And both parties understood that the Constitution secured some mix of states' rights and federal power. So they were arguing over the recipe, not the ingredients. Nonetheless, each side was quick to see its opponents as agents of foreign powers, traitors to the nation, and betrayers of Revolution and Constitution alike. In this way, they led the United States into its first and most florid culture war.

Today Jefferson's face adorns Mount Rushmore alongside Washington, Lincoln, and Theodore Roosevelt. He is lauded for inventing the nation (as the principal author of the Declaration of Independence) and then reinventing it (via the Louisiana Purchase, which set the country on its march to the Pacific). Yet even in 1796 he had enjoyed a long and distinguished career in public service. In fact, his credentials—delegate to the Continental Congress, governor of Virginia, envoy to France, secretary of state—were surpassed only by Washington himself.

Nonetheless, Federalists attacked him as un-American. An unmanly coward and a woolly intellectual, Jefferson had turned tail in Monticello in 1781 rather than face British invaders, they argued. His talents were largely literary and scientific, and his thoughts ran to abstract philosophy, not pragmatic politics. Federalists also attacked Jefferson as a traitor, a stealth abolitionist, a cheat in business, an erstwhile dictator, and a spendthrift who ran up massive personal debts. They even blamed him for the bitterness of the new party politics, on the theory that the Federalists were the only party the United States needed or could endure. South Carolina Federalist Robert Goodloe Harper called Jefferson "a weak, wavering, indecisive character," fit, perhaps, "to be a professor in a College, President of a Philosophical Society, or even Secretary of State; but certainly not the first magistrate of a great nation."[25]

The lowest blows concerned Jefferson's faith. Federalists read his call for national church–state separation—his disestablishmentarianism—as a fig leaf over his alleged atheism. He was, after all, a friend of Thomas Paine, that "filthy little atheist" (Theodore Roosevelt's words) who had described the religions of the world as "human inventions, set up to terrify and enslave mankind, and monopolize power and profit."[26] Federalists were committed to preserving a uniform and hierarchical social order, which rested on a culture of deference. So their attacks on Jefferson's faith were not just attacks on heresy. They were defenses of clerical elites.

This fight for Federalist culture was made urgent by the terrors of the French Revolution, which illustrated to many conservatives what happened when a society gave up on God and deference. To be an American, in their view, was to oppose the godlessness and "leveling" of the French Revolution. By this measure, Jefferson was no American. "We are not Frenchmen," wrote a critic from Connecticut, "and until the Atheistical Philosophy of a certain great Virginian shall become the fashion (which God in his mercy forbid) we shall never be."[27]

When the vitriol gave way to voting, Adams won 71 electoral votes to Jefferson's 68. According to historian Jeffrey Pasley, this election established two key precedents:

> It set the geographic pattern of New England competing with the South at the two extremes of American politics with the geographically intermediate states deciding between them. It established the basic ideological dynamic of a democratic, rights-spreading American "left" arranged against a conservative, social order–protecting "right," each with its own competing model of leadership.[28]

Today New England is associated with the Left and the South with the Right, but in 1796 these roles were reversed: New England (where Jefferson won zero electoral votes) was the homeland of the Federalists, and the South (where Adams garnered only two votes) was the homeland of the Democratic-Republicans.

Washington's Apotheosis

TWO YEARS AFTER this 1796 election, Rev. Timothy Dwight, Yale's president and a staunch Federalist, was still preaching a politics of fear and anxiety. Should the "enemies of Christ" (the Democratic-Republicans) ever come to power, he prophesied, America could well see the end of both religion and family:

> We may see the Bible cast into a bonfire, . . . our children, either wheedled or terrified, uniting in the mob, chanting mockeries against God . . . our wives and daughters the victims of legal prostitution; soberly dishonoured; speciously polluted; the outcasts of delicacy and virtue, and the lothing of God and man.[29]

That same year, Jefferson, in a letter to his daughter Martha, lamented the "rancorous passions" of even women in Philadelphia: "Politics and party hatreds destroy the happiness of every being here."[30] Virginia's Patrick Henry, in his last public speech, delivered in March 1799, tried (in vain) to cool this partisan fever. "United we stand, divided we fall," he said. "Let us not split into factions which must destroy that union upon which our existence hangs. Let us preserve our strength for the French, the English, the Germans, or whoever else shall dare invade our territory, and not exhaust it in civil commotions and intestine wars."[31]

A few months later, Washington fell ill after riding a horse through a snowstorm. On December 14, 1799, after a series of ineffectual treatments, including the draining of perhaps half of his blood, the only man who had any chance of uniting this no longer indivisible nation was gone. There was grief, of course, and thirty days of official mourning after "the Father of His Country" spoke his final words ("'Tis well.").[32]

But all was not well. America's seat of government was moving

at the time from Philadelphia to the "Federal City in the District
of Columbia." Washington's secretary of treasury Oliver Wolcott Jr.
complained that there was "no industry, society, or business" there.
"Most of the inhabitants are low people," he wrote, "and as far as
I can judge, they live like fishes, by eating each other."[33] And so it
went with the politicians maneuvering to move there. As the election of 1800 loomed and Washington metamorphosed into memory,
America remained dangerously divided.

Election of 1800

THE ELECTION OF 1800 was a turning point in U.S. history.[34] It
pitted a president against a vice president. It took negative campaigning to historic lows. It ended in a tie that produced a constitutional crisis. And it bequeathed to subsequent generations the ways
and means of the culture wars.

There were some new issues. Congress had voted in May 1798
for a "Provisional Army" of ten thousand soldiers and in July of that
same year for an "Additional Army" of twelve infantry regiments
and six mounted infantry companies—all to combat a possible invasion by France, which had been making sport of capturing American
ships. But Democratic-Republicans feared that the mustering of
these forces was one giant step toward a standing army, which might
be used against their fellow citizens. Also hotly debated were the
Alien and Sedition Acts of 1798, which outlawed the publication
of "any false, scandalous and malicious writing" against the U.S.
government or its elected officials and empowered the president to
deport almost any foreigner for almost any reason.

As in later culture wars, conservatives scapegoated immigrants as
"hordes of ruffians" and "revolutionary vermin."[35] Washington had
justified legislation against these undesirables by accusing them of
"poisoning the minds of our people, and sowing dissensions among
them."[36] Jeffersonians had responded by accusing the Federalists

of attempting to "excite a fervor against foreign aggression only to establish tyranny at home."[37] They then passed resolutions in Kentucky (written by Jefferson) and Virginia (written by James Madison) declaring these acts unconstitutional and therefore null and void.

Federalists, meanwhile, accused their opponents of sedition. But with each arrest for this crime—twenty-five in total, almost all of them of Jeffersonian journalists—came a growing outcry that the Federalists were abusing their power. According to Democratic-Republicans, these arrests betrayed not only the Spirit of 1776 but also the First Amendment of 1791 by, in essence, outlawing the opposition press.

None of these new issues changed the basic conflict, however. Once again, it was Adams and the Federalists versus Jefferson and the Democratic-Republicans. Once again, each side resorted to battlefield metaphors to describe the contest. (Federalist John Ward Fenno called it "a warfare of confusion against order, an insurrection of every vile propensity, against every good."[38])

The election of 1796 had been held in the aftermath of the Reign of Terror and the beheading of Louis XVI. This time the news of the day was the November 9, 1799, coup d'état of Napoleon Bonaparte. Democratic-Republicans pointed to rising navy and army appropriations as proof that the United States was aping France's military dictatorship. Again, Federalist rhetoric approached the apocalyptic. "Behold France, that open hell, still ringing with agonies and blasphemies, still smoking with sufferings and crimes, in which we see their state of torment, and perhaps our future state," wrote Massachusetts Federalist Fisher Ames. If the "mobocracy" should triumph, "the people would be crushed, as in France, under tyranny more vindictive, unfeeling, and rapacious, than that of Tiberius, Nero, or Caligula."[39]

Character assassination persisted, but this time the smears were more partisan and more personal, with the Federalist *Connecticut*

Courant telling its readers to think of each and every Jeffersonian "as a ravening wolf, preparing to enter your peaceful fold, and glut his deadly appetite on the vitals of your country."[40] In fact, the venom flowing between the Jefferson and Adams camps made Watergate-era politicking look like an Emily Post tea party. Jefferson spoke of Federalists as "enemies of our Constitution" and of their time in power as a "reign of witches."[41] Hamilton spoke of saving America from the "fangs of Jefferson" even as Democratic-Republicans spoke of saving America from the "talons of Monarchists."[42] "Citizens choose your sides," urged the Federalist *Daily Advertiser* of New York:

> You who are for French notions of government; for the tempes-tuous sea of anarchy and misrule; for arming the poor against the rich; for fraternizing with the foes of God and man; go to the left and support the leaders, or the dupes, of the anti-federal junto. But you that are sober, industrious, thriving, and happy, give your votes for those men who mean to *preserve the union* of the states, the purity and vigor of our excellent consti-tution, the sacred majesty of the laws, and the holy ordinances of religion.[43]

Soon each side was openly questioning whether this either-or nation could survive rule by the other. "The country is so divided and agitated, as to be in some danger of civil commotions," Secre-tary of the Treasury Wolcott told Hamilton.[44] *The Connecticut Cou-rant* wrote that there is "scarcely a possibility that we shall escape a Civil War."[45]

This time things looked better for the underdogs. The Federalists, who controlled both branches of Congress, had been in power since the start of the republic, so unpopular taxes and unpopular laws were theirs and theirs alone. Moreover, the party of Washington and Adams was at odds with itself, divided between moderate Federalists and Ultra (or High) Federalists, much as the GOP was divided by Goldwater conservatives in the 1960s and the Tea Party in the 2010s. While moderates praised Adams for attempting to end an undeclared naval war with France (the so-called Quasi-War), Ultras criticized Adams as a peacenik who had gone soft on France. In a letter that circulated widely as a fifty-four-page pamphlet, Hamilton wrote that Adams was not presidential material because of "great and intrinsic defects in his character," including "disgusting egotism," "distempered jealousy," and "ungovernable indiscretion of temper."[46] In a response that did little to disprove the allegation, Adams lashed out at Hamilton as "a bastard brat of a Scotch pedlar" and "a man devoid of every moral principle."[47]

But Adams was also set upon by Jeffersonians. James Thomson Callender, a rabble-rouser who made his name by exposing Hamilton's affair with a married woman, blasted Adams as a trigger-happy warmonger, urging his readers to "take your choice between Adams, war and beggary, and Jefferson, peace and competency." The Adams administration, he wrote, was "one continued tempest of malignant passions." As for Adams himself, he was a "repulsive pedant" and a "hideous hermaphroditical character which has neither the force and firmness of a man, nor the gentleness and sensibility of a woman."[48]

Ultimately, all this was a sideshow. The election did not turn on whether Adams was a warmonger (as the Democratic-Republicans insisted) or a peacenik (as many Ultra Federalists complained), or whether the freethinking Aaron Burr was "the most unfit man in the U.S. for the office of President."[49] In the end, Democratic-Republican claims that Hamilton, still the brains behind the Federalist outfit, was "a confessed and professed adulterer" canceled out Federalist claims that Charles Pinckney, Jefferson's campaign manager in South Carolina, had seduced, impregnated, and then abandoned "an unhappy female of a respectable family in Paris."[50]

Even more than the election of 1796, the election of 1800 came down to a referendum on Jefferson, whose character was *the* issue of the day. And once again, the shots were fired first and most often from the right, and not infrequently by ministers. "The question is not what he will *do*" should he win the presidency "but what he *is*," wrote Rev. William Linn, a New York–based Presbyterian minister who had served as the House of Representatives' first chaplain.[51] And what he was, Federalists said, was a saboteur of everything sacred.

Archpriest of Infidelity

AS IN 1796, Federalists attacked Jefferson as unmanly—a coward and a bookworm who preferred the solitude of his library and the companionship of ideas to the rough-and-tumble of political life. He was an enemy of the Constitution determined to remake America in the image of France, they said, and an impractical dreamer whose antediluvian nostalgia for agrarian life would bury America's mercantile economy. Pointing to a 1796 letter he wrote to his Italian friend Philip Mazzei, Federalists charged him with disrespecting Washington (who had already begun his apotheosis into an American saint). And though rumors of an illicit sexual relationship with "Dusky Sally" Hemings would not see their way into print until 1802, more generic gossip about "Mr. Jefferson's Congo Harem" spread far and wide.[52] Nonetheless, this referendum on Jefferson's character boiled down to a referendum on his religion, which became "the most defining issue" of the election.[53]

Jefferson may have been a libertine—DNA analysis has confirmed, to the satisfaction of most historians, that Jefferson likely fathered a child with Hemings—but he was not an atheist. Though he said he was "of a sect by myself," he also self-identified as a Christian.[54] But theologically he came down somewhere between Deism and Unitarianism, which is to say that he was in roughly the same company as John Adams, George Washington, and Alexander Hamilton. Each of these men believed in God and in afterlife rewards and punishments. None followed a path anything like the evangelical faith of the firebrands of the Second Great Awakening, the religious revolution that would ignite at Cane Ridge, Kentucky, in 1801 before spreading up and down the Eastern Seaboard and into the western frontier. Like Adams, Jefferson attended church (Anglican in his case), but Jefferson was more sharply critical of both clerics and organized religion. Still, the theological similarities between these two men were pronounced. Though both respected Jesus as a great moral teacher, neither would be recognized as a Christian today, since each rejected his divinity.

Federalists were more than happy to overlook this inconvenient truth. Embracing Adams as their candidate, they blasted Jefferson as a friend of Paine and an enemy of God whose hostility to revealed religion threatened to undermine public order and the Federalist way of life. Was Jefferson, as Massachusetts Federalist Theophilus Parsons divined, the "great arch priest of Jacobinism and infidelity"?[55] Or was he, as *The Connecticut Courant* intimated, a secret Jew or Muslim?[56]

In one of the first shots in this conservative attack, Linn admitted that Jefferson was perfectly well qualified to be president, except for one thing: "his disbelief in the Holy Scriptures . . . and open professions of Deism." In heated debates that preceded the Constitution's ratification in 1788, proponents of a religious test for higher office had said that the absence of such a test amounted to an "invitation to Jews and heathens" and made it "most certain that Papists may occupy [the presidency], and Mahometans [Muslims] may take it." Linn knew that the Constitution prohibited religious tests in federal elections, but he hoped that voters would impose one of their own for the presidency. "No professed deist, be his talents and achievements what they may, ought to be promoted to this place by the suffrages of a Christian nation," he wrote. "Would Jews or Mahometans, consistently with their belief, elect a Christian?"[57]

Political cartoonists also attacked Jefferson's faith. An anonymous cartoon called *The Providential Detection* depicted Jefferson preparing to offer the Constitution as a burnt offering on the "altar to Gallic despotism" while God watched from on high and an American eagle swooped down to stop the sacrilege. The fire on the altar before which Jefferson is kneeling is fueled by the radical writings of Voltaire, Paine, and other freethinkers, and Jefferson's notorious Mazzei letter is tumbling from his hand (and incriminating him in the process).[58]

The most famous theo-smear on Jefferson originated with Hamilton ("our Buonaparte," in Jefferson's words), who called his rival "an atheist in religion and a fanatic in politics."[59] Meanwhile, New England divines, convinced that human reason was as depraved as human will, got up what Paine referred to as a "war whoop of the pulpit" against Jefferson, whom they labeled "a confirmed infidel" notorious for "vilifying the divine word, and preaching insurrection against God."[60] Pamphleteers and editorialists pointed out that he worked on Sundays and did not even make a show of attending church, prompting the Federalist *Gazette of the United States* to reduce the upcoming choice of citizens to this simple either-or proposition: "Shall I continue in allegiance to God—and a Religious President; Or impiously declare for Jefferson—and No God!!!"[61]

Some New England ministers also saw a conspiracy afoot between Jeffersonians and the Order of Illuminati, a secret society of freethinkers that had supposedly masterminded the French Revolution and was now dedicated to creating a post-Christian "New World Order." Rev. Jedidiah Morse of Charlestown, Massachusetts, believed the Illuminati, if unchecked, would bring its "plagues" to America. "We have in truth secret enemies," he said in a widely printed 1799 sermon, "whose professed design is to subvert and destroy our holy religion and our free and excellent government" and to spread in the process "infidelity, impiety and immorality."[62] Federalists even went so far as to concoct fictional critics of Jefferson's faith, including a fake Jew named Moses S. Solomons who wrote in the *Philadelphia Gazette* that as a "follower of Moses and the Old Testament" he was in "common cause" with Christians against Jefferson and atheism.[63]

Today Jefferson's faith is an open book, thanks to his extensive writings on religion, including the so-called Jefferson Bible, which have come to light since his death.[64] In 1800, however, Jefferson's theology was a closely guarded secret. The man who gave us the metaphor of a "wall of separation between church and state" also believed in a wall of separation between the public and the private, and for him faith fell on the private side of the ledger. "Our particular principles of religion are a subject of accountability to our God alone," he would later write. "I inquire after no man's, and trouble none with mine."[65] So when his critics blasted him as a "hardened infidel" practicing the "morality of devils," he refused on principle to disabuse them of their errors.[66]

This principled silence led critics to scour Jefferson's only published book, *Notes on the State of Virginia* (1785), for signs and portents of infidelity. Here, Federalists argued, Jefferson called into question the story of the Great Flood and opposed teaching the Bible to schoolchildren. He also attacked religious establishments in the name of religious liberty, arguing in a now infamous passage, "It does me no injury for my neighbor to say there are twenty gods, or no god. It neither picks my pocket nor breaks my leg." Opponents saw these words as proof of Jefferson's godlessness, and Linn reasoned that any ship of state captained by such a man would run aground on the rocks of anarchy. "Let my neighbor once persuade himself that there is no God, and he will soon pick my pocket, and break not only my *leg* but my neck," he wrote. "If there be no God, there is no law."[67]

Most Americans at the time believed that social order depended on morality, that morality depended on religion, that the only true religion was Protestantism, and that the only firm foundation for

Protestantism was the King James Bible. So any perceived slights on Protestantism or its Bible were seen as theological errors and threats to social order. A victory by "the greatest villain in existence" could well lead to the sorts of attacks on Christianity that had convulsed postrevolutionary France.[68] "Should the infidel Jefferson be elected to the Presidency," wrote an alarmist in *The Hudson Bee*, "the *seal of death* is that moment set on our holy religion, our churches will be prostrated, and some infamous prostitute, under the title of the Goddess of Reason, will preside in the Sanctuaries now devoted to the worship of the Most High." Outside the churches, "murder, robbery, rape, adultery, and incest will all be openly taught and practiced," prophesied *The Connecticut Courant*.[69] The American people, a "Christian Federalist" from Delaware added, would become "more ferocious than savages, more bloody than tygers, more impious than demons."[70]

A Jefferson victory would also challenge traditional Federalist deference to clergy and could provoke God to withdraw his blessing from his chosen nation. From colonial times, many Americans had seen themselves as the New Israel. If they acted in accordance with their new covenant with the Almighty, God would bless them. But if they broke that sacred compact, God would curse them. According to Linn, the election "of a manifest enemy to the religion of Christ" would constitute "a rebellion against God." So a vote for Jefferson was a vote "to destroy religion, introduce immorality, and loosen all the bonds of society."[71]

Liberal Counterattack

IN THEIR COUNTERATTACK, Democratic-Republicans appealed not only to freethinkers but also to Catholics and Jews, Baptists and other revivalist upstarts, by contrasting Jefferson's firm faith in individual conscience and religious liberty with Adams's antidisestablishmentarianism. They also introduced to American public life the now familiar claim that, when preachers get involved in politics, they inevitably bow down at the altar of party and demand that the Almighty genuflect with them. Jefferson didn't want to destroy real religion, argued his Connecticut supporter Abraham Bishop, he wanted to destroy "that kind of religion, which is made a foot-ball or stalking horse, and which operates only to dishonour God and ruin man." True religion would suffer "a gradual, certain, and painful extermination," in Bishop's view, if politicians continued to manipulate it for political purposes.[72] In this way, Jeffersonians promoted their candidate as a *defender* of the faith, a bulwark against the reduction of religion to a political stratagem.

In the end, the presidential campaign of 1800 proceeded on fear more than facts. Each party trafficked in horror stories of an impending shipwreck should the traitors come to captain the ship of state. Both sides claimed to be defending the Constitution; each accused the other of declaring war on it. The Federalists insisted that Jefferson's vision of an underpowered federal government and overpowered states undermined the Constitution by rendering the federal government powerless and returning the No-Longer-United States to the chaos of the Articles of Confederation. Jeffersonians insisted that Federalists were intent on trampling the Bill of Rights and on trading in their hard-won republic for a crypto-monarchy made in the image of England.

What was most palpable in this election was the hatred. Rather than viewing members of the other party as patriotic Americans with different understandings of America's past and different visions of its future, each saw the other as enemies of the nation, heretics to the true faith, and betrayers of everything real patriots held dear.

In a December 1800 letter to his son, John Adams wrote that the new party politics was leading toward "a dissolution of the Union and a civil war."[73] And with each new accusation this nightmare seemed increasingly likely. According to the Federalists, Jefferson and his ilk mistrusted government. These French-loving Jacobins were determined to overthrow Christianity, morality, and social order. If Jefferson triumphed, God would be dishonored, Bibles would be confiscated, social chaos would reign, and blood would run in the streets. According to the Democratic-Republicans, Adams and the Federalists fundamentally mistrusted the people. These British-loving monarchists were stealth Tories, enemies of religious freedom who wanted to restore, in the name of social order, European patterns of hierarchy and deference. Adams's heart's desire was for a quasi-monarchy, with himself as king, and Hamilton (who was even more feared among Jeffersonians) wanted to raise a strong central army in order to suppress dissent. If Adams triumphed, the country would be run by an unholy alliance of powerful clergy and rich merchants hell-bent on overturning Revolution and Constitution alike.

These differences did not seem to brook compromise. But surely the election of 1800 would settle them. That is what elections are supposed to do. When the electors cast their ballots, however, nothing was settled.

Deadlock

As in 1796, New England voted for Adams and the South for Jefferson. No surprise there. But thanks to effective campaigning by the savvy and charismatic Aaron Burr, New York flipped. Its 12 electoral votes, won by Adams in 1796, went to Jefferson in 1800. So when the ballots of electors from the sixteen states (the original thirteen plus Vermont, Kentucky, and Tennessee) were counted on February 11, 1801, the Democratic-Republicans had won. Improbably, however, the election had ended in a tie, with 73 votes for Jefferson, 73 for Burr, 65 for Adams, and 64 for Pinckney.

Since the ratification of the Twelfth Amendment in 1804, electors have voted for presidents and vice presidents on party tickets. Through 1800, however, the Constitution had mandated one ballot to determine both the presidency and the vice presidency. Whoever got the most electoral votes became president, and whoever came in second became vice president. In the case of a tie, the election would be decided by the House of Representatives, which in the winter of 1801 was dominated by Federalists. The Jeffersonians should have instructed one of their electors not to vote for Burr, but they had neglected that crucial detail, so Jefferson and Burr had tied. What ensued was the sort of fight you would expect if a House controlled by Tea Party Republicans were charged with deciding whether Barack Obama or Hillary Clinton should be president.

The House balloting dragged on for days amid death threats and talk of secession. Each state had one vote and no candidate was able to command a majority. Federalists feared that Jefferson might call in France to settle the matter by force, while Jeffersonians feared that Adams might pull the same trick with England. Meanwhile, governors of Virginia and Pennsylvania prepared their militias to march on Washington to reverse a rumored Federalist coup. Jefferson warned Adams that further Federalist maneuvering "would probably produce resistance by force, and incalculable consequences."[74] Meanwhile, Joseph Nicholson, a gravely ill Republican representative from Maryland, was carried back and forth each day through the snow on a stretcher in order to cast his vote for Jefferson and prevent his state from going to Burr.

A week passed, and thirty-five ballots. Convinced "that we must risk the Constitution and a civil war or take Mr. Jefferson," James Bayard, a Delaware Federalist and his state's sole representative, let it be known that he (and Delaware) had decided to take Jefferson.[75] It is not clear what changed Bayard's mind. He may have won secret concessions from Jefferson's camp. He may have come to fear that anything short of a Jefferson victory would throw the country into chaos. In the end, Vermont and Maryland Federalists, hearing of Bayard's change of heart, decided to abstain, throwing their states to Jefferson. On the thirty-sixth and final ballot, held on February

17, 1801, Jefferson carried ten states, with four for Burr and two (Delaware and South Carolina) abstaining. The United States thus became the first country in modern history to peaceably pass control over its government from a ruling party to the opposition. However, in a fit of partisanship that anticipated today's Capitol, not one Federalist congressman cast a vote for Jefferson. And Adams refused to attend the inauguration.

Jefferson's Inaugural Address

JEFFERSON'S FIRST INAUGURAL address, though not typically classified as a masterpiece, is one of the great speeches in U.S. history. In 1795, Jefferson had written that it was "*immoral* to pursue a *middle line*" when the division was "between the parties of Honest men, and Rogues." Now he inaugurated not only his presidency but also his country's "great tradition of conciliation." Foreshadowing Lincoln's irenic first inaugural ("We are not enemies, but friends. We must not be enemies."), he nudged America's first culture war cycle beyond attack and counterattack into the stage of compromise and negotiation.[76]

Jefferson called the election "the revolution of 1800"—"as real a revolution in the principles of our government as that of 1776 was in its form."[77] And the common-man optics of the new capital's first inauguration contrasted sharply with President Washington's coronation-style festivities. On the eve of his March 4, 1801, swearing in, Jefferson slept in a boardinghouse and dressed for the day as "a plain citizen, without any distinctive badge of office."[78] Rather than riding in a coach, he walked to the Capitol. He did not powder his hair. He did not carry a sword. His ordinary brown-and-green suit was made in America. And he delivered his inaugural address in "so low a tone that few heard it."[79]

Noting that the task before him was above his talents (it wasn't), Jefferson confessed that as president he would "often go wrong

through defect of judgment." He tipped his cap to Washington—
"our first and greatest revolutionary character, whose preeminent
services had entitled him to the first place in his country's love"—
and to the Constitution, whose core commitments he succinctly
conveyed. In an olive branch to his clerical critics, he invoked "that
Infinite Power which rules the destinies of the universe" and that
"overruling Providence, which by all its dispensations proves that it
delights in the happiness of man here and his greater happiness
thereafter." The United States he described in mythic terms—as
both "a chosen country, with room enough for our descendants to
the thousandth and thousandth generation" and "a rising nation . . .
advancing rapidly to destinies beyond the reach of mortal eye." At
the heart of this speech lay a conciliatory effort to restore the "harmony and affection without which liberty and even life itself are
but dreary things."[80] Jefferson took aim at the view that the political battle between his party and the Federalists was also a cosmic
battle pitting God's angels against Satan's minions. In short, he was
trying to bring America's first culture war to an end by beating into
ploughshares its swords.

Long before the election of 1800, both Jefferson and Adams had
railed against political parties. "There is nothing which I dread so
much as a division of the republic into two great parties, each ar-
ranged under its leader, and concerting measures in opposition to
each other," Adams said in 1780.[81] Nine years later, Jefferson wrote,
"If I could not go to heaven but with a party, I would not go there at
all."[82] But this election had delivered to Americans a permanent two-
party system, turning partisanship and factionalism into the inhala-
tions and exhalations of American political life. Jefferson was not so
impractical as to imagine he could pull the plug on this new machine.
But he sought to atone for his not insignificant contributions to it, and
to return America's body politic to some measure of civility.

"Political intolerance" can be as dangerous as "religious intolerance," Jefferson said, "as despotic, as wicked, and capable of as bitter

and bloody persecutions." So he called on his fellow citizens to be "united with one heart and one mind." This unity had once been ensured by the charisma of America's first president, and Jefferson was under no illusion that he was Washington's Second Coming. So he sought to unite the American people around a simple idea. In this speech's most celebrated passage (and one of the most important in American political thought), he reminded his "brethren" that they were all Americans:

> But every difference of opinion is not a difference of principle. We have called by different names brethren of the same principle. We are all Republicans, we are all Federalists. If there be any among us who wish to dissolve this Union, or to change its republican form, let them stand undisturbed as monuments of the safety with which error of opinion may be tolerated, where reason is left free to combat it.[83]

Though both parties had their partisans, all were Americans first, Jefferson said. Few were ultras of any sort. Most were moderates, committed to republicanism rather than monarchy and to a federal system that honored both national power and states' rights. So the Alien and Sedition Acts could go the way of the Inquisition. Reason would triumph over foolishness without government intervention.

Legacy

JEFFERSON'S FIRST INAUGURAL did contribute to a great tradition of conciliation that serves, even today, as a counterpoint to the poisonous partisanship of the culture wars, but it did not usher in a golden age of political moderation. In fact, one of the most revolutionary legacies of the "revolution of 1800" was the two-party rancor of today's culture wars. Newspapers did not repent of partisanship. Conservatives and liberals continued to accuse each other of betraying the Revolution and trampling on the Constitution. On the very day he administered Jefferson's oath of office, Chief Justice John Marshall told Charles Pinckney that there were two types of Jeffersonians: "speculative theorists" and "absolute terrorists" (though he was generous enough to include Jefferson among the former rather than the latter).[84] Later that year, John Adams would lament that "we have no Americans in America."[85]

Meanwhile, nothing Jefferson did to counteract accusations of heresy—his inaugural day references to God, his attendance at Sunday worship services, his financial contributions to churches, or his extensive theological correspondence with friends and acquaintances—was able to convince his religious despisers that he was on the right side in the cosmic battle between the forces of light and darkness.

After the nation's library went up in smoke at the hands of the British in August 1814, Jefferson (now retired to Monticello) offered to sell Congress his extraordinary personal library, which included among its more than six thousand volumes a British translation of the Quran. Some Federalists objected to the price ($24,950), but the central objection was to the contents, which included in the judgment of Rep. Cyrus King of Massachusetts "many books of irreligious and immoral tendency." Some even suggested that the United States should buy the overall collection and burn the "atheistical" volumes.[86]

Congress did agree to buy (and not to burn) the collection, which became the foundation for the Library of Congress, and few of the horrors Jefferson's books were supposed to visit on the country came to pass. The United States did not become a nation of atheists. Americans did not start speaking French. Those who had buried their Bibles were able to dig them up and read them unmolested. Jefferson's "revolution" did not lapse into anarchy or terror or dictatorship. There was no coup d'état, and neither Jefferson nor Adams was assassinated. By 1812, Adams and Jefferson had not just made peace, they had entered into a wide-ranging correspondence that historian Lauren Winner has described as one of the classic expressions of American literature.[87]

As for the Federalist Party, it never returned to power. Voters cooled to its conservative nostalgia for Old World aristocracy and monarchy, and in 1804 they reelected Jefferson in a 162 to 14 landslide. Thanks to a coalition of "rationalists cool about religion and pietists hot for it," liberals did more than win this culture war.[88] They put their conservative opponents out of business and Federalist culture to rest. The Federalist Party enjoyed a brief resurgence thanks to its staunch opposition to the War of 1812, which pitted the United States against England. But by that war's end in 1815, the Federalist Party had for all intents and purposes vanished, fatally injured by calls at its 1814–15 Hartford Convention for New England's secession from the union.

What did not vanish with the Federalists were the culture wars themselves. In the election of 1800, we hear in Jefferson's despisers a new voice: the voice of modern American conservatism, anxious about the fate of deference, stability, and hierarchy in a world in which liberty, democracy, and emotionalism are running amok. We see conservatives turning religion into an engine of political partisanship and evangelicalism starting to become "a quasi party of its own."[89] We see a nation divided into North and South over cultural questions, though in this case the North was the hotbed of political and religious conservatism. (What Susan Jacoby calls the "reversal of southern and New England patterns of religious intolerance" will come later.[90]) We also see Americans wrestling with the tensions and ambiguities bequeathed to them by the founding compromises of the Constitution, trying to turn shades of gray into black and white. As a group, the founders never approved of either the strict separation of church and state or their fusion. Neither did they settle, once and for all, the question of federal power versus states' rights, or the question of the relative importance of liberty and equality (for that matter, what these two key words were to mean). Part of the genius of the founding was its equivocation, which was both a product of compromise and a model for more to come. But all this gray all but commanded future conflict, including the Civil War itself, calling to arms individuals and movements intent on transforming by some time-traveling alchemy the complexity of the founders (and the Constitution itself) into some unambiguous "original intent."

But the Jefferson wars did produce—as culture wars typically do—some agreement. As Americans debated the virtues and vices of Adams and Jefferson, religious uniformity and religious freedom, a culture of hierarchy and a culture of inclusion, they agreed that their leaders did not need to meet a religious test. Citizens did not yet agree that their presidents could be avowed atheists. But they did agree that their presidents need not be traditional Christians. Though America's population was then (as it is today) overwhelmingly Christian, its leaders did not need to check the "evangelical" box to take up residence in the White House.

Voters also agreed to move beyond the aristocratic airs of Washington and Adams to a more egalitarian style. They agreed not to resurrect the conservative culture of deference that had characterized New England from the Puritans to the Federalists. Instead they decided to move forward into an unknown future, "advancing rapidly to destinies beyond the reach of mortal eye." Their cultural disagreements were by no means behind them, however. As they moved into that unknown future, they would continue to turn "differences of opinion" into "differences of principle." They would also continue to denounce one another as betrayers of everything U.S. citizens were supposed to hold sacred. In short, the view of the pro-Jefferson *National Intelligencer* that Americans were "universally agreed" that "religion ought to be kept distinct from politics" would prove to be hopelessly naïve.[91] Thanks to this first of America's many culture wars, the faith of political figures had become a proxy for character, and religion had become a wedge issue in American politics. Later conservatives would work hard to insert that wedge into questions as diverse as immigration, polygamy, alcohol consumption, abortion, and gay marriage. And they would come to question the Americanness of Catholics, Mormons, and Muslims alike.

2

Anti-Catholicism

TODAY THERE ARE SIX Catholics on the Supreme Court and anti-Catholicism is largely a thing of the past. Some Americans make sense of recent Catholic sex scandals by drawing on ancient tropes of priests as perverts preying on the young. But most criticisms of Catholicism today are rooted in policy rather than prejudice—in disagreements over abortion, gay marriage, or contraception. Few question whether Catholics can be patriotic Americans, and those who do are rightly dismissed as cranks. But anti-Catholicism runs deep in American culture, and it took a long and bitter culture war to uproot it.

This culture war erupted on a hot August evening in 1834 in Charlestown, Massachusetts, when a mob of largely working-class Protestant men assembled outside an Ursuline convent and boarding school for girls built on Ploughed Hill, within earshot of Bunker Hill, the site of the first major battle of the American Revolution. Precisely what happened next is difficult to determine, since the events of the night were veiled at the time by smoke and are obscured today by the fog of memory.

It appears from eyewitness testimony, however, that many of the men wore masks or concealed their identities behind faces painted American Indian–style. Carrying "No Popery" banners, they spoke against "the abuses of convents in the old country and the cruelties of the catholic religion." They wielded clubs and drank from rum and whiskey bottles—liquid courage for the violence to come. "Down with the Pope! Down with the Bishop! Down with the convent!" they shouted. One nun tried to defuse the situation with a simple appeal: "Did you not all come of women? Then for the love of your mothers & sisters, leave us unprotected females, & disperse." The convent's mother superior, Mary Anne Moffatt, also known as Madame Saint George (after the soldier martyr and dragon slayer), responded less diplomatically. Moffatt, who would later be dismissed as "a woman of masculine appearance and character, high-tempered, resolute, defiant, with stubborn, imperious will," scolded the men as "dirty vagabonds of the city." Then, according to John Buzzell, a local brickmaker and the mob's ringleader, she answered their threats with one of her own: "If you meddle with us, the Bishop has 30,000 men, who will burn your houses over your heads." After this tense exchange, gunshots rang out, perhaps as a warning to the rioters to disperse, perhaps as a warning to the inhabitants to flee, perhaps as a signal for the assault to begin.[1]

Six years earlier, in 1828, nuns from the Ursuline order—the first to come to North America (via France in 1639)—had moved into a three-story convent in Charlestown (now in Somerville) that doubled as an elite boarding school for girls. At Mount Benedict, as this school was known, ten or so nuns taught approximately fifty girls. Curiously, most of these girls were Protestants and many hailed from Boston's Unitarian aristocracy. Boston is now an Irish Catholic stronghold (until Thomas Menino, an Italian Catholic, was elected mayor in 1993, Irish Catholics had run the city for over a century), but Protestants lorded over Boston in the 1830s, so when the angry mob assembled on that August evening in 1834, the nuns had every reason to wonder whether local officials would come to their defense.

During the 1830s, as the refined republicanism of the Federalists was giving way to the rough-and-tumble populism of the Age of Jackson, a "contagion of rioting" swept across the country as citizens struggled with a litany of ills: "ethnic hatreds; religious animosities; class tensions; racial prejudice; economic grievances; moral fears over drinking, gaming, and prostitution; political struggles; the albatross of slavery."[2] In fact, 1834 was, in the words of one observer, America's great "riot year," a time when, according to Unitarian theologian William Ellery Channing, it seemed to many as if American "society were shaken to its foundations, all its joints loosened, all its fixtures about to be swept away."[3] That year saw riots from Louisiana to Massachusetts—labor riots, bank riots, election riots, ethnic riots, anti-abolitionist riots, race riots, anti-Mormon riots, and anti-Catholic riots. The next year the nonpartisan *Niles' Weekly Register* would complain that "brute force has superseded the law, at many places, and violence become the 'order of the day.'"[4] Or, as a citizens' petition from upstate New York put it:

> The maxim of Jefferson, that "error may always be safely tolerated, so long as truth is left free to combat it," . . . seems to have been left for this age to have discovered that a stone or a brick-bat thrown from the hand of a mob is a short and improved method of introducing the truth within the scull.[5]

On that hot night in Charlestown, there were some middle-class merchants in the mix, including a dry-goods merchant, a shoe dealer, and a factory owner. But the mob comprised for the most part truckmen and brickmakers—working-class men worried about losing jobs to Irish immigrants and likely resentful of the aristocratic education the school was supplying to Boston

Brahmins' daughters.[6] The mob was also driven by religious factors, including a rising tide of anti-Catholicism set off by a new immigration wave from Ireland. Undergirding all these factors was the conservative conviction that lies at the heart of all U.S. culture wars—that something dear was being lost, so it was up to all true patriots to recover it.

Chivalrous Violence

IN THE WEEKS and months leading up to August 1834, a dog was shot and killed on convent grounds; ringleader John Buzzell, who reportedly stood a Bunyanesque six feet six, dished out a brutal beating to an Irish groundskeeper, also on convent land; and Charlestown's selectmen butted heads with bishop of Boston Benedict Fenwick concerning his effort to bury two Catholic children on land he had purchased on Bunker Hill for use as a Catholic cemetery. Most ominously, rumors circulated of a nun held against her will at Mount Benedict.

A few years earlier, a convert to Catholicism named Rebecca Reed had left Mount Benedict and begun speaking of abuse there. These stories would later find their way into print as *Six Months in a Convent* (1835). But allegations that Reed had been abused by Catholic authorities were already circulating in and around Boston. Two weeks before the riot, a nun named Elizabeth Harrison (a.k.a. Sister Mary John) had also run away, only to be coaxed back by Bishop Fenwick (who had served in 1817 as president of Georgetown and was responsible for opening in 1827 what would become Boston College). Rumor had it that Harrison had been forced to return to Mount Benedict and was now held captive there, perhaps in an underground dungeon. Some even speculated that she had been buried alive. So when the rioters assembled outside Mount Benedict on the evening of August 11, 1834, they were not merely drunken Protestants threatening violence against the pope, the bishop, and the convent. They were chivalrous young knights intent on delivering fair maidens from distress.[7]

Precisely what mobilized these men is difficult to determine. Beginning on Saturday, August 9, handbills addressing Charlestown's selectmen appeared, demanding swift action in the matter of Elizabeth Harrison—or else. One read:

> GENTLEMEN—Unless there is a legal investigation of the nunnery affair by Thursday night, August 14, it will be demolished by the truckmen of Boston. Take notice, and govern yourselves accordingly.

Another handbill skipped over the preliminaries to a feverish call to arms:

> GO AHEAD! To arms!! To arms!! Ye brave and free, the avenging sword us shield! Leave not one stone upon another of that curst nunnery that prostitutes female virtue and liberty under the garb of holy religion. When Bonaparte opened the nunneries in Europe, he found crowds of infant skulls!![8]

Into this hair-trigger situation rode the Presbyterian minister Lyman Beecher, who had recently left the pulpit at Boston's Hanover Street Church to run Lane Theological Seminary in Cincinnati, Ohio. On Sunday, August 10, the day before the riot, he delivered anti-Catholic sermons at three different Boston churches. In these sermons—"oratorical hell fire" on the "whoredom of Babylon" and the "foul beast of the papacy," according to one local paper[9]—Beecher urged Bostonians to work to win the West for Protestantism. In *A Plea for the West* (1835), which grew out of these sermons, Beecher would write that rank-and-file Catholics already held "in darkness and bondage nearly half the civilized world." Now Catholic leaders were secretly plotting to infiltrate the Mississippi Valley, seize it on behalf of the pope, and smother American liberties in the process. According to Beecher, the purpose of Catholic schools was not to nurture young Catholics but to convert young Protestants, and he pointed to Mount Benedict, with its mostly Protestant student body, as exhibit A in this soul-robbing conspiracy. Catholic schools were intended to convert Protestants, overthrow Protestantism, and turn the United States into a papal colony, he reasoned. To send your daughter to a convent school was not only to risk her virtue and her heavenly reward but also to imperil the nation. "Is it not treason," Beecher asked, "to commit the formation of republican children to such influences?"[10]

Second Great Awakening

THE UNITED STATES was at the time in the throes of the Second Great Awakening, that resurgence of religious enthusiasm that rewrote the denominational map, promoting Baptists and Methodists to the head of the religious class and introducing to the American religious family new homegrown religious options, including the Church of Jesus Christ of Latter-day Saints (the Mormons). Thanks to a series of successful "new measures" instituted by Charles Grandison Finney, the lawyer-evangelist who spearheaded this revival by presenting his brief for Jesus, the Second Great Awakening also turned evangelicalism into the dominant religious impulse of the early republic, displacing the predestination theology of colonial-era Puritanism with a freewill theology, called Arminianism, that offered everyone the choice to accept or reject Jesus for themselves. This Awakening also gave a more prominent public role to women and blacks, and produced a series of populist preachers who offered the nation a form of faith that was more emotional and more egalitarian—a freewheeling spiritual style appropriate to the Age of Jackson and America's newfound cultural independence.[11]

The most obvious by-product of this religious populism was revivalism, a tradition that would give the nation soul-winning preachers, from Billy Sunday to Billy Graham. But the Second Great Awakening was not just about saving souls. It also aimed to save the nation. Americans had steered their ship of state through the rocks of the Revolutionary War and the shoals of the "revolution of 1800." Now evangelicals labored to make the nation worthy of God's choosing. As Baptist farmer-preachers and Methodist circuit riders traveled far and wide to make converts, voluntary associations such as the American Bible Society (est. 1816), the American Tract Society (est. 1825), the American Temperance Society (est. 1826), and the American Anti-Slavery Society (est. 1833) strove to transform the United States into something approaching the kingdom of God.

These social reformers dreamt of a "benevolent empire" in which Christianity would reign by persuasion, not coercion. But this vision of what founding father Samuel Adams called a "Christian Sparta" excluded many Christians.[12] It saw a nation of Protestants, by Protestants, and for Protestants. Or, as one Philadelphia editor put it, "When we remember that our Pilgrim fathers landed on Plymouth rock to establish the Protestant religion, free from persecution, we must contend that this was and always will be a Protestant country."[13]

The growing presence of Catholics troubled this vision, threatening to turn the dream of Protestant freedom into a nightmare of Catholic control: a puppet nation run by a dictator in Rome. According to evangelical social reformers, Catholics represented a theological, moral, and political threat to the American way of life. Catholic teachings about God and the Bible were false. Their priests were debauched. And their parishioners' slavish obedience to a tyrannical pope was at odds with America's love of liberty.

All these themes found expression in a budding anti-convent literature. Borrowing from the tropes of colonial captivity narratives— stories of innocent young maidens kidnapped and held against their will by bloodthirsty Indians—anti-convent narratives depicted nunneries as prisons and brothels where conniving priests violated their vows of celibacy with the young inmates they held captive as nuns. These narratives also gave voice to the passion of Protestants to reclaim their country in the name of the pure, primitive Protestantism.[14]

Burning the Convent

THE ASSAULT ON Mount Benedict began late in the evening of August 11, 1834. The mob began by tearing down fences and unhinging the convent gate, forcing open this cloistered community to the wider world. Rioters broke windows and pockmarked the convent with stones. After checking to be sure that the nuns and their pupils had escaped into the night, they ransacked the building, moving from room to room, throwing musical instruments (including valuable harps and pianos) out of windows, and piling broken-up furniture onto a makeshift pyre. Around midnight, the conflagration began, with the contents of the convent, including a cross from the chapel altar and a "great bible," lit in all likelihood from a torch carried by a local fire brigade.[15]

The atmosphere was carnivalesque, with rioters singing songs, smoking cigars, and cavorting in schoolgirls' dresses. In another form of cross-dressing, the ringleader, John Buzzell, donned a bishop's robe in what he called "a spirit of deviltry."[16] One teenage rioter held an ersatz auction of books, asking for bids before consigning each volume to the flames. Communion wafers found their way into rioters' pockets and sacramental wine into their stomachs. A thousand dollars in cash went missing. In the cemetery, someone broke open the resting places of the dead—perhaps for sport, perhaps out of curiosity—to see whether they might find Elizabeth Harrison entombed there, dead or alive.

Before the night was over, the mob had destroyed in the name of the Protestant God and the American nation every structure on the premises, including a lodge for the bishop, an icehouse, a cooking shed, a farmhouse, and a barn. It did this unmolested. None of the thousand or more onlookers seems to have raised a hand in protest. In fact, the firefighters, who routinely toasted at their banquets such genteel virtues as "order, restraint, discipline, and obedience," either stood idly by or took part in what one historian has termed "one of the most infamous acts of arson in American history."[17]

The next day, this "mob of demons," as one paper called them, returned to finish what it had started, laying waste to rosebushes and grapevines, fruit trees and vegetable gardens, as if to ensure that even the soil itself would never again nurture a single Catholic soul.[18] The Ursulines carried twelve thousand dollars in insurance on the buildings and another two thousand dollars on their contents, but that covered only acts of God. So the nuns and their students were not only terrorized and exiled, they were also robbed.

Catholicism on Trial

ROMAN CATHOLIC AUTHORITIES responded by turning the other cheek. Haunted by the possibility of further violence, and mindful of rumors of crowds of angry Irish railroad workers preparing to march on Harvard's library, Fenwick appealed to his fellow Catholics in a homily the next day not to follow the "eye for an eye, tooth for a tooth" ethic of the Old Testament but Jesus's admonition to "love your enemies" instead. "Turn not a finger in your own defense," he said, "and there are those around you who will see that justice is done."[19] But justice (at least of the earthly kind) would not be done.

There was a lot of scolding. Boston's Protestant elites spoke eloquently against the violence. "We remember no parallel to this outrage in the whole course of history," the *Boston Evening Transcript* wrote.[20] Unitarian minister Caleb Stetson called the arson "one of the foulest crimes that ever disgraced humanity." According to most of these elites, however, this crime offended law and order more than religious liberty. It represented a fall, in Stetson's words, from "the government of law and reason" into "the reign of will and passion," and threatened not only Catholic life and limb but also the harmonious way of life of proper Bostonians.[21]

In "The Late Outrage of Charlestown," the Unitarian *Christian Examiner* denounced mob violence as warfare "upon civil society" by its "vilest class." The "diabolical frolic" in Charlestown exposes the "depth of evil" lurking "in the bosom of our community," it lamented. "We are not the people whom we thought ourselves to be."[22]

But the *Christian Examiner* did not stop at blaming the mobs. It also took a swipe at Lyman Beecher:

> We doubt not that religious fanaticism, in its lowest and most brutalizing form, had some influence in producing the wickedness which has been perpetrated at Charlestown. It was excited . . . in part perhaps by writings and preaching of some one or more of those pests of our community, who seem to have little other notion of religion, than that it is a subject about which men's passions may be inflamed, and they may be made to hate each other.[23]

At a meeting convened by the mayor at Boston's Faneuil Hall on Tuesday, August 12, the "Protestant citizens of Boston" condemned the riot as "a base and cowardly act" against their "Catholic brethren."[24] The next day, Cambridge passed resolutions condemning the convent burning as a "criminal and disgraceful attack upon a building occupied only by defenceless women and children" and expressing its "desire that the perpetrators may be discovered and brought to justice."[25] Two days later, on August 15, Governor John Davis announced a five-hundred-dollar reward intended to fulfill that desire. But the perpetrators were not brought to justice. Threatening signs scattered throughout Charlestown made it difficult for the thirty-eight-person investigative committee (all Protestants) to gather evidence. "All persons giving information in any shape, or testifying in court against any one concerned in the late affair at Charlestown," one sign read, "may expect assassination."[26]

In the end, there were two criminal trials for a total of thirteen men. Each drew national interest and packed crowds hoping to espy from a safe distance the inner workings of mob psychology and convent life. But the real sensation was Catholicism itself, which served in both trials as the lead defendant. Testimony focused more on the exotic beliefs and practices of the victims than the violence of the perpetrators—on the confessional, the Virgin Mary, the Catholic Bible, and the sleeping arrangements of nuns. The mother superior—"the sauciest woman I ever heard talk," according to Buzzell—was widely blamed for the riot.[27] In fact, according to one historian, Moffatt "attracted an invective conventionally reserved for the pope (as Antichrist)."[28]

In these trials, America's culture war on Catholics starts to come into focus, and with it two very different interpretations of the nation. During the election of 1800, participants debated whether the United States was to become more like England or France. Now the question was whether it was to become Rome. Rather than banishing infidels, conservatives in the 1830s sought to banish Catholics. Throughout these trials, defense attorneys portrayed Protestant witnesses as "domestic" (and trustworthy) and Catholics as "imported" (and suspect). As foreign agents of a foreign power, Catholic nuns were not just undeserving of American justice. They were a threat to it. Informing this rhetoric was an understanding of the United States as a Protestant nation whose core values were undercut by Catholic immigrants, who read a different Bible and followed a different chief executive. But a very different understanding of the nation lurked outside the courthouse, in denunciations of the convent burning as an assault on the freedoms granted to all Americans by God and the Constitution. From this liberal perspective, the United States was a multiethnic and multireligious nation—a refuge for immigrants and religious minorities—threatened not by "foreign" Catholics but by "native" Protestants whose hatred of Catholics was un-American to the core.

During the Buzzell trial, Attorney General James Austin made an impassioned plea for this sort of cosmopolitanism. "We seem to be rolling back the tide of improvement—arresting the march of mind—and becoming more bigoted, instead of more liberal," he told the jury. "We proclaim toleration in our statutes, and are in reality less liberal than our ancestors, when they persecuted the Baptists and Quakers." Chivalry lay at the heart of his appeal, however. Members of the mob had portrayed their actions as part of a gallant rescue of helpless women—a liberation of enslaved maidens from the clutches of the Whore of Babylon. Austin turned the tables, referring to the riot as a "war upon women and children." In this war, waged hard by Bunker Hill—a site "consecrated by the best blood in the country, an altar to liberty and the rights of man"—no one came to the defense of these defenseless females. No magistrates, no militia, no neighbors appeared to defend their lives, their liberty, or their property. "It will be inscribed in our history," Austin concluded, "that here, at least, the age of chivalry is gone."[29]

Buzzell and the seven other men accused of the capital crimes of arson and burglary were acquitted because, as one of the prosecutors observed, key witnesses had been stunned into silence by threats of assassination. Decades later, an unrepentant Buzzell would tell *The Boston Globe* that "the testimony against me was point blank and sufficient to have convicted twenty men, but somehow I proved an alibi, and the jury brought in a verdict of not guilty."[30] When this verdict was delivered on December 12, 1834, shouts of joy erupted from the courthouse crowd.

The second trial went almost as well for the accused. Here five men were tried for lesser crimes. Only one, Marvin Marcy, a teenage boy who had played the role of mock auctioneer while burning the convent's books, was convicted. His sentence was life in prison, but thanks to impassioned appeals for mercy from Fenwick and Moffatt (intended, one suspects, to damp the anti-Catholic fire) the governor pardoned him after a few months.

In the absence of justice, money might have partly compensated the Ursulines for one of the most notorious acts of anti-Catholic terror in U.S. history. But no money was forthcoming. In its final report, the investigative committee had called for Massachusetts to indemnify the nuns. "If this cruel and unprovoked injury, perpetrated in the heart of the commonwealth, be permitted to pass unrepaired," it concluded, "our boasted toleration and love of order, our vaunted obedience to law, and our ostentatious proffers of an asylum to the persecuted of all sects and nations, may well be accounted vain glorious pretentions, or yet more wretched hypocrisy."[31] But efforts to make the nuns whole stalled in the legislature, as did the investigators' pluralistic vision of America as an asylum for the oppressed.

Riotous Reasoning

IT IS COMMON to think of riots as spontaneous and irrational, but the burning of the Ursuline convent was both planned and, in its way, principled. It followed fairly strict social conventions for mobbing—for example, directing violence at property rather than persons—cultivated in Europe and brought to North America in the eighteenth century. Like the Boston Tea Party, a riot redeemed in memory by the conviction that its cause was just, the Charlestown riot exposed fissures in American society even as it acted them out. It, too, was performed in the name of liberty and democracy. But religion was also at play, since the rioters justified their actions on the theory that Catholics, like the British in 1776, hated liberty and democracy alike.

During the 1796 and 1800 elections, Federalists and Jeffersonians had fought over the mix of order and liberty needed to produce the "well-ordered liberty" that had eluded both the British (too much order) and the French (too much liberty). In the "turbulent era" of Jackson, the pendulum was swinging toward something approaching lawlessness.[32] To be sure, Boston's Brahmins rushed to defend order, the nuns, and those Protestant parents who had placed their children's hearts and minds in the hands of Mount Benedict's mother superior. But the mob also had its principles. Like Boston's Tea Party rebels, the convent rioters had violated good order. But they had done so for a reason: to beat back a foreign power hostile to the interests of freedom-loving America. Here we see one of the paradoxes of this culture war: Protestants battled Catholics not *despite* America's commitment to religious liberty but *because* of it. Because convents were "bad," one agitator explained, they "ought not to be allow[e]d in a free country."[33]

In the short term, this logic triumphed. After a brief stay in Roxbury, Massachusetts, where they were again threatened and harassed, the Ursulines decamped for Canada in 1838.

Anti-Catholicism in the Colonies

TODAY AMERICANS PRIDE themselves on their tolerance, so it is tempting to see the Ursuline convent burning as an aberration—a violation of the same American values at play in the "Ground Zero Mosque" controversy: religious liberty and private property. But anti-Catholicism is as American as apple pie. Arthur Schlesinger Sr. called it "the deepest bias in the history of the American people."[34] John Higham said it was "the most luxuriant, tenacious tradition of paranoiac agitation in American history."[35]

In fact, anti-Catholicism has been part of Western civilization since the Reformation of the sixteenth century, when efforts to reform the Roman Catholic Church produced a new branch of

Christians whose identity (as "protesters") was tied up in *not* being Catholics. So Protestants have long carried with them both a mistrust of priests and the conviction that Catholicism is fraudulent Christianity. Martin Luther, who spearheaded the German Reformation, denounced the Roman Catholic Church as a "blood-thirsty, unclean, blasphemic whore of the devil." But Luther's rhetoric was not his own. Throughout early modern Europe, Protestants blasted Catholicism for its false theology and debased morality. Fusing these two complaints, a British historian referred to the history of the papacy as a corrosive combination of "avarice, ambition, sacrilege, perjury, an absolute contempt of everything sacred, the most amazing dissoluteness, every species of debauchery in excess, a total depravity and corruption of doctrine and morals."[36]

North America had been colonized by Catholics in New Spain and New France, but New England was established by Protestants for Protestants. Fear and loathing of priests and popes came to the New World on the *Mayflower* and quickly spread to all thirteen original colonies. The Catholic population in these colonies probably never topped 25,000—about 1 percent of a 2.5 million population—but colonial legislators treated Catholics like a real and present danger. In 1642, Virginia prohibited Catholic settlers. In other colonies, priests were banished, Catholic schools were outlawed, officeholders were required to forswear allegiance to the pope, and voting rights were denied to people who attended Catholic Mass. New York passed An Act Against Jesuits and Popish Priests in 1700. Maryland, which had been founded by Sir George Calvert, a Roman Catholic, and had served for a short time as a safe haven for Catholics, reversed course in 1704 with An Act to Prevent the Growth of Popery Within This Province. In Virginia, Catholics were not allowed to serve as guardians or witnesses. In Maryland, they were prohibited from bearing arms. In North Carolina, liberty of conscience was the birthright of everyone except Catholics. And New Hampshire did not allow Catholics to hold state office until

1876. Only in Rhode Island, founded by Roger Williams as an island of religious liberty in a sea of religious coercion, were Catholics left largely unmolested. Still, Williams referred privately to the "Romish wolf" as "the common enemy."[37]

New England was the mecca for colonial anti-Catholicism. There children entertained themselves with a parlor game called Break the Pope's Neck, the popular *New England Primer* warned Protestant children to "abhor that arrant Whore of Rome," and on Pope Day each year New Englanders burned the pope in effigy. Anti-Catholic prejudice was particularly strong among the Puritan governors and preachers who lorded over political and intellectual life in the Massachusetts Bay Colony. Heirs of the Reformation of John Calvin's Geneva, Puritans got their name from their determination to "purify" the Church of England from any hint of Catholicism. Their task was to build a "city upon a hill" for all the world to see, and they didn't want papists to ruin the view.[38]

It is true that New England Puritans cherished religious freedom, but they held that freedom close. It was illegal to celebrate Mass in public in colonial Massachusetts. Also outlawed was celebrating Christmas, which Puritans (in the original war on Christmas) saw as a popish festival. Harvard established a lecture series in 1750 dedicated to "detecting & convicting & exposing the Idolatry of the Romish church, their tyranny, usurpations, and other crying wickedness in their high places."[39] And in 1768 Samuel Adams asserted that "much more is to be dreaded from the growth of POPERY in America, than from Stamp-Acts."[40]

Protestant fears of "popery" were theological (a 1743 Georgia act required officeholders to swear an oath against transubstantiation) and moral ("crying wickedness in her high places"). They were also political. Catholicism functioned as a foil that helped to define what it was to be an American in an era in which the meaning of America was up for grabs.

Colonists worried that the pope and his minions were conspiring

to tyrannize the New World. One motivation for the Revolutionary War was widespread revulsion against the Quebec Act of 1774,
which guaranteed religious liberty to Quebec Catholics. The First
Continental Congress, which had only one Catholic member, responded to this legislation (one of the so-called Intolerable Acts)
with a letter to the British people expressing its "astonishment that
a British parliament should ever consent to establish in that country
a religion that has deluged your island with blood, and dispersed impiety, bigotry, persecution, murder, and rebellion through every part
of the world." The fear was that foreign powers might use these immigrants to Quebec in order "to reduce the ancient, free, Protestant
Colonies to the same state of slavery with themselves."[41]

There was talk at the founding of turning the United States into
a Protestant nation, but the founders decided on a secular state with
guarantees of religious liberty and without religious tests. They
did not pursue the strict separation of church and state favored by
Jefferson and Madison, however. In fact, whatever "wall of separation" they constructed was short and weak. Many early presidents
declared national days of fasting and prayer. Congress funded
military chaplains and opened its sessions with supplications to the
Almighty. So American politics has never been as godless as the
Constitution, or as religiously neutral.

We now associate the founders with religious liberty, but most
stood knee-deep in this anti-Catholic muck. John Adams referred to
Catholicism as slavery—"a great and detestable system of fraud, violence and usurpation" that reduced the minds of ordinary Catholics "to
a state of sordid ignorance and staring timidity" and thereby chained
them into "cruel, shameful, and deplorable servitude."[42] Jefferson was
of a similar mind. "In every country and in every age, the priest has
been hostile to liberty," he wrote. "He is always in alliance with the
despot, abetting his abuses in return for protection to his own."[43]

Washington, however, denounced Pope Day celebrations in 1775
and cracked down on anti-Catholicism in his army and in the early

republic. As a general charged with uniting his troops and a president charged with uniting his country, he needed loyal Catholic soldiers and citizens. And thanks in part to his influence, a "wave of toleration" washed over the country under his watch.[44] Before the end of the eighteenth century, Vermont, South Carolina, and New Hampshire took anti-Catholic language out of their state constitutions, and Delaware and Georgia allowed Catholics to vote. But anti-Catholic bigotry did not disappear. The first person prosecuted under the Alien and Sedition Acts—the printer-politician Matthew Lyon, who had brawled with Roger Griswold on the floor of the House in 1798—came from an Irish Catholic family. And as immigration from Ireland and Germany picked up in the second quarter of the nineteenth century, many Americans were anxious yet again about the "papal menace."

Anti-Catholicism in the Age of Jackson

IN THE 1830S, immigration quadrupled to 600,000 newcomers, and during the 1840s it tripled to nearly 1.7 million—about a third of them Irish.[45] By 1850, the U.S. population included 1.6 million American Catholics (up from 660,000 ten years earlier), making the Catholic Church the largest Christian body in the United States.[46]

But anxiety about immigrants boomed, too. Nativists—conservators of "native" American privilege—worried about losing control of their country to the foreign-born. They denounced immigration for economic, social, and even hygienic reasons, arguing that immigrants were far more likely than "natives" to be paupers, criminals, and carriers of disease. But the core complaint was not that immigrants were caught in the grip of poverty, crime, or cholera. It was that they were servile to the pope—"a perverted religion was the primary source of all their misfortunes."[47]

In the first third of the nineteenth century, dozens of new Protestant newspapers appeared, and each attacked Catholicism. The American Tract Society produced a series of tracts with titles such as *False Claims of the Pope* (1842). But hatred of Catholics also spread via local and national anti-Catholic societies, which published such newspapers as *Priestcraft Exposed, Priestcraft Unmasked, Anti-Romanist, The Downfall of Babylon,* and *The American Protestant Vindicator* (all inaugurated in the 1830s). The output in this genre was vast, extending to "primers, children's stories, travel books, novels, plays, verse, histories, gift books, almanacs, pamphlets, and sermons."[48] Even the Book of Mormon got into the act, denouncing a "great and abominable church" with the devil as its founder (1 Nephi 13:6).

Initially, this literature targeted Catholic theology—the mission statement of *The Protestant* promised "to defend that revealed truth . . . against the creed of Pope Pius IV"—but it quickly extended to moral and political attacks.[49] The announcement of a new Boston newspaper called *American Patriot* demonstrates not only how these theological, moral, and political concerns intertwined but also how nativism and anti-Catholicism were tied up with economic anxieties. In a litany of grievances that recalls the brief against King George III in the Declaration of Independence (and looks forward to similar laments by the Religious Right), it portrayed the Protestant supermajority as an oppressed minority:

> We are burdened with enormous taxes by foreigners. We are corrupted in the morals of our youth. We are interfered with in our government. We are forced into collisions with other nations. We are tampered with in our religion. We are injured in our labor. We are assailed in our freedom of speech.[50]

In the end, the core arguments of these conservators of Protestant America were three: Catholicism was not Christian; it was not moral; and it was not American. In short, Catholics were theological imposters, amoral villains, and traitors. To do battle with them was not to violate First Amendment protections of religious liberty and free speech. It was to protect both.

Theological Imposters

THE THEOLOGICAL ATTACK on Catholics was straightforward: Catholicism was not Christianity. The pope was an imposter, a pretender to the throne rightly occupied by Jesus alone. And the Catholic claim to apostolic succession—an uninterrupted chain of command from Jesus to Peter to the current pope—was thin cover for the fact that Catholics were, like Judas, betrayers of Jesus and his gospel. Catholic feast days owed more to paganism than to Paul, and Catholic homilies owed next to nothing to the Bible. In short, Catholicism was wrong in both doctrine and practice.

Recycling Reformation-era arguments, Protestants blasted the Catholic teaching of transubstantiation (the transformation of bread and wine into Jesus's body and blood) as cannibalism. The "lucrative fiction of purgatory" was "one of the most unscriptural dogmas and pick-pocket doctrines in the Romish church." Holy water was superstition. So was crossing yourself. Celebrations of the Latin Mass were "mummeries of prayers in unknown tongues."[51] Critics also derided as idolatry such Catholic practices as prayers to the saints and adoration of the Virgin Mary. Confession was to them an insertion of the priest into an interaction that belonged to God and the believer alone, and it persisted solely because it allowed priests to worm their way into the intimacies, wallets, and bedrooms of those who put their trust in them. Finally, all those gaudy pictures of Catholic saints violated the prohibition against graven images in the Ten Commandments (unless, of course, yours was a Catholic Bible, in which case that part would be mysteriously excised).

Where in the Bible did it say that priests had the power to forgive sins? Or had to be celibate? Where in the Word of God did it say not to eat meat on Fridays? Or to go as a pilgrim to Rome? Or to obey the pope as if he were God? Nowhere. No wonder Catholic priests, bishops, and popes went to such lengths to keep the Bible out of the hands of their people. The Bible did say, however, to expect a deceiver called a "Man of Sin" who "exalteth himself above all that is called God" (2 Thessalonians 2:3–4). That Antichrist, many U.S. Protestants believed, was none other than the pope himself.

Amoral Villains

NOT EVERYONE IS a theologian, so for more popular tastes there were convent captivity narratives, such as *Rosamond; or, A Narrative of the Captivity and Sufferings of an American Female Under the Popish Priests in the Island of Cuba* (1836), which, depending on your point of view, was either the apex or the nadir of this genre. In this melodrama of sex, race, and torture, author Rosamond Culbertson, the reputed mistress of a Cuban cleric, uncovered a plot to abduct "Negro" boys, murder them, and grind them into spicy sausages.

Other anti-Catholic writers had criticized the cruelty of the Inquisition, but the sort of torture thought to have ended in the Dark Ages was alive and well in these Gothic tales of horror in which priests used the intimacy of the confessional to seduce young women, lure them into nunneries, and despoil their innocence. One scholar has called these stories "crypto-pornographic anti-Catholic tales of abduction and seduction."[52] She might have added liberation, because these nuns ultimately escape, like the Israelites across the Red Sea, from slavery into freedom.

Rebecca Reed's *Six Months in a Convent* (1835) sold ten thousand copies in its first week. *Awful Disclosures, by Maria Monk, of the Hotel Dieu Nunnery of Montreal* (1836) sold three thousand copies before 1860, making it the bestselling book in antebellum America until it was surpassed by *Uncle Tom's Cabin* by Lyman Beecher's daughter, Harriet Beecher Stowe. Both of these anti-Catholic novels told of innocence lost and freedom found, but Reed's *Six Months in a Convent* was tamer, focusing on the obsessive rituals, absurd superstitions, and rigid authoritarianism of the Ursuline convent and its mother superior. *Awful Disclosures* was wilder, sexier, and more sadistic—anti-Catholicism's answer to Edgar Allan Poe.[53] Sold as a tell-all by "Maria Monk," *Awful Disclosures* was really fiction masquerading as memoir. The book ends with our heroine foiling a plot to murder the unborn child she shares with a priest. Along the way it tells of priests who demand absolute obedience in body and soul, exploit the intimacies of the confessional, and force nuns into "criminal intercourse."[54] The babies born to these unholy unions are strangled shortly after birth, but not before receiving (via baptism) their heavenly reward.

Like other books in this genre, *Awful Disclosures* depicted nunneries as places where innocent young women were incarcerated, indoctrinated, and abused. Or, as the baroque title of another such book put it, *Priests' prisons for women; or, A consideration of the question, whether unmarried foreign priests ought to be permitted to erect prisons into which, under pretense of religion, to seduce or entrap, or by force compel young women to enter, and after they have secured their property, keep them in confinement and compel them, as their slaves, to submit themselves to their will, under the penalty of flogging or the dungeon?*[55] (The answer was no.)

Convent captivity narratives sold for many reasons. First, they made the moral case against Catholicism and, in so doing, allowed Protestant readers to stand in judgment over debauched priests and duped nuns. Second, they promised to reveal what had been kept hidden, to cross over into the dark depths and secret passageways of clandestine organizations and reveal what *really* went on behind closed doors. Third, they broke taboos, offering sexually charged entertainment largely unavailable elsewhere and combining that titillation with torture chambers—Eros and Thanatos between two covers. Finally, they fed what one literary scholar has referred to as the "attraction of repulsion" many Protestants felt in the face of Catholicism.[56]

Antebellum Protestants knew they were supposed to detest Romanism, but some were strangely drawn to it—its sumptuous art, its ancient cathedrals, even Rome itself. Why were convents able to lure innocent young women? Why were priests able to enchant them? Because Catholicism was alluring and enchanting. When John Adams accompanied George Washington on a visit to a "Romish chapel" in Philadelphia, he dutifully scoffed at the rosaries, the Ave Marias, the genuflecting, the altarpiece, the candles, and the full-length crucifix of Christ "in the agonies, . . . the blood dropping and streaming from his wounds." But the congregation "chanted most sweetly and exquisitely," and Adams was smitten: "Here is everything which can lay hold of the eye, ear, and imagination— everything which can charm and bewitch the simple and ignorant. I wonder how Luther ever broke the spell."[57]

Traitors to the Nation

THE MOST IMPORTANT theme in this anti-Catholic literature was that Catholicism was a political threat to the American experiment in republican government. How so? Because it was despotic and authoritarian, at home with monarchy, not democracy. Because it was absolutist, intent on blotting out freedom of thought and freedom of speech. And because it was a sworn enemy of both religious liberty and church–state separation. Catholicism was not just a foreign faith. It was a form of indentured servitude—a "slave creed" incompatible with American values.[58] From this perspective, the fight against Romish tyranny found a direct analogy in the patriots' fight against British tyranny.

In this political critique of Catholicism, the leading voices belonged to Lyman Beecher, who made the Vatican's secret plot to take over America the centerpiece of *A Plea for the West*, and

Samuel Morse, who is best known today as the inventor of the tele-graph and Morse code. A native of Charlestown, Massachusetts, Morse sounded the alarm against these "enemies of all liberty" in *Foreign Conspiracy Against the Liberties of the United States* (1835). "Popery is a *Political system*," he wrote, "*despotic* in its organization, *anti-democratic* and *anti-republican*, and cannot therefore coexist with American republicanism."[59] So it was imperative for Protes-tants to set aside their denominational bickering and unite against Catholic immigration, Catholic schools, and Catholic politicians.

In the early twenty-first century, American critics of Islam warned that tolerance was a Trojan horse secreting enemies into the heartland. Liberals who defended Muslims' freedoms were naïfs who didn't understand that sometimes you have to restrict the liberty of a minority in order to secure it for the majority. Some even claimed that Islam was a purely political project and *not* a religion. Morse made similar claims regarding Catholicism. "We are the dupes of our hospitality," he wrote. Because of our toler-ance, this "infallibly *intolerant*" faith was spreading "into every nook and corner of the land; churches, chapels, colleges, nunneries and convents, are springing up as if by magic every where." We must not allow the "political designs" of the Vatican to "be shielded from attack" by the "sacred cloak" of "religion."[60]

Morse described ordinary Catholics more as victims than as perpetrators—"senseless machines" who "obey orders mechanically." But he was irate over the machinations of the Jesuits, whom he de-scribed as "a *secret* society, a sort of Masonic order, with superadded features of revolting odiousness, and a thousand times more danger-ous." Regarding "the impression that the order of Jesuits is a purely religious Society . . . and therefore comes with the protection of our laws, and must be tolerated," Morse wrote, "there cannot be a greater mistake. It was from the beginning a *political* organization, an absolute Monarchy masked by religion."[61]

Morse's provocation was plain: The clash of civilizations between

Protestantism and Catholicism had come to America, so it was time for U.S. Protestants to join the fight. The pope was intent on conquering the United States and running it as a Catholic colony. When faced with a line separating church and state, his priests would step right over it without the least pang of conscience. So, what would it be: the sovereignty of the people or the sovereignty of the pope? If Americans did not rise up against this "conspiracy against our liberties," Morse wrote, the Vatican would be lording over the nation from abroad, acting through puppet politicians and ignorant immigrants who "obey their priests as demigods."[62]

Morse saw the irony of refusing to tolerate the intolerant, and of denying freedom of conscience in the name of freedom of conscience, but he refused and denied nonetheless. "Americans will not be cowed into silence by the cries of *persecution, intolerance, bigotry, fanaticism,* and such puerile catchwords, perpetually uttered against those who speak or write ever so calmly against the dangers of Popery," he wrote. "But if detestation of Jesuitism and tyranny, whether in a civil or ecclesiastical shape, is in future to be called *intolerance,* be it so; only let it be generally understood, and I will then glory in *intolerance.*"[63]

Catholic Counterattack

LIKE OTHER CULTURE wars, this one started on the right. It, too, was asymmetrical.

The deluge was on the anti-Catholic side, and few liberals defended their Catholic neighbors on religious-liberty grounds. But Catholics—the cultural liberals in this tale—did respond with a sprinkling of new Catholic journals, beginning with the Charleston-based *United States Catholic Miscellany* in 1822 and with new Catholic organizations, such as the Catholic Tract Society, founded by Bishop John Hughes in Philadelphia in 1827. The movers and shakers behind this Catholic counterattack represented a range of responses from accommodation to confrontation.[64]

The best-known accommodater was Orestes Brownson, an early Transcendentalist (alongside Emerson and Thoreau) who converted to Catholicism in 1844. Most Irish Catholics in the United States were "quiet, modest, peaceful, and loyal citizens," Brownson wrote, yet "hanging loosely on to their skirts is a miserable rabble, unlike any thing which the country has ever known of native growth." In another passage that revealed how his allegiance to class seemed to outweigh his allegiance to religion, he observed that most foreigners "are not republican in their spirit, their interior habits, and their interior life and discipline." This defect he attributed to European politics rather than Catholic faith. Catholicism is "not a foreign religion," he wrote, and it is not "hostile to American nationality."[65]

Bishop John Hughes, also known as "Dagger John," took a more confrontational approach. In 1830, he contributed to the anti-Catholic weekly *The Protestant* a series of fake dispatches, under the pen name "Cranmer," intended to demonstrate the lack of scruples (and good sense) among Protestant writers and editors. His "alarming reports of the progress of Catholicity" spoke of nunneries and Jesuit seminaries that did not exist and Catholic churches overflowing with parishioners—anything to get the Protestants' dander up. He then exposed his own con (and the "editorial depravity" of *The Protestant*) in the pages of the Catholic *Truth Teller*.[66] After learning of an October 1842 incident in Corbeau, New York, where a Catholic priest made a bonfire of Protestant Bibles, Hughes didn't just refuse to apologize. He celebrated this affront with gusto. "To burn or otherwise destroy a spurious or corrupt copy of the Bible, whose circulation would tend to disseminate erroneous principles of faith or morals," his *Freeman's Journal* editorialized, "we hold to be an act not only justifiable but praiseworthy." And when Hughes heard of spreading Bible riots, he channeled his inner Mary Anne Moffatt. "If a single Catholic Church were burned in New York," he vowed, "the city would become a second Moscow."[67]

In this culture war, Protestants denounced Catholicism as the enemy of the True, the Good, and the American Way, and Catholics defended themselves in turn. But as the Ursuline convent burning demonstrates, anti-Catholicism was not just an "ism." Anti-Catholic ideas had the power to make things happen, and among those things were riots, arson, and even murder. Protestant–Catholic mob violence broke out regularly during the "turbulent era" of the 1830s, 1840s, and 1850s. In Philadelphia, riots in May and July of 1844 left the City of Brotherly Love in a state of civil war. To critics, such mob violence was senseless. But rioters have their reasons, too, and in this case the reason was to "save the Bible," and America with it.

Philadelphia Bible Riots

DURING THE PROTESTANT Reformation, Protestants had distinguished themselves from Catholics by their mantra of *sola scriptura*. Whereas Catholics claimed that Christian authority resided in both scripture and tradition, Protestants insisted on the authority of the "Bible alone." Given this legacy, it should not be surprising that virtually every American public school in the early nineteenth century taught the Bible not as literature but as truth, and not only as truth but as "the fountainhead of morality and all good government."[68] One of the core objectives of public schooling was to create moral citizens. But the only way to instill morality was through religion, the only true religion was Protestantism, the only sure foundation for Protestantism was the Bible, and the only real Bible was the Protestants' King James Version. Or so went the prevailing logic.

This use of public schools as de facto Protestant schools went on without much complaint until immigration brought sufficient numbers of Catholics into cities such as New York and Cincinnati, where Catholic parents and priests started to ask why public school teachers were making their children read the wrong Bible. Pitched battles ensued, but nowhere was the conflict sharper, or more deadly, than in Philadelphia.

On November 14, 1842, the Dublin-born Bishop Francis Kenrick addressed a letter to the board of controllers of Philadelphia's public schools, protesting an 1838 decision mandating the reading of the King James Bible in the city's schools. Evoking "religious liberty" and "equal rights" and drawing on an 1834 school board ruling against sectarian religious instruction, Kenrick asked that Catholic schoolchildren be allowed to read from the Catholic Bible and that they be excused from class during prayers and the singing of Protestant hymns.[69]

In language anticipating white Southern protests against "outside agitators" during the civil rights movement, Protestant ministers objected to "the interference of foreign prelates, and of a foreign ecclesiastical power" in their local affairs. One Philadelphia resident reported that "the Pope was coming to this country with an army of cassocked followers, . . . [each] trebly armed with weapons, concealed under the folds of 'Babylonish robes.' "[70] The board did not exempt Catholic schoolchildren from prayers and hymns, and it continued to prohibit annotated Catholic Bibles on the grounds that the only truly nonsectarian Bibles were those that, like the King James, proceeded "without note or comment." But it did rule in January 1843 that no children should be required to read from the King James if their "parents were conscientiously opposed thereto."[71]

Over the next few months, nativists stewed and tensions simmered. "Native Americans" warned that a "papal ascendency" was turning their city, the birthplace of independence, into the "American Rome."[72] In November 1842, ninety-four Protestant ministers from twelve different denominations formed the American Protestant Association in an effort to combat the contagion they deemed "subversive of civil and religious liberty, and destructive to the spiritual welfare of men."[73] Under the leadership of nativist editor and orator Lewis Levin, the American Republicans dedicated themselves in December 1843 to keeping the vote out of the hands of immigrants and the King James Bible in the hands of schoolchildren.

The Bible, they argued, was "the basis of the American Republic, and the superstruction of their civil and religious liberty." And the King James Bible, accepted as scripture by Baptists, Methodists, Presbyterians, and Episcopalians, was *not* a sectarian book.[74]

Catholics tried to explain that they were not opposed to Bible reading in schools; they just wanted to see Catholic civil liberties respected. But nativists gathered in Independence Square on March 11 saw things differently, resolving that the bishop's actions were a brazen "attempt to banish the Bible from our public institutions."[75] If the Catholics get their way, *The Presbyterian* argued, Philadelphia's entire public school system should be "leveled to the dust."[76]

These fighting words erupted into fistfights and then gunfire in May 1844. On May 3, the American Republicans met in Kensington, a manufacturing suburb and stronghold of Irish laborers, and began denouncing immigrants, the Irish, Catholics, and Rome. They were beaten back by an Irish mob. Anti-Catholics responded by announcing another meeting for May 6 and calling on all "Natives" to "sustain them against the assaults of Aliens and Foreigners."[77]

One time-honored strategy among culture warriors is to present your legions as a besieged minority under the thumb of infidels or Mormons or secular humanists, and the several thousand "no popery" activists who assembled on May 6 did just that. At the time, 121 of the 128 churches in Philadelphia were Protestant, but the nativists said the city was being overrun by Irish Catholic hordes. This message was interrupted first by an Irish laborer, who dumped a pile of either dirt or manure at the base of the speakers' platform, and later by a torrential rain. The weather (or was it the smell?) drove the crowd into the Nanny Goat Market (another Irish stronghold), where shouts of "On, On Americans. Liberty or Death" were interrupted by volleys of rotten vegetables, then pushing and shoving, and finally gunfire.[78]

A teenage marcher named George Shiffler was shot and killed and instantly martyred. Lithographs depicted him bloody and dying, draped in a torn and tattered American flag. Sheet music also immortalized him:

"I die, I die," he nobly said,
"But in a glorious cause,
In exercise of Freedom's Right,
My Country and her Laws."[79]

That night, angry nativists rampaged through Kensington, destroying Irish homes. After they set their sights on a school run by the Catholic Sisters of Charity, they were met with gunfire, which killed one nativist and wounded another. Soon the nativists were likening the riot to the Saint Bartholomew's Day massacre, which had left thousands of French Protestants dead in 1572. "The bloody hand of the Pope has stretched itself forth to our destruction," wrote *The Native American* on May 7. "We now call on our fellow-citizens, who regard free institutions, whether they be native or adopted, to arm."[80]

Later that day, nativists assembled by the thousands in Independence Square, near where the Declaration of Independence and the Constitution had been drafted. One group carried a torn American flag with a banner that read, "This is the flag that was trampled by Irish Papists."[81] Protesters then marched to Kensington, where once again Protestants and Catholics locked in mortal combat. Nativists demolished the Hibernia Hose house and an Irish American volunteer firehouse. Before the night was over, more than thirty Irish Catholic homes had been burned to the ground, and families were fleeing what had become a war zone.

This did not end the terror, however. The next day, May 8, nativist mobs chanting anti-popery slogans marched again through Kensington, looting homes and setting entire blocks of houses on fire. They then vented their rage on Catholic houses of worship, burning down Saint Michael's church and rectory, and the Sisters of Charity female seminary. Next they headed downtown, burning to the ground Saint Augustine's church and rectory. Taking a page out of the Ursuline convent riot, they also sacked the home of the Irish Catholic school controller Hugh Clark and burned his books in a bonfire. Governor David Porter responded by placing Philadelphia under martial law, but not before at least a dozen people had died and forty or fifty were seriously injured. Fearing for their lives, some Catholic priests took off their clerical collars and Bishop Kenrick closed the city's Catholic churches on Sunday, May 12. It wasn't safe to be a Catholic in Philadelphia anymore.

Even *The Native American* was chastened by this "wanton and uncalled for desecration of the Christian altar," but rank-and-file nativists were not done.[82] On the Fourth of July, a parade of several thousand people marched in an anti-foreign, anti-Catholic parade in Kensington, showcasing widows and orphans of the martyrs. Floats were strewn with icons of George Washington, the Declaration of Independence, and the flag. The Bible became, according to one observer, a "rallying point" for nativist politics, "like the hickory pole or the coonskin" of Andrew Jackson.[83]

The next day the rioting resumed. Catholics had prepared for the defense of the Church of Saint Philip de Neri in the Southwark district by stockpiling rifles there. So Catholics, anti-Catholics, and soldiers alike converged on that church. After some efforts at negotiation, anti-Catholics forced their way into the sanctuary with a battering ram. When they fired a cannon, and the Catholics fired back, it seemed as if Philadelphia was descending into a long war. Once peace was restored three days later, the accounting for this second riot was more than a dozen killed and fifty or so wounded. The City of Brotherly Love was again under martial law.

Like Boston's Brahmins a decade earlier, Philadelphia's scions of social order stood up for liberty in this affair, responding to the anti-Catholic violence with a combination of shame and outrage. The Democratic *Spirit of the Times* blamed an "unholy alliance" of agents provocateurs in the American Republican Party and the American Protestant Association, while the antislavery *Pennsylvania Freeman* wrote that "incendiarism and human butchering" proved that Protestant leaders were no better than the pope.[84] The real traitors, in other words, were not those who built up these Catholic churches but those who burned them down.

As in Boston, some Philadelphians reflected on what the bloodshed said about themselves. Evoking Shakespeare, the law-and-order *Public Ledger* wrote:

> The State is at war, and it is at war with treason, raising a parricidal hand against the law. This is worse, much worse, than a foreign war. . . . [S]omething is rotten in the state of Pennsylvania. Corruption is at work within us; the elements of mischief are among us, a part of ourselves.[85]

Catholics used these riots as an opportunity to look back at the Ursuline riot and reflect on the shortcomings of religious liberty in America:

> In spite of the lesson which may still be read, upon the blackened walls of Mount Benedict, we had thought, that under the guaranties of the American constitution, even a Catholic might worship God without being shot for it, and build a church, without danger of its being burned. . . . It has been our fate, however, to learn from our new experience, the folly of our confidence and hope. We have lived to see persecution for opinion's sake triumph.[86]

For the most part the city's fathers were unrepentant. Whereas Boston's official investigation had blamed the Protestant mob, Philadelphia's investigators faulted Catholics—for trying to exclude the Bible from the public schools, for violating the free speech and assembly rights of nativists, and for stockpiling guns at Saint Philip de Neri. But the real culprits, Protestants said, were not rank-and-file Catholics. The real culprits were alien priests who led their followers like lambs to the slaughter—"foreign ecclesiastics, foreign in birth, foreign in education, and foreign in the objects of their mission."[87]

Anti-Catholic Hysteria

THE "CONSTANT STREAM of riots" that beset the United States in the 1830s through the 1850s distinguished itself from earlier rioting by its violence against life and limb.[88] Earlier rioting had targeted property rather than persons, as in the Ursuline convent burning. But mob actions became increasingly bloody, as the Philadelphia Bible riots demonstrate. "Americans could kill each other," according to one historian of rioting in this period, "because they did not identify with each other."[89]

One positive effect of this new bloodletting was a national weariness with anti-Catholic ire, which produced in turn a hiatus in anti-Catholic rioting. Aware of the power of words to provoke violence, critics of Catholicism promised a kinder, gentler approach. *The American Protestant Magazine*, established in 1845, vowed to proceed "not in a controversial manner," and with benevolence toward its Romanist "friends."[90] What this new approach meant in practical terms was that some anti-Catholic organizations and newspapers returned for a time to theological disputes, focusing on converting Catholics to true Christianity and exposing errors associated with prayers to the saints, indulgences, relics, and transubstantiation.

This more conciliatory voice was met by increasing stridency in the Catholic ranks, not least by "Dagger John" Hughes. In a November 1850 homily delivered at Manhattan's Saint Patrick's Cathedral, Hughes told his parishioners that the "paranoia" of anti-Catholic ranters and ravers wasn't paranoia at all. There *was* a Catholic plot to overrun America:

Protestantism pretends to have discovered great secrets. Protestantism startles our eastern borders occasionally on the
intention of the Pope with regard to the valley of the Mississippi, and dreams that it has made a wonderful discovery. Not
at all. Everybody should know it. Everybody should know that
we have for our mission to convert the world, including the inhabitants of the United States, the people of the cities, and the
people of the country, the officers of the navy and the marines,
commanders of the army, the Legislatures, the Senate, the
Cabinet, the President, and all![91]

Nicholas Murray, an Irish-born convert from Catholicism to
Presbyterianism who had addressed (under the pen name "Kirwan")
a series of public letters to Bishop Hughes beginning in 1847, responded to these inflammatory words with fire of his own. First
delivered to a near-capacity crowd in the Broadway Tabernacle in
1851, "The Decline of Popery and Its Causes" drew on the anti-
Semitic trope of Judaism as a dying force and Christianity as young
and vibrant:

While popery may be compared to a decrepit, nervous,
and wrinkled old man, whose hearing is obtuse, and whose
memory is short, and who, heedless and forgetful of the events
passing around him, is always prattling about the past, Protestantism is strong, and active, and zealous, and enterprising, and
attractive, and looking to the future.[92]

But the contrast was not just old age versus youth. It was victory
versus defeat. In classic culture war language, Murray declared that
"the combat may be protracted, but the victory is certain." Catholicism, he wrote, "is like a vessel bound by a heavy anchor and a short
iron cable to the bottom of the stream, while the tide of knowledge
and freedom are rising around it." But Murray was not content to

watch it sink. He prophesied its destruction: "The Lord will consume it with the breath of His mouth, and will destroy it with the brightness of His rising."[93] Anti-Catholicism was returning to its bellicose past.

A new immigration wave, which saw over a hundred thousand new arrivals annually beginning in 1845 (roughly a third of them Catholics, and many fleeing the Irish potato famine), led nativists to argue once again that Catholics were paupers and criminals, draining public coffers, crowding pubs and hospitals, troubling the streets, and corrupting local and national politics. Following in her father's footsteps, novelist Harriet Beecher Stowe issued an urgent call in 1846 for Protestant schools in the West to counterbalance the "insidious, all-pervading, persevering" Roman Catholics.[94] But international affairs also played a role in keeping the anti-Catholic fever piping hot. The Mexican–American War, which U.S. citizens waged with their largely Catholic neighbor from 1846 to 1848, produced appeals in Mexico for American Catholics to side not with their nation but with their coreligionists. At least one fighting force, the Saint Patrick's Battalion, did just that. Meanwhile, the Italian revolutions of 1848, waged against the foreign rule of the Austrian empire, led Pope Pius IX to flee Rome. This show of weakness might have reassured U.S. citizens anxious about a Catholic crusade on America. If Catholics couldn't even hold on to the Vatican, how could they take Missouri? But nativist logic was becoming increasingly unmoored from reason.

Protestant–Catholic rioting was in the 1850s "more violent and more frequent than in any previous age." Anti-Catholic hysteria returned to Charlestown, Massachusetts, in the guise of a young Irish girl who, after converting to Protestantism, was allegedly stolen away by a Catholic priest and her mother. And New York City became a "madhouse of street violence."[95] During the early 1850s, dozens of churches were either burned to the ground or blown up. Priests were tarred and feathered. A new spate of bestselling anti-convent narratives again put nunneries under suspicion and attack.[96] And when Pope Pius IX donated a block of marble to be used in the Washington monument, vigilantes took the situation into their own hands, stealing the stone and, according to some reports, dumping it into the Potomac.

Amid this hysteria, it almost seemed as if "every Catholic woman who goes to confession is lewd, every priest a sworn foe to our liberties, and every Roman Catholic an incipient traitor to the constitution."[97] In one particularly egregious fit of paranoia, Massachusetts citizens petitioned their legislature to create a committee to investigate the nefarious designs of convents against their liberties, only to learn that the commonwealth no longer had any convents.

Alessandro Gavazzi, an ex-priest and former chaplain to Italian revolutionaries, was the poster boy for this revitalization of anti-Catholic pique. While Murray predicted war, Gavazzi demanded it. During a U.S. tour organized by the American and Foreign Christian Union, he told New Yorkers in March 1853 that he wasn't a "protestant" because Catholicism wasn't worth protesting:

No! No! Popery cannot be reformed. . . . Destruction to Popery! No Protestantism, no protestations. Nothing but annihilation! Therefore, I do not call myself a Protestant; I am a Destroyer.[98]

Gavazzi made his mark via attacks on Archbishop Gaetano Bedini, who arrived in the United States in June 1853 as the first papal representative to the United States and met the next month with President Franklin Pierce. Gavazzi stalked Bedini, holding him responsible for the killings of his fellow Italian revolutionaries and branding him the "Bloody Butcher of Bologna"; meanwhile, Bedini sparked riots almost everywhere he went. Amid banners that read, "NO PRIESTS, NO KINGS, NO POPERY" and "DOWN WITH THE RAVEN BUTCHER," he was burned in effigy in Boston,

Baltimore, and Cincinnati, and targeted for assassination in New
York City.[99] An anti-Catholic riot during his Christmastime visit to
Cincinnati in 1853 prompted sixty-three arrests and left one dead
and fifteen wounded. Critics charged that Bedini had come to the
United States to start a secret society or an American Inquisition
or both. Sen. Lewis Cass (D-MI) denounced the rioting in January 1854, but anti-Catholics defended it as free speech. In this way,
Bedini became in the mid-1850s *the* face of Catholic evil to a Protestant population still wary of papal designs on U.S. sovereignty.

Know-Nothings

LIKE MANY SOCIAL movements, anti-Catholicism burned hot-
test just before it flamed out. Thanks to an anti-Catholic tradition
that extended from the Age of Luther through the Age of Jackson,
and from schoolbooks and sermons to poems and plays, "the average Protestant American of the 1850's had been trained from birth
to hate Catholicism."[100] Capitalizing on this training, conservative
politicians in the 1850s turned fear of immigrants and Catholics
(categories that were becoming increasingly indistinguishable) into
a political force.

This political movement had its roots in local nativist organizations in the 1840s. Most of these groups, including the Order of
United American Mechanics of New York, were not affiliated with
a party. But they targeted Democrats, who had become the party
of immigrants and Catholics. Initially, many of these organizations
vented their frustrations on immigrants in general rather than Catholics in particular, expressing their demands in largely economic
terms—as efforts to protect American-born laborers against cheap
foreign labor.

Then the Order of the Star-Spangled Banner was born, in New
York in either 1849 or 1850. Because this "America for Americans" fraternity was secret, it could operate behind the scenes. And

operate it did. Critics tittered at its passwords, rituals, and secret handshakes. But after James Barker became its leader in April 1852, its membership and influence expanded rapidly. Nativists got a big boost from the 1852 presidential election, which was won by Democrat Franklin Pierce on the strength, many said, of the foreign-born vote. Anger over this outcome pushed many conservatives toward "native Americanism," which in the next few years went from triumph to triumph. By November 1853, when *New-York Tribune* editor Horace Greeley first called them "Know-Nothings" in print, they had become a national political party.

Some have viewed the Know-Nothings merely as an anti-immigrant organization. And they did work for legislation to exclude the foreign-born from public office and to require twenty-one years of residency for naturalization. But as historian Ray Billington has argued, "the motive behind their movement was hatred of Catholicism."[101] In an era in which the question of slavery was dividing almost every political group, anxiety about Catholics held the Know-Nothings together. At their initiation ceremonies, candidates needed to prove not only that they were born in the United States but also that their parents were not Catholics, that they had been raised Protestant, and that they were not married to a Catholic. Initiates then pledged to "vote only for native born American citizens" to the "exclusion of all foreigners and Roman Catholics in particular."[102]

While the Know-Nothings denounced their enemies as un-American, their liberal critics returned the favor. Rep. William H. Witte (D-PA) said that the "existence of secret, oath-bound political associations" was "inconsistent with, and dangerous to, the institutions of republicanism, and directly hostile to the genius of this government."[103] Ironically, critics of anti-Catholicism drew on anti-Catholic tropes themselves. "Which is the most proscriptive, intolerant, bigoted and slavish—the Jesuit oath or that of the Know Nothing?" asked one New York legislator, while another lawmaker from the same state called a Know-Nothing gathering an "abominable, dangerous assumption of despotic powers . . . equaled only by the Inquisition of Spain." New York senator William Seward added that the Know-Nothings were doing what culture warriors always do: "breaking society into two classes."[104]

Writing in *The Washington Union* against the spate of anti-Catholic violence that roiled the nation in the mid-1850s, "A Native Protestant" posed a tough question about this effort to slice American society in half: "If the Catholic is to be attacked, who, indeed will be safe? . . . [T]he house of an Episcopalian or a Methodist will burn as readily as that of an Irish Romanist, and we suspect that his blood will in the end be fully as acceptable and sweet to many of those who are prominent in this work of hate." Citing the Golden Rule, this author posed another hard question to "the Presbyterian, the Methodist, the Baptist, the Unitarian":

Is it so short a time since your faith has felt the iron heel of persecution that you are ready and eager to apply to others those practices of persecution and proscription of which your fathers in England and elsewhere so justly complained? And if so, in what sense can you call yourselves followers of Him who said to you and to all men, *"Do unto others as you would that they should do unto you"*?[105]

Henry Wise, a Democrat who beat a Know-Nothing to win Virginia's governorship in 1855, was one of the era's most eloquent defenders of multireligious America. Convinced that "the fate of one is the fate of all," Wise praised founders of different religions—"Hancock the Puritan, Penn the Quaker, Rutledge the Huguenot, Carroll the Catholic, Lee the Cavalier, Jefferson the Free Thinker"—for coming together to found a new nation. In the beginning, he wrote, "there was tolerance . . . there was a mutuality of pledge . . . and there was a common stake of sacrifice."[106] But now the Know-Nothings were trying to get half the country to hate the other half.

Wise's arguments against the Know-Nothings were practical, historical, biblical, and constitutional. The Know-Nothings' secret politicking was, in his words, "against the spirit of Magna Charta," *"against the spirit of our laws* and the facts of our history," "against the spirit of the Christian Reformation, against the whole scope of Protestantism, against the faith, hope, and charity of the Bible," "against American hospitality and comity," and "against Americanism in every sense and shape!"[107]

Wise spoke eloquently against fighting bigotry with bigotry. "There is no homœpathy in moral disease," he wrote. Just as Jeffersonians "rolled back the tide of federalism" in 1800, he and his Democrats "will roll back the tide of fanaticism." But Wise, too, used anti-Catholic language against anti-Catholic fanatics:

> Do Protestants now mean to out-Jesuit the Jesuits? . . . Will they wear the Monkish cowls? . . . Will they bloat themselves into that bigotry which would burn non-conformists? . . . Will they visit us with dark lanterns and execute us by signs, and test oaths, and in secrecy? Protestantism! Forbid it![108]

By Wise's calculations, natives outnumbered the foreign-born in the United States by eight to one and Protestants outnumbered Catholics twenty-one to one. So Protestants could take care of themselves without government assistance. Unless, of course, Know-Nothings undermined their efforts. How, Wise asked, are Protestant missionaries going to save a single Catholic soul if they are suspected of being secret agents for Know-Nothingism? There are only two sure consequences of the intermingling of church and state, he argued: "the state will corrupt the church, and the church will destroy the liberties of the state."[109]

This was vintage Jefferson, but a more innovative argument concerned, oddly, miscegenation. Since "the children of all are crossed in blood," what does it really mean to say one person is "native" and another person is "foreign"? "Who were *our protoplasts?*" Wise asked. "English, Irish, Scotch, German, Dutch, Swedes, French, Swiss, Spanish, Italian, Ethiopian—all people of all nations, tribes, complexions, languages and religions!" And who are the original Americans? "Why, the Indians! *They* are the only true *natives.*"[110]

Election of 1856

IN 1854, ROUGHLY seventy-five Know-Nothings were elected to the U.S. Congress, and Know-Nothings took control of the Delaware and Massachusetts legislatures. The victory in Massachusetts was particularly spectacular, with Know-Nothings capturing the governorship, the entire Senate, and all but two seats in the House. In 1855, Connecticut, New Hampshire, Rhode Island, and California went to the Know-Nothings, who also won elections in Tennesse, Maryland, and Kentucky. Declaring war on Catholics seemed to be smart politics—so smart, in fact, that the only goal left for Know-Nothings seemed to be the White House itself.

The presidential election of 1856 proved, however, to be the Know-Nothings' last. The Native American Party candidate, Millard Fillmore, who had served as president from 1850 to 1853, carried only Maryland. Know-Nothings did manage, however, to shoot down the presidential hopes of John C. Frémont, who ran on the ticket of the newly formed Republican Party (no relation to Jefferson's Democratic-Republicans) against Fillmore and Democrat James Buchanan.

Although Frémont professed to be an Episcopalian, Native Americans and Democrats alike charged him with being a closet Catholic. There was some plausibility to the charge (advanced in campaign tracts such as *Romish Intrigue: Fremont a Catholic!*) since his father was a French Catholic, he attended a Catholic school, and he was married (albeit in a civil ceremony) by a Catholic priest. In fact, the ever-pugnacious Bishop Hughes called efforts to distance Frémont from Catholicism "the most audacious attempt on the credulity of the American people that has ever been tried." But the most damning evidence was an account of a widely published conversation in which Frémont was asked whether he believed in the transubstantiation of the wafer at Mass into the body of Christ, and he supposedly answered, "I do."[111]

The Frémont camp rightly understood that many conservatives were anxious that the election of a Catholic would allow the pope to rule the country by proxy. So it countered with a four-page leaflet called Col. Fremont Not a Roman Catholic, which claimed to offer "proof positive, that Col. Fremont is and always has been a Protestant," including testimonials of his confirmation in an Episcopal Church and the baptism of his children in that same congregation.[112] Like Jefferson, however, Frémont refused to confess his faith publicly, on the grounds that religion was a private matter and that "introducing sectarian issues into politics" was improper.[113]

Frémont carried eleven states but none farther south than Ohio. So Buchanan became the last U.S. president before Abraham Lincoln (and, according to many historians, one of the worst). Frémont was doubtless hurt by his abolitionism, and by the fact that he was the first presidential candidate of the Republican Party. Still, the Catholic rumors did not help in an era in which images were circulating of Pope Pius IX crumbling the Constitution in his right hand and spearing an American eagle with his left. The New-York Mirror thought Frémont's alleged Catholicism was his biggest liability. "Tens of thousands of the more bigoted Protestants," it wrote, "persist in the belief, after all denials, that Col. Fremont is a little fishy on the Catholic question."[114]

Still, this election was the end of the Know-Nothings. Just as quickly as these upstarts won political power, they squandered it. In fact, their downfall was more rapid than their ascent. The real story of the 1850s, therefore, was the failure of anti-Catholicism as a political force.

What happened? First, the Know-Nothings failed to govern. Even in Massachusetts, where they monopolized state politics, they were unable to pass meaningful legislation. So they quickly earned a reputation as "do-nothings." Second, the country blamed them for ongoing anti-Catholic rioting, including a November 1856 melee that left "8 to 17 dead and 64 to 150 wounded" in Baltimore.[115] Third, the question of slavery overtook the question of Catholicism. The Kansas-Nebraska Act of 1854 opened up two new territories and allowed settlers to decide whether their territories would allow slavery. By effectively repealing the Missouri Compromise of 1820, which had prohibited slavery in the Louisiana Territory, this legislation sent national politics into a tailspin, splitting existing political organizations and shifting power to the Republican Party, which opposed both the Kansas-Nebraska Act and the expansion of slavery it endorsed. This act also prompted the famous Lincoln–Douglas debates, where Lincoln's spirited and principled opposition to slavery launched him onto the national political stage.

In this battle between nativists and Catholics, the culture wars cycle took some time to play out. Conservatives started the cycle by attempting to banish Catholics from the American family. Catholics and a few non-Catholic liberals struck back, arguing for a more inclusive understanding of the nation. Catholics like Bishop Hughes relished the fight and were reluctant to compromise. So anti-Catholicism did not disappear with the Know-Nothings. As the prospect of a civil war loomed, Americans increasingly divided their nation into Northerners and Southerners rather than Protestants and Catholics, but anti-Catholicism resurfaced in the 1880s, for example, when an illustration in *Puck* magazine depicted the pope dreaming of "A Roman Catholic America,"[116] and in the 1920s with vicious attacks on Al Smith, the Democratic governor of New York and the first Catholic to run for president. But the argument for liberty and inclusion eventually prevailed.

Repeatedly, rank-and-file Catholics pledged their allegiance to the

United States, and Catholic priests eventually affirmed the separation of church and state, opening the way for the inclusion of Catholics under America's sacred canopy. The moment when Catholics most visibly joined America's unofficial religious establishment—when the lost cause of anti-Catholicism was certifiably lost—came in 1960, when John F. Kennedy became the first Catholic elected president. But it was really the Cold War that gave liberals the victory in this culture war. By the time Americans were preoccupied with "atheistic communism" in Russia and China, Catholics had proved their Americanness by fighting for their country in two world wars and by enlisting in the Cold War with gusto. They had also moved into cities, suburbs, and rural areas alike, becoming the friends and coworkers of Protestants and, in some cases, their spouses. So when Americans thought of their common religion in the 1950s, many thought no longer of Protestantism or even Christianity but of the "Judeo-Christian tradition." In 1955, in an influential book called *Protestant-Catholic-Jew*, sociologist Will Herberg spoke for many of his compatriots when he referred to Protestantism, Catholicism, and Judaism as the "three great faiths"—"equally legitimate, equally American"—undergirding the "American Way of Life."[117] And in the early twenty-first century, six Catholics sat on the Supreme Court.

A century and a half earlier, however, that way of life had been sorely tested. As the 1850s gave way to the 1860s, the Protestant–Catholic culture wars of the "turbulent era" gave way to a conflict over slavery that would plunge the United States into civil war. When that war was over, as the nation was doing what it could do to heed its dead president's admonition to "bind up the nation's wounds,"[118] Americans turned their attention from south to west—to the Salt Lake City basin where a strange sect was doing strange things with family and society alike.

3

The Mormon Question

ON JANUARY 29, 1844, Joseph Smith, founder of the Church of Jesus Christ of Latter-day Saints, translator of the Book of Mormon, and mayor of Nauvoo, Illinois, met with Church leaders in his mayor's office and announced his candidacy for president. Roughly a week later, in a manifesto for his presidential campaign, he called on Congress to put an end to slavery by purchasing slaves from slave owners. He weighed in on issues from prison reform to congressional salaries to national banking, quoting from Benjamin Franklin, George Washington, John Adams, Thomas Jefferson, Andrew Jackson, and other "venerated fathers of freedom."[1]

Not many non-Mormons saw such a neat fit between Mormonism and Americanism. In the sole issue of the *Nauvoo Expositor*, published June 7, 1844, dissident Mormons charged that America's newest presidential candidate was a preacher of "false and damnable doctrines," a swindler, theocratic despot, secret polygamist, and the mastermind behind an intra-Mormon inquisition as vile as any tyranny in medieval Spain.[2]

Smith and his city council answered these charges in a manner that seemed intended to prove them—by ordering the destruction of the *Nauvoo Expositor*'s printing press. Smith and his brother Hyrum were then arrested and imprisoned for treason in Carthage, Illinois. On June 27, 1844, an anti-Mormon mob stormed the jail where the Smiths were being held and shot them both dead. Many thought this would be the end of Smith's church. But what killed their founder only made them stronger. Smith became a martyr and model for millions of Mormons to come.

Smith's assassination was part of a culture war on Mormonism that began even before the publication of the Book of Mormon in 1830. It played out in some respects like the culture war on Catholicism. Once again, Protestant conservatives saw a religious minority as a threat to the American way of life. Once again, they attempted to banish members of that religious minority from the American family, arguing that, because of their enslavement to a religious despot, their liberty was incompatible with American liberty. The anti-Mormon wars were more bitter and bloody than the anti-Catholic wars, however. Mormon leaders would be sued, jailed, beaten, stripped naked, tarred and feathered, and murdered. Members would be chased from New York to Ohio to Missouri to Illinois to the Utah Territory. Politicians would call for anti-Mormon genocide. But the Mormon counterattack was fiercer, too. Almost every LDS leader took up the bellicose posture of "Dagger John" Hughes, refusing until the bitter end to assimilate or compromise.

Today members of the Church of Jesus Christ of Latter-day Saints are widely regarded as incontestably American. They run for president, captain football teams, write bestselling novels, win on *Jeopardy*, serve in Congress, wear the Miss America crown, and star (and win) on reality shows such as *American Idol* and *Dancing with the Stars*. But as Smith's ill-fated run for the White House indicates, it has not always been thus. In fact, Americans were at war with Mormonism even before it was born.[3]

Prior to the publication of the Book of Mormon in March 1830, critics were denouncing Smith's "Golden Bible" as "a 'new thing' in the history of superstition, bigotry, inconsistency, and foolishness."[4] Within days of its appearance, that book was decried in print as "evidence of fraud, blasphemy and credulity, shocking to the Christian and moralist."[5] Later criticism proceeded almost at the pace of today's social media. Within months a satire ("The Book of Pukei") had appeared, and by the next New Year's Day a local paper was reporting that "one of Jo Smith's Gold bibles was lately burnt at the stake."[6] By 1831, critics as far away as Ohio were already comparing the "abject slavery of the mind" of Smith's followers with "the chains of Popery."[7] They were also referring to these "slaves" as "Mormonites" (later shortened to "Mormons") because of their use of the Book of Mormon, which was itself named after the ancient prophet said to have compiled much of the book.[8]

In some respects, Mormonism was just another product in the rough-and-tumble spiritual marketplace of early-nineteenth-century America. Like others swept up in the ecstasies of the Second Great Awakening, Mormons praised Jesus, spoke in tongues, sang hymns, visited with angels, and baptized converts. But Saints (as Mormons called themselves) refused to see their Church as yet another Protestant denomination. In an era that genuflected to self-reliance and individual experience, Mormons emphasized collective practices such as plural marriage, baptism for the dead, and ritual adoption, each of which brought the faithful together into an extended family of God. "If men are not saved together, they cannot be saved at all," said Smith's successor Brigham Young.[9]

But Saints did not simply separate themselves from the "Gentiles" (as they called non-Mormons). They also believed themselves to be superior. While still a teenager, Smith had knelt down and begged God to tell him "which of all the sects was right . . . and which I should join."[10] None of the above, God replied, and Mormonism was born. After the Book of Mormon appeared, Mormons described

their organization as the one true church and denounced as apos-
tates Christians who refused to join them in restoring the gospel to
its original glory. Like Protestants, Mormons accepted the Bible as
true. Unlike Protestants, they did so only "as far as it is translated
correctly"[11] Rejecting the "Bible alone" slogan of the Protestant Reformation, they insisted that the Book of Mormon was scripture and
that revelation was ongoing.

"Gentiles" did not take kindly to these provocations. In fact,
over ensuing decades, LDS members would endure the most wide-
ranging assault on any religion in U.S. history. The State of Missouri
and the U.S. Army would wage war against them. Mobs would
shoot at and kill their missionaries, burn down (and blow up) their
homes and places of worship, and threaten members with whippings
and worse if they did not pack up their belongings and get out of
town. In one particularly outrageous case, the good citizens of Fleming County, Kentucky, went to the trouble of tearing down an LDS
church stud by stud in order to prevent members from collecting
fire insurance.[12] Meanwhile, revivalists railed against Mormonism
in the pulpit and in print, denouncing its founder as "a compound
of ignorance, vanity, arrogance, coarseness, stupidity and vulgar-
ity."[13] Newspapers attacked Saints as "lawless and licentious fanatics," "scoundrels," and "moral lepers."[14] Political cartoonists depicted
them with horns.[15] Anti-Mormonism would also make its way into
novels and onto party platforms.

James Garfield had been president for only a few months when
he found time to denounce the Mormons for offending "the moral
sense of manhood by sanctioning polygamy."[16] President Chester
Arthur would decry polygamy in all four of his State of the Union
addresses. Governors would issue executive orders to end it. Judges
would fine and imprison members. Congress would take away the
suffrage of Saints and seize Church property. The House of Representatives would vacate the seat of a Mormon delegate and refuse to
seat another. And when a Mormon was finally elected to the Senate,

senators would debate for four years whether to admit him. Even the Supreme Court would weigh in. Its justices, in their first-ever decision on the First Amendment's free-exercise clause, would rule that religious liberty extended only to belief, not to the controversial Mormon practice of plural marriage.

Through it all—through the threats, the name-calling, the mob violence, the lawsuits, the imprisonments, the arsons, the murders, and the mobilization of the coercive powers of all three branches of the federal government against them—Mormons rarely compromised. Instead of making nice to their Protestant neighbors, they continued to insist that theirs was the one true church and that all other churches had left Jesus behind. Instead of making nice to their fellow Americans, they denounced the United States as a "wicked nation," its legislators as "liars, thieves, whoremongers, gamblers, and drunkards," and its people as "steeped in sin and ripened for the damnation of hell."[17] Meanwhile, Mormon theology became *less* orthodox over time and Mormon rites *more* distinctive. Rather than blending in, Mormons followed a policy of "gathering" in close-knit communities where they could build temples, perform rituals, patronize one another's businesses, vote in blocs, and otherwise enjoy the economic, political, social, cultural, and spiritual benefits of living in close proximity to one another. These places of gathering, however, quickly became magnets for anti-Mormon violence.

So the Mormons moved and gathered and moved again. And wherever they gathered, trouble was never far behind. From Palmyra, New York, where the Book of Mormon was criticized before it was published, they moved to Kirtland, Ohio, where Smith was arrested for bank fraud. Next they moved to Missouri, where Smith was arrested for treason, and to Nauvoo, Illinois, where Smith met his maker at the trigger finger of a mob. According to historian Patrick Mason, "The pattern was depressingly familiar: the arrival of Mormons followed by a gradual rise in community violence, culminating in extralegal violence, and finally concluding with forced expulsion."[18] But as this pattern played out—from New York to Ohio to Missouri to Illinois and beyond—Mormons wrote in their own blood a narrative of persecution in a land supposedly dedicated to the proposition that all religions are created equal. They were God's chosen people, modern-day Israelites forever leaving Egypt behind, wanderers in search of a New Zion. In this case, however, Babylon was in hot pursuit.

Local Anti-Mormonism

IN THE BEGINNING, both Mormonism and anti-Mormonism were local, confined to areas where Saints gathered or their missionaries were active. Focusing on the founder rather than the Church, and on scripture rather than ritual, early critics argued that Smith was a fraud and the Book of Mormon a hoax. Resurrecting his past as "a noted money-digger," they insisted that Smith—"a man of questionable character, of intemperate habits"—had given up treasure hunting for revelation forging, all in pursuit of the almighty dollar.[19] Anyone who believed that the LDS prophet was out for anything other than profit they dismissed as a dupe.

In the first anti-Mormon pamphlet, *Delusions: An Analysis of the Book of Mormon* (1832), Disciples of Christ preacher Alexander Campbell took on Smith and his scripture. According to Campbell, "this Atheist Smith" was "as ignorant and impudent a knave as ever wrote a book." And his book—an "impious fraud"—was no Bible. "I would as soon compare a bat to the American eagle [or] a mouse to a mammoth," wrote Campbell, " . . . as to contrast it with a single chapter in all the writings of the Jewish or Christian prophets." But above all Campbell charged Smith with anachronism. Though Smith slathered his book with ancient sounding "Smithisms"—"all the King James' *haths, dids* and *doths*"—the volume he produced had all over it the fingerprints of upstate New York in the 1820s. In the Book of Mormon, Smith includes "every error and almost every truth discussed in N. York for the last ten years," Campbell wrote. "He decides all the great controversies—infant baptism, ordination, the trinity, regeneration, repentance, justification, the fall of man, the atonement, transubstantiation, fasting, penance, church government, religious experience, the call to the ministry, the general resurrection, eternal punishment, who may baptize, and even the question of freemasonry, republican government, and the rights of man."[20]

Many early critics saw Mormonism through the lens of anti-Catholicism, sneering at "Pope Joseph the First" and LDS "priest-craft."[21] In 1842, former Mormon leader John Bennett charged Smith with plotting "a daring and colossal scheme of rebellion and usurpation" that would crown him as "emperor and pope" of "a despotic military and religious empire" stretching from Ohio to Iowa.[22] In a political cartoon, Thomas Nast drew a crocodile called "Roman Church" and a turtle called "Mormon Church" crawling onto the Capitol dome. The caption read: "Religious liberty is guaranteed— but can we allow foreign reptiles to crawl all over us?"[23]

Other critics compared Mormonism with Islam, calling the Book of Mormon "a new Alcoran" and Smith the "Yankee Mahomet."[24] This was not meant as a compliment. Like Muhammad, these critics argued, Smith was a false prophet peddling a false Bible and willing to advance his false religion by force. Writing from Henderson, Illinois, in 1841, Congregationalist minister S. G. Wright referred to Mormonism as "a second edition of Mohammedanism," adding that there was "cause to fear" this Second Coming because LDS members were "intending to support their claims to this country at the point of the bayonet."[25] According to some witnesses, Smith wore the "Mormon Mahomet" sobriquet as a badge of honor.[26] Ex-Mormon Thomas Marsh swore in an 1838 affidavit, "I have heard the prophet say that he should yet tread down his enemies, and walk over their dead bodies; that if he was not let alone he would be a second Mahomet to this generation, and that he would make it one gore of blood from the Rocky Mountains to the Atlantic Ocean; that like Mahomet, whose motto, in treating for peace, was 'the Alcoran, or the Sword,' so should it be eventually with us, 'Joseph Smith or the Sword.' "[27]

But early anti-Mormonism was not driven entirely by theological concerns, or by unflattering comparisons with Catholicism and Islam. Wherever Mormons gathered, local critics found social, political, economic, and cultural reasons to hate them. They were poor and unkempt. They were wealthy and they inflated land prices. They opposed slavery. They stuck to their own. Missouri's "old settlers" were particularly concerned about bloc voting. Critics saw this Mormon practice as an affront to republican virtue in a country where each individual was supposed to cast his own vote in keeping with his own conscience. They also saw bloc voting as a political threat. "It requires no gift of prophecy," read an 1833 citizen declaration demanding the removal of Mormons from Jackson County, Missouri, "to tell that the day is not far distant when the civil government of the county will be in their hands; when the sheriff, the justices and the county judges will be Mormons, or persons wishing to court their favor from motives of interest or ambition."[28]

Efforts to bar Mormons from voting led to an election riot in 1838 in Gallatin, Missouri, which sparked a "Mormon War" in the northwestern part of the state. During this conflict, critics denounced LDS members as a "tribe of locusts" who threatened "to scorch and wither the herbage of a fair and goodly portion of Missouri."[29] Others compared the LDS influx to a black cloud or a volcano. But it wasn't just names that hurt them. Mormons were driven from Jackson County to Clay County to Caldwell County by Missourians who destroyed their houses, tarred and feathered their leaders, and threatened graver harms if the Mormons in their midst did not take their fanaticism elsewhere. Naïvely, Mormons appealed to the courts and the governor to protect their lives, liberty, and property. When these appeals fell on deaf ears, Mormons decided to fend for themselves.

Following the Ursuline convent riot of 1834, Bishop Fenwick had told Boston's Catholics to turn the other cheek. On July 4, 1838, LDS leader Sidney Rigdon chose another path, delivering a stern "declaration of independence" from mobocracy in which he solemnly swore that the Mormons were done with suffering passively at the hands of bloodthirsty mobs. After warning enemies of his church "to come on us no more forever," he pledged that, for anyone who did, "it shall be between us and them a war of extermination, for we will follow them till the last drop of their blood is spilled, or else they will have to exterminate us."[30]

This fiery rhetoric fired up the Mormons, who mobbed people they suspected of plotting to mob them and burned down buildings in the process. It also fired up the opposition, sparking battles between Mormon and anti-Mormon militias. On October 27, 1838, Missouri governor Lilburn Boggs, finding the Mormons in defiance of the laws of the state and at war with its people, issued a notorious executive order that read: "The Mormons must be treated as enemies, and must be exterminated or driven from the state if necessary for the public peace."[31] Three days later, in the bloodiest day of Missouri's Mormon War, a mob attacked an LDS settlement at Haun's Mill, killing at least seventeen men and boys. Shortly thereafter, Joseph Smith and other LDS leaders were captured and imprisoned. Held for months on charges of treason, they narrowly avoided execution by firing squad.

As Missouri was emptied in the late 1830s of Mormons (including Smith himself, who escaped from prison on April 15, 1839), it became plain that the governor, his militia, and the mobs had won. But there was some sympathy in more liberal quarters for members of an upstart religion who, according to many eastern newspapers, were (to quote Shakespeare) "more sinned against than sinning."[32] Unitarian minister William Henry Channing contributed to this tepid liberal counterattack by describing the "madness" of Missouri anti-Mormonism as "a tragedy of almost unequalled horror." He also connected the dots between anti-Catholicism and anti-Mormonism, decrying both the "unbridled mobocracy" unleashed on the Mormons and "the burning of the convent at Charlestown."[33] Such sympathy from eastern liberals swelled in the years after Missouri's Mormon War, as Saints scattered and gathered and scattered again.

Invited to Illinois by citizens sympathetic to their suffering and a governor keen for their votes, Mormons built Nauvoo, Illinois, into the second largest city in the state (after Chicago) in the early 1840s. Given the sorrows that had accompanied their separatism, Smith might have opted for a strategy of accommodation. Instead he introduced theological and ritual innovations that piqued the curiosity of locals and outraged critics. As R. Laurence Moore has argued, Smith deliberately invented and aggressively advertised "Mormon difference," inviting persecution (and attracting followers) along the way.[34] Rather than assimilating, Mormon leaders repeatedly doubled down, staking a claim to their Americanness by emphasizing their outsiderhood. "Let us alone and we will evangelize the world and not make much fuss about it," the ever-defiant Brigham Young said in 1844. "Mob us & we will do it sooner."[35]

In Nauvoo, Smith taught that God was corporeal, with "flesh and bones," and that divinity was many, not one—that we, too, could be gods.[36] He instituted (secretly) the practice for which his movement would become notorious: plural marriage. And by the Church's own admission he took as many as forty wives himself. But Smith did not just lord over a church increasingly at odds with nearby Methodists and Baptists. He also crafted a "theodemocracy" (his term) in which he personally controlled the executive, legislative, and judicial branches of government plus a local militia called the Nauvoo Legion. These actions provoked the mobs that cost Joseph Smith his life and the Mormon people yet another Zion.[37]

After Smith's assassination in 1844, Mormons went west under the direction of their second president and prophet, Brigham Young. Long-standing believers in the promises of America and the divine inspiration of the Constitution, LDS leaders by the 1840s had come to see the United States as a site of corrupted Christianity *and* corrupted republicanism—a reprobate republic that had betrayed its founding promises. So with Missouri laid waste and Nauvoo besieged, they began an epic journey into what was then Mexico—across the Great Plains and into the Great Basin between the Rocky Mountains and the Sierra Nevada. As they left a country they had come to see as unjust, Mormon matriarch Eliza Snow urged them on:

> *Let us go, let us go where our rights are secure,*
> *Where the waters are clear and the atmosphere pure,*
> *Where the hand of oppression has never been felt,*
> *Where the blood of the Prophets has never been spilt.*[38]

National Anti-Mormonism

THIS EXODUS MIGHT have put an end to the bloodshed, but a series of events conspired, first, to reconnect these expats to other Americans and, then, to metamorphose the "Mormon menace" from a local concern into a national crusade.

Less than a year after the first Mormons arrived in lands surrounding the Great Salt Lake in 1847, the discovery of gold at Sutter's Mill in northern California in 1848 put an end to their brief isolation by sending entrepreneurs from the east scurrying across their lands. Also in 1848, the Treaty of Guadalupe Hidalgo, which concluded the Mexican–American War, transferred control over the Salt Lake Valley from Mexico to the United States. In the Compromise of 1850, Congress turned that land, home to over eleven thousand Mormons, into the Utah Territory. That same year President Millard Fillmore appointed Brigham Young Utah's governor, turning any "Mormon problem" that might develop there into literally a federal case.

A more crucial catalyst for the nationalization of anti-Mormonism came in August 1852, when the LDS Church, in an announcement literary critic Harold Bloom characterized as "the most courageous act of spiritual defiance in all of American history,"[39] went public with its doctrine of plural marriage (also known as "celestial marriage" or "the Principle"). Joseph Smith may have believed in this doctrine as early as 1831, and as the *Nauvoo Expositor* controversy indicates, polygamy had been an open secret among Mormon leaders from the early 1840s forward. In January 1852, Ohio congressman David Cartter observed that this practice was being "whispered, and more than whispered" in the Utah Territory.[40] At a special conference in Salt Lake City in August 1852, that whisper turned into a shout when Orson Pratt, a member of the Quorum of the Twelve Apostles (the highest LDS governing body after the presidency), announced publicly "that the Latter Day Saints have embraced, as part and portion of their religion, the doctrine of a plurality of wives." Pratt defended that doctrine on the basis of the Bible, ongoing revelation, anthropology, and sociology. Four-fifths of the world is polygamous, he observed, and in monogamous nations "whoredom, adultery, and fornication" predominate. Moreover, plural marriage had been practiced by Abraham and other biblical patriarchs. Anticipating legal battles to come, Pratt also argued for plurality of wives on religious-liberty grounds. He rejected the view that this doctrine was "something that pertains to domestic pleasures, in no way connected with religion." In fact, it was "part and portion of our religious faith . . . necessary for our exaltation to the fullness of the Lord's glory in the eternal world." To forbid this "essential doctrine" would be to forbid Mormonism itself. Therefore, "it is constitutional."[41]

After Pratt concluded his Great Announcement, Brigham Young endorsed this "essential doctrine" with his trademark gusto, observing matter-of-factly that Smith "had more wives than one" and prophesying that plural marriage will one day "ride triumphantly above all the prejudice and priestcraft of the day; it will be fostered and believed in by the more intelligent portions of the world, as one of the best doctrines ever proclaimed to any people." Thomas Bullock then read a previously undisclosed "revelation on celestial marriage" from 1843 in which God instructed Joseph Smith to embrace marriage for eternity and a plurality of wives.[42]

This epiphany opened the door to a nationwide culture war, and critics of the "Mormon menace" rushed in. During the second half of the nineteenth century (and particularly after the end of the Civil War put an end to the slavery debate), these critics founded antipolygamy societies, wrote and read antipolygamy novels, delivered and listened to antipolygamy sermons and lectures, chuckled at antipolygamy political cartoons, laughed at antipolygamy jokes, applauded at antipolygamy plays, read antipolygamy editorials, and agitated for antipolygamy legislation. Mark Twain and *New-York Tribune* editor Horace Greeley traveled to Salt Lake City and filed reports. So did the British adventurer and *Kama Sutra* aficionado Sir Richard Burton (who found, to his regret, that Mormon marriages were as boring as monogamous ones). Before the "Mormon question" was settled, the nation would also hear from congressmen, senators, presidents, and Supreme Court justices.

Some of this talk would be civil. But much of it bordered on hysteria. For the leader of a church, Young used surprisingly smutty language, calling lesser Mormon leaders "my niggers" and delighting in shocking reporters.[43] "The only difference between your system at the East and ours," he told the *New York Times*, "is that you keep your whores and treat them like brutes, and we keep ours and treat them like human beings."[44] Meanwhile, Young's critics struggled to outscream one another. A book called *The Mormon Monster* gave this queasy history of the Mormon movement: "It was born in the womb of imposture, nursed in the lap of fraud, rocked in the cradle of deception, clothed in the garments of superstition, fed on the milk of ignorance, and fattened on the strong meat of sensualism, despotism, fanaticism, crime, bloodshed, and rebellion."[45] Even church historian Robert Baird let his emotions get the best of him, calling Mormonism "the grossest of all the delusions that Satanic malignity or human ambition ever sought to propagate."[46] Apparently these delusions had some real-world effects, or so said Southern preachers who blamed a spate of cyclones on Mormon missionaries.[47]

As in other culture wars, conservatives launched the first attacks. Mormons counterattacked by chastising their opponents for warring on religious liberty and trampling the Constitution. Anti-Mormons responded by arguing that the Constitution provided no cover for tyranny and licentiousness. "Polygamy marks the line . . . between all that is depraved, selfish, and corrupt, and all that is pure, noble, and exalted," argued Rep. Hiram Walbridge (D-NY) in 1854. It may be fit for "the semi-barbarous nations of China, Turkey, Tartary, and the savages of our forest, and the barbaric tribes of benighted Africa," he said, but it is unfit for a U.S. territory. "It wars against virtue, the spirit of public liberty, and the dignity of our race. It is an enemy not only to be resisted, but overcome, not only to be held in check now, but put down forever."[48]

When the center of gravity of anti-Mormon concerns shifted in the 1850s from a person (Smith) to an institution (the LDS Church) and from a scripture (the Book of Mormon) to a practice (polygamy), Mormons ceased to be seen as a threat to good order in Kirtland or Nauvoo alone. They came to be seen as a threat to a still fragile republic. Decades earlier, conservatives had feared a Catholic takeover of the Midwest. Now they feared a Mormon takeover of the West—"a vast military domination . . . from California to Cape Horn."[49] Some came to believe it was time to put an end to "Mormondom" itself. Rep. Emerson Etheridge, a former Know-Nothing from Tennessee, called for the "extirpation of Mormonism in Utah."[50] A preacher (also from Tennessee) argued in a commencement speech for genocide. "The strong arm of government should be employed," he said, "to wipe from the face of civilization every Latter-day Saint in Utah, men, women and children."[51]

A few liberal "Gentiles" defended the Mormons against their conservative despisers. Illinois's Stephen Douglas, now remembered for sparring with Abraham Lincoln in the Lincoln–Douglas debates, advocated for the Mormons so forcefully that some accused him of being a closet Mormon. Viewing antipolygamy as a hammer that threatened to smash not only the "peculiar institution" of Utah but also the "peculiar institution" of the South, he argued on the basis of the principle of popular sovereignty against federal interference in either polygamy or slavery. Rabbi Louis Weiss, in a letter to the *Chattanooga Times*, called on the governor of Georgia to come to the defense of Mormons who had been assaulted by mobs in that state. Of this mob violence, Weiss wrote: "I can safely say that such action is not Christian; it is surely not religious; and it is positively not in accord with biblical injunction."[52]

As they debated how to answer the Mormon question—would "gunpowder and cold steel" be necessary, or would a war of words do the trick?[53]—Americans once again considered whether the United States was a secular nation or a Christian one, and if Christian, what manner of Christian should it be. The Great Basin may have been, in the words of Brigham Young, "a good place to make Saints," but it was also a good place to make (and find) trouble.[54] And for the rest of the century the Mormons did some of both.

Buchanan's Folly

IN 1856, THE new Republican Party listed polygamy alongside slavery as one of the "twin relics of barbarism" and urged Congress to outlaw it in all U.S. territories. But when Democrat James Buchanan was elected president that year, his party initially sidestepped the Mormon question on the theory that any meddling with the domestic arrangements of husbands and wives in the West might justify meddling with the domestic arrangements of slaveholders and slaves in the South. In April 1857, however, barely a month after Buchanan's inauguration, an adviser urged him to stir up trouble in Utah in order to divert attention from slavery. "I believe," Robert Tyler (son of former president John Tyler) told Buchanan, "that we can supersede the Negro-Mania with the almost universal excitements of an Anti-Mormon Crusade . . . and the piping's of Abolitionism will hardly be heard amidst the thunders of the storm we shall raise."[55] One month later, Buchanan declared the Utah Territory to be in a state of rebellion against the United States, dismissed Young as its governor, and ordered the U.S. Army to march on Salt Lake City to install his replacement by force. This ill-fated effort to combat what Buchanan called the "despotic power" of Young and the "frenzied fanaticism" of his followers bogged down in winter weather and never engaged Mormon militias.[56] But "Buchanan's Folly" did prompt a tragedy that helped to turn the nation against the LDS Church.

Long before Buchanan's soldiers were anywhere near Salt Lake City, Young made it clear he would neither compromise nor accommodate. He had reasons to resist, including popular sovereignty and religious liberty. But most of his rhetoric was emotional, even apocalyptic, referring to territorial officers as "poor, miserable blacklegs, broken down political hacks, robbers and whoremongers," and to the impending "Utah War" as a battle between "kingdoms of darkness" and "the kingdom of God."[57]

In an August 5, 1857, gubernatorial proclamation, Young rehearsed the sorry saga of Mormon persecution in the New World:

> For the last twenty five years we have trusted officials of the Government, from Constables and Justices to Judges, Governors, and Presidents, only to be scorned, held in derision, insulted and betrayed. Our houses have been plundered and then burned, our fields laid waste, our principal men butchered while under the pledged faith of the government for their safety, and our families driven from their homes to find shelter

in the barren wilderness and that protection among hostile savages which were denied them in the boasted abodes of Christianity and civilization.

And why did this Christian civilization persecute them? "Because of our religious faith," and because of the prejudices of "hireling priests and howling editors who prostitute the truth for filthy lucre's sake."[58]

Recalling American Revolution patriots and Mormon martyrs (and anticipating the "by any means necessary" rhetoric of Malcolm X), Young asserted the right of self-defense against "oppression" and vowed to exercise it. "Our duty to ourselves, to our families, requires us not to tamely submit to be driven and slain, without an attempt to preserve ourselves," he wrote. "Our duty to our country, our holy religion, our God, to freedom and liberty, requires that we should not quietly stand still and see those fetters forging around, which are calculated to enslave." Young then forbade the U.S. Army from entering Utah, called on Utah militias to prepare to fight, and declared martial law.[59] But he did more than ready for war. He also got up a religious revival now remembered as the Mormon Reformation. Church leaders preached hellfire and damnation. Church members were rebaptized. Men and women were encouraged to enter into plural marriages.

As federal soldiers approached, non-Mormon migrants from Arkansas and Missouri were driving cattle through Utah on the way to California. On September 11, 1857, Mormon militiamen, accompanied by Paiute Indians, massacred more than one hundred twenty migrants, demonstrating that the violence in this culture war could be inflicted *by* Mormons as well as *on* them. Reports and illustrations of the Mountain Meadows Massacre, as it came to be called, seared into the nation's consciousness the image of Mormons as western vigilantes. But according to Patrick Mason, this tragedy did more than that. It demonstrated "the dangerousness of 'fanaticism,' the utter depravity of Mormonism, and the lawlessness of Utah."[60]

Still, Congress did not take on polygamy, at least not before the Civil War. Efforts to twin slavery and polygamy energized many Northern Republicans, who argued that, like slavery, polygamy was "a great moral, social, and political evil" "at war with all true liberty" and at odds with "the law of God" and "the law of every State in the Union."[61] But the family resemblance between these two "peculiar institutions" boxed in Southern Democrats. As Rep. Lawrence Branch (D-NC) put it, "If we can render polygamy criminal, it may be claimed that we can also render criminal that other 'twin relic of barbarism,' slavery."[62] In congressional debates, Southerners typically expressed their personal disdain for the "nauseating and disgusting crime" of polygamy only to conclude that any effort to outlaw it would be unconstitutional.[63] Some spoke of limits on federal power. "Sir, I think polygamy a burning shame upon any community . . . and I will extirpate this disgraceful evil as quickly and as sharply as any man, if I can but see the power of Congress to do it," said Laurence Keitt (D-SC).[64] Others emphasized religious liberty. "What right has this Government to interfere with the religious relations of the people in this Territory?" asked William Boyce of South Carolina.[65] Alexander Stephens of Georgia said, "If we discriminate to-day against *Mormons*, to-morrow, perhaps, we shall be asked to discriminate against Baptists, Methodists, Presbyterians, or Catholics."[66]

By 1862, the Confederacy had seceded from the Union and Southern Democrats had left the House and Senate, so Congress was able to pass legislation criminalizing polygamy in the territories. This bill, the Morrill Act, was sponsored by Justin Morrill of Vermont (the birth state of both Smith and Young), who as early as 1857 had argued on the House floor against both "the foul abomination of spiritual wifery" and any notion "that we must tamely submit to any burlesque, outrage, or indecency which artful men may seek to hide under the name of religion!"[67]

On July 1, 1862, President Lincoln signed the Morrill Act, which proved to be a dead letter. It provided no means for enforcement in a territory in which the executive, legislative, and judicial branches (juries included) were dominated by Mormons. And there was little will in Washington to try to enforce it. When asked by an LDS member what he intended to do about the Mormons, Lincoln told this story:

> When I was a boy on the farm in Illinois there was a great deal of timber on the farms which we had to clear away. Occasionally we would come to a log which had fallen down. It was too hard to split, too wet to burn and too heavy to move, so we plowed around it. That's what I intend to do with the Mormons. You go back and tell Brigham Young that if he will let me alone, I will let him alone.[68]

But the Morrill Act was not without effect. As many Southern defenders of the Mormons had feared, federal interference with the domestic institution of polygamy *did* prepare the way for federal interference with the domestic institution of slavery. On January 1, 1863, just six months after Lincoln signed the Morrill Act, he issued the Emancipation Proclamation, which declared "all persons held as slaves . . . shall be . . . thenceforward, and forever free."[69]

After the nation settled the slavery question by blood and bayonets, Lincoln's live-and-let-live attitude gave way to a consensus in the nation's capital that plowing around the not-so-saintly Saints had gone on long enough. The ensuing clash, which the Atlanta-based *Christian Index* deemed "the most important that has ever engaged the attention of our National Government," stretched across the Atlantic Ocean to England, where A. Conan Doyle gave Mormon polygamy a prominent place in his first Sherlock Holmes story, "A Study in Scarlet," and Pope Leo XIII condemned it (and Mormonism itself) in an encyclical.[70]

Back in the United States, polygamy became *the* cultural preoccupation of the 1880s.[71] Efforts to effect a "Second Reconstruction" in Utah brought together "southerners with northerners, states with the federal government, Democrats with Republicans, and clergy and lay members of various Protestant denominations."[72] This conservative coalition also included presidents of both major parties. Beginning with Rutherford Hayes, five consecutive presidents denounced what Chester Arthur referred to as the "odious crime" of polygamy.[73] After the paroxysms of the Civil War and Reconstruction, Mormons helped to bind up the nation's wounds by providing it with a common enemy.

This culture war proceeded on two fronts, one moral and the other political, as conservatives blasted the LDS Church for spreading polygamy and theocracy. For some conservative culture warriors, this was a fight for Christian civilization. For others, it was a defense of the American republic. But for most, these two agendas blurred into one moral crusade—for democracy, Christianity, and the American family. "Let Mormonism prevail," said Rev. William Strickland of Tennessee, "and we sap the very foundation of society and wipe out the Christian home."[74]

The Moral Argument Against "White Slavery"

ACCORDING TO ONE critic, the list of Mormon offenses against the nation and its God included "infidelity, deism, atheism; lying, deception, blasphemy; debauchery, lasciviousness, bestiality; madness, fraud, plunder; larceny, burglary, robbery, perjury; fornication, adultery, rape, incest; arson, treason, and murder."[75] But polygamy topped the list. This "scarlet whore," in the words of Rep. John McClernand (D-IL), was a key theme in anti-Mormon literature before the LDS Church publicly proclaimed the doctrine in 1852, but thereafter it was *the* preoccupation.[76] Polygamy was primitive, according to the racist logic of secretary of the Territory of Utah Benjamin Ferris, belonging not to advanced nations but "to the indolent and opium-eating Turks and Asiatics, the miserable Africans, the North American savages, and the Latter-day Saints. It is the offspring of lust, and its legitimate results are soon manifest in the rapid degeneracy of races."[77] (In this way, Mormons, like Jefferson before them, were also "twinned" to Muslims [a.k.a. "Turks"].)

Like anti-Catholics, anti-Mormons promoted their cause through a variety of literary genres. Some of these works were marketed as fiction. Others were, in the words of scholar Eric Eliason, "pseudononfictional"—"true life" tales that refused to allow the facts to get in the way of a good story.[78] This literature presented Mormonism (like Catholicism in convent captivity narratives) as a religion that sacrificed the innocence of women on the altar of male lust. Tabloid titles and purple prose showcased the tragedies of innocent heroines duped by despotic religious leaders. Instead of being forced into nunneries to satisfy the carnal desires of Catholic priests, however, these women were forced into "harems" lorded over by "libidinous 'Saints' and lecherous 'prophets.'"[79] Once again, Gothic tropes of horror predominated: demonic men, innocent women, lust, madness, imprisonment, seduction, betrayal, rape, and underground torture chambers. In this case, the stories were set in the Wild West and unveiled the mysteries of Salt Lake City, "the biggest whorehouse in the world."[80]

Following Harriet Beecher Stowe, who used her talents as a sentimental novelist to bring down slavery in *Uncle Tom's Cabin*, antipolygamy writers sought to stir the sympathies of their readers against this grave threat to women and their families. In other words, they portrayed polygamy as an assault on family values—"an organized, systemized attack on the permanence and purity of the Christian home."[81] Mormon wives were "enslaved, hopeless, helpless."[82] Their husbands were the "hyenas of society," sexual predators whose unbridled lust turned homes into harems and Salt Lake City into "the Sodom of the Occident."[83] Ministers, social reformers, and journalists denounced this "congregation of sensualists" in pulpits, newspapers, and magazines.[84] Also joining this conservative opposition

were leaders of the Reorganized Church of Jesus Christ of Latter
Day Saints, a breakaway group that flatly denied that Joseph Smith
ever practiced plural marriage and condemned the "Brighamites"
for introducing it.[85] But the most powerful antipolygamy voices
belonged to Mormon defectors, whose memoirs read like a combination of Puritan-era captivity stories and slave narratives.

Wife No. 19 (1875), a memoir by Ann Eliza Young, who left
the LDS Church and sued Brigham Young for divorce in the early
1870s, was a huge hit. Billed as "The Rebel of the Harem," she went
on a nationwide lecture tour that included a stop in Washington,
DC, where President Ulysses Grant and members of Congress heard
her describe her "life in bondage" to the Church and her exodus
from the clutches of a Mormon pharaoh. Mormonism's "chief 'beauties,'" she contended, were "incest, murder, suicide, mania and
bestiality."[86]

The "pseudononfictional" answer to Maria Monk's *Awful Disclosures* was Maria Ward's *Female Life Among the Mormons* (1855),
which presented Mormon plural wives as victims of (among other
things) mesmerism and cannibalism. In a lurid passage on "Mormon
Barbarities," a plural wife who dared to criticize Mormonism's signature institution "was taken one night when she stepped out for
water, gagged, carried a mile into the woods, stripped nude, tied
to a tree, and scourged till the blood ran from her wounds to the
ground, in which condition she was left till the next night, when
her tormenters visited her again, took her back to her husband's
residence, and laid her on the door-step, where she remained till
morning."[87]

As this story intimates, antipolygamy novelists drew frequent
parallels between African slavery in the South and "white slavery"
in the West. Repeatedly, conservatives described polygamy as bondage and the movement to uproot it as the new abolitionism. After
witnessing female converts on a boat heading to America under the
aegis of a "snaky" Mormon missionary, Jennie Fowler Willing wrote:

My heart ached for them, for I knew the plunge into the awful sea of sensuality that awaited them. They would be taken to Utah, and at each station, the men would flock about the train, picking out the girls that suited their fancy, paying the missionary for them, each loading his purchases into a wagon, and driving off to the farm where the poor thing would be set to raising pigs, poultry, and babies, for her master's enrichment and aggrandizement.[88]

In *Boadicea: The Mormon Wife* (1855), Alfreda Eva Bell wrote that Mormon wives are "white slaves" who "are required to do all the most servile drudgery; are painfully impressed with their nothingness and utter inferiority . . . and are frequently . . . subjected to personal violence and various modes of corporeal punishment."[89] In her dedication "to the Mormon wives of Utah," which appeared in *Wife No. 19*, Ann Eliza Young prayed "for your deliverance from the worse than Egyptian bondage in which you are held." "Come out of the house of bondage!" she commanded these "Mormon wives." "This Christian realm is not 'Babylon,' but THE PROMISED LAND!" Later in the book, Young argued that polygamy was "more cruel than African slavery ever was, since it claims to hold body and soul alike."[90]

Harriet Beecher Stowe hit similar notes in a preface to a book by another runaway from polygamy's chains. After commending Fanny Stenhouse's *Tell It All* (1874) as "a plain, unvarnished tale of truth, stranger and sadder than fiction," Stowe wrote:

Our day has seen a glorious breaking of fetters. The slave-pens of the South have become a nightmare of the past; the auction-block and whipping-post have given place to the church and school-house; and songs of emancipated millions are heard through our land.

Shall we not then hope that the hour is come to loose the

bonds of a cruel slavery whose chains have cut into the very hearts of thousands of our sisters—a slavery which debases and degrades womanhood, motherhood, and the family?[91]

In a later piece in the *Anti-Polygamy Standard* of the Ladies' Anti-Polygamy Society, Stowe made a similar appeal to the "Women of America": "Let every happy wife and mother who reads these lines give her sympathy, prayers and effect to free her sisters from this degrading bondage."[92]

Stowe's appearance on this cultural battlefield might suggest that the real liberals in this culture war were the anti-Mormons, who labored to end the sin of "white slavery" just as abolitionists labored to end the sin of black slavery. And antipolygamists *did* draw on liberal themes, presenting themselves as champions of religious liberty and women's rights. But appearances can be deceiving. Throughout the history of America's culture wars, conservatives have latched on to the rhetoric of the Left. Today conservatives quote Martin Luther King Jr. to oppose affirmative action and cite Gandhi to justify blowing up abortion clinics. During the nineteenth century, proponents of Protestant America drew on abolitionist tropes in their efforts to eliminate their religious rivals. So while Stowe was a progressive evangelical on the slavery question, she was a conservative evangelical when it came to Mormons (and Catholics). The ligature connecting these positions was her commitment to the traditional family.

As literary critic Nancy Bentley has observed, antipolygamists such as Stowe described slavery and polygamy as "nearly identical crimes against the family."[93] In a society committed to the "cult of true womanhood," each of these "twin barbarisms" compromised the piety of American women, the purity of the American home, and the strength of the American republic.[94] In this way, polygamy came to be seen as both a corruption of female virtue and "a form of treason" against the nation.[95]

Given this identification of polygamy with "white slavery," out-siders struggled to understand why any woman would choose to become one wife among many—to receive one-half (or less) of her husband's affection.[96] And what most Mormon critics decided was that little choice was actually involved. In the antipolygamy novels of the second half of the nineteenth century, women were either brainwashed or duped into polygamy. Some fell under the hypnotic talents of Mormon con men. Others set sail from England and en-tered into marriages in Utah in good faith, only to discover to their horror that they were wife number two or three or more.

The Political Argument Against Theocracy

POLYGAMY WAS NOT the Mormons' only sin. Theocracy was, ac-cording to many, an equal danger, because it undermined the patrio-tism of "traitorous" LDS leaders and rank-and-file Mormons alike.[97]

"Is not Mormonism inimical to the institutions of our country?" asked William Harris in *Mormonism Portrayed* (1841). After all, Mormons were obliged to follow Smith's revelations wherever they might lead, and often they led headlong into politics. According to Harris, Mormons "have voted, almost to a man, with Smith"—a clear violation of the "civil compact," which says that "all shall think and act for themselves." Suppose that Mormons became a major-ity in a state. "Would it be right that such a majority, controlled by *one man*, should rule? Would not such a state of things be a total subversion of Republicanism, and the establishment, in effect, of a despotism?"[98]

The *Nauvoo Expositor*'s attack on Smith featured sharp critiques of his post–Book of Mormon innovations, including polygamy and "the doctrine of many Gods," but the main issue was abuse of power. In his "attempt to unite church and state," Smith had set himself up as "king or law-giver" and thus created a "religious despo-tism . . . incompatible with our free institutions." Moreover, Smith had used his nearly unlimited power in Nauvoo for personal gain. The practice of the gathering "has been taught by Joseph Smith and others for the purpose of enabling them to sell property at most exhorbitant prices, not regarding the welfare of the Church." In this way, "the wealth which is brought into the place is swallowed up by the one great throat, from whence there is no return."[99]

Later critics were convinced that Young's appetite for economic and political power was equally prodigious. In 1851, an LDS envoy returning from Washington told Young that President Fillmore "hoped you would not mingle your religion with your public duties."[100] But mingle he did. In fact, Young lorded over Utah like Smith had lorded over Nauvoo. Utah's economy ran across his desk. And thanks to Mormon militias, both rumored and real, Young was the most powerful military man west of the Mississippi.

On postcards and in political cartoons, Young was depicted as the fat man from Utah with more wives (and crying children) in his bed than he (or his biographers) could count. In Utah, critics described "the old Boss" as the territory's robber baron, monopolizing not only ecclesiastical, political, and military power but also economic life. According to Representative Morrill, Young wielded "more despotic power than is now exercised by any ruler on the globe where written constitutions are observed." Moreover, because of a tithing policy requiring members to contribute 10 percent of their income to his church, Young was making "a princely revenue."[101] According to the *New York Times*, Young—"as thorough a despot . . . as ever held the scepter"—served as Utah's de facto "Prophet, Priest and King."[102]

In making these arguments against LDS tyranny, anti-Mormon critics drew on anti-Catholic and anti-Muslim tropes of earlier decades. This time they raged against Young instead of Smith, conjuring up the specter of a new Vatican in the West. "An ecclesiastical hierarchy exists in Utah, with a plenitude of power greater than that which can to-day be exercised by the Pope of Rome," Morrill contended. "Its grasp is more merciless and far more selfish than Pius IX would dare attempt."[103]

Josiah Strong's *Our Country* (1885) is typically remembered as a nativist attack on Roman Catholicism, but it also includes an anti-Mormon chapter. There Strong argues that the real peril of Mormonism was political, not sexual. "Polygamy is not an essential part of Mormonism" (since the movement began without it) "nor is polygamy a very large part of Mormonism" (since a very small percentage of Mormons practiced it). The real peril of Mormonism is its "ecclesiastical despotism." There existed, in Strong's judgment, an "irrepressible conflict between Utah Mormonism and American republicanism." Unlike democratic America, in which "we the people" ruled, the LDS Church was "ruled by a man who is prophet, priest, king and pope, all in one." And its power was growing day by day, via missions, childbirth, and the "systematic colonization" of "vast tracts of land."[104]

Picking up on earlier attempts to tar Mormons with the stain of Islam, critics denounced the LDS Church as a false religion with a false prophet peddling false revelations. This time, however, the despot was "the Mohammed of Salt Lake."[105] Observers continued to complain that both Mormonism and "Mohammedanism" supplemented the Bible with "a volume of miserable fables" and a "spurious prophet."[106] But in searching for what the *Methodist Review* called "the points of contact and resemblance between the Mohammedanism of the East, and the Mormonism of the West," critics after the Great Announcement of 1852 also homed in on polygamy.[107] According to Jennie Fowler Willing, whose *On American Soil; or, Mormonism the Mohammedanism of the West* (1906) gave voice to more than half a century of anti-Mormon anxiety, Utah's "Mohammedanism" aped Islam by offering its followers polygamy in this world and "a sensual, material heaven" in the next. But Willing also took aim at political and economic life among the Saints, arguing that both Islam and Mormonism "proselyte by violence" and "aim at universal domination." The LDS isn't a religion of salvation, she wrote in a claim that would be resurrected in the twenty-first-century Islam wars. It is "a great financial and political scheme"—a "bossism" of the West in which the Saints' reigning prophet serves as "absolute ecclesiastical ruler" and "political monarch."[108]

Attempts to prove the Church's guilt by association with Islam were so widespread that as early as 1861 the LDS paper *The Millennial Star* found itself plea-bargaining. "Nearly everybody who has heard or read of 'Mormonism' and the 'Mormons' from Gentile sources has found the name of Joseph and Mahomet coupled, and the religious systems founded by the Eastern and Western Prophets classed together and likened one to the other," Mormon missionary E. W. Tullidge observed. The purpose of trotting out this "caricature" was to "blacken" Smith and the Church. Nonetheless, the analogy was "much more in our favour than against us," since it illustrated "the Saints as empire-founders." Unlike Islam, Tullidge reasoned, Mormonism "has not a military mission, nor has it been built up by the sword, nor will it be built up or extended by military aggression and conquests." Saints built their empire by preaching and gathering. "Their forced exoduses from the Gentiles," rather than shrinking their numbers, only augmented them.[109]

Still, many critics saw "Mormondom" as a threat to the Christian family and the American republic. To bring this point home, critics depicted Mormon women as serfs and Mormon men as tyrants. The suffragist and freethinker Matilda Joslyn Gage classified Mormonism among the religions that "subjugate the many to the caprice of the few." She, too, objected to polygamy, but chiefly in political terms. "The Mormon marriage formula," wrote Gage, "directs the man to look to God, but enjoins the woman to look toward her husband as God, rendering him the same unquestioning obedience that has been demanded from all Christian wives through the ages."[110] Women's rights activist Kate Field, who lectured widely on "The Mormon Monster" in the 1880s, described polygamy as "only a secondary evil." The real crime was tyranny, which turned rank-and-file Mormons into "slaves to the church and traitors to the United States Government."[111]

Utah women were the first Americans of their gender to vote (in 1870), but what good was female suffrage if wives were forced to cast their ballots as their husbands saw fit? "It does not take much arithmetic," wrote Willing, "to see that the man who can march to the polls with the votes of ten wives, and twenty daughters in his vest pocket, is a powerful man. He has multiplied himself by thirty-one."[112]

A memorial opposing Utah statehood and passed in 1889 by both houses of the Idaho legislature broadened this critique to cover the control exercised by the leaders of this "treasonable" church over their flocks:

> The turning over of a State government to said Mormon Church, or the leaders thereof, would be unsafe and impolitic, because said church is composed by a large majority of the lowest and most densely ignorant classes of the Old World peasantry, who are in no way Americanized, and who have nothing in common with our aims or our republican institutions. They are serfs, and serfs only—slaves to the most tyrannical and despotic organization in existence. They are absolutely under the control of their leaders, and the use of the ballot in their hands would be entirely under the direction of said leaders, and a travesty of the elective franchise.[113]

Mormon Defenses of Polygamy

ONE SCHOLAR HAS observed that, in the "war of words" between Mormons and their opponents, "both sides delivered as many blows as they observed."[114] That is incorrect. Mormons did fight for their civil rights and their religious freedom. At times they provoked their opponents to violence. They also inflicted violence themselves. But like all U.S. culture wars, this one was lopsided. In fact, it was the most lopsided culture war in American history. Mormons were a tiny minority in this fight, and liberal defenders of religious liberty largely abandoned them. Even legislators who opposed antipolygamy legislation went out of their way to denounce the LDS Church. And the wider crusade of "the home against the harem," which preoccupied not only legislators but also novelists, journalists, and ministers, was even more one-sided.[115] By the time Utah statehood came in 1896, Mormons likely had absorbed a thousand blows for every one they had delivered. But Mormons did strike back.

Anti-Mormons had repeatedly argued that polygamy was hazardous to one's health, likening it to the "plague," "malaria," a "cancer in the breast of the nation," and an "Asiatic and African pestilence."[116] Senator Douglas, who had previously supported the Mormons, turned on them in a debate with Lincoln on June 12, 1857, calling on Congress "to apply the knife and cut out this loathsome, disgusting ulcer."[117] But Mormons saw plural marriage as a cure. Taking their cues from Orson Pratt's famous defense of polygamy, they argued for plural marriage on biblical, theological, sociological, and constitutional grounds.[118]

Biblically, Mormons argued that polygamy was better than monogamy at fulfilling God's commandment to "multiply, and replenish the earth" (Genesis 1:28). They described plural marriage as an "everlasting covenant," underscoring the fact that Abraham, Moses, and David had taken more than one wife.[119] And they said that God had reaffirmed this covenant in a revelation to Joseph Smith. Some even found warrant for "Abrahamic marriage" in the New Testament, claiming that Jesus (who was born into the polygamous line of David) married many wives and fathered many children.[120]

When it came to polygamy and the Bible, fair critics had to concede that the Mormons had a point. *The New York Herald* hoped for the "subjugation" of Mormonism and gave voice to the genocidal fantasies of others to see the "fields of Utah laid waste, and the Mormons hung by hundreds." It admitted, however, that the LDS Church had "unanswerable evidence" from scripture on its side: "So far, therefore, as the Holy Bible is concerned, the Mormons are, according to strict logic, much better qualified to persuade us to take four wives, than we are to induce them to stick to one."[121] "The Great Agnostic" Robert Ingersoll wryly described polygamy as "one of the institutions of Jehovah." "It is protected by the Bible," he wrote. "It has inspiration on its side."[122] If the Mormons had the Bible, however, they did not have the Book of Mormon. There God calls polygamy as "abominable before me" (Jacob 2:24).[123]

Theologically, Mormons placed the practice of polygamy inside a theology that spanned time and eternity. According to this theology, human souls live before they are incarnated on Earth, and polygamy is a way to bring more of these preexisting souls into the world. But Mormons looked forward as well—to their "exaltation" and even deification. Plural marriage brought husbands, wives, and children together into eternal glory.

Mormons also argued that monogamy was unnatural: by nature, men seek variety in sexual relations, and in monogamous societies they will do so in brothels and extramarital affairs. Look at Paris, said Orson's brother Parley Pratt, where one-third of the children are illegitimate, or to cities on America's Eastern Seaboard, which breed sexual sins. Turning the tables on antipolygamists, Pratt argued that the fruits of monogamy included "whoredoms, intrigues, seductions, wretched and lonely single life, hatred, envy, jealousy, infanticide, illegitimacy, disease and death."[124] But prostitution was unknown in Utah, which also had strict laws against adultery and fornication. No wonder monogamy is the outlier in world history, Mormon apologists said.

In defending polygamy on social grounds, Mormons did the math. The U.S. Census reported more female than male births, and the killing of men in wars further upset the gender balance. In an exclusively monogamous society, these numbers would doom many women to single life, but polygamy solved this demographic problem.

Mormons also worked hard to refute the claim that polygamy was antiwoman, responding to books such as *Wife No. 19* with stories of wives who not only consented to plural marriages but thrived in them. *Defence of Polygamy, by a Lady of Utah* (1854) began as a letter from Belinda Pratt, the sixth wife of Parley Pratt, to her sister in New Hampshire. Pratt made some familiar arguments (about how monogamy is unnatural for men because "it is his to move in a wider sphere"), but she also spoke surprisingly candidly about how polygamy gave women respite during menstruation from the otherwise overwhelming sexual needs of their husbands.[125]

Mormon women also hit back on the pages of the *Woman's Exponent* (est. 1872), a periodical run mostly by women. And Mormon women in both monogamous and polygamous marriages gathered en masse in favor of polygamy as divine commandment and common sense—"the only family system that safely contained men's sexual urges."[126] On January 13, 1870, prompted by proposed legislation that would have denied the right to vote to anyone who even *believed* in polygamy, a few thousand Mormon women protested at an "indignation meeting" at the Old Tabernacle on Salt Lake City's Temple Square. At a similar meeting that same year in Provo, Mormon women gathered "to stand up and defend this heaven-revealed principle."[127] The bill was defeated.

Religious Liberty and the First Amendment

MORMONS AND A few liberal defenders also argued that efforts to outlaw polygamy violated the First Amendment's free-exercise clause. Mormons were convinced that their opponents were driven first and foremost by religious animus—that Protestant ministers were the masterminds behind the anti-Mormon crusade. They sharply denounced their critics' efforts to run around the First Amendment by pretending that polygamy was not a religious matter. Polygamy was a keystone of Mormon faith, they insisted, and deserving of constitutional protection.

Utah delegate William Hooper, speaking on the House floor against the bill that would have criminalized belief in plural marriage, delivered an impassioned brief for religious liberty on behalf of the "most vigorously lied about of any people in the nation." He spoke of the Puritans who had "fled from their homes in Europe to the wilds of America" so "that they might worship God in accordance with the dictates of conscience." He raised the specter of those "fearful days of the Spanish inquisition, or the days when, in New England, Quakers were persecuted or banished, and witches burned at the stake." And he denounced the bill as "a disastrous precedent for future tyranny . . . in direct opposition to that toleration in religious belief which is characteristic of the nation and age." Channeling his inner Jefferson, he described belief in plural marriage as "an essential feature in our religious faith" and called on House members to cast a vote for religious liberty:

> It is not permitted, Mr. Speaker, that any one man should sit as the judge of any other as regards his religious belief. This is a matter which rests solely between each individual and his God. . . . Our Constitution throws over all sincere worshipers, at whatever shrine, its guarantee of absolute protection. The moment we assume to judge of the truthfulness or error of any creed the constitutional guarantee is a mockery and a sham.[128]

To such constitutional salvos, anti-Mormons responded in two ways. Some conceded that Mormonism was constitutionally protected but that polygamy and theocracy were not. "It is not a matter of religion," said a Virginia congressman. "It is a matter of vice."[129] Others made a more radical claim. Again anticipating twenty-first-century arguments against Islam, they asserted that Mormonism wasn't *really* a religion. It was a polygamous scheme, or a money-making racket, or a power grab, or all of the above. This argument circulated as early as the 1830s, when critics called Smith's "Gold Bible" yet another attempt by a money digger at self-enrichment and self-aggrandizement. It caught on in the 1870s and 1880s, when critics argued that the LDS Church was really a front for sexual license, political skullduggery, and economic gain. Moving far beyond those who had denounced Mormonism as a *false* religion, these critics drew on metaphors of disguise and anxieties about confidence men to argue that Mormonism was a *non*-religion. Mormonism "is not a religion according to the American idea and the United States Constitution," wrote a Congregationalist critic.[130] Some even put the term in scare quotes, as in "the vileness and villainies of Brigham Young's 'religion.'"[131] From this perspective, freedom of religion was inviolate, but did not extend to LDS polygamists and theocrats because they were only acting "under the guise of religion."[132] Whatever religion there was in Mormonism was a "cloak" for something else—an "excuse for unbridled license."[133] Legislators thus had every legal right to outlaw polygamy, disenfranchise Church members, and seize Church property.

Mormon leaders objected strenuously to efforts to deny Mormons their constitutional rights. In a debate with John Taylor, who would go on to become the third LDS president, U.S. vice president Schuyler Colfax denied that polygamy was "a question of religion." Taylor replied, "If a revelation from God is not religion, what is?"[134]

This constitutional debate also extended to the First Amendment's establishment clause, which states that "Congress shall make no law respecting an establishment of religion." Some legal scholars have argued that strict separationism—the view that the First Amendment requires what Jefferson referred to as a "wall of separation between church and state"—did not become a mainstream legal theory until the twentieth century when (ironically) it was used as a cudgel to beat Roman Catholics (who allegedly refused to respect that "wall"). Legal scholar Sarah Barringer Gordon finds a parallel development much earlier, when nineteenth-century Americans embraced something like strict separationism as a cudgel to beat Mormons and in the process "remade legal history and constitutional law."[135]

Setting the establishment clause aside, some evangelicals had argued against bringing Utah into the union on the theory that the United States was a Christian country. "As a Christian nation can we consent to take anti-Christian states into the union?" the *Christian Advocate and Journal* asked in 1855.[136] But Morrill based his novel argument on strict church–state separation. At the time, disestablishment was mandated at the federal level, not in the states. But just how separate church and state should be in the territories was up for grabs. "If Congress is prohibited from making an established religion, a Territory must be equally prohibited, for a Territory is the creature of Congress, and Congress cannot authorize a Territory to authorize an incorporated company of priests to do what it may not do itself," Morrill reasoned. He then turned to Utah to bring his argument home. "The republican form of government in Utah is a dead letter . . . while the real *bona fide* government is that of the Mormon priesthood."[137]

Reynolds v. United States

IN A STEM-WINDER of a House speech, Morrill asked whether there was any limit to the crimes one could commit under the guise of religious liberty. "Could a man, charged with burglary or rape, find privilege and excuse before any of our courts on a plea that it was an act done in accordance with the religion of the prophet Mercury, or the prophet Priapus, and that our Constitution permits the *free exercise* of religion?"[138] The Supreme Court settled this question in *Reynolds v. United States* (1879). George Reynolds, Young's secretary and the husband of two wives, argued that his arrest under the 1862 Morrill Act violated his religious liberty. Rejecting this argument, the Supreme Court ruled that Mormons had every right to *believe* in polygamy but no right to *act* on that belief. This historic ruling—the Supreme Court's first on the free-exercise clause—closed the door on constitutional questions regarding polygamy even as it opened the door to new antipolygamy legislation.

In 1882, the U.S. Congress responded with the Edmunds Act, followed by the Edmunds-Tucker Act in 1887. This one-two punch put muscle into antipolygamy legislation for the first time by targeting individuals *and* the LDS Church. The Edmunds Act forbade polygamists from voting, holding public office, or serving on juries. The Edmunds-Tucker Act, in an effort to smash what Sen. George Edmunds of Vermont saw as a Mormon monopoly over the Utah economy, disincorporated the LDS Church and seized much of its property. On the theory that votes for women in Utah gave outsize influence to husbands with many wives, this act also abolished woman suffrage in the territory.

By the 1880s, Mormonism was no longer just a local nuisance or a theological error. It had become criminal. All told, roughly a thousand men in Utah were convicted of polygamy, unlawful cohabitation, and similar charges.[139] Many female Saints were arrested for refusing to testify against their husbands. Pregnant plural wives were indicted for fornication. And all efforts to grant statehood to Utah were put on hold.

During this period—Mormons call it "The Raid"—virtually the entire LDS leadership (including George Q. Cannon, who in 1882 lost his job as territorial delegate to the U.S. House) went into hiding, where they ate, slept, and conducted Church business in their own version of the Underground Railroad. Meanwhile, LDS president John Taylor vowed massive resistance to U.S. authority. "Are we going to suffer a surrender of this point? No, never. No, never," he said in an August 20, 1882, sermon that foreshadowed

Alabama governor George Wallace's 1963 "Segregation now!" speech.[140] On July 4, 1885, Taylor called for American flags to be lowered to half-staff to mourn the death of religious liberty.

The Manifesto

AS THE STORY is typically told, all this drama—the indictments, the convictions, the running, the hiding, the charges, the countercharges—came to an end on September 24, 1890, when LDS president Wilford Woodruff finally bowed to government pressure and proclaimed Mormon opposition to "any marriage forbidden by the law of the land."[141] The language of "The Manifesto," as it came to be called, was advisory only, but it was enough. Property seized from the Church was returned. Many convicted polygamists were pardoned, and existing prosecutions were set aside. In 1896, Utah finally became the forty-fifth state.

"The Manifesto" did not stop anti-Mormon activism, however. Neither did it stop LDS polygamy, since those who were in plural marriages often remained in them and new plural marriages continued to be celebrated.[142] In 1898, Utah elected as its congressman B. H. Roberts, who had multiple wives. The House refused to seat him. In 1902, Utah elected Reed Smoot (who was *not* a polygamist) to the Senate, which held four years of hearings before seating him in 1907. This was only possible, however, after Joseph F. Smith, who had succeeded Woodruff as LDS president, issued a "Second Manifesto" in 1904 denying that the Saints were still secretly performing plural marriages, and promising to excommunicate those who continued to do so.

Of all the culture wars explored in this book, this one was the closest to a draw. In the nineteenth century, at least, the anti-Mormons won. In fact, as historian Cristine Hutchison-Jones has observed, anti-Mormonism survived even this "Second Manifesto."[143] Congress backed off, as did presidents and the Supreme

Court. But anti-Mormon exposés continued to appear in popular magazines such as *Collier's*, *Cosmopolitan*, and *McClure's*. And Hollywood produced a series of anti-Mormon films, including *A Mormon Maid* (1917) and *Trapped by the Mormons* (1922), which indulged in sex, murder, and suicide alongside long-standing stereotypes, from Mormon leaders converting comely maidens in order to bed them to Mormon vigilantes slaying opponents for sport.

Nonetheless, the anti-Mormon culture wars have been over now for nearly a century. Like Catholics, Mormons accepted the separation of church and state. And while some breakaway Mormon groups continued to practice polygamy, the LDS Church conformed to the norm of monogamy. Increasingly, Mormons found their identity as a "peculiar people" in more socially acceptable markers, including prohibitions against tobacco, alcohol, tea, and coffee they refer to as the Word of Wisdom. These compromises bought Mormons some measure of respectability in the early twentieth century. In fact, according to historian Jan Shipps, positive media depictions of Mormons were outweighing negative depictions as early as the 1930s.[144]

Back in 1857, *Harper's Weekly* had struggled to find reasons for the U.S. Army to march on Utah: "It may be said that marriage, as we understand it, is a Christian rite, and that we are a Christian people; and that no abomination like polygamy can be tolerated in a Christian country." Yet its editors were fair-minded enough to ask their readers (and themselves) whether "in the cold, clear eye of the Law and of the Constitution, we are a Christian people." They also allowed themselves to entertain the possibility (however briefly) that there were no easy answers to that question. In the end, however, *Harper's* editors determined that there is "no doubt" that "this is very certainly a Christian country." Therefore, the Mormon question would not be settled by debate but "on feeling and sympathy, or, rather, on hatred and disgust." Americans "never would, and never will, tolerate a set of obscene, licentious wretches as their fellows and equals. They never would, and never will, permit a horde of creatures, in every respect worse than Turks, to defy our habits, our tastes, our feelings, and our civilization."[145]

Americans continue to debate whether we are "a Christian country" and "a Christian people," but there is no longer any debating whether there is space for Mormons among us. Once again, a bitterly fought culture war produced a new cultural consensus. In this case, Americans agreed that their sacred canopy would cover not only Protestants and Catholics but also Mormons. Today almost no one claims that Mormons cannot be patriotic Americans. Liberals and conservatives alike affirm the freedom of members of the LDS Church to believe what they believe and to practice their religion as they see fit. In fact, Mormons—"quintessential Americans," in the words of conservative columnist George Will[146]—are *overrepresented* both in popular culture and on Capitol Hill. During the 2012 presidential election campaign, some cultural conservatives threatened to refuse to vote for Mitt Romney because they did not want a Mormon to become president. But when the votes were counted, white evangelicals voted for Romney in even greater numbers than they had voted for George W. Bush four years earlier. Romney may have lost, but Mormons won.

4

———

Prohibition and Pluralism

I N THE RUN-UP TO midnight, January 16, 1920, when the
Eighteenth Amendment to the U.S. Constitution was to go
into effect, drinkers mourned the death of the legal liquor
trade at mock funerals of that icon of alcohol John Barleycorn. At
a party at the American House Rathskeller in Boston, officiated by
waiter-undertakers in black hats and mourning clothes, there were
liquor bottles with candles burning at both ends of the dance hall
and empties littering a makeshift coffin. A skull-and-crossbones on
the wall read: "In Memory of John Barleycorn, Not Dead—Only a
Trance."[1] A flu epidemic kept many revelers at home in Chicago on
this Black Friday, and in New York City bitter cold did the same.
But nothing could chill a last-call party on Park Avenue in Manhattan featuring black bottles, black glasses, and black caviar, with funeral dirges mourning the passing of "Wet America."

The "wets" were not partying alone, however. The Anti-Saloon
League (ASL), the leading force behind constitutional prohibition, put out a Prohibition Day press release wishing Americans "a

happy Dry Year."[2] In small towns across America, members of the Women's Christian Temperance Union (WCTU) held their own funerals bidding good riddance to John Barleycorn. At a jazz funeral at Temple Baptist Church in Los Angeles, a quartet sang "The Brewers' Big Horses Can't Run Over Me" while four pallbearers "dressed in hobo costumes" committed a demijohn "dressed in grave clothes" to the great beyond. Barleycorn's fate, according to Rev. Henry Miles Cook, who preached the joys of the "Water Wagon," was "eternal extinction without the hope of resurrection."[3] In Chicago obsequies, after a six-foot-high liquor bottle was embalmed, cremated, and buried to the delight of congregants at local churches, Frank Ebbert of the ASL spoke of plans to take the dry gospel global—"to Sahara-ize the rest of the world."[4]

In the most publicized of these dry ceremonies, "baseball evangelist" Billy Sunday put Barleycorn to rest in Norfolk, Virginia, where twenty pallbearers carried a twenty-foot-long coffin through the streets with an actor playing "His Satanic Majesty" trailing close behind. Sunday, who had quit his job patrolling the outfield for the Chicago Cubs in order to labor in the fields of his Lord, was at the time America's most famous evangelist. He was also one of the liquor trade's foremost critics. In a slangy sermon on "Booze" he delivered hundreds of times, Sunday described the liquor question that would consume the nation during the 1920s as a matter of "prosperity against poverty, sobriety against drunkenness, honesty against thieving, heaven against hell." To Sunday, the saloon was "the mother of sins"—"the deadliest foe to the home, the church and the state." But the saloon wasn't just a "sneak," a "coward," a "thief," and a "liar." It was also an infidel:

It has no faith in God; has no religion. It would close every church in the land. It would hang its beer signs on the abandoned altars. . . . It is the moral clearing house for rot, and damnation, and poverty, and insanity, and it wrecks homes and blights lives today.[5]

When faced with such villainy, everyone had to make a choice. Would it be God and family? Or sin and the devil? In 1920, America had made the right choice. "The reign of tears is over," Sunday thundered in his anti-eulogy in Norfolk. "The slums will soon be only a memory. . . . Hell will be forever for rent."[6]

But soon America's Dry Decade was over and prohibition itself was only a memory. The saloon that Sunday had described as a "free pass to hell" never rose from the dead, but thirteen years after these John Barleycorn parties, alcoholic beverages did. Beer came first, resurrected on April 7, 1933, when a law signed by that icon of liberalism President Franklin Delano Roosevelt legalized the sale of beer containing up to 3.2 percent alcohol. To celebrate this milestone, the Anheuser-Busch Clydesdales delivered a case of Budweiser to former New York governor (and prohibition opponent) Al Smith at the Empire State Building and another to President Roosevelt at the White House. Distilled spirits were legalized next, when the ratification of the Twenty-First Amendment on December 5, 1933, overturned the Eighteenth and brought an end to what President Herbert Hoover had described as a "noble" experiment.[7]

This lurching from prohibition to repeal is often told as a watershed in American political history, with scholars focusing on how "drys" pioneered a new form of single-issue pressure politics to ensure prohibition's passage and how "wets" returned the favor to ensure its repeal. Historians also debate more practical matters: Did prohibition work? Did it reduce alcohol consumption and deep-six the saloon? Or did it produce, as Pulitzer Prize–winning author Robert Lewis Taylor wrote, "an orgiastic and prolonged era of hard drinking, immorality, racketeering, gun molls, gang wars, political corruption, bribed police and judges, poisoned booze, speakeasies, irreligion, emancipation of women to fresh vistas of impudence . . . short skirts, saxophone-tooting . . . and additional decadence"?[8] Finally, what are we supposed to take away from this story of prohibition and repeal? That efforts to legislate morality are doomed to failure in a land of liberty? Or that such efforts fail only when good Americans lose their moral bearings, and their nerve?

Answers to these questions must begin with the fact that battles over prohibition and repeal were never just about booze, or just about politics. They were battles in a wider culture war that featured, in addition to wets and drys, flappers and gangsters, immigrants and the Ku Klux Klan, F. Scott Fitzgerald and *The Great Gatsby*, Babe Ruth and the cult of celebrity, talking movies and the Model A, prosperity and the Great Crash, and endless debates about alcohol, sex, crime, and liberty. When Dr. Arthur James Barton of Atlanta told a convention of Southern Baptists in May 1930 that "there is no neutral ground in this war," he wasn't talking about just alcohol. When he said "it is a 'war to the knife and knife to the hilt' between the forces of sobriety and orderly government on the one hand and the forces of liquor and lawlessness on the other," he was talking as well about fast cars, fast women, political corruption, and organized crime.[9]

Like most culture wars, this one featured a series of overlapping battles—between youth and the elderly, pluralists and exclusivists, scientists and clergy, immigrants and nativists, libertarians and communitarians, and a new culture of leisure and self-fulfillment versus a more traditional culture of hard work and self-denial. In an era in which Americans found themselves drawn simultaneously to progress and nostalgia, the Victorian mother stared down the flapper for the right to define "the cult of true womanhood" even as Protestants battled Catholics (once again) for the soul of the nation.[10] To those who reveled in them, the glory of the 1920s was that things were changing. But to those who reviled them, the problem was that things were moving too fast, and in the wrong direction.

If you follow the booze alone, it can be difficult to determine just who the conservatives and the liberals were in this culture war. Was the Eighteenth Amendment puritanical or progressive? Was prohibition reactionary and repressive—"a pinched, parochial substitute for reform . . . carried about America by the rural-evangelical virus?"[11]

Or could prohibitionists stand with pride in a lineage of liberal social reformers—alongside "the movements for industrial safety, electoral reform, world peace, fair labor laws, food regulation, urban planning, good government, and (nearest cousin of all) woman suffrage"?[12]

Prohibition *was* a product of Progressivism—an effort at social reform aimed at bettering the lives of women and children and undercutting the political power of saloon-based bosses. Yet many of the arguments for repeal were conservative ones, rooted in concerns about law and order and the family. But when the alcohol debate is viewed more broadly, as one front in a wider culture war on dancing and immigration and smoking (evils all), then the sides are much easier to assign. Of course, there were people who were on the left on one issue in these culture wars and on the right on another. But Billy Sunday and his fellow drys were typically conservative. Anxious about the emergence of a multicultural America in which Protestantism was but one religion among many, they fought for a more exclusive America. Wets were typically liberals, committed to individual liberty in religion, dancing, dress, and alcohol. Theirs was a more pluralistic understanding of America that allowed citizens to decide for themselves whether to go to Mass or drink a glass of wine (or both).

Still, this culture war was dominated by the liquor question, which drew all other questions to itself. If you hated the talkies, you probably hated them because the starlets they featured were smoking and drinking (and suggesting much more). If you wanted to cut off immigration, your goal may well have been to keep Irish and German drunks out of the country. If you supported votes for women, it may have been because you expected them to vote dry. If you favored William Jennings Bryan over Clarence Darrow in the Scopes "Monkey" Trial of 1925, it might have been because you rejected evolution (as Bryan did) or because you found Bryan's "Case Against Alcohol" more compelling than Darrow's account of "The Ordeal of Prohibition."[13] And if you attacked Democrat Al Smith in the election of 1928 because you believed (as Methodist bishop and ASL leader James Cannon did) that Smith's Catholicism was "the Mother of ignorance, superstition, intolerance and sin" or that he would give the country away to "the Italians, the Sicilians, the Poles and the Russian Jew," you were probably also concerned about the prospect of your commander in chief belting down a rumored "four to eight cocktails a day."[14]

For much of the 1920s the liquor question was *the* question in American culture. As Americans debated this question, they were arguing about the alcohol content of beer and the intoxicating effects of the martini, but they were also debating American values. Was prohibition an unjust and un-American attack on individual liberty—an unconstitutional intrusion of federal power into private life? Or was it a quintessentially American defense of innocent women and children? "To believe that Prohibition will stand," wrote journalist Michael Monahan, "is, in my view, to believe that the Republic has lost her way and is without the guiding light of her noblest traditions."[15] But dry Americans were just as convinced that the country would be on the up-and-up only once its saloons had been shut down.

In his famous "Booze" sermon, just after he had blasted the saloon as an infidel, Billy Sunday had fixed on the saloon as an assassin. "It sent the bullet through the body of Lincoln; it nerved the arm that sent the bullets through Garfield and William McKinley," he said. "Every plot that was ever hatched against the government and law, was born and bred, and crawled out of the grog-shop to damn this country." But "we the people" do little in response. "People will drink anyway," we figure. And isn't that their right as free citizens? But what, Sunday asked, does "personal liberty" really mean when it comes to the liquor question?

"Personal liberty" is for the man who, if he has the inclination and the price, can stand up at a bar and fill his hide so full of red liquor that he is transformed for the time being into an irresponsible, dangerous, evil-smelling brute. But "personal liberty" is not for his patient, long-suffering wife, who has to endure with what fortitude she may his blows and curses; nor is it for his children, who, if they escape his insane rage, are yet robbed of every known joy and privilege of childhood, and too often grow up neglected, uncared for and vicious as the result of their surroundings and the example before them.[16]

As the twenties roared, others were less sure that what ailed America was alcohol. In fact, many were morally certain that *prohibition* was the problem. Prohibition didn't prohibit much except our liberties, they argued. But it opened the door to all sorts of social and cultural problems, including organized crime, gang warfare, and political corruption, which visited plagues on the nation far worse than those prohibition was designed to cure.

In a 1928 speech accepting the Democratic Party's presidential nomination, Al Smith, a son of second-generation immigrants and a product of the tenements of Manhattan's Lower East Side, argued that "there is as much, if not more, [liquor] than there was in pre-prohibition days." "I believe in temperance," he said, but prohibition had not achieved that goal. In fact, it had given us "bootlegging, hijacking, racketeering, corruption and lawlessness." Smith also blasted the Anti-Saloon League as a "propaganda association" peddling "prejudiced and bigoted ideas"—a "twin brother," in fact, of the racist Ku Klux Klan "for the destruction of American principles and American ideals."[17]

Despite efforts to distance himself from the Roman Catholic hierarchy—"I recognize no power in the institutions of my Church to interfere with the operations of the Constitution of the United States . . . I believe in the absolute separation of Church and State," he said[18]—Smith was savaged as a Catholic throughout the 1928 campaign. Fundamentalist preacher Ben Bogard called him a "friend of negro rapists."[19] The nativist Fellowship Forum warned that "if

Smith wins, Rome and whiskey Rule. If Hoover wins, America is saved for Americans."[20] The liberal (Smith) lost to the conservative (Hoover) in a landslide.

Temperance: The Long War

THIS STORY OF alcohol and its antagonists isn't restricted to Billy Sunday and Al Smith, of course, or even to prohibition and repeal. But it isn't as old as the United States either.

Some early temperance activists tried to cloak their cause in the mantle of antiquity by arguing that "prohibitory laws" are as old as the Ten Commandments and the Garden of Eden. Others cast their nets wider, citing the Buddhist precept "not to use intoxicating liquor or drugs" or a Quranic passage describing the "sinfulness" of intoxicating beverages. In the colonies and the early republic, however, hardly anyone had anything bad to say about alcohol. The *Arbella*, which ferried John Winthrop and the first members of the Massachusetts Bay Colony to the New World, arrived with three times as much beer as water. And the colonists we might expect to have worked themselves up over this topic—the Puritans—were in fact heavy drinkers who staggered to work and to church in something of an "alcoholic haze."[21]

Echoing Martin Luther, who in 1530 urged true believers to "drink, and right freely,"[22] Puritan divines referred to drink as "a good creature of God."[23] Their congregants drank throughout the day and throughout their lives, but they drank particularly hard at funerals. In fact, according to one colonial historian, "entire communities, children included, became intoxicated" at some funerals.[24] The colonial army gave soldiers daily rations of rum or whiskey, and in the home women chugged alcohol-laced medicines, ostensibly for health reasons. George Washington, Benjamin Franklin, and Thomas Jefferson all made their own alcoholic beverages. So we should not be surprised that Americans borrowed the tune for

"The Star-Spangled Banner" from a British drinking song, or that they consumed more alcohol per capita between 1790 and 1830 than at any point in their history. "Until well after the American Revolution," writes historian Norman Clark, "to refuse a drink in New England was to deny God, reject fellowship, and stand as a fool before custom and medicine."[25]

In an era when clean water was hard to come by and tea and coffee were expensive, early Americans drank huge amounts of distilled spirits, which they saw as both medicine, good for whatever might ail you, and food: barley, corn, or wheat literally distilled into liquid form. Americans drank beer, wine, and hard cider, too. But wine, which was typically imported, was considered an elite beverage, and beer and hard cider did not travel well before widespread refrigeration. Men, women, and children took healthful "drams" as they awoke and went to bed, and washed down their meals with distilled spirits. In public, early Americans drank when signing a contract, bidding at an auction, raising a barn, and casting a vote. (When George Washington sought office in Virginia's House of Burgesses in 1758, he spent thirty-four of his thirty-seven-pound election budget on liquor for supporters at the polls.) They drank at births, baptisms, weddings, and funerals. They drank particularly hard on the Fourth of July, in part because they saw it as patriotic to partake of spirits distilled from native corn or native rye, but also because drinking to intoxication gave early Americans "a feeling of independence and liberty": "to be drunk was to be free."[26]

One English visitor to America in the 1830s, after waxing eloquent about mint juleps and American ladies (and American ladies with mint juleps), described the "propensity to drink," always and everywhere, as part of the American character:

If you meet, you drink; if you part; you drink; if you make an acquaintance, you drink; if you close a bargain, you drink; they quarrel in their drink, and they make it up with a drink. They

drink, because it is hot; they drink, because it is cold. If successful in elections, they drink and rejoice; if not, they drink
and swear—they begin to drink early in the morning, they
leave off late at night; they commence it early in life, and they
continue it, until they drop down into the grave.[27]

Still, there were isolated protests. In *The Mighty Destroyer Displayed* (1774), Philadelphia Quaker and abolitionist Anthony Benezet attacked this "bewitching poison" as a slave master that saps
body, soul, and will alike. "Unhappy dram-drinkers are so absolutely
bound in slavery to these infernal spirits," he observed, "that they
seem to have lost the power of delivering themselves from this
worst of bondage."[28] True freedom, Benezet wrote, was the liberty
to make your own choices, free from the fetters of slave driver and
rum alike.

The physician and Declaration of Independence signer Benjamin
Rush also challenged the conventional wisdom that alcohol was "a
good creature of God." "Spirituous liquors" drained not only money
and morals but also health, by causing palsy and madness (among
other diseases), he said. Like most early temperance advocates,
however, Rush believed that fermented drinks, such as wine, beer,
and cider, were good for you. According to his "Moral and Physical
Thermometer," while toddy and grog led to lying, swearing, and suicide, "small beer" produced happiness, and wine produced "strength
and nourishment."[29]

Despite the strong words against strong drink, the idea that alcoholic beverages were heaven-sent died hard. Yes, Alexander Hamilton argued in *The Federalist* papers (no. 12) for an excise tax on
spirits. But when he got that tax in 1791, it was quickly and forcefully resisted, most notoriously in the Whiskey Rebellion of 1794.
That rebellion was put down. So was the tax, in 1802.

During the Second Great Awakening, when evangelicalism displaced Puritanism as the nation's dominant religious impulse and

millions of early-nineteenth-century Americans were born again, temperance emerged as the most enduring social reform movement in U.S. history. As the Calvinist belief that God had predestined each of us to heaven or hell gave way to the more flattering conviction that we could choose (or reject) salvation for ourselves, evangelicals got about the business of saving souls and society. Many were convinced that, just as the soul could be sanctified, society could be perfected. So the Second Great Awakening fueled a variety of reforms aimed at protestantizing the nation. Many came to see alcohol as "Demon Rum" and drunkenness as sin. In 1814, a New England Tract Society pamphlet likened "the great destroyer" of intemperance to "war . . . the plagues of Egypt . . . a fire . . . a burning fever . . . [and] a sweeping pestilence."[30] "A nation of drunkards" was also a nation under the condemnation of God.[31]

As the rhetoric of revivalism spilled over into the temperance movement, compromise became difficult, even unchristian. The distinction between distilled and fermented alcoholic beverages became as blurry as the vision of those who imbibed them, and temperance came to mean abstinence from beer and wine as well as whiskey and rum. Some zealots even argued that Christians should stop using wine at Communion and that ministers should refuse to offer that sacrament to anyone in the liquor trade.

Among those who preferred teetotalism over moderation was Rev. Lyman Beecher, the popular preacher who would deliver impassioned anti-Catholic sermons in Boston in the days leading up to the Ursuline convent burning of 1834. "Intemperance is the sin of our land," Beecher argued in six influential sermons on the topic in 1825:

[I]f anything shall defeat the hopes of the world, which hang upon our experiment of civil liberty, it is that river of fire, which is rolling through the land, destroying the vital air and extending around an atmosphere of death. . . . It obliterates the fear of the Lord and a sense of accountability, paralyses the

power of conscience, hardens the heart, and turns out upon
society a sordid, selfish, ferocious animal.[32]

Abraham Lincoln, in an 1842 speech, seemed to take aim at
Beecher when he targeted pious perfectionists who pilloried sellers
and users of alcohol as "damned without remedy" and blamed them
for "all the vice and misery and crime in the land." But he saved his
strongest condemnations for "the demon of intemperance" itself.
Though he favored persuasion over legislation, Lincoln praised "the
temperance revolution" as a transformation even more important
than the revolution of 1776. "In *it*," he concluded, "we shall find
a stronger bondage broken; a viler slavery, manumitted; a greater
tyrant deposed."[33]

Temperance advocates also took a page out of revivalism's ritual
manual, calling on their fellow citizens to die to old lives of sin
and rise up to new lives of virtue. This marriage of revivalism and
temperance was plain at Baptist and Methodist altar calls where
accepting Christ meant repenting of drinking. But the temperance
movement was revivalistic (and conservative) in another sense: it
sought to recover a Protestant past many conservatives believed was
slipping away.

In an effort to solve the problems alcohol abuse brought to
homes, factories, and farms, temperance societies of the sort Lincoln
later addressed in Illinois began to appear across early-nineteenth-
century America. By 1834, the heavily Protestant American Temperance Society claimed 7,000 local organizations with 1,250,000
members. Other groups founded before the Civil War included the
Washington Temperance Society (or "Washingtonians"), who appealed to a more secular constituency, as well as fraternal groups,
such as the Sons of Temperance and the Independent Order of
Good Templars. There were also groups for women (the Daughters
of Temperance) and African Americans (the New England Colored
Temperance Society). These societies popped up as well in the

South, but white Southerners kept temperance at arm's length for many of the reasons they sidestepped the polygamy question: they feared that allowing the federal government into their bedrooms or liquor cabinets would allow it to meddle in slavery.

Members of temperance associations sang temperance songs, recited temperance poems, took abstinence pledges, patronized temperance theaters, and checked into temperance hotels. They also played the patriotism card, depicting the struggle for temperance as a struggle for "Our SECOND INDEPENDENCE!"[34] Like Benezet, they argued that real liberty wasn't about the freedom to drink yourself drunk. Drinkers were not really free; their wills were bound to their desire for alcohol. True liberty expressed itself in virtue, not vice. It was a product of self-control, not self-indulgence. With this understanding of liberty in mind, temperance editor Jesse Goodrich rewrote the Declaration of Independence:

> We hold these truths to be self-evident; that all men are created *temperate*; that they are endowed by their Creator with certain natural and innocent desires; that among these are the appetite for COLD WATER and the pursuit of happiness![35]

In speeches and songs at cold-water Fourth of July celebrations, temperance advocates borrowed from the rhetoric of independence and antislavery to damn the "voluntary bondage" of the time-honored Independence Day binge and to praise those who had taken back "from the tyranny of appetite their long-lost liberty."[36] The nineteenth-century war on "King Alcohol," they argued, was like the eighteenth-century war on George III. It should be fought with the same passion and toward the same end: the redemption of a people from a foreign enemy.

Enslavement to drink was a key theme in popular theater. In fact, "temperance dramatists stressed the theme of voluntary slavery in practically every script they wrote."[37] Offstage, temperance found ready support among antislavery activists, including William Lloyd Garrison, Theodore Weld, and Lucy Stone, all of whom, to borrow from Lincoln, looked forward to a day "when there shall be neither a slave nor a drunkard on the earth."[38] In fact, many abolitionists echoed Lincoln in arguing that the liquor trade was *worse* than the slave trade—that the "chains of intoxication" were "heavier than those which the sons of Africa have ever worn."[39] In *Parallel Between Intemperance and the Slave-Trade* (1828), Heman Humphrey, a white Congregationalist cleric, president of Amherst College, and cousin of the abolitionist rebel John Brown, argued that chattel slavery was a "mere sting of an insect" when compared with "the fangs of a tiger" of strong drink. But Humphrey was no apologist for the "diabolical" slave trade. Though he acknowledged that New World slavery was "dripping with gore," he saw intemperance as "a worse evil"—"heavier with wo, and guilt, and death." Why? Because it inflicted more illness and death, because it fettered both body and mind, and because it endangered American democracy. "Much as I love my children," wrote Humphrey, "let them all grind in chains till they die, rather, infinitely, than become the slaves of strong drink."[40]

Some African Americans also argued that drunkenness was worse than slavery—because it affected every race and class, and because it extended its tentacles worldwide. The former slave and abolitionist Frederick Douglass saw slavery and temperance as roughly equivalent evils. "It was about as well to be a slave to *master*," he wrote in *My Bondage and My Freedom* (1855), "as to be a slave to *rum* and *whisky*."[41] Other African American temperance advocates sided with Humphrey. "Bad as was American slavery the slavery of intemperance is worse," wrote the black abolitionist and poet Frances Ellen Watkins Harper.[42] William Whipper, in a presidential address to the Colored Temperance Society of Philadelphia, contended that the "blighting monster" of intemperance was "an evil . . . in the history of the world . . . without a parallel"—"a still greater tyrant" than the "obsequious degradation, multiplied injuries and tyrannical barbarity" of slavery.[43]

Nonetheless, temperance advocates relied at first on persuasion rather than coercion. They aimed to convince individuals to forgo liquor, not to force them to do so. Most early temperance activists followed Rush in distinguishing between the evils of distilled spirits and the pleasures of fermented beverages, such as beer, wine, and hard cider. In fact, the Massachusetts Society for the Suppression of Intemperance served wine at its meetings, and an early temperance tract called cider and beer "nutritious and palatable drink."[44] So while there were teetotalers in their ranks, the initial aim of temperance advocates was simply to convince Americans to drink less. Borrowing heavily from revivalists, who sought to save souls first, they aimed at individual conversion over social transformation. Their cold-water gospel challenged drunken sinners to repent and take on new lives of sobriety. It soon became apparent, however, that many of those who "took the pledge" broke it. So persuasion gave way to coercion, and the crusade against alcohol moved from parlor and pulpit into political campaigns.

Timothy Shay Arthur, one of nineteenth-century America's most prolific authors, began his temperance career as an advocate of moral suasion. His novel *Ten Nights in a Bar-Room, and What I Saw There* (1854) was one of that century's bestselling books. It reads at first like a Washingtonian tract. The town drunk, Joe Morgan, turns from a life of inebriation (and ruin) to a life of sobriety (and success) after his pious daughter, "Little Mary," is killed by a shot glass thrown across the Sickle and Sheath Tavern. In the end, however, Morgan makes an impassioned plea for legal prohibition, and his fellow citizens respond by closing their town's taverns, destroying their liquor, and outlawing the sale of "intoxicating drink."[45]

This shift from persuasion to coercion came to Maine in 1851, when Portland mayor and temperance activist Neal Dow steered through his state's legislature a bill, later known as the Maine

Law, that prohibited the manufacture and sale of alcoholic beverages except for "medicinal and mechanical purposes."[46] During the 1850s, twelve more Northern states went dry via similar legislation. Many of these bills were unpopular and short-lived, shot down by state courts or overturned by later legislators. Following a much-publicized Portland Rum Riot, which left one man dead and seven wounded, the Maine Law itself was repealed in 1856.

After the Civil War, in a second wave of temperance activity, groups such as the Women's Christian Temperance Union (est. 1874) and the Anti-Saloon League (est. 1893) pushed for "local option" legislation that would allow towns and counties to decide for themselves whether to license or prohibit alcohol. This effort—popular sovereignty applied to the drink problem—got a boost from a series of high-profile supporters, including P. T. Barnum, who featured a temperance melodrama, *The Drunkard, or The Fallen Saved*, at his American Museum, and "The Great Agnostic" Robert Ingersoll, who harbored no doubts about "this damned stuff called alcohol."[47] After many localities decided to go dry, Kansas, Iowa, and North Dakota did the same in the 1880s. In another flurry of prohibitionist activity, ten Southern states joined the drys between 1907 and 1915 (though the real purpose of this Southern campaign may have been "to keep liquor from the poor whites and negroes"[48]).

Sin and the Saloon

LIKE OTHER CULTURE wars, this battle between the wets and the drys was a symbolic fight. Its key symbol was the saloon, which one prohibitionist described as the "great enemy of the home, the church, the school, and the State."[49] As the name of the Anti-Saloon League implies, prohibitionists pointed their fingers not at drink or drinkers but at the saloon, and the drunkenness, prostitution, gambling, profanity, poverty, sickness, and political corruption it was said to foster. Although temperance advocates included distillers, bartenders, corner grocers, and pharmacists as "central figures in their demonology," they hated with a special hatred the saloon owner, whom they saw as the right-hand man to Satan and "Demon Rum."[50]

Violent attacks on saloons and their proprietors were justified as efforts to protect the home—to prevent men from wasting their wages on drink when they should be bringing money home to support wives and children. But they were also attacks on immigrants: German brewers who supplied the saloons and Irish immigrants who staffed and patronized them. The attack on the saloon was also advertised as an effort to redeem the nation, since temperance advocates often argued that what was at stake was not simply the future of individuals, families, and communities but the fate of the republic itself. Like other culture warriors, prohibition's prophets charged their enemies with treason as well as vice, conjuring up an impending apocalypse in which an unrepentant nation would be destroyed not by fire or ice but by the gin and tonic.

Of all the attacks on saloons and their proprietors, the most dramatic were the "hatchetations" of Carry Nation, an imposing woman (nearly six feet tall) who described herself as "a bulldog running along at the feet of Jesus, barking at what He doesn't like." For Nation, these dislikes were legion. WCTU president Frances Willard had famously pledged to "do everything," so, in addition to "home protection and saloon destruction," her organization had agitated for women's suffrage, the eight-hour workday, marriage and divorce reform, prison reform, world peace, and the right of workers to organize. Nation stuck more closely to cultural questions, nipping at the heels of tobacco, extramarital sex, and the Masonic Lodge. At a time when Teddy Roosevelt—a "blood-thirsty, reckless, cigarette-smoking rummy," in her estimation—was said to "speak softly, and carry a big stick," Nation spoke harshly, carried a small hatchet, and, beginning in ostensibly dry Kansas in 1899, attacked saloons in the name of Jesus Christ.[51]

Previously, in the Women's Crusade of 1873–74, tens of thousands of housewives had knelt down outside saloons and prayed for saloonkeepers to shut their doors in the name of the sacred trinity of God, home, and country. Nation, whose failed first marriage to an alcoholic wedded her to the temperance cause, took a more confrontational approach. Her performances, which repeatedly landed her in jail, featured the smashing of liquor bottles, glassware, and pictures of scantily clad women—all with her trademark hatchet. Neither side in the temperance debate was particularly fond of this Madam of Mayhem, who was widely dismissed as a crank, especially after she outraged a Coney Island crowd in 1901 by cheering the assassination of President William McKinley ("a friend of the rumsellers and the brewers," she said, "[who] did not deserve to live").[52]

It is difficult to gauge Nation's influence, though it may well be that the "New Kansas 'Twister,'" as the *Los Angeles Times* called her, did the temperance cause "infinitely more harm than good."[53] Nonetheless, her anger attested to a growing unease in the country with the culture of the saloon and, more broadly, with the self-indulgence that many Americans were coming to associate with modernity itself. Few would call wets, as Nation did, "rum-soaked, whiskey-swilled, Saturn-faced rummies" or take up a hatchet while calling down God's vengeance on saloonkeepers.[54] But the temperance cause cannot be dismissed as easily as Nation can. The Eighteenth Amendment did not pass because America had become a nation of prudes and Puritans possessed, as journalist H. L. Mencken once put it, by "the haunting fear that someone, somewhere, might be happy."[55] It passed because, as historian Ronald Walters wrote, "Americans had a drinking problem," and because prohibitionists had a plan to fix it.[56]

The House Prohibition Debate

THIS NOT-SO-MODEST PLAN, advanced by ministers, doctors, social scientists, novelists, playwrights, and politicians, was to put an end to the liquor trade. It was debated most exhaustively in the U.S. House in 1914, after Rep. Richmond Hobson, an Alabama Democrat and naval war hero, sponsored a resolution to turn the Constitution against alcohol. In this debate, which offers a snapshot of this culture war on the eve of prohibition, supporters of a constitutional ban on liquor sales began by cataloging the dangers of alcohol, which they regarded as "the worst evil that is cursing the human race to-day." Alcohol, argued Pennsylvania Progressive Willis Hulings, "corrupts the youth, beggars its victims, robs the household, and fills the land with disease, distress, and vice." Or, as Hubert Stephens (D-MS) put it, rather more at length and with greater oratorical flourish:

> It creates moral leprosy, it blights the intellect, and it wrecks the physical body. . . .
> It makes demons of men and women; it destroys the best instincts of mankind; and it causes many of those made in the likeness and image of God to degenerate into brutes. . . .
> It blights love; it wrecks homes; it destroys affection; it mars all that is beautiful and good and true in human nature. . . .
> It destroys reverence for the highest and best things in life; it creates contempt for virtue; and it mocks at religion.[57]

In all these ways, argued Hobson, the "protoplasmic poison" of alcohol created more havoc than "war, pestilence, and famine combined." It made slaves out of Caucasians and savages out of American Indians and African Americans. It also struck "deadly blows at the life of the Nation itself."[58]

Seizing on the emerging discipline of statistics, some tried to translate these sentiments into data, calculating that the liquor traffic was "responsible for 25 per cent of the poverty, 37 per cent of the pauperism, 45.8 per cent of child misery, 25 per cent of insanity, 19.5 per cent of divorces, and 50 per cent of the crime."[59] Hobson himself reckoned that "there are 5,000,000 heavy drinkers and drunkards in America."[60]

Many also underscored the dangers this "great destroyer" posed to American democracy. The narrower problem was the saloon itself, which often doubled as a polling place. Here, in a clear analog to the kept wives of the Utah polygamist (who allegedly voted with their husbands) and to hypnotized Catholics (who were said to vote with the pope), the votes of drinking men were secured for wet candidates, giving "the saloon keeper . . . greater political influence than any preacher" in many towns. Another problem was the cabal of brewers and distillers, which Hulings called "a powerful coordinated banditti carrying on guerilla operations between the lines of the great political parties," supporting Republicans here and Democrats there, depending solely on how wet they were. In an era in which "trust busters" such as Theodore Roosevelt were leading the charge against monopoly power, prohibitionists attacked the "National Liquor Trust" as "treason to the common welfare." Raising the specter of a government "of the liquor dealers, for the liquor dealers, and by liquor dealers," Rep. M. Clyde Kelly (R-PA) insisted that this trust, too, "must be eliminated if the Republic is to endure."[61]

Pointing to France and China, which had outlawed absinthe and opium, respectively, prohibitionists argued that the United States had to follow suit in order to survive. "No family, no State, no nation, no empire, no civilization can permanently flourish and prosper and survive unless it is sober," Hobson concluded. "Zeppelins, submarines, bombs, and siege guns are not the only things that can destroy a nation," added Rep. Andrew Volstead (R-MN), who would later sponsor the controversial Volstead Act for the enforcement of the Eighteenth Amendment. "We do not need to wait for a foreign foe to invade our land to find it in peril. Our nation is already in peril, and the foe is within our borders."[62]

But the argument against strong drink was not just utilitarian and political. It was also moral and theological. Echoing the claim of ASL founder Howard Russell that "the Anti-Saloon League movement was begun by Almighty God," partisans of prohibition referred repeatedly to the United States as a "Christian nation" and insisted that Christ's legions—from pew to pulpit to heaven itself—were on their side.[63] On the other side were those whom Representative Kelly described as "vultures of vice"—"the grafters and gangsters, the parasites that clothe themselves in the proceeds of woman's shame, the inhuman ones that bathe themselves in the tears of little children, the wastrels who wreck and ruin material things while they contaminate childhood, debauch youth, and crush manhood." Like Kelly, Rep. James Bryan (P-WA) saw but "two sides to the question": "There are those here who are going to help the dives and brothels, and the dirty, low places where liquor is sold in this country, and there are others who are going to oppose it." Equally certain that this question pitted "the good Christian people of the United States" against "the forces of evil," Rep. Percy Quin (D-MS) presented his fellow lawmakers with a Billy Sunday–style choice: "Are you with the forces of evil and corruption, or are you with the good people who are trying to build up your country?"[64]

Given this stark dualism, it should not be surprising that prohibitionist thought waxed utopian; if the saloon is hell on earth and you are able to destroy it, then the kingdom of God cannot be far away. Or so it seemed to Rep. Daniel Garrett (D-TX), who looked forward to "the day when we may have a saloonless Nation, forever at peace with itself, the world, and all mankind."[65]

The Case Against Prohibition

ANTIPROHIBITIONISTS IN THE House responded to these arguments by invoking Jefferson on local sovereignty and states' rights. The effort to force prohibition upon wet citizens was "unjust and undemocratic"—a violation of "every true principle of individual liberty and American government." Consolidating power in the federal government is what empires do, not republics, they said. The effort to dry up the nation by force was, in the words of Rep. Oscar Underwood (D-AL), a "tyrannous scheme to establish virtue and morality by law." Echoing Underwood, Rep. Andrew Barchfeld (R-PA) asked, "What prohibitionist from the corn fields of Kansas, the cotton fields of Alabama, or the seacoast of Maine, where the bootlegger votes for prohibition, has a right to command a steel worker in my district that faces 2,800° F. at the furnace door that he may not have his beer when his heat is ended?"[66]

The Civil War and Reconstruction hovered over these states' rights arguments, especially among Southerners. A constitutional amendment against booze, argued Rep. Robert Henry (D-TX), invited "an amendment providing that certain States shall not have separate schools and churches and graveyards, and that the races shall not be separated socially, and that there shall be no State laws against the intermarriage of the races."[67] Other states' rights champions said that to cede DC the power to outlaw alcohol was to cede the power to insist on votes for women.

Then there was this practical objection: Laws can be enforced only where public sentiment (and juries) support them. In the absence of local support, constitutional prohibition could either be ignored or enforced. "If it is not enforced and remains a dead letter, it will breed deceit, hypocrisy, disrespect of law, and encourage evasion, lying, trickery and lawlessness," observed Henry. "If it be enforced, it will require an army of United States officials, paid spies and informers, who will go into the business house and the home, invade the sacred liberties of our people." This is why, as opponents of the Eighteenth Amendment repeatedly put it, "prohibition doesn't prohibit." In the many states where it has been tried, observed Charles Coady (D-MD), "prohibition has been a lamentable and miserable failure."[68]

Why? Human nature, for one. Whereas prohibitionists blamed drunkenness on the "National Liquor Trust," Rep. Martin Morrison (D-IN) traced it back to Noah's drunken binge in the biblical book of Genesis. Barchfeld spoke of the temptation, as old as Adam and Eve, to partake of the "forbidden fruit." Why do people violate prohibition laws? he asked. "It is simply the old prejudice against . . . having one man say you shall not eat pork, or roast beef, or oysters, or drink Potomac water, or beer, or something stronger."[69]

Given human nature, antiprohibitionists argued, the solution was not coercion. "You cannot make a nation sober by act of Congress or by constitutional amendment," said Edward Pou (D-NC).[70] The only way to do that was through persuasion—through temperance.

Antiprohibitionists also objected to the confiscation of millions of dollars' worth of property—California vineyards, say—without compensation. They fretted about replacing jobs lost when breweries and distilleries shut down, and about the $250 million shortfall in annual revenues from beer, wine, and liquor taxes. But the most common objection was that prohibition infringed on personal liberty. Wets repeatedly denounced their opponents' efforts to force unpopular legislation upon U.S. citizens. "We are trying to regulate all human conduct by laws, laws, laws," complained Julius Kahn (R-CA). "Today it is prohibition," said J. Hampton Moore (R-PA), "tomorrow it may be tango dancing or cigarette smoking."[71]

Opponents of prohibition also objected to efforts by the Anti-Saloon League to turn the alcohol question into a contest between believers and nonbelievers. Many wet cities had a higher percentage of church members than did dry rural areas, they pointed out. Many ministers opposed prohibition, too. So, according to Rep. James Gallivan (D-MA), "to say that a man who takes a drink cannot be a

Christian" is intolerant at best. Appealing to Jefferson's understanding of strict church–state separation, antiprohibitionists demanded that legislators leave moral questions to religious institutions. "Our national policy has been to reserve for the churches the preservation of the morals of the people and to withhold for the statesmen the material problems of politics and economy," said Moore. "This is a policy we should still adhere to." But opponents of prohibition were of two minds about church and state, and some were quite happy to match their opponents Bible quote for Bible quote. In a speech aimed at becalming the "tornado of fanaticism" stirred up by prohibitionists, Rep. Henry Vollmer (D-IA) cited the sterling examples of "George Washington, the brewer; Thomas Jefferson, the distiller; Abraham Lincoln, the saloon keeper; and Jesus Christ of Nazareth, who turned water into wine."[72]

While objecting to prohibitionist "hysteria," the wets whipped up plenty of their own. Rep. Richard Bartholdt (R-MO) compared the "madness" to "the days of witchcraft." Pou said any attempt to force prohibition upon U.S. citizens would be "the first step toward civil war." But the most overheated "NO!" rhetoric had come a few decades earlier from Rep. Roger Mills (D-TX):

> [Prohibition] is wrapped in the livery of heaven, but it comes to serve the devil. It comes to regulate by law our appetites and our daily lives. It comes to tear down liberty and build up fanaticism, hypocrisy, and intolerance. It comes to confiscate by a legislative decree the property of many of our fellow citizens. It comes to send spies, detectives, and informers into our houses; to have us arrested and carried before courts and condemned to fines and imprisonments. . . . It comes to bring us evil—only evil—and that continually.[73]

Finally, wets objected to the "intemperate" utopianism of their opponents. Denouncing the "mischievous Utopian dreams" and "Puritanic tyranny" of prohibitionists, Rep. James Buchanan (D-TX) said, "It must be borne in mind that human perfection can never be attained." Bartholdt, too, rejected the view that prohibition would do away with all that ails us. Just look at nations of "Mohammedans," who are prohibited from drinking alcohol, he said. Are they really happier than Christian societies?[74]

The Prohibitionist Rejoinder

ON STATES' RIGHTS, some drys sided with Hamilton and federal power. "The fiction that we are 48 different peoples finds no logment in my mind," said Rep. John McKenzie (R-IL). "Our rivers cross State lines as they go murmuring on their way to the sea; our mountain ranges link together the different States; our railroad, telephone, and telegraph lines cement the different Commonwealths together as one great country." But most prohibitionists sided with Jefferson and states' rights, even as they insisted that alcohol was a national problem demanding a national solution. In an argument that paralleled the claim that even one polygamous territory was a threat to monogamous marriages nationwide (a claim that found a mate in twenty-first-century same-sex marriage debates), prohibitionists said that wet states imperiled dry states. No cry of "States' Rights!" went up when Congress came down on opium and cocaine trafficking, they observed. Or when the federal government spent millions "killing boll weevils, destroying ticks, and saving sick hogs." Why should things be any different with the "interstate nuisance" of alcohol?[75]

Prohibitionists also claimed that *they* were "the real friends of liberty." Liberty and license are two separate things, they observed, and only in the anarchic state of nature is liberty absolute. According to Kelly, "wherever there is law there are limitations of personal liberty":

The highwayman is prohibited from taking property by force. The embezzler is prohibited from taking money by deceit. Men are prohibited from damaging a city sidewalk. They can not send certain matter through the mails. They can not kill game out of season. In fact, every man is hedged about by thousands of restrictions upon his personal liberty solely because such restrictions advance the comfort, virtue, and welfare of the general public.[76]

Hulings made a similar point in more graphic language: "A man has a natural right to own a hog and sleep with him if he chooses, but society will not permit him to keep a pigsty to the annoyance of his neighbors."[77]

On practical matters such as lost tax revenue, some drys insisted that legislators must not "place the value of the almighty dollar above that of human life." Others said that what the IRS lost on liquor taxes it would more than make back in reduced costs for "courts, jails, hospitals, and poorhouses." Regarding the "prohibition does not prohibit" mantra, drys conceded that a constitutional amendment prohibiting liquor traffic would not stop every drop of alcohol from flowing. But why set the bar so high? "Larceny laws do not prevent stealing" and "homicide laws do not prevent the killing of men," said Rep. Edwin Webb (D-NC). Does that mean we should repeal them?[78]

The Hobson resolution debate took over ten hours and involved over eighty representatives. In the end, the resolution passed 197 to 190, well below the two-thirds required for a constitutional amendment. But a major push by the Anti-Saloon League during the 1916 elections produced a Congress with twice as many drys as wets, and in April 1917 the United States declared war against Germany. This decision may or may not have made the world "safe for democracy" (as President Woodrow Wilson put it), but it made the United States a dangerous place to oppose prohibition. Instead of distracting citizens from the liquor question, as the Civil War had distracted them from polygamy, World War I made prohibition palpable, even necessary. Patriotic legislators denounced German Americans as un-American and demanded that grain be used to feed the troops rather than inebriate them. As one Wisconsin prohibitionist wrote, "We have German enemies across the water. We have German enemies in this country too. And the worst of our German enemies, the most treacherous, the most menacing are Pabst, Schlitz, Blatz, and Miller."[79]

On December 22, 1917, in the midst of World War I, the House and Senate voted for a constitutional amendment banning the manufacture, sale, and transport of intoxicating beverages. By January 16, 1919, the required three-quarters of the states had ratified the amendment, which *The Baptist Observer* characterized as "the crystallization of national Christian sentiment" and the bête noire of "whiskey-loving aliens."[80] But what exactly had the Eighteenth Amendment, slated to go into effect one year hence, prohibited? Was beer an intoxicating beverage? Was wine? Via the Volstead Act—passed on October 28, 1919, in an effort to clarify and enforce the Eighteenth Amendment—Congress defined "intoxicating liquors" as beverages containing more than 0.5 percent alcohol by volume and thus forbade trade in beer, wine, and cider as well as whiskey, gin, and rye. But the bone-dry Volstead Act did not forbid possessing alcohol, and it allowed doctors to prescribe whiskey and families to purchase sacramental wine.

After the Eighteenth Amendment

ONE MIGHT IMAGINE that the great debate over alcohol would have taken place *before* the Eighteenth Amendment was enacted, and in some respects it did. Temperance had been discussed since the early nineteenth century, and the House debated Hobson's prohibition resolution exhaustively in 1914. But not all citizens are activists, and there was more than a little complacency among wets in the years leading up to constitutional prohibition. "It is probably inherent in the nature of a reform movement that those who favor the reform should be more alert and better organized than those who are opposed to it," journalist Charles Merz has observed. "The reformer sees in the existing situation an immediate menace to morals or to public safety which spurs him into action. The opponent of the reform is usually self-satisfied."[81] And so it went with prohibition. Before January 17, 1920, the conservatives were on the offensive in this culture war, outlawing the liquor trade in a majority of U.S. states. The self-satisfied wets lost by default, without really landing a blow. After January 17, 1920, however, wets started throwing punches of their own. But first they had to let things play out—to demonstrate to the American public that the one-two combination of the Eighteenth Amendment and the Volstead Act was a fool's errand. Luckily for them, that didn't take long.

During the 1914 House debate, wets had argued repeatedly that nationwide prohibition was unenforceable. From day one of the Dry Decade, the federal and state governments seemed to concede as much. In fact, the key impact in most cities was simply to drive prices up and the liquor trade underground.

On the evening of January 16, 1920, as prohibition was going into effect, six masked men had tied up two railroad employees and locked away six more before stealing roughly one hundred thousand dollars' worth of "medicinal" whiskey from two boxcars. Then things got worse. As Congress, presidents, governors, and judges— all eager to be done with the prohibition mess—looked the other way, a massive underground industry boomed, funneling all manner of "intoxicating liquors" to thirsty Americans and untold wealth to moonshiners, rumrunners, bootleggers, speakeasy proprietors, corrupt field agents, and icons of organized crime. One popular preacher bellowed that prohibition "ought to be enforced if every street in America had to run with blood and every cobble stone had to be made of a human skull."[82] But there was no stomach for that. So law-abiding citizens became lawbreakers, and respect for the rule of law eroded. Soon many were blaming prohibition itself for the litany of social ills they had once placed at the feet of the liquor trade. Yes, supporters of prohibition continued to put on a happy face. Basking in the glories of "this saloonless land," the Anti-Saloon League claimed credit for 1920s prosperity. Mrs. Harry Newton Price, owner of two DC beauty parlors, credited the Eighteenth Amendment for a boom in her industry. "It is very easy to trace the growth of the beauty parlor business to prohibition," she said in 1922. "When men drank, they were not so critical. Their wives and sweethearts looked attractive to them without the assistance of beauty parlors. Now, however, men remain clear-eyed all evening and notice wrinkles, pallor, straight hair and unsparkling eyes. As a result, the women are flocking to beauty parlors."[83]

But women, who had previously taken their alcohol at home, were flocking to speakeasies too. The 1920s saw a huge spike in demand for sacramental wine (both Jewish and Catholic) and a massive shift from saloon beer to bathtub gin. Meanwhile, speakeasies popped up like dandelions (and dandelion wine), and bootleggers to supply them, and organized crime to hit up both for a portion of the profits, and corrupt police officers to look the other way. Americans probably drank less during prohibition, thanks to higher prices, which, in a bizarre new form of social inequality, shut out low-income customers. But given the utopianism that had attached itself to prohibitionism, that "less" was considerably "more" than expected.

Not long after national prohibition went into effect, President Warren Harding referred to failed enforcement efforts as "the most demoralizing factor in our public life."[84] In 1922, journalist H. L. Mencken concluded that "prohibition is a failure, and it grows a worse failure every day." "In every American city, and in nine-tenths of the American towns, every known alcoholic beverage is still obtainable . . . and even in the most remote districts there is absolutely no place in which any man who desires to drink alcohol cannot get it."[85] In 1924, Mencken added:

> Five years of prohibition have had, at least, this one benign effect: they have completely disposed of all the favorite arguments of the Prohibitionists. None of the great boons and usufructs that were to follow the passage of the Eighteenth Amendment has come to pass. There is not less drunkenness in the Republic, but more. There is not less crime, but more. There is not less insanity, but more. The cost of government is not smaller, but vastly greater. Respect for law has not increased, but diminished.[86]

Clarence Darrow, that champion of liberty, secularity, and modernity who would battle William Jennings Bryan and evolution in the Scopes Trial, attacked prohibition (which Bryan supported) as "a radical and revolutionary change" passed by "zealots" as a "war measure, at a time when the great majority of citizens were engrossed in graver matters." Darrow explained:

> Most [laws] grow out of the habits and customs of the people. These customs grow into mores and are finally embodied in laws. Long before statutes are passed, the great mass of men have formed their attitudes and ways of living and the statutes are simply codifications of existing folkways.

Prohibition, by contrast, was passed by an "active minority, moved by religious zeal" and contemptuous of public opinion. Given the "impossibility" of repeal, Darrow argued for something like the campaign Southern segregationists would employ during the civil rights era against federal desegregation mandates. Instead of trying to enforce an unpopular law, let prohibition die of "opposition, neglect and disuse," he argued.[87]

As Americans debated the pros and cons of prohibition, they were debating what Americans should and should not be allowed to pass over their lips and gums. But like Carry Nation, whose rage extended far beyond the beer tap and the saloon, they were also debating sexual license, Christian theology, and law and order.

Consider Rev. Mark Matthews, minister of Seattle's First Presbyterian Church, the largest Presbyterian congregation in the United States at the time. Matthews was one of America's most outspoken critics of the liquor trade, which he referred to as "the most fiendish, corrupt and hell-soaked institution that ever crawled out of the slime of the eternal pit." But Matthews's critique of alcohol was part of a broader critique of "smoking, cosmetics, modern novels, Sunday golf," and other modern American amusements. Conjuring Lincoln's famous "house divided" speech, Matthews insisted that "the nation cannot exist half-drunk and half-sober." Neither could it survive half-flapper and half-Victorian mother.[88]

Percy Andreae, a spokesman for Ohio brewers, saw the war on alcohol as a religious war in which evangelical Protestants like Matthews were scheming to impose their customs on Catholics, Jews, and liturgical Protestants. How else to explain the "two-tiered legal system" in which wealthy, white Americans drank like honored guests at a Gatsby party while authorities cracked down on alcohol use among African Americans and German and Irish immigrants? Or Henry Ford's claim that "bootlegging is a 95 percent controlled Jewish industry"? Or efforts by an ASL spokesman to pin the failures of the Eighteenth Amendment on "unwashed and wild-eyed foreigners who have no comprehension of the spirit of America"?[89] The prohibitionist cause "has for its object the supremacy of a certain form of religious faith," namely, the belief "that the Creator frowns upon enjoyment of any and every kind, and that he has merely endowed us with certain desires and capacities for pleasure in order to give us an opportunity to please Him by resisting them," Andreae argued. "How many Roman Catholics are prohibitionists?

How many Jews? . . . Or Lutherans? Or German Protestants generally? What is the proportion of Episcopalians to that of Methodists,
Baptists and Presbyterians, and the like, in the active prohibition
army?" According to Andreae, the "religious zealots" behind prohibition were the heirs of dour Puritan divines. They stood for "a
Sunday without a smile, no games, no recreation, no pleasures, no
music, card-playing tabooed, dancing anathematized, the beauties
of art decried as impure—in short, this world reduced to a barren,
forbidding wilderness in which we, its inhabitants, are to pass our
time contemplating the joys of the next."[90]

Parties of the Past and the Future

DECADES BEFORE MATTHEWS and Andreae, Transcendentalist
Ralph Waldo Emerson had written of "two parties which divide the
state": the parties "of Past and Future, of Memory and Hope."[91] Liberal critics of prohibition were the party of hope. "I like the dreams
of the future better than the history of the past," they said with
Jefferson.[92] To them, the Eighteenth Amendment was an effort by
the U.S. government to turn their society back—to teleport it to a
mythical era of monocultural uniformity when everyone read the
same Bible and Victorian values such as thrift, sobriety, and hard
work seemed ordained by God. These critics reveled in the art and
literature of the "lost generation" and welcomed into American society the "new woman" (who won the vote in 1920) and the "new
Negro" (of the Harlem Renaissance). They loved blurring the sharp
lines laid down—in morality, culture, and religion—by the conservative party of the past. They felt liberated by the sudden shift in
social values and intoxicated by "black and tan" jazz clubs, which
to them were less about the mixing of drinks and more about the
mixing of cultures—of whites and blacks, men and women, the
rich and the poor. The cabaret is a powerful solvent of racism,
wrote Chandler Owen in the African American literary magazine

The Messenger in 1922: "It is breaking down the color line. It is destroying the psychology of caste. It is disseminating joy to the most humble and the most high. It is the dynamic agent of social equality."[93] Because they valued "cultural pluralism"—a term coined in 1924 by the Jewish philosopher Horace Kallen—members of this party of hope sneered at immigration legislation meant to make the nation more white and European.[94] Equally un-American, in their view, were efforts to turn voters against Al Smith because he was Catholic.

This liberal "party of the future" reveled in the pace of change of the Roaring Twenties without worrying much about where things were headed. Its members never tired of pointing out that the Eighteenth Amendment seemed far better at organizing crime than discouraging drinking. They opposed prohibition as an infringement on individual liberty, an imposition of prudery on progress. And they joined Columbia University president Nicholas Murray Butler and Reform Rabbi Stephen Wise in denouncing the "persecuting spirit" and "Ku Klux Klanism" that possessed the nation in the 1920s. The "chief danger" confronting the country, Butler concluded, was not drunkenness but "bigotry and intolerance."[95]

On the conservative side of this cultural divide, defenders of prohibition were the party of memory and the past. Members of this party feared the loss of an America that was whiter and more rural than the nation was becoming in the 1920s. They were anxious about what the Great Migration of African Americans to Northern cities would do to those cities, and about the jazz clubs these migrants frequented in places like Harlem. They applauded legislation such as the Asian Exclusion Act, which effectively cut off immigration from Asia in 1924. They lamented the short skirts, bobbed hair, and lipstick of the "new woman." They cheered for Jesus the businessman in Bruce Barton's bestseller *The Man Nobody Knows* (1925). And they sent a series of Republican presidents—Warren Harding, Calvin Coolidge, Herbert Hoover—to Washington, DC.

Evangelist Bob Jones, whose racially segregated Bob Jones University would get caught up in a later culture war, spoke for this pro-Protestant party when he said during the 1928 presidential campaign, "I'd rather see a saloon on every corner than a Catholic in the White House."[96]

This party of the past criticized journalists who wrote of the failures of prohibition and songwriters, advertisers, and movie producers who used their creative powers to make drinking seem cool. To these conservatives, the problem with the 1920s was not so much that prohibition boosted organized crime or youthful rebellion but that these vices were quickly becoming virtues, at least among the privileged white folks of *The Great Gatsby* set. In other words, the problem wasn't Al Capone; it was his elevation to American folk hero. Or, as Mencken put it (gleefully, in his case), the business of evading prohibition was becoming "a sort of national sport."[97]

This contest between hope and fear was nothing new, of course. It had simmered in the nineteenth century under the pressure of industrialization, urbanization, and immigration, which together turned American culture away from Victorian values of hard work, thrift, and sobriety toward a new culture of leisure, consumption, and self-fulfillment. And it anticipated in many ways the culture wars of recent decades, which are a referendum on the sex, drugs, and rock 'n' roll of the 1960s much as the prohibition debate was a referendum on the sex, cocktails, and jazz of the 1920s. (If the joint symbolized youthful rebellion in the 1960s, the highball did that work in the 1920s.) But to those who were engaged in it, the "family values" debate of the 1920s felt new: scary new for those who experienced the decade as decadence and loss, and exhilarating new for those who experienced it as liberation and gain.

The 1920s was an era of sexual freedom, or of sexual debauchery, depending upon your point of view. It was an era of cars and contraceptives, jazz and the radio, the Charleston and the Black Bottom. It was also a time when celebrities seemed to be unintentionally paving the path to hell. Greta Garbo, Mae West, Clark Gable, and Humphrey Bogart all drank in their movies. Sports heroes were rarely celebrated for hard work or self-control. Both Babe Ruth and Walter Hagen were consumers par excellence. Each was known to show up at the ballpark or the first tee late, drunk, overweight, and perhaps with a "new woman" on his arm. In the Dry Decade, writes social worker Martha Bensley Bruère, drinking was "an adventure, a gesture of daring, a sign of revolt."[98] The same can be said of the Roaring Twenties themselves, a post-Victorian riot of nonconformity and freedom.

The Roaring Twenties was also the decade when, thanks to Sigmund Freud's "pleasure principle," a nation (or part of one) learned to stop repressing its desires. But one person's id is another person's sinful nature, so Americans were profoundly divided over the direction the country was going. "Drinking Man," writes historian Norman Clark, "is Cowboy Man and Gangster Man, determined to be the creator of his own circumstance, the master of his own soul." As such, he exemplifies "moral freedom." But he also exemplifies "moral nihilism."[99]

To conservatives who saw 1920s licentiousness as the wrecking ball of American society, the problem with the speakeasy wasn't so much that people could drink and get drunk there. It wasn't even that (unlike the saloon) it welcomed men and women alike and did nothing to keep their glistening bodies apart. The problem with the speakeasy was that it was racing at a Bugatti's pace away from an increasingly distant culture that had put family and community first. In the speakeasy the self was king (or queen) and he (or she) was charged with nothing more exalted than self-expression and self-fulfillment. For Clark, at least, the 1920s witnessed a great "unraveling" of "bourgeois family values," such as "duty, delayed gratification, unity, loyalty, continuity." As the cult of the individual gained ground, Americans flitted from "the church-of-one's choice to the sexual indulgence-of-one's choice to the family-of-one's choice and surely to the drink-or-drug-of-one's choice."[100]

A Failed Experiment

HENRY FORD VOWED in 1929 that he would stop making cars if prohibition were repealed. (He didn't.) But other business leaders, many of whom had enthusiastically bankrolled prohibition, turned against it in the late 1920s. So did Hollywood executives and leading lawyers. The fight against prohibition got another lift from a newspaper industry that seemed as eager for repeal as for the latest story about bootlegging. (The *New York Times* alone printed 16,231 stories about prohibition—few of them favorable—between 1920 and 1927.[101]) But Protestants continued to fight the good fight. Officers of the mainline Federal Council of Churches told Congress in pro-prohibition testimony in 1926 that "in dealing with gigantic social evils like disease or crime, individual liberty must be controlled in the interest of the public welfare."[102] An editorial in *The Christian Century* called "This *Is* Armageddon," published in 1933 as public opinion against prohibition was skyrocketing, promised that "we shall fight to the limit of our powers" against repeal.[103]

Also among the conservatives in this fight were many women, who had won the right to vote with the ratification of the Nineteenth Amendment in 1920. Over the course of the 1920s, however, women demonstrated that not all of their gender thrilled to WCTU moralism. Some young women bobbed their hair, bared their legs, and sipped cocktails, of course. But there were also more traditional women, such as Pauline Sabin, a Republican Party stalwart and Gotham socialite who formed the Women's Organization for National Prohibition Reform as a protest against the WCTU's claim to speak for all of her gender. Like the prohibitionists they opposed, these activists made their case in the name of home protection. "Women feel that something must be done to protect their children," Sabin told the House in 1930. Only this time they were protecting their children from the "co-educational speakeasy" rather than the saloon.[104]

Angered by years of "snooping, spying, keyhole-peeping and

interference with fundamental rights and liberties by fanatics and professional busybodies," newspaper magnate William Randolph Hearst conceded in 1929 that the Eighteenth Amendment was "not only the most flagrant violation of the basic American principle of personal liberty that has ever been imposed on the American public, but the most complete failure as a temperance measure that has ever been conceived and put into impractical operation." As an unelected yet powerful overseer of American culture, Hearst fretted about a clash in which citizens were sharply "divided into two classes—drys, who want to make the country bone-dry, and wets, who want to make the country souse-wet." But he took solace in the fact that the vast majority of Americans were moderates who "realize that temperance can be secured without prohibition, and never can be secured with prohibition."[105]

As Hearst's conversion testifies, many Americans grew weary in the 1920s of what prohibition had wrought, including gang warfare, a resurgent Klan, intrusive government, anti-Catholic bigotry, and an unmistakable drift toward hard liquor and binge drinking. By 1922, 61 percent of respondents in a massive *Literary Digest* poll said they were dissatisfied with the Eighteenth Amendment; four years later, that figure had jumped to 81 percent.[106] This frustration gave way to resolve after the stock market crash of October 1929 put an end to 1920s prosperity. The Great Depression that followed did for repeal what World War I had done for the Eighteenth Amendment: it made urgent what had previously been merely desirable. As banks failed, factories closed, and unemployment lines snaked around city blocks, economic considerations came to the fore, just as military ones had in 1917. Soon opponents of prohibition were arguing that this not-so-noble experiment was dragging down an already sinking economy, costing jobs and tax revenues.

This protest also gained from the emergence of organizations critical of the Eighteenth Amendment and the Volstead Act. Previously, the only real organized opposition had come from industry groups such as the Distillers' Association of America and the United States Brewers' Association. Now organizations such as the Association Against the Prohibition Amendment (est. 1918), which rejected prohibition in the name of individual liberty and local control, gave the protesters ASL-style muscle.

Initially, these groups pushed simply to modify the Volstead Act, by allowing for the sale and distribution of beer and wine. But in 1930, the American Bar Association voted for outright repeal. In 1931, the blue-ribbon Wickersham Commission, charged by President Herbert Hoover with investigating prohibition, found widespread contempt for anti-liquor laws among U.S. citizens and widespread corruption among police. In 1932, Franklin Delano Roosevelt ran for president on a Democratic Party platform opposing what businessman and AAPA chief John Raskob called the "damnable affliction" of prohibition.[107] FDR (and liberalism) won in a landslide, in part because Hoover, his conservative Republican opponent, had become associated with a stay-the-course strategy on both alcohol and the economy, and because an increasingly pluralistic population was coming to associate the GOP with intolerance and bigotry toward immigrants and Catholics.

During the historic House debate of 1914, Bartholdt had somehow anticipated both prohibition and repeal. Prohibition would pass, but there could be "no doubt about the final outcome," he said. "A nation which has thrown off the shackles of despotism will not, for any length of time, tyrannize over itself."[108] That length of time turned out to be just under fourteen years. On December 5, 1933, Utah became the thirty-sixth state to ratify the Twenty-First Amendment, which overturned the Eighteenth. That evening, in the nation's capital, President Roosevelt praised "this return of individual freedom" while directors of the AAPA gathered for a victory dinner at the Waldorf-Astoria in New York City.[109] As the champagne flowed, multimillionaire Pierre du Pont presented each AAPA director with a commemorative cocktail glass. FDR reportedly had a cocktail at the White House, while Mencken retired to a Baltimore hotel to drink in the moment with a cold glass of water and a Menckenesque quip. "My first in thirteen years," he said.[110]

Diversity and Homogeneity

THE CULTURE WARS of the 1920s were about many things, alcohol included. But what really drove them was the contest between diversity and homogeneity. Posed narrowly, the question of the decade was whether the nation would impose one culture of alcohol—a progressive and Protestant culture—on an increasingly multiethnic and multireligious society. Posed more broadly, the question was whether the nation could abide the multiplicity that modernity had wrought. Was the United States "a blend of all the peoples of the world" in which each of us is forever assimilating ourselves to others?[111] Or was it a country of white Anglo-Saxon Protestants into which immigrants were required to assimilate in order to be considered "one of us"?

The 1920s witnessed a series of conservative efforts to homogenize American culture—to create a twentieth-century analog to the Federalist culture of uniformity and deference. A rapidly expanding Klan insisted that only native-born, white Protestants were real Americans. Immigration restrictions intended to rid the country of supposedly unassimilable newcomers from Eastern Europe and Asia passed in 1921 and 1924. The anti-Catholicism of the 1928 presidential campaign aimed at keeping the White House a Protestant preserve. And prohibition made the United States more evangelical at the expense of Catholics and Jews.

These efforts at homogenization were consistent with Victorian culture, which gloried in custom and tradition. For Victorians on both sides of the Atlantic, it was a blessing to be given the same name as your mother, to be married in the same church, and to be buried in the same graveyard with the reassurance of the same words. Victorian society was hierarchical, divided into people who mattered and those who did not, and the people who mattered were expected to look, think, dress, and act like one another. This combination of stasis and homogeneity was a legacy of John Winthrop's famous *Arbella* sermon, which championed the sort of organic order later safeguarded by the Federalists. It was personified by President Warren Harding, who spoke for conservatives throughout U.S. history when he said that "there is more happiness in the American small village than in any place on earth,"[112] and it resurfaces today whenever Tea Party Republicans side with small-town values against the culture of Washington fat cats.

Victorians drew sharp lines between Christians and heathens, men and women, blacks and whites, natives and immigrants. The Jazz Age blurred these lines, calling the exclusivism of Christianity into question, integrating nightclubs, and introducing the androgynous figure of the flapper, with short hair, a short skirt, small breasts, and a cigarette in one hand and a highball in the other. The 1920s also upset the monoculture of the small town. It did so through immigration and urbanization, through the Great Migration of African Americans from the rural South to Northern cities, and through the explosion of new cultural forms, including jazz and the Charleston. During the 1920s, the United States was becoming less homogeneous by the day, and the great question of the age was whether you found the new pluralism exciting or disturbing (or both). Did the drinking and dancing that dizzied you make you feel (like F. Scott Fitzgerald) that "it is the beginning of everything"?[113] Did it make you feel, like old-moneyed Tom Buchanan in *The Great Gatsby*, that everything was coming to an end—that "civilization's going to pieces"? Or did you, like *Gatsby* narrator Nick Carraway, fall somewhere "within and without"—"simultaneously enchanted and repelled by the inexhaustible variety of life."[114]

Occupying that middle ground with Carraway was journalist Walter Lippmann, who criticized prohibitionists, Klansmen, funda-

mentalists, nativists, and other conservatives as adherents of "the religion of the older American village civilization making its last stand
against what looks to it like an alien invasion."[115] But Lippmann, who
shared the anxieties of many 1920s conservatives about what America was leaving behind, also wrote with nostalgia about the ways in
which "the acids of modernity" were wearing away at theological
certainties and moral norms, creating a centrifugal society in which
(to quote from Aristophanes) "Whirl is King."[116] Where you stood
on the 1920s depended on what you made of these acids, and of this
whirl. Was this dissolving and this whirling destructive, evidence of a
society unraveling at the seams? Or was it constructive, spinning out
new hues for an increasingly polychromatic society?

In the melting-pot camp was Teddy Roosevelt, who once warned
American mothers against "race suicide."[117] In the last letter he
wrote before his death in 1919, he said that he supported immigration, but only if the immigrant was to become "an American and
nothing but an American":

> There can be no divided allegiance here. Any man who says
> he is an American but something else also, isn't an American
> at all. We have room for but one flag, the American flag . . .
> We have room for but one language here and that is the Eng-
> lish language, for we intend to see that the crucible turns our
> people out as Americans, of American nationality, and not
> as dwellers in a polyglot boarding house; and we have room
> for but one, soul loyalty, and that is loyalty to the American
> people.[118]

Other conservative critics of hyphenated Americanism included
state legislators who passed laws in the 1920s prohibiting the teaching of foreign languages in public schools and national legislators
who instituted in 1924 an immigration quota system intended "to
preserve the ideal of American homogeneity."[119]

The pluralist camp included writer Randolph Bourne, who praised the United States as "the first international nation,"[120] and Rabbi Wise, who called for "an end of the spirit which limits the possession of America to any group of Americans."[121] But chief among these multiculturalists was Horace Kallen, who pushed against the centripetal force of the melting-pot metaphor with the centrifugal force of "cultural pluralism." The United States is a "symphony of civilization," Kallen had written in 1915.[122] In this symphony each race, each ethnic group, has its own instrument to play—something to contribute to the orchestration of America. "Democracy involves not the elimination of differences but the perfection and conservation of differences," Kallen believed. "It aims, through Union, not at uniformity, but at variety, at a one out of many, as the dollars say in Latin, and a many in one."[123]

Republicans largely sided with homogeneity and the conservative party of the past, but Calvin Coolidge, in a rebuke of Klan intolerance, told the American Legion in 1925 that it was time for Americans to "cast off our hatreds." During World War I, he observed, "well-nigh all the races, religions, and nationalities of the world were represented" in the U.S. armed forces:

> No man's patriotism was impugned or service questioned because of his racial origin, his political opinion, or his religious convictions. Immigrants and sons of immigrants from the central European countries fought side by side with those who descended from the countries which were our allies; with the sons of equatorial Africa; and with the Red men of our own aboriginal population, all of them equally proud of the name Americans.

That "respect for different kinds of good" needed to be carried over to the rest of American society. "Divine Providence has not bestowed upon any race a monopoly of patriotism and character,"

Coolidge said. "Whether one traces his Americanism back three centuries to the *Mayflower*, or three years to the steerage . . . we are all now in the same boat."[124]

Americans descended from those who arrived here on wooden boats or in 747s (or on foot across the Bering Strait) would debate multiculturalism and monoculturalism into the twenty-first century, but they would do so under the shadow of the Roaring Twenties. FDR's New Deal is typically credited with endearing liberals to big government and with gestating an economic conservatism allergic to federal taxing and spending, but prohibition, too, brought on a massive expansion of the federal government's size and scope. It also gave evangelicals the sense that they could have a real impact on American politics. Without the 1920s, the "moral federalism" of the Moral Majority is unthinkable.[125] But this culture war, too, ended in a liberal victory.

During the 1914 House debate over prohibition, Barchfeld had observed that the proposed amendment would place inside the Constitution "something that is not there now and has never been there—a limitation upon the personal liberties of the citizen."[126] All other amendments had increased individual liberties—by ensuring freedom of speech or protecting the right to bear arms or guaranteeing due process. The ratification of this outlier seemed to give the lie to the maxim that liberals win America's culture wars. But prohibition was repealed. After "tyrannizing" over themselves for thirteen years, Americans decided that they had had enough. This victory did not just belong to the thirsty, however. The pluralists won, too.

Back on January 16, 1920, the last day of legal liquor before the Eighteenth Amendment went into effect, the Anti-Saloon League had said that "a new nation will be born" with prohibition. According to *The New York World*, which opposed prohibition, this moment was a different sort of turning point—a time when "the Government of the United States as established by the Constitution and maintained for nearly 131 years will cease to exist."[127] Neither prophecy was accurate. No nation died that day. No nation was born. But prohibition's lifespan was a mere thirteen years, and over the course of the 1920s and early 1930s more and more Americans decided yet again to side with inclusion over exclusion—with cultural liberalism over cultural conservatism.

Earlier in American history, any given culture war might take a century or more to play out. This one took less than two decades. The 1920s saw the rise of mass communications with nationwide reach—of new national media, such as radio and talking movies. But social changes, spurred on by immigration and industrialization, also came faster and more furiously. As a result, the culture-war cycle accelerated, moving from attack to counterattack to negotiation to resolution more quickly than ever before.

Although prohibition was repealed, there *are* still prohibitionists of a sort among us. Cigarette smoking is outlawed in many public places, and New York mayor Michael Bloomberg famously attempted in the 2010s to outlaw extra-large sodas for public health reasons. But as the 1920s and 1930s lurched toward the 1960s and 1970s, the pluralistic culture we now associate with the Roaring Twenties took to the air and flew. With the end of World War II and the rise of the counterculture, more and more Americans reveled in the diversity that modernity had wrought, tuning in to our "symphony of civilization." But all this reveling sounded discordant to conservatives, who worried that their values—"traditional values"— were being sacrificed to the next new thing. Disoriented by the buzz of the modern world, they, too, would long to return to the village or the small town, which was characterized (at least in their imaginations) by unity and sameness—by "modesty in women, rectitude in men, and thrift, sobriety, and hard work in both."[128] In the late 1970s, these traditionalists would claim once again to speak for the "moral majority," and yet another culture war would be on.

5

The Contemporary Culture Wars

I N THE LORE OF the Religious Right, the first shots in today's culture wars were fired from the left. "Who started this? Who is on the offensive?" asked conservative political commentator Pat Buchanan in 2004. "The answer is obvious. A radical Left aided by a cultural elite that detests Christianity and finds Christian moral tenets reactionary and repressive is hell-bent on pushing its amoral values and imposing its ideology on our nation."[1]

There is some truth to this claim. The Supreme Court did escort God out of public school classrooms in the early 1960s; the New Left targeted racism, sexism, and warmongering later that same decade; an increasingly multicultural academy revised college reading lists in the 1970s and 1980s; and San Francisco mayor Gavin Newsom issued marriage licenses to gay and lesbian couples in 2004. But the view that liberals started these culture wars is more conservative spin than careful history. There were radicals in the antiwar, feminist, black power, and gay liberation movements who wanted to turn American society upside down, perhaps "by any means necessary." But the Supreme Court was not girding for battle, cultural or otherwise. The browning of faculty and curriculum in higher education was viewed by most on the left as a social reform rather than a religious crusade. At least a thousand bras were burned in the imaginations of cultural conservatives to every one burned in real time. Even the gay rights movement was not radical so much as reactionary—a response to long-standing bigotry against homosexuals.

It was cultural conservatives who injected into these debates the rhetoric of war, precisely because they saw the issues as matters of absolute morality and eternal truth. They started the contemporary culture wars because once again they saw American society drifting away from them, erasing forms of culture they held dear. Channeling Cold War rhetoric into domestic politics, they blasted "liberal elites" as socialists undermining the country from within. If liberals in this era were wide-eyed parents-to-be, hoping for a better future for their children, conservatives were anxious parents, clutching their daughters and sons close and willing to fight not to lose them in an increasingly bewildering world.

In other words, the contemporary culture wars began in the fight over the sixties, not in the 1960s themselves. And that fight did not begin until the Right started to protest. Reagan declared war on the "bad sixties" as early as 1966, when he launched his political career by denouncing student protesters and sympathetic faculty at the University of California, Berkeley.[2] Neoconservatives, who rejected their New Left roots around the time the Democratic Party selected George McGovern as its standard-bearer in 1972, declared war on the counterculture. But these fights did not go national until the late 1970s and early 1980s, when Reagan ran for (and won) the presidency and the Religious Right broadcast its critique of the sixties far and wide. That decade was not about peace, love, and understanding, conservatives insisted. It was about drug overdoses, race riots, flag burnings, promiscuity, angry feminists, and even angrier blacks—all quite predictable in a society that had lost its moral compass, its respect for authority, and its unifying faith. Undergirding and accompanying this attack on the "bad sixties" was nostalgia for the "good fifties," a golden age for cultural conservatives even today.

Liberals defended themselves (and the sixties) from this conservative attack, criticizing the 1950s in turn. But like the culture wars of the 1920s and 1930s, the culture wars of the 1970s and beyond played out relatively quickly. While the culture wars cycle accelerated in the Roaring Twenties in part because of the rise of national media, it sped up even more in recent decades because of the emergence of the Internet and the twenty-four-hour news cycle. Gay marriage, all but unthinkable in the late 1980s, was legal in nearly three out of every four states when the Supreme Court declared it the law of the land in 2015.

With this acceleration came increasing divisiveness, as decades of bitterness were compressed, in some cases, into months. In the contemporary culture wars, the maw of cultural politics opened wide and nearly swallowed civil society whole. Culture warriors continued to fight over religion, family, sexuality, race, education, and evolution, but now they fought as well over issues that had previously been considered nonpartisan. As the modus operandi of cultural warfare became the MO of politics writ large, Americans were drawn into a Culture War of Everything, which saw liberals and conservatives taking up sides on the arts, sports, and foreign policy.

Like other family feuds, today's culture wars began not with a single shot but with an accumulation of grievances that finally bubbled up and boiled over. In 1954, in *Brown v. Board of Education*, the Supreme Court mandated public school integration. In 1962 and 1963, it banned official prayer and devotional Bible reading in public schools. In 1971, it upheld busing as a means to desegregate those schools. In 1972, Congress sent the Equal Rights Amendment, which guaranteed equal rights for women, to the states for ratification. In 1973, in *Roe v. Wade*, the Supreme Court affirmed abortion rights. In 1976, the IRS stripped Bob Jones University of its tax-exempt status because it prohibited interracial dating. And then there were the 1960s themselves and their less talented stepchild the 1970s—that bacchanalia of "sex, drugs, and rock and roll" followed by the hangover of Farrah Fawcett posters, Atari, and disco. As these decades crested and crashed, many on the right came to fear that American culture had come unmoored and was drifting onto the rocks of secularity and moral relativism. Our indivisible country was breaking apart and sinking.

But this anxiety did not yet catalyze those who would come to be known as the Religious Right. Evangelicals and fundamentalists initially ignored *Brown*. Protests against *Engel v. Vitale* (which outlawed official prayers in public schools in 1962) and *Abington School District v. Schempp* (which outlawed devotional Bible reading in public schools in 1963) were muted. "They put the Negroes in the schools and now they've driven God out," Rep. George Andrews (D-AL) said of the *Engel* decision, which also "shocked and disappointed" evangelist Billy Graham.[3] But Graham's Southern Baptist Convention praised both decisions for upholding church–state separation. And fundamentalist Carl McIntire refused to fuss over *Engel* because the vague prayer the Court deemed unconstitutional in that case—"a pagan prayer," in his view—did not mention Jesus.[4] Regarding *Roe v. Wade*, Protestants left the protesting of that decision to Catholics for most of the 1970s. In fact, *Baptist Press* praised *Roe* for advancing "the cause of religious liberty, human equality and justice," and as late as 1980 the evangelical magazine *Moody Monthly* was observing that "evangelicalism as a whole has uttered no real outcry" against abortion.[5]

Historians have long observed that evangelicals retreated from the public square after the embarrassments of the Scopes "Monkey" Trial of 1925 and prohibition repeal in 1933 only to emerge, Rip

Van Winkle–like, from their long slumber in the 1970s. Whereas their spiritual ancestors worked to save souls *and* reform society, mid-twentieth-century evangelicals effected a "great reversal," separating themselves from "worldly things." That is not quite right. "Plain-folk" evangelicals dug deep into politics in the Sunbelt as early as the 1930s and 1940s. The Family, a secretive group founded in 1935, vigorously opposed FDR's New Deal in Christ's name. The National Association of Evangelicals was established in 1942 and the National Religious Broadcasters in 1944. Billy Graham, no shrinking violet in the field of politics, befriended President Eisenhower and made the cover of *Time* magazine in 1954. And the evangelical magazine *Christianity Today* published its first issue in 1956.[6]

However, none of the above wielded much political power (Graham was more pawn than king in the Great Game of national politics) and rank-and-file evangelicals *did* devote less time to re-forming America in the half century after the Scopes Trial. Many separated themselves from sinful society, withdrawing into their own private Idahos, worshiping in their own churches, forming their own denominations, attending their own secondary schools and col-leges, patronizing their own camps, reading books from their own publishers, listening to their own radio stations, and watching their own television programs.

As they observed their fellow citizens grinding their hips like James Brown, evangelicals were able to imagine that their subcul-ture would never be seduced by the counterculture's "sex machine." *Their* daughters would not engage in premarital sex. *Their* sons would not succumb to the "homosexual lifestyle." But the rulings of the Supreme Court in the 1960s and 1970s called this faith into question. Evangelicals began to wonder whether they could continue to hold off the barbarians at the gate. Then came Jimmy Carter and the IRS.

"Segregation Academies" and the IRS

THIS TIME THE threat was not to public school prayer but to private school segregation, more specifically to the tax-exempt status of the hundreds of "segregation academies" that had sprung up post-*Brown*. The Supreme Court's effort to desegregate public schools had been met by "massive resistance" in the South. Many segregated school districts had ignored the decision. Others had shut down rather than admit blacks, funneling their students into new, all-white private schools (which were not subject to the Court's desegregation mandate). After the Civil Rights Act (1964) prompted stricter federal enforcement of desegregation, enrollment at these "schools that fear built" exploded, creating "a new dual system of schools—one, white and 'private'; the other, disproportionately black and 'public.'"[7]

In May 1969, in *Green v. Kennedy* (later *Green v. Connally*), black parents in Holmes County, Mississippi, had sued to end tax exemptions for three new "white flight" academies. The Nixon administration initially sided with the academies, but reversed course in July 1970, announcing that it could "no longer legally justify allowing tax-exempt status to private schools which practice racial discrimination." In 1971, the DC Court of Appeals ruled for *Green's* plaintiffs, finding that segregated private schools were not charitable and therefore not tax-exempt.[8] In the early 1970s, the IRS issued a series of ineffective guidelines that required nondiscriminatory policies, but did not require private schools to follow them.[9] Under this "farcical" policy, critics said, "a private school [is] nondiscriminatory just because it says it is."[10]

In 1977, Jimmy Carter carried his born-again piety from rural Georgia to the White House, thanks to strong support among evangelicals (who now constituted perhaps one-third of the U.S. population), including 59 percent of Southern Baptists.[11] There was hope in the heartland that Carter would use his bully pulpit to denounce the nation's moral bankruptcy, and perhaps even to do something about it. Then Carter's IRS commissioner Jerome Kurtz cracked the whip. Under stricter IRS rules published in August 1978, the burden of proof shifted to these private schools, which were *presumed* to be racially discriminatory if they opened or expanded in the *Brown* era and if their minority enrollments were under one-fifth of the minority school-age population in their communities.

At this juncture, what came to be known as the Religious Right found its voice and its power. It also found common cause with political conservatives. "There was an overnight conversion," recalled Paul Weyrich—the conservative strategist who coined the term "moral majority" and would go on to become a kingmaker in the Religious Right—as conservative Christians realized that "big government was coming after them as well."[12] Observes historian Grace Hale, "Distance had been created to promote godliness. Maybe distance would have to be violated to save it."[13]

According to Ralph Reed, who would later lead the Christian Coalition, many white evangelicals decried the IRS decision as "a declaration of war on their schools, their churches, and their children."[14] But it was the Religious Right that declared that war, reintroducing to American politics the rhetoric of the cultural battlefield and a mind-set of spiritual struggle: no compromise, no negotiation, no surrender.

With evangelicals mobilized as they had not been in decades, the IRS and Congress fielded close to half a million protest letters. Some pastors and parents simply wanted the feds to butt out of their schools (segregated or otherwise). Others insisted these schools were *Christian* academies, not *segregation* academies, and had been unfairly and illegally targeted.

This mass protest united evangelicals and Catholics on education long before they found common ground on abortion. It prompted a series of hearings in 1979 at the IRS and in Congress, which effectively vetoed the new policy by refusing to appropriate funds to carry it out. The controversy also caught the attention of GOP leaders, including California governor Ronald Reagan, who said that the IRS rule "threatens the destruction of religious freedom itself."[15] Rather than perpetrators of racial discrimination, parents and administrators at these Christian schools were, in his view, victims of religious discrimination at the hands of an overreaching federal government. This sentiment made its way into the 1980 GOP platform, which vowed to "halt the unconstitutional regulatory vendetta launched by Mr. Carter's IRS commissioner against independent schools."[16]

In this way, the Religious Right did more than start another culture war. It began a radical reevaluation of the role of Christianity in public life. At times its members cast themselves, like evangelicals from the 1830s to the 1930s, as insiders charged with bending American society toward God and the Good. In this morality play, they were benevolent overseers of American politics—part of Nixon's "silent majority." More often they cast themselves as the oppressed—rebels who, like folk singers and Beat poets, drank deep of "the romance of the outsider" in American life.[17] Expanding this victim mentality to the breaking point, Robert Billings, who would later serve as executive director of the Moral Majority, compared white evangelicals to slaves under the yoke of DC masters:

> The cost of political negligence is slavery! As our government increases its crippling pressure on the Christian home, school and church, the need for Christian action becomes increasingly critical. If Christians do not master politics, we will, most certainly, be mastered by those who do.[18]

Bowing to this newly awakened political giant, the IRS scrapped its 1978 guidelines, instructing local IRS officials to review segregated private schools on a vague (and ineffectual) case-by-case basis. For many evangelicals, this mass protest was their first taste of political power. They indulged that taste by serving up a wide-ranging culture war targeting such matters as abortion, busing, feminism, pornography, art, history, affirmative action, rock music, divorce, violence on television, drug use, gambling, secular humanism, liberalism, high school textbooks, the literary canon, school prayer, Vietnam, and the legacy of the 1960s. All of these subjects were in their view moral and religious. None was subject to negotiation or compromise.

Jerry Falwell and the Moral Majority

BACK IN 1965, in a sermon delivered the day Rev. Martin Luther King Jr. led civil rights marchers from Selma to Montgomery, Alabama, Jerry Falwell, a fundamentalist preacher at Thomas Road Baptist Church in Lynchburg, Virginia, and the host of *The Old-Time Gospel Hour* television program, suggested that King was a communist. He also criticized "left-wing" leaders of the "so-called freedom movement" for stirring up hatred and violence. "Preachers are not called to be politicians but to be soul winners," Falwell said.[19]

In 1976—*Newsweek's* "The Year of the Evangelical"—Falwell seemed to be having a change of heart. In this bicentennial year, he organized I Love America rallies in 141 cities in an effort to bring "America Back to God." On July 4, 1976, he told his followers that "this idea of 'religion and politics don't mix' was invented by the devil to keep Christians from running their own country." In 1977, he worked with actress Anita Bryant and her Save Our Children campaign to repeal a gay rights ordinance in Dade County, Florida. In 1978, he helped to defeat a Virginia referendum to legalize pari-mutuel betting. In 1979 in Lynchburg, he joined forces with Weyrich and others to form the Moral Majority—a "pro-life, pro-family, pro-moral, and pro-American" organization. So it was no surprise when in 1980 he repudiated as "false prophecy" his earlier stance against mixing religion and politics. "All the moral issues that matter today are in the political arena," Falwell said. "There's no way to fight these battles except in that arena."[20]

In addition to saving individual souls, Falwell was now committed to saving the soul of the nation, stopping "the growing tide of permissiveness and moral decay" from "crushing our society." But Falwell was not just beckoning America "back to biblical morality" and "back to patriotism." He was urging its citizens both to oppose the SALT II treaty, teachers unions, and the Occupational Safety and Health Administration, and to support capitalism, Israel, nuclear weapons, a balanced budget amendment, tax cuts, and massive increases in military spending. "The free-enterprise system is clearly outlined in the Book of Proverbs of the Bible," he said.[21]

The marriage Falwell officiated between religious and political conservatives worked because he and his flock came to see big government as morally wrong. The federal government was not just telling him how to run his schools and his family. It was using its coercive power to spread secular humanism. So members of the Moral Majority did not stop at agitating for "family values." They also agitated for limited government. When Reagan said "government is not the solution to our problem; government is the problem," they said "Amen," and when Pat Robertson called government "public enemy number one," they joined in the chorus.[22]

Falwell was not the only conservative Christian to convert in the Carter years to the gospel of conservative political activism. In 1977, psychologist James Dobson founded Focus on the Family and Donald Wildmon founded the American Family Association. Two years later, Beverly LaHaye formed Concerned Women for America with the goal of "reversing the decline in moral values in our nation" and televangelist James Robison organized the Religious Roundtable.[23] On August 22, 1980, Robison delivered a rousing wake-up call in front of fifteen thousand enthusiastic evangelicals at a Dallas rally for Reagan. "I'm sick and tired of hearing about all of the radicals and the perverts and the liberals and the leftists and the Communists coming out of the closet," he said. "It's time for God's people to come out of the closet."[24] At this same rally, Reagan offered his famous endorsement of the Religious Right: "I know you can't endorse *me*. But I want you to know that I endorse *you*."[25]

Many of these leaders were inspired by the popular books, lectures, and films of the goateed evangelical theologian Francis Schaeffer. Schaeffer, who opposed on biblical grounds the "non-compassionate use of accumulated wealth," was to the left of the Moral Majority on many economic and environmental issues.[26] But his argument that the God of the Bible called Christians to involve themselves in every aspect of human life influenced many born-again Christians to pop their spiritual bubbles and get into politics. "If it hadn't been for Francis Schaeffer, I would have been a pastor in Lynchburg, Virginia, but otherwise never heard of," Falwell said. "He was the one who pushed me out of the ring and told me to put on the gloves."[27]

As they looked back on the birth of the Religious Right and told their own creation stories, other evangelical leaders credited Schaeffer. But more often they pointed to *Roe v. Wade*. According to this "abortion myth," as historian Randall Balmer calls it, the leaders of the Religious Right portrayed themselves as "new abolitionists" fighting for the unborn just as abolitionists had fought against slavery.[28] Ed Dobson, a founding member of the Moral Majority, put it in these terms: their focus was on the family. This is a good story, but it is not how it happened. Falwell did not preach his first anti-abortion sermon until 1978, and the Southern Baptist Convention did not oppose abortion until 1980.[29]

"The Religious New Right did not start because of a concern about abortion," says Dobson. "I sat in the non-smoke-filled back room with the Moral Majority, and I frankly do not remember abortion ever being mentioned as a reason why we ought to do something."[30] Weyrich's recollection is similar:

What galvanized the Christian community was not abortion, school prayer, or the ERA. . . . I am living witness to that because I was trying to get those people interested in those issues and I utterly failed. What changed their mind was Jimmy Carter's intervention against the Christian schools, trying to deny them tax-exempt status on the basis of so-called de facto segregation.[31]

The IRS rule "kicked the sleeping dog," says conservative icon Richard Viguerie. "It was the spark that ignited the religious right's involvement in real politics."[32]

Since the early 1960s Weyrich (a Catholic) had tried to bring white evangelicals and political conservatives together in order to raise money and stir up votes on such issues as school prayer, abortion, and pornography. But well into the 1970s he was like the man in the New Testament parable casting seed upon rocky ground. The IRS's Kurtz, who according to the Moral Majority's executive director did "more to bring Christians together than any man since the Apostle Paul," unwittingly replenished that soil, in no small part because so many in the Religious Right were tied so closely to "white flight" academies.[33]

In Lynchburg in 1967, the same year public schools were finally desegregated in Virginia, Falwell had established a private school called Lynchburg Christian Academy. At its opening it had zero black students, the same number of black members at Falwell's massive Thomas Road Baptist Church. Although he would later repent of his segregationism (and admit blacks to his school and his church), Falwell was at the time a white supremacist.[34]

Ronald Reagan

To WAGE THEIR "civil war of values,"[35] the conservative Christians who formed the Moral Majority needed soldiers on the ground, in state capitals, and in Washington, DC. They drafted plenty—into "policy institutes, political action committees, fund-raising and direct mail organizations, publishing networks, hundreds of state and local groups, and dozens of national umbrella political organizations."[36] But they also needed a general. They recruited him not from the Deep South but from the western reaches of the Sunbelt in Southern California.

Unlike Falwell, who seemed to have been born to lead troops in this war, Reagan looked at first to be miscast. While endorsing the GOP presidential candidate Barry Goldwater in 1964 in his nationally televised speech, "A Time for Choosing," Reagan had endeared himself to conservatives by calling on U.S. citizens to choose between free enterprise and big government, individual liberty and totalitarian collectivism, the freedom of capitalism and the slavery of the welfare state. Invoking Moses and Jesus, he spoke for what is "morally right."[37] Reagan knew that conservatism was not just about economics. It was also driven by cultural concerns and shot through with nostalgia for a golden age when men were men, morality was absolute, and America was exceptional. But Reagan was a B-movie actor, rather than an A-list preacher, and the former head of a labor union (the Screen Actors Guild). For much of his adulthood he had been a Democrat, and throughout his life he praised FDR. As California's governor, Reagan signed a bill allowing women to end their pregnancies in order to safeguard their own health and he opposed a campaign to prohibit gays and lesbians from serving as public school teachers. Equally important, Reagan never showed much interest in Christianity before the late 1970s. He was an irregular churchgoer. He was divorced. And his second wife, Nancy Reagan, had been pregnant when they married. For a man who would come to be identified with "family values," he had horribly strained relationships with his four children. His son Ron called him "distant and inattentive"; he didn't meet his grandchildren until the 1980 presidential campaign necessitated it; and when his daughter Maureen ran for the Senate in 1981 he refused to endorse her.[38]

Like Federalist ministers who ignored John Adams's heterodoxy in the election of 1800, conservative Christians were pragmatic enough to overlook these shortcomings. So they endorsed Reagan just as enthusiastically as he had endorsed them. Thanks in part to the Moral Majority's voter mobilization efforts (the Iranian hostage crisis was also key), Reagan defeated Carter in 1980, and during his presidency, which ran from 1981 to 1989, Reagan thanked the Religious Right repeatedly for its support.

One "thank you" came in January 1982, when the Reagan administration intervened in litigation between the IRS and Bob Jones University. BJU had not enrolled African American students until 1971; from 1971 to 1975 it had enrolled only married blacks; and in 1975 it had adopted a series of rules against interracial dating and interracial marriage (including advocating for either). BJU had appealed on religious liberty grounds the IRS decision to revoke its tax-exempt status, arguing that its racial policies were based on the religious conviction that "the Bible forbids interracial dating and marriage" and were therefore protected under the First Amendment.[39] The courts agreed first with BJU and later with the IRS. In 1982, as the Supreme Court was about to hear oral arguments, Reagan sided with the University, ordering Treasury and Justice officials to drop the case. This action produced an outcry on the left nearly as fierce as the Religious Right's reaction to the 1978 IRS guidelines. Why would a president, nearly three decades after *Brown*, support such a blatantly racist institution? In 1983, the Court ruled against BJU, ordering it to pay a million dollars in back taxes.

As these IRS disputes demonstrate, the culture wars of the 1970s and beyond *were* to some extent (and sometimes to a great extent) about race. In 1983, culture warrior Sen. Jesse Helms spent sixteen days filibustering a bill to create a federal holiday in honor of Martin

Luther King Jr. Reagan himself was not above playing the "race card" by denouncing Cadillac-driving "welfare queens" and "strapping young bucks" buying T-bone steaks with food stamps.[40] (He also called the popular television miniseries *Roots* "rather destructive" because of "the bias of all the good people being one color and all the bad people being another."[41]) The Religious Right first flexed its muscles and felt its power in the fight against IRS "segregation academy" rules. And the rhetoric on the right about small government, states' rights, and welfare cheats was always also about race. But race was not the central concern in the culture wars. The racial anxiety that got the movement going in the South also resonated in the heartland. But it could not have sustained a nationwide movement without two key pivots from the Religious Right.

Pivoting from Race to Religion

THE FIRST WAS a pivot from race to religion, which Falwell and his friends pulled off in the IRS protest. Conservative culture warriors have a long history of co-opting liberal rhetoric—of "talking left while walking right."[42] In the nineteenth century they opposed religious liberty for Catholics and Mormons in the name of preserving religious liberty for Protestants. In the contemporary culture wars they described abortion as a "holocaust," the ERA as a violation of women's rights, and affirmative action as "reverse discrimination." But nowhere was this rhetorical reversal as inventive as in the debate over segregation academies.

Although Falwell obviously supported segregation academies (he was, after all, the founder of one), he did so in the name of religious liberty, not white supremacy. The 1978 IRS rule was not about integrating private schools, he argued. It was about controlling Christian ones. In its 1962 and 1963 rulings, the Supreme Court had launched a war on God in the public schools. Now the federal government was bringing that fight to private schools.

The genius of this first pivot was that it redefined the Religious Right as victims of bigotry rather than bigots themselves. The schools they were defending were *Christian* academies, not *segregation* academies, they argued. Their aim was to protect schoolchildren from secularization, not integration. As the Religious Right put it, those who wanted to close their schools were motivated not by racial equality but by anti-Christian bias. Unbelievers wanted to impose their own religion—"secular humanism"—on everyone else, insisting, as Lutheran minister Richard John Neuhaus would later frame it, on a "naked public square" denuded of religious reasoning.[43] "In one fell swoop," writes political scientist Corey Robin, "the heirs of slaveholders became the descendants of persecuted Baptists, and Jim Crow a heresy the First Amendment was meant to protect."[44]

As the 1980s arrived and the Reagan Revolution advanced, culture warriors leapt gleefully over Jefferson's famous wall of church–state separation. Reviving imagery from Gov. Winthrop's *Arbella* sermon (imagery that itself was derived from Matthew 5:14), Reagan spoke of the United States as a "shining city on a hill." And what was shimmering was not just political or economic freedom but also Christian liberty. In an effort to reintroduce God to the classroom, Reagan supported school prayer and the teaching of creationism. He adopted the rhetoric of sin and evil, he spoke of Americans as God's chosen people, and he turned "God bless America" into a coda for all future presidential proclamations. "The First Amendment was not written to protect the people and their laws from religious values," he told the National Religious Broadcasters in 1983. "It was written to protect those values from government tyranny."[45]

Pivoting from Race to Family

THE SECOND PIVOT of Falwell and the Religious Right was from race (where the Bible was not particularly helpful) to family (where it was).[46] Like Pope Paul VI, who referred to the family in his

1968 encyclical *Humanae Vitae* as "the primary unit in the state,"[47] conservative Christians rejected the classical liberal view (of John Locke and others) that society is a compact of individuals. The family, Falwell argued, is "the fundamental institution of society, an immutable structure established by our Creator."[48] That institution was now in danger of being lost at the hands of an overreaching federal government.

Yes, abortion was murder and homosexuality was unnatural. But each also undermined family life. Similarly, feminism was dangerous because (among other things) it confused the distinct roles men and women and boys and girls were to play in *the* "traditional family," which Falwell and his followers understood to be of a singular sort: one male breadwinner and one female homemaker, married, with children, living under one roof and the patriarchal authority of the man of the house. The ERA, which the Religious Right sent down to defeat in 1982, confused these responsibilities, luring women out of their roles as housewives and challenging the role of the husband as "head of the wife." "Breadwinner conservatism thus largely replaced, or incorporated in subtle ways, white supremacy as the public face of southern conservatism," writes historian Robert Self.[49]

As they turned their attention to abortion, homosexuality, feminism, and "family values," conservative Christians joined the perennial American battle over the one and the many—the battle between those who believe the alternative to a unified society is chaos and those who embrace pluralism as a positive good. "No one has a monopoly on the family," said Bella Abzug, giving voice at the 1977 National Women's Conference to the feminist position that family, like abortion, should be a matter of choice.[50] Women didn't have to be homemakers. They didn't have to marry or have children. And they didn't have to restrict their sexual lives to marriage or even to men. When it came to family, liberals said, let a thousand flowers bloom.

Conservative culture warriors rejected this multiplication of family types, insisting that there is *one* eternal and unchanging design for *the* family. (They were livid when the Carter administration reimagined its 1980 "Conference on the Family" as the "Conference on Families.") Deviations from this godly design had created a social crisis visible in skyrocketing divorce rates, abortion on demand, urban crime, rampant pornography, government-funded child care, two-worker households, and homosexuality. Again this issue helped to fuse political and cultural conservatives, by providing a moral and religious justification for antipathy to government. The reforms of FDR's New Deal and Johnson's Great Society had turned the powers of the federal government against the "traditional family." Now culture warriors were determined to redirect those same powers toward supporting it.

Christian America

After making these two pivots—from race to religion and family—conservatives needed a master narrative to bring everything together. They found it in the story of the rise and demise of "Christian America." Instead of defending white superiority and the "Southern way of life," they defended "Christian America."

According to this narrative of loss and recovery, the United States is not an experiment in Enlightenment virtue undertaken by Deists and Unitarians who wrote a godless constitution. It is a Christian project initiated by men who followed Jesus Christ as their Lord and Savior. The Declaration of Independence spoke of a "Creator" who "endowed" U.S. citizens with "certain inalienable rights." And the First Amendment's establishment clause was designed to protect the church from state interference, not the state from church interference. Sixties liberals spat in the face of this legacy, as the Supreme Court banished God and the Bible from the public square and the sexual revolution replaced sexual restraint with sexual license. From this perspective, only Eisenhower-era Christians (or, in some versions of the story, Judeo-Christians) were true Americans. The secular sorts in nonclerical robes who ruled in *Engel, Schempp,* and *Roe* were not defenders of the American faith but enemies of it. "Secular humanism," too, was un-American. And those who proselytized for it were guilty of treason as well as apostasy.

The broad outline of this quintessentially conservative tale derived from the narratives of loss and recovery of other culture wars, but the most intimate antecedent was what Southern historian Charles Reagan Wilson has referred to as "the religion of the lost cause."[51] After the Civil War, he argues, Southerners embraced a civic theology that cast them as martyrs: God's chosen people even in the jaws of defeat. More than a century later, a cherished way of life was again under attack, and the fact that the righteous were losing only made them all the more righteous. As of the late 1970s, however, this way of life was no longer confined to one region. It drew its sustenance from "Christian America" and the "traditional family"—two symbols that acquired an air of sacrality before melting into each other under the pressure of the Religious Right: one nation under the providence of God and the family patriarch.

Yes, the Religious Right was born of anxieties over racial mixing and the demise of white supremacy. But if it had continued to speak as Falwell spoke in his pro-segregation sermons, it would not have traveled much farther than the five Southern states Alabama governor George Wallace carried against Richard Nixon and Hubert Humphrey in the 1968 presidential election. What gave the Religious Right reach was its leaders' decision to harness the anger and frustration conjured up by the demise of legal segregation to causes that traveled better. Instead of rushing to the barricades of white superiority and the "Southern way of life," they rushed to the defense of "Christian America" and the "traditional family." Instead of denouncing the federal government's interference in racial segregation, they denounced its intrusion into family and religious life—except, of course, when they were *demanding* its intrusion into individual choices about the religions Americans would affirm and what sorts of families they would form.

Liberal Counterattack

THESE CONTEMPORARY CULTURE wars were again asymmetrical; the Right fired far more shots than the Left returned. But the Left did respond. Historian Henry Steele Commager criticized the Religious Right for its preoccupation with "private sin" at the expense of "social evil." "They have much to say about the wickedness of limiting posterity, whether by birth control or abortion," he wrote, "but very little if anything to say about the kind of world children will be born into or about the systematic destruction of a rightful inheritance of natural resources."[52]

Bart Giametti, a classicist turned Yale president who would later serve as Major League Baseball's commissioner, attacked the Moral Majority as a threat to liberty, liberal arts education, and religious pluralism in a blistering August 1981 address to incoming Yale freshmen. These "peddlers of coercion" are "angry at change, rigid in the application of chauvinistic slogans, absolutistic in morality," he said. They "presume to know what justice for all is . . . which books are fit to read, which television programs are fit to watch, which textbooks will serve for all the young" and "when human life begins." For them, "there is no debate, no discussion, no dissent. . . . There is only one set of overarching political and spiritual and social beliefs; whatever view does not conform to these views is by definition relativistic, negative, secular, immoral, against the family, anti-free enterprise, un-American." This isn't just "nonsense," Giametti continued. It is "dangerous, malicious nonsense." It rejects "the very pluralism—of peoples, political beliefs, values, forms of merit, and systems of religion—our country was founded to welcome and foster."[53] There is not just one way to love one's family, one's country, and one's God.

Canon Wars

DESPITE GOP ELECTORAL gains in the Reagan era, conservatives *did* feel "dispossessed by change."[54] As the counterculture went mainstream, they experienced a litany of losses: the loss of the patriarchal family in which mothers and fathers, daughters and sons, all played their appointed roles and demonstrated the appropriate deference; the loss of a Christian America, where the authority of the biblical witness was unchallenged by Hindus, Buddhists, or nonbelievers; the loss of a white society, in which it seemed either natural or divinely ordained that those who occupied the White House and corporate boardrooms would be sturdy stock of European descent; and the loss at the end of the Vietnam War of faith in Americans as God's chosen people. These losses triggered anxieties in many, and their anxieties found expression in "canon wars" about history and literature, and "art wars" about ethics and aesthetics.

Since the emergence of public schooling in the 1820s, Americans had fought over what should be taught in public schools, colleges, and universities. The deadly "Bible wars" of the 1840s were about which Bible would be read in public schools, and the Scopes Trial of the 1920s turned on whether those schools could teach evolution. In the twentieth century, Southern conservatives denounced textbooks that glorified Lincoln's fight against the Confederacy, and laissez-faire capitalists denounced those that lauded FDR's New Deal. Irish Americans and German Americans demanded to be seen and heard in textbooks, and African Americans and American Indians did the same, protesting racial slurs and negative stereotypes and demanding not only recognition of their contributions to U.S. history but also acknowledgment of the evils visited upon them. The Civil Rights Act (1964) and the Voting Rights Act (1965) prepared the way for many African Americans to enter high school and college teaching jobs. And as 1960s activists moved from the streets into tenured positions, high school textbooks and college curricula started to reflect what abolitionist Frederick Douglass once described as our "composite nation."[55] In secondary schools, textbooks championed Douglass, W. E. B. Du Bois, and Eleanor Roosevelt alongside Washington, Franklin, and Jefferson.[56] In higher education, departments of African American Studies and Women's Studies proliferated.

Bennett's Legacy

WILLIAM BENNETT, WHO served under Reagan as National Endowment for the Humanities chairman and secretary of education, aimed to reverse these trends with a controversial manifesto. Based on consultations with a study group of thirty-one educators, *To Reclaim a Legacy: A Report on the Humanities in Higher Education* (1984) fired the first shot across the bow of the new pluralism in U.S. colleges and universities.

Like any good conservative, Bennett started with a lament. Most students who graduate from U.S. colleges, he argued, are "lacking even the most rudimentary knowledge" of Western civilization because professors are either ignoring the humanities or teaching them as "one subject among many." The humanities, which Bennett defined (following Matthew Arnold) as "the best that has been said, thought, written," had once fostered community by transmitting "a common culture" to students. But educators no longer agreed on a common core, because they had succumbed to the false view that "all meaning is subjective and relative to one's own perspective." The humanities were also suffering from the intrusion of "special interest politics" and a shift from delivering content to cultivating skills.[57]

We need "a common curriculum with humanities at the core," he said. This curriculum would include

- an understanding of the history of Western civilization;

- "a careful reading of several masterworks of English, American, and European literature";

- "an understanding of the most significant ideas and debates in the history of philosophy"; and

- "demonstrable proficiency in a foreign language."[58]

Bennett knew that American colleges and universities could not turn the clock back to a "classical curriculum" taught to "only a privileged few." He also knew that his "common curriculum"—"the glue that binds together our pluralistic nation"—would need to be "sensitive to the long-overlooked cultural achievements of many groups." So he included in it "some familiarity with the history, literature, religion, and philosophy of at least one non-Western culture or civilization."[59] All that came with a caveat, however, and a big caveat it was:

> But the core of the American college curriculum—its heart and soul—should be the civilization of the West, source of the most powerful and pervasive influences on America and all of its people. It is simply not possible for students to understand their society without studying its intellectual legacy. If their past is hidden from them, they will become aliens in their own culture, strangers in their own land.[60]

Hirsch's Cultural Literacy

IN HIS MANIFESTO, Bennett had offered a list of a few dozen canonical authors and titles—from classical antiquity, medieval and modern Europe, and American history and literature—including Homer, Plato, Dante, Shakespeare, Locke, Twain, and the Bible. In his 1987 bestseller, *Cultural Literacy: What Every American Needs to Know*, University of Virginia English professor E. D. Hirsch Jr. offered a list of over four thousand building blocks of "cultural literacy." Whereas Bennett's list was prescriptive (what we *should* know), Hirsch's was descriptive (what literate Americans *actually* know). Moreover, Hirsch set a lower bar, insisting only that his "common reader" know the terms "Huckleberry Finn" and "I Have a Dream," not that she actually read them.[61]

Like *To Reclaim a Legacy*, Hirsch's *Cultural Literacy* was driven by a perceived "decline of literate knowledge." Three-quarters of American seventeen-year-olds could not identify Henry Thoreau or Walt Whitman, Hirsch warned, and two-thirds could not place the Civil War in the second half of the nineteenth century. Hirsch, a Democrat, understood cultural literacy as an "avenue of opportunity for disadvantaged children." His book's central insight was this: In order to succeed in society, you need to be able to communicate effectively, and in order to communicate effectively you need to possess the "shared culture" upon which communication depends. Cultural literacy was that "shared culture"—"the network of information that all competent readers possess"—and Hirsch was determined to deliver it to underprivileged children. Taking possession of this prize would enable American youth of all races and classes to make sense of the Declaration of Independence, but it also would enable them to read the Black Panther Party platform of 1972, which referred to "the Declaration of Independence, the Pledge of Allegiance to the Flag, the Gettysburg Address, and the Bible." You need "traditional culture," Hirsch wrote, to understand "progressive ideas."[62]

Bloom's Closing of the American Mind

IN *CULTURAL LITERACY*, Hirsch focused on elementary education. In *The Closing of the American Mind* (1987), University of Chicago political philosopher Allan Bloom focused on higher education. "The truth is the one thing most needful," he wrote in the book that came to define the canon wars, and that most needful thing was under attack in the very citadel built to defend it.[63] This book was not, as cultural critic Camille Paglia once claimed, "the first shot in the culture wars," but it definitely hit the bull's-eye.[64] Reviewer after reviewer scratched heads trying to figure out how a nerdy volume that included extensive meditations on Plato, Machiavelli, Heidegger, and Nietzsche could become a bestseller and transform its author from an unknown academic into a celebrity scold.

Bloom thrilled conservatives by taking on feminism, deconstructionism, historicism, rock music, the New Left, black power, the cult of progress, secularization, divorce, equality, radicalism, democracy, affirmative action, the sexual revolution, immodesty, modernity, nihilism, the Soviet Union, the feminization of American culture, and the "decomposition of the university." These woes he traced to the "bad sixties," when radical youth spurned the powers that be, and to ancient Athens, when those same powers put Socrates to death. But his central target was relativism. "There is one thing a professor can be absolutely certain of: almost every student entering the university believes, or says he believes, that truth is relative," he wrote. And his book was devoted to demonstrating that relativism is for the faint of heart. Bloom attacked relativism because he believed in discriminating between truth and falsehood, good and evil, the profound and the superficial, the educated and the uneducated. All cultures were not equal, and no book was trapped in the historical moment in which it was written. But he also attacked relativism because he was convinced that it sapped students of passion.[65]

Bloom saw in his students nothing of the intellectual eros—the longing for truth, beauty, and the good—that had characterized the "Great Books" education he had received at Chicago in the glory years of the 1940s and 1950s. He wanted to bring longing back to the student body, and to stir students' souls in the process. (*Souls Without Longing* was the book's original title.)

Political philosopher Albert Hirschman has written of a "rhetoric of reaction" that "delights in almost automatic inversion, whereby increased liberty leads to slavery" and "open-mindedness is a form of fanaticism."[66] Bloom drew on this conservative rhetoric, fretting about "the great democratic danger" that, by liberating the individual from tradition, only enslaved him to the banality of the here and now. While the university once shaped students into lovers of ancient wisdom, it now contorted them into parrots of their peers. As a result, young people were trapped inside the illogic of a democratic society that fetishized the useful, sneered at the theoretical, and lauded tolerance more than truth. Ironically—and this is the point of the title—all this "open-mindedness" closed the minds of American youth to the thinkers and ideas that might actually liberate them. These soulless students exhibited none of the "humanizing doubts" that infuse the dialogues of Plato. Among them, the "great-souled man, who loves beautiful and useless things" had gone missing.[67]

Much of the passion in this diatribe seems to have derived from Bloom's experience of a Cornell student rebellion in the late 1960s and early 1970s—a period he recalled as "an unmitigated disaster" for higher education. In this rebellion, as he tells it, reason collapsed under the force of emotion as students, faculty, and administrators conspired to politicize and trivialize the university. Although student radicals saw themselves as enemies of authority and partisans of nonconformity, they were in Bloom's view conformists to the core and their age a "period of dogmatic answers and trivial facts."[68]

Bloom knew that the Reagan era had witnessed a revival of core curriculum requirements, but this revival failed to stir his soul, since universities still refused to put philosophy and the humanities atop the disciplinary pecking order. In fact, they refused to recognize any pecking order at all. Neither would they weigh in on what made for an educated person. Bloom's solution was to return to "the good old Great Books approach." This meant "trying to read [the classics] as their authors wished them to be read" (i.e., closely and slowly) and wrestling in the process with the perennial questions they posed: "Is there a God? Is there freedom? Is there punishment for evil deeds? Is there certain knowledge? What is a good society?"[69]

Backlash

AS BENNETT WORKED Washington, DC, and Bloom and Hirsch charged up the bestseller lists (at one point occupying the top two nonfiction slots), liberals launched a canon wars counterattack.

University of Chicago professor Jonathan Z. Smith compared the authorial voice in *To Reclaim a Legacy* to British administrators at the twilight of the Indian Raj who spoke "with the smug, yet wistful voices of dying colonialism." Bennett's imagined past "appears to lack women, Jews, Byzantines, and Muslims," Smith observed. How can he speak so blithely of "*the* western mind" as a singular entity? Doesn't he know that even inside his list of a few dozen canonical texts "there are differences and dissonances"—that the work of the humanities always involves the complexities of "translation, interpretation, and historical consciousness?" "The nostalgic tone of his Report is apt," Smith wrote, for what Bloom awaits is "the coming of last year."[70]

African American literature scholar Henry Louis Gates Jr. said that Bennett's study offered a "nostalgic return" to "the 'antebellum aesthetic position,' when men were men, and men were white, when scholar-critics were white men, and when women and persons of color were voiceless, faceless servants and laborers, pouring tea and filling brandy snifters in the boardrooms of old boys' clubs." To return to *this* canon, Gates continued, is to return to "an old order in which my people were the subjugated, the voiceless, the invisible, the unrepresented, and the unrepresentable. Who would return us to that medieval never-neverland?"[71]

Literary critic Robert Scholes attacked Hirsch for claiming that memorizing lists of key terms would raise living standards, improve social justice, extend democracy, and make the United States more competitive in global markets. ("Voodoo education," he called it, echoing George H. W. Bush's critique of "voodoo economics."[72]) The authors of *Multi-Cultural Literacy* (1988) deemed Hirsch's

list "alarmingly deficient in its male and European bias." They then
offered a list of their own, which included Cinco de Mayo, Betty
Friedan, Toni Morrison, Wounded Knee, beatnik, ashram, condom,
karma, Little Red Book, rap music, and Swahili.[73]

Still, Bloom got the lion's share of the criticism (and the book
sales). When neoconservative Norman Podhoretz called his bestseller "the most devastating assault on the liberal culture that
anyone has produced in our time," he meant it as a compliment.[74]
Liberals and radicals were less kind. Writer and editor David Rieff
called *The Closing* "a book decent people would be ashamed of
having written."[75] Philosopher Robert Paul Wolff wrote a tongue-in-
cheek review in which he pretended that Saul Bellow had written a
"funny novel in the form of a pettish, bookish, grumpy, reactionary
complaint against the last two decades."[76] Other reviewers called
Bloom's book sexist and racist. They criticized his esoteric writing and shoddy scholarship. They lamented his misanthropy. They
called him to task for scapegoating his students and for blindly following the Straussian orthodoxy of his teacher, political philosopher
Leo Strauss. In a book called *The Opening of the American Mind*
(1996), historian Lawrence Levine insisted on making room in the
canon for non-Western sources.

The core complaint was that *The Closing* was elitist and, therefore,
anti-American. Political scientist Benjamin Barber referred to Bloom
as a "Philosopher Despot" and to his bestseller as "one of the most profoundly antidemocratic books ever written for a popular audience."
Why, he asked, are American readers so enamored of this "raging
assault on liberal tolerance and democratic education"—a book that
exalts "the *few* who embody philosophy" and sneers at "the *many* who
embody America"? Barber knew that lots of conservative readers
were "anxious about the loss of fixed points, wishing for simpler, more
orderly times," and he acknowledged that these "anxious ones" were
wary about liberty lapsing into anarchy and equality into mediocrity.
But Barber cast his vote for American values nonetheless.[77]

Unyielding, Bloom wore his elitism with glee. In a 1988 Harvard speech, he greeted his audience as "Fellow Elitists!" Hadn't he observed in *The Closing* that real education was not for everyone? Philosophy is a way of life, he wrote, and only a "tiny band of men" are equipped to do it.[78]

You won't get this from reviews, but neither *Cultural Literacy* nor *The Closing* was lacking in nuance. Praising "the virtues of multicultural education," Hirsch wrote that "tolerance of diversity is at the root of our tradition."[79] And Bloom, who sneered at "impoverishing certitudes," seemed to disdain blind conservatism nearly as much as blind liberalism.[80] In fact, Bloom repeatedly refused to label himself a conservative, noting that "any superficial reading of my book will show that I differ from both theoretical and practical conservative positions."[81] If he were alive today, Bloom would be no friend of the anti-intellectual populism of Rush Limbaugh, Ann Coulter, and Bill O'Reilly. The point of philosophy, in his view, was not to arrive at the truth; it was to deliver one from dogma. Still, both authors were drafted into the "right" side of the culture wars, where (as in all warfare) nuances go to die.[82]

"The Closing of the Stanford Mind"

AMID THIS FUROR, Stanford University opened up another battlefield in the canon wars when it reexamined its Western Culture requirement—a yearlong core curriculum course that required all freshmen to read fifteen classics in Western literature, from the Bible, Homer, and Plato to Dante, Galileo, Marx, and Freud. In the spring of 1986, the Stanford Black Student Union denounced the course's "core list" as racist. The message of Western Culture, said former Black Student Union president Amanda Kemp, was "nigger go home."[83] Soon Hispanic, Asian, and feminist groups were piling on, arguing that Western civilization was nothing to celebrate and calling Western Culture sexist and Eurocentric.

In January 1987, on Martin Luther King Jr.'s birthday, Democratic presidential candidate Jesse Jackson marched in solidarity with Stanford student protesters, who chanted, "Hey, hey, ho, ho, Western Culture's got to go." That spring, minority students occupied the offices of Stanford president Donald Kennedy, demanding curricular changes. In March 1988, the Stanford Faculty Senate voted 39 to 4 to replace its old requirement with a new, more pluralistic sequence, Cultures, Ideas, and Values (CIV), which would include, in addition to Western classics, "works by women, minorities and persons of color," attention to at least one non-Western culture, and at least one work focusing on race, class, or gender.[84] Days after that vote, William Bennett came to Palo Alto to denounce "the closing of the Stanford mind." The decision to axe Western Culture, he said, was political rather than educational—the result of "pressure politics and intimidation," not "enlightened debate." "Those who attack Western values and accomplishments do not see an America that—despite its imperfections, its weaknesses, its sins— has served and continues to serve as a beacon to the world," he said. "Instead, theirs is an America hopelessly tainted—tainted by racism, imperialism, sexism, capitalism, ethnocentrism, elitism."[85]

Novelist Colman McCarthy accused Bennett of "academic nationalism" and of treating Stanford students like "invading Huns," but a chorus of conservative applause drowned out the liberals.[86] Harking back to the corruption of Boss Tweed's Tammany Hall, columnist George Will denounced Stanford's "academic spoils system," which was designed not to promote the truth but "to satisfy racial, sexual and ethnic groups."[87] "Affirmative action for great books is an embarrassment," wrote conservative columnist Charles Krauthammer.[88] "If Jane Austen and Virginia Woolf appear in the curriculum," added City University of New York (CUNY) professor Gertrude Himmelfarb, "there should be no ambiguity about the grounds of their inclusion—not as women novelists but as first-class novelists."[89]

The canon wars did not end at Stanford, of course. Conservatives

reacted with horror as universities across the country tried to address "multicultural illiteracy" with requirements that emphasized
non-Western cultures and the contributions of women and minorities to U.S. history.[90] Local fights concerned whether *The Adventures
of Huckleberry Finn* was an appropriate book for high school classrooms or hometown libraries. Is Twain's novel "racist trash," as one
educator argued, or is it "a matchless satire on racism, bigotry, and
property rights in human beings"?[91]

Similar questions bedeviled the overseers of state and national
standards for secondary education. As New York State revised its
social studies standards in the direction of multiculturalism, CUNY
professor Arthur Schlesinger Jr. gave voice to the anxiety of many
traditionalists that America's *pluribus* was overrunning its *unum*.
In his bestseller *The Disuniting of America* (1991), Schlesinger acknowledged the importance of women's history and Latin American, Asian, and African history but described "Europhobia" and "the
new ethnic gospel" as dangers to the long-standing American ideals
of assimilation and integration, and to our "common ideals" and
"common culture." "The bonds of national cohesion in the republic
are sufficiently fragile already," he wrote. "Public education should
aim to strengthen those bonds, not to weaken them. If separatist
tendencies go on unchecked, the result can only be the fragmenta-
tion, resegregation, and tribalization of American life."[92] Schlesinger
also made an important historical observation: that universalist
arguments for unity used to be regarded as liberal, but with the rise
of identity politics, they had come to be seen as conservative. In a
similar turnabout, many Republicans today oppose the Common
Core State Standards.

Piss Christ

IN 1989, THE culture wars visited the art world, as cultural conservatives found in the museum a new site for airing fears about the

rise of homosexuality and the decline of the West. Again combatants debated the one and the many, objectivity and subjectivity. Again they politicized a venue that was supposed to be free from political influence. In these fights, culture warriors grew increasingly attuned not simply to symbols such as the flag and the cross but also to images—visual representations of naked black bodies and aborted fetuses.

Back in 1981, pundits and politicians had debated the winning design for a proposed Vietnam War memorial on the National Mall. Critics of that design, by Yale College undergraduate Maya Lin, objected to its minimalism and to its refusal to celebrate the war as (in Reagan's terms) a "noble cause."[93] Noting that its two sunken walls were to be black granite instead of the white granite favored elsewhere in the capital, one critic termed the proposed memorial "a black gash of shame and sorrow." Journalist Tom Wolfe called it "a tribute to Jane Fonda." Others judged it inane, elitist, depressing, perverse, insulting, antiwar, and nihilistic. Lin's defenders charged that these critics were motivated less by artistic or even political calculations than by sexism, racism, and anti-intellectualism. (Lin was a woman, an Asian American, and a Yalie.) Look at her simple design without prejudice, they said, and you will see an eloquent piece of art—a perfect expression of a nation deeply divided over the Vietnam War.[94]

In the late 1980s, debates over art turned from memorials to photographs, and from patriotism to family values. Donald Wildmon of the American Family Association stirred the pot with an April 5, 1989, public letter denouncing Andres Serrano's *Piss Christ*—a photograph of a wood and plastic crucifix awash in the artist's urine. Previously, Wildmon had attacked the indecencies of popular culture, pressuring 7-Eleven to stop selling *Playboy* and *Penthouse*, and CBS to remove a scene from a cartoon supposedly depicting Mighty Mouse sniffing cocaine. Now he turned to high art. "The bias and bigotry against Christians, which has dominated television and movies for the past decade or more," he contended, "has now moved over to the art museums." First came *The Last Temptation of Christ* depicting "Jesus as a tormented, deranged, human-only sinner," then Madonna's "Like a Prayer" video depicting "Christ having sex with a priest," and now Serrano's "desecration of Christ," Wildmon wrote. "Maybe, before the physical persecution of Christians begins, we will gain the courage to stand against such bigotry."[95]

Piss Christ had been shown without fuss or fury in Manhattan, Los Angeles, Pittsburgh, Richmond, Virginia, and Winston-Salem, North Carolina. According to Serrano, it was "absolutely not calcu-lated to offend."[96] But offend it did. Members of the AFA's massive mailing list barraged Congress and the National Endowment for the Arts (NEA) with protest letters and phone calls. So did viewers of Pat Robertson's *700 Club* television program and members of Phyllis Schlafly's Eagle Forum. When Pat Buchanan looked at *Piss Christ* he saw an "anti-Christian, anti-American, nihilistic" society in which liberals were repeatedly coming out on top. "While the right has been busy winning primaries and elections, cutting taxes and funding anti-communist guerrillas abroad, the left has been quietly seizing all the commanding heights of American art and culture," he said, before calling for "a cultural revolution in the '90s as sweeping as its political revolution in the '80s."[97]

On May 18, 1989, senators Alfonse D'Amato (R-NY) and Jesse Helms (R-NC) denounced "this piece of trash" and the "jerk" who had produced it.[98] And on June 8, Rep. Dick Armey (R-TX) sent NEA director Hugh Southern a letter threatening NEA budget cuts signed by over one hundred members of Congress. Stop paying for "morally reprehensible trash" and develop new grant-making guide-lines that respect "public standards of taste and decency," Armey demanded. Otherwise, the House would "blow their budgets out of the water."[99]

Since Congress created the NEA in 1965, its funds had been al-located through peer-review panels meant to insulate it from political interference and the artists it supported from infringements on artistic freedom. Serrano had received fifteen thousand dollars in NEA funds via the Southeastern Center for Contemporary Art in Winston-Salem, North Carolina. That drove D'Amato and Helms to distraction. In "a ritual counter-desecration," D'Amato tore up a copy of *Piss Christ* on the Senate floor.[100] "This is not a question of free speech," he said. "This is a question of abuse of taxpayers' money." Taking a more pious tack, Helms called Serrano's "so-called artwork" a blasphemous effort to "dishonor our Lord." But Helms, too, followed the money. The Constitution may allow Serrano to produce and display his photographs, he argued, but "it certainly does not require the American taxpayers or the Federal Government to fund, promote, honor, approve or condone it." The remedy? An amendment to appropriations legislation that would prevent the NEA from funding "obscene or indecent materials" (including homoeroticism); "materials which denigrate the objects or beliefs of the adherents of a particular religion or non-religion"; and "material which denigrates, debases, or reviles a person, group, or class of citizens on the basis of race, creed, sex, handicap, age, or national origin."[101]

Robert Mapplethorpe and the NEA

ON JUNE 12, 1989, Christina Orr-Cahall, director of the Corcoran Gallery of Art, located one block from the White House, abruptly canceled an exhibition of Robert Mapplethorpe photographs slated to open July 1. *Robert Mapplethorpe: The Perfect Moment* had been organized by the Institute of Contemporary Art at the University of Pennsylvania, which had received thirty thousand dollars in NEA funding for it. Orr-Cahall reportedly feared that the exhibition, which included homosexually explicit images, could provoke Congress to cut NEA funding (or eliminate the agency altogether).

The conservative *Washington Times* called this turn of events "the best thing to happen in American arts since Philip Roth lost the manuscript of a novel in a New York men's room." Other traditionalists judged Mapplethorpe's photos to be pornography, not art. Real art ennobles, they argued, expressing and reinforcing eternal values such as "the good, the true, and the beautiful." Mapplethorpe's "snapshots of a tourist in hell" sneered at those values and at the ordinary Americans who held them dear.[102]

Repeatedly critics referred to Mapplethorpe as a "homosexual artist" whose death by AIDS in 1989 was a just punishment for his sins. In a bizarre op-ed piece, *Washington Times* columnist Richard Grenier fantasized six separate times about locating Mapplethorpe's corpse, dousing it with kerosene, and setting it on fire. As for the "shocking and depraved" photographs, many could not even bring themselves to describe them. Others seemed to relish the opportunity, focusing on images that (by their gaze) featured "a little girl with her dress up, one man about to urinate in the mouth of another, an elephantine penis hanging out of a pair of pants, and the 'artist's' nude photo of himself, with a bullwhip sticking out of his rectum."[103] In short, Mapplethorpe seemed to epitomize everything that had gone wrong with music, literature, and the arts since the salacious 1960s. He, too, glorified the "libertinism and polymorphous perversity" that led through the drug-induced haze of Woodstock to the violence of Altamont.[104]

Echoing parallel disputes over education, art warriors accused the Left of seeking to destroy, in the name of "primitivism, feminism, racialism, multiculturalism, and homophilia . . . every traditional social institution, beginning with the church . . . and ending with the family." In the name of uniformity, hierarchy, and deference, *The New Criterion* publisher Samuel Lipman took aim at multiculturalism, which he defined as "a widespread assault on what is variously called Western, or European, or white-dominated or male-dominated civilization." According to Lipman, the "multicultural agenda" functioned in the arts as a sort of aesthetic relativism, asserting "that the art of all peoples is equally worthy of preservation and presentation." In the absence of a clear commitment to a hierarchy of values, the "imperishable masterpieces" of the European tradition were reduced to "no more than one kind of ethnic manifestation."[105]

The Right also accused the Left of putting advocacy before art, but the conservatives in this battle were advocates too—for premodern art over the avant-garde, and for heterosexuality over the "florid and variant sexualities" of Mapplethorpe's pictures.[106] Every dollar given to an African American artist or a lesbian was a dollar snatched from a straight, white male.

In this era, which historian Daniel Rodgers has characterized as an "age of fracture," Lipman held on to the dream of one "common civilization" and an NEA committed to preserving "our common cultural and artistic inheritance."[107] But liberals, unafraid of fracture, spoke of civilizations in the plural, criticizing any appeal to universality as a political attempt to valorize *one* artistic vision and to render invisible the rest.

Mapplethorpe's opponents kept returning to taxpayer funding, however. Censorship is not the issue, they said. Neither is artistic freedom. The issue is federal funding. Artists cannot expect to receive grants without *some* congressional oversight, especially if they are going to produce "pornography and anti-Christian bigotry." "If art and religion are to be free of state influence, then they must indeed be free of state influence," reasoned Sen. Slade Gorton (R-WA). "If they are to be free of censure, they cannot depend on subsidy." Or, as Helms put it, "People who want to scrawl dirty words on the men's room wall should furnish their own walls and their own crayons." It was high time for this "so-called art" to come to grips with the laws of supply and demand. "Let the NEA and the artists they support meet the same tests as other artists in our society—the demand of the marketplace," said the American Family Association.[108]

Defending the NEA

AS LIBERALS WERE quick to point out, this was precisely what the NEA was created *not* to do. It was designed to insulate artists from the vagaries of the marketplace—to support through public funds art that would not be supported privately. What the nation was now witnessing was the erosion of that buffer—the blatant interference of conservative lawmakers in aesthetic matters quite beyond their ken.

Echoing Garrison Keillor, who thanked the NEA for funding in its infancy his *A Prairie Home Companion* radio show, Arthur Levitt Jr., former chairman of the American Stock Exchange, observed in *The Wall Street Journal* in 1990 that "all four Pulitzer Prize winners this year received NEA funds at important junctures in their careers."[109] Sen. Ted Kennedy (D-MA) characterized the controversial grants as "aberrations," adding that "Congress must not put itself in the position of serving as a board of censors for the arts." Others drew a straight line from Helms and his "cultural Mafia" to Nazi Germany, Soviet Russia, Red China, and other totalitarian haters of free speech and artistic freedom. "Once we allow lawmakers to become art critics," warned Robert Brustein of the Cambridge-based American Repertory Theater, "we take the first step into the world of Ayatollah Khomeini, whose murderous review of *The Satanic Verses* still chills the heart of everyone committed to free expression."[110]

An arts coalition representing symphony orchestras, dance companies, opera companies, theater groups, museums, and state and local arts agencies vigorously defended federal funding for the arts, noting how, since the NEA's founding in 1965, "37 professional dance companies have grown to 250 dance companies . . . 60 professional orchestras have grown to 210 professional orchestras . . . [and] 27 professional opera companies have grown to 113 professional opera companies." And all this for a cost of just 68 cents per taxpayer per year![111] Other NEA supporters said that the Helms amendment was so vague and far reaching that, if passed, it would prohibit the NEA from funding almost anything. Sen. John Danforth (R-MO) noted that the Helms amendment would probably preclude NEA funding for *The Color Purple* (for denigrating men), *Huckleberry Finn* (for denigrating blacks), and *The Merchant of Venice* (for denigrating Jews).[112]

In the canon wars, Bloom and his supporters had defended "Truth" against "truths." At the heart of this arts controversy was another debate about the one and the many. Is there a single standard of beauty by which all art can be objectively judged? Is beauty in the eye of the beholder? And what of morality? Is it one or many?

Casting their lot with objectivity and uniformity, conservatives claimed that there was *one* American public committed to *one* universal standard of beauty and *one* universal standard of morality (which also turned out to be their own). Liberals saw a society made up of different publics with competing ethical and aesthetic standards. Helms wanted to punish the NEA whenever "it strays from what he fancies to be the center line of American ethical belief," wrote Brustein. Yet "no such line exists—not in a society as vast, various and eclectic as the real America."[113]

Sen. Daniel Patrick Moynihan (D-NY), who saw in this art war a return to the moralism of the party of the past of the 1920s, doubted that Mapplethorpe's critics were really speaking on behalf of universal beauty or a unified public:

> Do we really want it to be recorded that the Senate of the United States, in the 101st Congress of this Republic, is so insensible to the traditions of liberty in our land, so fearful of what is different and new and intentionally disturbing, so anxious to record our timidity that we would sanction institutions for acting precisely as they are meant to act? Which is to say, art institutions supporting artists and exhibiting their work?

More. Are we so little mindful of the diversity of our
Nation, and the centrality of censorship and persecution in the
experience of not just a few but I would almost say every religious and ethnic inheritance in this land?[114]

Magazine editor Steven Durland argued that the censors were
clinging to an obsolete view of their country as "white, Christian,
heterosexual and male." The arts should "embody our differences,"
said Rep. Pat Williams (D-MT). "A free society," added Harvard
Law professor Kathleen Sullivan, "can have no official orthodoxy in
art any more than in religion or politics."[115]

But conservatives again flipped the script, casting themselves as
Inquisitors' victims, naturalized citizens in our "nation of outsiders."[116] Homosexuality, feminism, and multiculturalism were the
new repressive orthodoxy. The real bigots were "Hollywood, homosexuals, abortionists, family planners, the sexually promiscuous,
failed spouses, failed parents, failed kids."[117]

Conservatives believed that *Piss Christ* and Mapplethorpe's
images spoke for themselves. Just as evangelicals saw the Bible as
self-interpreting, they could not imagine that different viewers
could see these photographs differently. So while Serrano, in a letter
to the NEA, contended that his most controversial photograph "has
multiple meanings and can be interpreted in various ways,"[118] blasphemy was by their sights its one and only meaning.

In a *New York Times* interview, Serrano described *Piss Christ* not
as a desecration of religion but as a critique of its desecration, "a protest against the commercialization of sacred imagery."[119] Elsewhere
he said that "the picture is meant as a criticism of the billion dollar
Christ-for-profit industry and the commercialization of spiritual
values that permeates our society . . . a condemnation of those who
abuse the teachings of Christ for their own ignoble ends."[120]

Frank Schaeffer, prodigal son of evangelical icon Francis Schaeffer, argued that *Piss Christ* "is no more blasphemous than most

religious television that so-called Christian organizations support. The idea of sending Oral Roberts ten dollars because he has told me God will bless me if I donate money to him is certainly just as much heresy and blasphemy as putting a crucifix in a jar of urine."[121] John Buchanan, president of People for the American Way, a nonprofit founded in 1981 to undercut the claim of the Religious Right to speak for the "real America," told senators that *Piss Christ* was, indeed, "shocking," "outrageous," and "offensive," but insisted it was "good theology" nonetheless—"a faithful portrayal of the shocking, outrageous, offensive reality of our sinfulness heaped upon Him."[122] One art critic discerned in Serrano's work "the victory of the spirit in the humiliation of the flesh."[123] Another wrote that *Piss Christ* "pays idiosyncratic homage to ideas that Christ originally stood for."[124]

Piss Helms

AS THIS ARTS drama moved into its last act, the Washington Project for the Arts agreed to host the Mapplethorpe exhibition that the Corcoran had canceled. The show then traveled to the Contemporary Arts Center in Cincinnati, where museum director Dennis Barrie was arrested on (and eventually acquitted of) obscenity charges.

Some conservative legislators, led by Rep. Dana Rohrabacher (R-CA), tried to eliminate all NEA funding. Others backed the content restrictions of the Helms amendment. In October 1989, Congress rejected that amendment and decided to fully fund the NEA, minus a symbolic forty-five thousand dollars (the amount previously granted Serrano and Mapplethorpe). But Congress did adopt language prohibiting the use of NEA funds for materials that "may be considered obscene, including but not limited to, depictions of sadomasochism, homoeroticism, the sexual exploitation of children, or individuals engaged in sex acts and which, taken as a whole, do not have serious literary, artistic, political, or scientific value."[125]

Many in the arts community feared that these content restrictions—the first in NEA history—would produce a chilling effect. The chill came quickly. One month after the compromise bill passed, NEA chairman John Frohnmayer took back a ten-thousand-dollar grant his agency had awarded to Artists Space in New York City for an AIDS-themed exhibition called *Witnesses: Against Our Vanishing*. In his view, the catalog crossed the line separating art from politics when artist David Wojnarowicz described Cardinal O'Connor as a "fat cannibal from that house of walking swastikas up on Fifth Avenue" and fantasized about dousing Helms with gasoline and setting him on fire.[126] Under intense pressure from the arts community, Frohnmayer restored the grant, but pressure continued to build from both sides. A group known as the NEA Four sued after Frohnmayer overturned decisions by NEA peer-review panels to grant them fellowships. And when the NEA announced it would require all its grant recipients to adhere to the new content restrictions, many artists turned down their grants, refusing to sign what they saw as a loyalty oath.

Meanwhile, People for the American Way ran a series of apocalyptic radio spots focused on the NEA controversy: "Imagine a world in which millions of people are at the mercy of a small band of extremists. In which works of art are subject to government censorship. And freedom of expression is a crime. Now stop imagining. Welcome to America, 1990."[127] In a song called "Jesse Don't Like It," Loudon Wainwright III criticized "Mr. Censorship":

If Jesse thinks it's dirty, it don't get any funds.
They use that taxpayer's money on tobacco and guns.
Your freedom of expression is being denied.
But if you're not sure what you like, then just let Jesse decide.[128]

Jos Sances's protest was more visceral: a serigraph—*Piss Helms*—depicting a naked black man urinating on Senator Helms. In another piece by the same name, Phoenix artist Cactus Jack immersed a photograph of Helms in a container of beer.

The Christian Coalition

IN 1989, AS the art wars were peaking, Jerry Falwell shut down the Moral Majority. It had played almost no role in the 1988 election of Reagan's successor, Republican George H. W. Bush. Its ability to raise money had been undercut by sexual and financial scandals plaguing Jimmy Swaggart, Jim and Tammy Faye Bakker, and other televangelists. And Falwell had thrown away the little political capital he had left in support of apartheid in South Africa. THE MORAL MAJORITY IS NEITHER, read one bumper sticker, and by the time Falwell pulled the plug, his organization *was* hugely unpopular, with unfavorables topping favorables even among white evangelicals.

Learning from the Moral Majority's mistakes, Pat Robertson used the political capital he had earned in his bid for the 1988 Republican presidential nomination to form, in 1989, a pressure group closely tied to the GOP and focused on local and state politics. The Christian Coalition, which under the leadership of Young Republicans leader Ralph Reed would come to dominate the Religious Right in the 1990s, got much of its early momentum from direct-mail appeals on the art wars.

"Last week I began a new organization to fight for our freedoms— The Christian Coalition," Robertson wrote in a direct-mail appeal dated October 25, 1989. That appeal began and ended not with segregation academies or abortion but with "TAX-PAYER FUNDED Photographs Too Vulgar to Print."[129] In 1990, Reed ran a series of newspaper, radio, and television ads calling on legislators to abolish the NEA: "Do you want to face the voters in your district with the charge that you are wasting their hard-earned money to promote sodomy, child pornography, and attacks on Jesus Christ?"[130] On the strength of this fusion of antigovernment conservatism and evangelical anxiety, the Christian Coalition quickly emerged as *the* political organization of the Religious Right in the 1990s.

In 1992, Buchanan famously brought the culture wars to the Republican primaries, attacking President Bush for allowing the NEA to fund *Tongues Untied*, a PBS documentary about gay black men, and pledging that, if elected, he would "shut down, padlock and fumigate" the NEA.[131] Buchanan lost the Republican nomination to Bush, who lost the general election to the Democratic governor of Arkansas Bill Clinton, but on the floor of the Republican National Convention he delivered his now famous "culture wars" speech. "There is a religious war going on in our country for the soul of America," Buchanan said. "It is a cultural war, as critical to the kind of nation we will one day be as was the Cold War itself."[132] In this speech (it "probably sounded better in the original German," quipped columnist Molly Ivins[133]), Buchanan praised Bush as "a defender of right-to-life, and lifelong champion of the Judeo-Christian values and beliefs upon which this nation was built." He then blasted "Clinton & Clinton" for promoting "abortion on demand, a litmus test for the Supreme Court, homosexual rights, discrimination against religious schools, women in combat." "That's change, all right," he said, but "it is not the kind of change we can tolerate in a nation that we still call God's country."[134]

Two years later, in the 1994 midterm elections, the Christian Coalition played the role the Moral Majority had played in the 1980 elections, helping to give control of both houses of Congress to Republicans and paving the way for the "Contract with America," crafted by House Speaker Newt Gingrich (R-GA). One year later, congressional Republicans slashed the NEA budget by 39 percent. In 1995 and again in 1996, House Republicans shut down the federal government in a miscalculated show of strength that would eventually force Gingrich to step down as Speaker of the House and propel President Clinton to reelection in 1996.

Homosexual Art

THE ART WARS were about art, of course, and about federal spending and Christianity. But antihomosexuality was the lost cause in this debate. At a time when "God's people" had, in James Robison's words, "come out of the closet," were gays and lesbians supposed to stay in?[135]

The object of conservative anxieties was to some extent displaced in these art wars—from homosexuality to "homosexual photographs" to public funding for the same. But the NEA's critics repeatedly blurred the categories of "obscenity" and "homosexuality," most plainly in 1989 NEA appropriations legislation, whose laundry list of potentially "obscene" art included "homoeroticism" alongside "the sexual exploitation of children."[136]

After the NEA reversed itself and provided funding for the AIDS-themed exhibition *Witnesses: Against Our Vanishing*, Pat Buchanan decided that both the gay rights community and the arts community were behaving like children. He reserved most of his paternal scolding for homosexuals, however, who in his view were getting precisely what they deserved in the AIDS epidemic. "The gays yearly die by the thousands of AIDS, crying out in rage for what they cannot have: respect for a lifestyle Americans simply do not respect; billions for medical research to save them from the consequences of their own suicidal self-indulgence," he wrote. "Truly these are lost souls, fighting a war against the Author of human nature, a war that no man can win."[137] During the 1992 presidential campaign, Buchanan referred to gay men as "sodomites" and called AIDS "nature's retribution" against homosexuals.[138]

Pat Robertson, in a *700 Club* interview with Frohnmayer, said he and other U.S. taxpayers were "fed up to here with using our money for homo-erotic art and anti-Christian diatribes by way-out fringe artists."[139] Helms, too, invoked an ostensibly uniform "American people," whom he said were "disgusted with the idea of giving the taxpayers' money to artists who promote homosexuality insidiously and deliberately." But Helms was also disgusted by homosexuality itself, and by Mapplethorpe's effort "to gain wider exposure of, and acceptance for," it.[140]

Impeaching the Sixties

AS THE REAGAN era yielded to the presidencies of George H. W. Bush and Bill Clinton, some sort of détente might have been expected. Bush played a culture warrior in the 1988 presidential campaign, which he won in part because his team was able to target his Democratic opponent, Massachusetts governor Michael Dukakis, as a sixties-style liberal who was soft on crime and hard on the military. But Bush, a moderate Republican and former U.N. ambassador, was a pragmatist at heart, a New England Episcopalian as allergic to cultural warfare as he was to speaking in tongues. In his acceptance speech at the 1988 Republican National Convention in New Orleans, Bush called for "a kinder, gentler nation."[141] His two nominees to the Supreme Court—a liberal, David Souter, and a conservative, Clarence Thomas—preserved the status quo on *Roe v. Wade*.

"New Democrat" Bill Clinton, who took the White House from Bush in 1992 with the mantra "It's the economy, stupid," also tried to turn down the temperature on hot-button social issues. Though he would be criticized as a tax-and-spend liberal, he, too, was a moderate who did more to complete the Reagan Revolution than overturn it, signing on to welfare reform and famously declaring in his 1996 State of the Union address that "the era of big government is over." Clinton supported *Roe v. Wade* but spoke often about his desire to make abortion "safe, legal, and rare." As homosexuality became a cultural battlefield, Clinton tilted right. In 1993, he codified a Don't Ask, Don't Tell policy that allowed gays and lesbians to serve in the military as long as they kept their homosexuality secret. In 1996, he signed the Defense of Marriage Act (DOMA), which defined marriage for federal purposes as a "union between one man and one woman." On church–state questions, Clinton refused the strict separation long preached by Democrats. The faith-based initiative often associated with George W. Bush was actually created in 1996 by Clinton, who also affirmed the rights of students to pray in public schools. "I have never believed the Constitution required our schools to be religion-free zones," he said, "or that our children must check their faiths at the schoolhouse door."[142]

Despite the moderating influences of these two presidents, the culture wars of the Reagan era persisted throughout the 1990s, not least because there were so many constituencies—think tanks, political action committees, talk show hosts, fund-raisers, legislators, and partisan newspapers and websites—that benefited from them. As it became clear that *Roe* was not in imminent danger of being overturned, Randall Terry and his Operation Rescue took the abortion fight to the streets, borrowing tactics from the civil rights movement in order to stop a "holocaust" at the hands of "baby killers." ("To vote for Bill Clinton," Terry told ministers in 1992, "is to sin against God.")[143] When this movement stalled, some turned to violence, murdering doctors, receptionists, and other abortion clinic employees in a spate of anti-killing killings between 1993 and 1998.

During the midterm elections of 1994, the realignment of the GOP begun by Goldwater, pursued by Nixon, and consolidated under Reagan, was finally complete. As Southern Democrats converted en masse to Republicanism, the GOP won control of both houses of Congress for the first time since 1954. Newt Gingrich's "Contract with America" steered clear of abortion, homosexuality, and school prayer, but culture warriors would not be sidelined for long. After Clinton vetoed legislation banning "partial-birth abortion" in 1996, the Watergate criminal turned evangelical activist Charles Colson compared the United States to Nazi Germany.[144] That same year, in a review of court cases on abortion, gay rights, and euthanasia, Richard John Neuhaus of the "theoconservative" magazine *First Things* did the same. Convinced that the judiciary had declared its independence from the American people and morality itself, he called for radical action—"from noncompliance to resistance to civil disobedience to morally justified revolution"—against "judicial tyranny."[145]

Culture warriors also used the 1998 sex scandal regarding Clinton's "not appropriate" relationship with intern Monica Lewinsky—*the* political event of the 1990s—to revisit the 1960s. Falwell railed against "the radical homosexuals, anti-family feminists, Godless atheists," and "the liberal media,"[146] but the Religious Right's central target was the draft dodger, adulterer, and marijuana inhaler Bill Clinton, who epitomized in its view the sexual immorality and moral relativism of the "bad sixties." In *The Death of Outrage* (1998), William Bennett denounced not only Clinton's "moral bankruptcy" but also the refusal of the nation to get as worked up about it as he and Falwell plainly were.[147]

In a case Harvard Law professor Alan Dershowitz denounced as "sexual McCarthyism," Clinton was impeached by the House only to be acquitted by the Senate.[148] Clinton's political survival prompted serious soul-searching among conservative Christians, who had worked (and prayed) so hard to oust "Slick Willie." The premise underlying the Moral Majority and the Christian Coalition had been that most Americans shared their values. Yet during the Lewinsky scandal Clinton's approval rose sharply—to 73 percent—and in the 1998 midterm election voters sent many Republican legislators packing.[149]

Looking back on the impeachment debacle after that punishing election, conservative strategist Paul Weyrich concluded that the liberals had won the contemporary culture wars. "I no longer believe that there is a moral majority. I do not believe that a majority of Americans actually shares our values," he wrote in 1999. "This is why, even when we win in politics, our victories fail to translate into the kind of policies we believe are important." His recommendation?

Evangelicals should "separate [themselves] from the institutions that have been captured by the ideology of Political Correctness."[150] That same year, in a book Randall Terry called "more dangerous than the child-pornography at Barnes and Noble,"[151] columnist Cal Thomas and pastor Ed Dobson (both evangelicals) argued that the Religious Right had failed because it had focused too narrowly on elections and legislation. You can't use government to force an immoral citizenry to become moral, they reasoned, before calling on the Religious Right to abandon the culture wars.[152] Weyrich was less apocalyptic. "We need," he concluded, "some sort of quarantine."[153]

The Islam Wars

THAT QUARANTINE WAS short-lived. During a Republican caucus debate in Iowa in December 1999, Texas governor George W. Bush was asked to name his favorite political philosopher. "Christ," he answered, "because he changed my heart."[154] When Bush won the presidency in 2000—in the closest presidential contest since the 1800 tie—white evangelicals were overjoyed to have one of their own in the Oval Office. When he won a second term, defeating Democrat John Kerry in 2004, pollsters and pundits credited "values voters" with turning the election his way and returning both houses of Congress to Republicans. Like his father, the second President Bush was a reluctant cultural warrior—a "compassionate conservative" who would rather break up a fight than instigate one. Nonetheless, he, too, was quickly drawn in.

Previous American presidents had invoked God, but in recognition of the population's religious diversity, they typically did so in vague generalities. Jimmy Carter tested this unwritten rule, but as a Southern Baptist believer in the separation of church and state, he always respected it. George W. Bush was different. In the first official act of his "faith-based presidency," he declared his inauguration day a National Day of Prayer and Thanksgiving. His cabinet meetings began with prayer.[155] And when journalist Bob Woodward asked him whether he consulted his father before invading Iraq in 2003, Bush said, "He is the wrong father to appeal to. . . . There is a higher father that I appeal to."[156] Bush's refusal to hide his light under a bushel exasperated "New Atheists," who attacked religion as a poison and a pox on American politics.

After Islamic extremists crashed hijacked jets into the World Trade Center, the Pentagon, and a Pennsylvania field early in his first term, Bush worked hard to live up to his pledge to serve as "a uniter, not a divider."[157] Putting on the hat of a cultural liberal (if only on this issue), he resisted the temptation to demonize Muslims the way prior presidents had demonized Catholics and Mormons. The nation is at war with terrorists, not with Muslims, he said repeatedly: "Islam is a religion of love, not hate."[158] Bush had no interest in returning to the frisson of prior religion wars, with Islam as the new religion you had to hate. He had even less interest in starting a twenty-first-century crusade with the world's 1.5 billion Muslims.

In a televised conversation with Pat Robertson, Falwell blamed 9/11 on those who had "mocked" God: "the pagans, and the abortionists, and the feminists, and the gays and lesbians who are actively trying to make that an alternative lifestyle."[159] But many conservative Christians blamed Islam. Shortly after 9/11, Rev. Franklin Graham, son of evangelist Billy Graham, blasted Islam on NBC Nightly News as "a very evil and wicked religion."[160] Pastor Jerry Vines, ex-president of the Southern Baptist Convention, called Muhammad a "demon-possessed pedophile."[161] In November 2001, Rep. Saxby Chambliss (R-GA), chairman of the House Subcommittee on Terrorism and Homeland Security, fantasized about empowering a Georgia sheriff to "arrest every Muslim that crosses the state line."[162] Provocateur Ann Coulter's plan was more ambitious: "We should invade their countries, kill their leaders and convert them to Christianity."[163] Others called for a ban on Muslim immigration, and for the expulsion of Muslims who were not U.S.

citizens. In a move straight out of earlier anti-Catholicism and anti-Mormonism, Pat Robertson claimed on his *700 Club* that Muslims did not enjoy First Amendment religious liberty protections because "Islam is not a religion. It is a worldwide political movement meant on domination."[164]

When Keith Ellison (D-MN), the first Muslim elected to the U.S. House of Representatives, announced in 2006 that he would use a Quran at his swearing-in ceremony, Rep. Virgil Goode (R-VA) blasted that choice as a threat to "the values and beliefs traditional to the United States of America."[165] FOX News personality Sean Hannity compared Ellison's plan to using the "Nazi Bible": Hitler's *Mein Kampf*.[166] Ellison deftly responded to the controversy by announcing that he would be sworn in on Jefferson's own "Alcoran of Mohammed," acquired by Congress in 1815. In this way, he explicitly linked today's Islam wars to earlier clashes over Jefferson's heresies.

During Reagan's two presidential terms, conservatives had cut taxes, raised military spending, slashed regulations, and brought the Cold War to a close, but Reagan frustrated conservative Christians by doing little more than empathizing with their plight. He talked a good game, affirming in his first inaugural address that "we are a nation under God" and denouncing the Soviet Union as an "evil empire" in a 1983 speech to the National Association of Evangelicals. He complained about the rise of abortion and pornography and the decline of the traditional family and Christian morality. He also called for constitutional amendments to restore prayer to the public schools and to prohibit abortion.[167] But he never made these issues a priority. And while he appointed Antonin Scalia, a pro-life Catholic, to the Supreme Court, he also appointed two swing voters, Sandra Day O'Connor and Anthony Kennedy, who continued to uphold abortion rights. "I knew conservatives would get the short end of the stick," Richard Viguerie said. "I just didn't know the stick would be this short."[168]

This may have been a case of taking the man out of Hollywood without taking the Hollywood out of the man. Perhaps Reagan never intended to do much about cultural issues. Perhaps his strategy was always to string white evangelicals along, "taking advantage of voters' anxiety about moral decline for partisan political advantage."[169] Then again, maybe there was nothing to be done. Perhaps the cultural tide was flowing so hard to the left that there was no rowing against it. In any event, many on the Religious Right felt disappointed, even betrayed. Some came to see themselves as victims of not only secular humanists but also Reagan himself.

In the end, George W. Bush disappointed conservative Christians even more than Reagan had, since he was so plainly one of their own. Bush, too, proved unable to hold back the liberal tide that continued to wash over American culture. In 2008, as Bush was finishing out his second term, Richard Cizik of the National Association of Evangelicals lamented the "unholy alliance" he had helped to cement between conservative Christians and the GOP. "Evangelicals have given everything and gotten nothing in return," he said.[170] Even in an era defined by Republican dominance in tax-and-spend policy—an era of plummeting marginal tax rates and rising defense budgets—liberals were winning the culture wars.

The Obama Wars

LIKE THE THREE presidents before him, Barack Obama came into office with little interest in serving as commander in chief in a culture war. He had made a name for himself at the 2004 Democratic National Convention in Boston, where he pledged his allegiance not to "red states" or "blue states" but to the "United States."[171] As America's first black president, he was determined to smooth over the racial divide rather than further erode it. Convinced it made no sense to be the standard-bearer of an anti-God party in a country with more Christians than any other in human history, he invited megachurch pastor Rick Warren to pray at his inauguration, spoke regularly of his faith in Jesus as "my Lord and Savior," sang "Amazing Grace" during a eulogy, and continued to fund faith-based organizations. To the exasperation of progressives, he tacked hard to the center on taxing and spending, and he refused to pick a fight over gun control, even after mass shootings at Fort Hood, Aurora, and Newtown. When it came to vicious personal attacks (rocker Ted Nugent called him a "subhuman mongrel" and Rev. Steven Anderson prayed for his death[172]), Obama turned the other cheek so fast and so often that he sometimes seemed to be spinning on his own axis.

When it comes to the culture wars, however, it only takes one to tango. And here again the conservatives got things going. During the 2008 presidential campaign, Alaska governor and GOP vice-presidential candidate Sarah Palin referred to the Illinois senator running for the Democratic presidential nomination as Barack *Hussein* Obama and many on the right suggested that Obama was a secret Muslim. During his presidency, conservatives attacked Obama from day one, most angrily via the Tea Party, which emerged in 2009 as a visceral substitute for an eviscerated Religious Right. Viewed initially as a purely political group intent on cutting taxes and shrinking government, the Tea Party quickly proved to be a culture wars organization even less amenable to compromise than the Moral Majority or the Christian Coalition.[173]

In fact, Obama ("Enemy Number One" according to one North Carolina congressman[174]) endured during his two terms a barrage of personal attacks unrivaled even by Jefferson. Refusing to accept the legitimacy of America's forty-fourth president, "birthers" questioned whether Obama really was born in the United States (a presidential requirement) and demanded to see his birth certificate. At a rally of veterans on the National Mall, Larry Klayman of the right-wing Freedom Watch blasted him as "a president who bows down to Allah"—"not a president of 'we the people'" but "a president of his people."[175] According to conservative talk show host Glenn Beck, Obama was "a racist" with "a deep-seated hatred for white people."[176] No wonder 71 percent of Tea Party conservatives came to believe that Obama would "ruin the country" and 30 percent of Republicans thought he was a Muslim.[177]

Perhaps the angry white men in the GOP base could not stomach a black man in the White House. Perhaps conservatives were sick and tired of electing Republicans who did nothing to roll back deficit spending and liberal creep. Perhaps the institutional power of culture wars television networks, culture wars PACs, culture wars websites, and culture war billionaires was too much to resist. The nation grew increasingly polarized during Obama's two terms, as moderates became as rare as a snowstorm on Capitol Hill and phrases such as "liberal Democrat" and "conservative Republican" became redundant. While Rep. Maxine Waters (D-CA) was calling Speaker of the House John Boehner (R-OH) a "demon" and Rep. Randy Weber (R-TX) was calling Obama a "Socialist dictator," Rep. Allen West (R-FL) cut to the chase, ordering the president to "get the hell out of the United States of America."[178]

Such spittle was not confined to cable news channels or Capitol Hill, however. As Americans were increasingly living in areas with like-minded voters and associating on social media with like-minded "friends," political antipathy increased. Study after study demonstrated that political partisanship was becoming the new normal with nearly two-thirds of Americans describing themselves as "strong" partisans of either Republicans or Democrats.[179]

True to form, these Obama wars were asymmetrical. Most of the thunder came from the Right—from talk show hosts and elected officials beholden to the Tea Party who accused the president of launching a "war on religion" and even a "war on whites."[180] The titles of books by bestselling author Ann Coulter—*Treason: Liberal Treachery from the Cold War to the War on Terrorism; Godless: The Church of Liberalism; Demonic: How the Liberal Mob Is Endangering*

America—show not only how "liberal" had become a fighting word but also how conservatives felt mugged by the traitors and demons in their midst.

Liberals did fight back, however, in a counterattack that included Keith Olbermann, the decade's iconic angry liberal. From his perch at MSNBC, Olbermann blasted Bush for "urinating on the Constitution" and the Tea Party for working to "march this nation as far backward as they can get, backward to Jim Crow, or backward to the breadlines of the '30s, or backward to hanging union organizers, or backward to the Trusts and the Robber Barons."[181] In one of his most notorious rants, Olbermann called Republican Scott Brown (who was running for Ted Kennedy's Massachusetts Senate seat in 2010) "an irresponsible, homophobic, racist, reactionary, ex-nude model, teabagging supporter of violence against women." In the Obama years, you weren't anybody until somebody labeled you a "fascist," a "socialist," or a "Nazi."[182]

Gay Marriage

THERE WERE ADDITIONAL cultural clashes in the early twenty-first century over public displays of the Ten Commandments, creationism in public schools, handguns, Mel Gibson's blockbuster movie *The Passion of the Christ*, immigration, stem-cell research, partial-birth abortions, hip-hop, the War on Christmas, and efforts to remove Terri Schiavo (a comatose woman) from a feeding tube. All were designed, according to Thomas Frank's *What's the Matter with Kansas?* (2004), not to reverse the course of American culture but to gin up the GOP's white evangelical base and return pro-business Republicans to Congress, where they could continue to pass pro-business bills hostile to the economic interests of heartland voters. "The trick never ages; the illusion never wears off," Frank writes. "*Vote* to stop abortion; *receive* a rollback in capital gains taxes. . . . *Vote* to strike a blow against elitism; *receive* a social order in which wealth is more concentrated than ever before in our life-times."[183] It is true that the contemporary culture wars have often been waged by politicians who have no intention of overturning *Roe v. Wade*. But Americans are not just economic animals. Here beliefs matter. Here moral, religious, and cultural concerns run deep. So when the culture wars during the Bush and Obama presidencies fix-ated on homosexuality—*the* cultural issue of the 2000s—they did so not only because Republican politicians stood to gain from com-plaining about "the gay lifestyle" but also because many heartland voters believed that homosexuality was contrary to natural law and divine commandments.

Same-sex marriage had been on the table since 1989, when, in the midst of the art wars, Andrew Sullivan made "the case for gay marriage" in a *New Republic* cover story.[184] But that case was not really heard until the turn of the millennium. The Right won early ballot initiatives defining marriage as the union of one man and one woman, and in 2000 the Supreme Court ruled that the Boy Scouts had a "constitutional right of expressive association" to bar gay troop leaders.[185] That same year, however, Vermont became the first state to recognize same-sex civil unions. In 2003, the House and Senate took up the Federal Marriage Amendment, a failed effort to declare same-sex marriage unconstitutional, which James Dobson, in a clas-sic example of culture war overreach, described as "our D-Day, our Gettysburg, our Stalingrad."[186] In June 2003, the Supreme Court struck down a Texas antisodomy law and (much to Justice Scalia's annoyance) enshrined in the process a right to sexual privacy. Then came a November 2003 decision by the Massachusetts Supreme Judicial Court—"the culture war equivalent of the sinking of the Lusitania"[187]—which, in a legal boon to the Left and a fund-raising bonanza for the Right, declared same-sex marriage legal in the commonwealth.

In 2010, a federal judge ruled that Proposition 8—a Mormon-backed voter initiative in California that defined marriage as the union of a man and a woman—was unconstitutional. In 2012, Obama became the first U.S. chief executive to endorse same-sex marriage. In 2013, the Supreme Court struck down the Defense of Marriage Act as a violation of the due process clause of the Fifth Amendment. After the Supreme Court dealt another blow to opponents of same-sex marriage in 2014, blogger and election prognosticator Nate Silver joked that "gay marriage is on pace to be legal in 73 states by next Tuesday."[188] The following year, in *Obergefell v. Hodges*, the Supreme Court made marriage equality the law of the land. "The right to marry is a fundamental right inherent in the liberty of the person," wrote Associate Justice Anthony Kennedy for the majority, "and under the Due Process and Equal Protection Clauses of the Fourteenth Amendment couples of the same-sex may not be deprived of that right and that liberty."[189] On a matter as fundamental as matrimony, this was an extraordinarily quick turnabout. And another victory for the cultural Left.

CONCLUSION

Will the Culture Wars Ever End?

CONSERVATIVES DID NOT LOSE every battle in the contemporary culture wars. They defeated the Equal Rights Amendment in 1982. They slashed the budget of the National Endowment for the Arts in 1994. They put an unprecedented number of drug offenders behind bars, turning the United States into an incarceration nation with the highest ratio of prisoners to citizens anywhere in the world. They expanded the role of religion in public life, turning explicit God talk into the new normal inside both major political parties. Finally, cultural conservatives turned "liberal" into a dirty word, "recast[ing] liberalism for large numbers of Americans as a moral threat rather than as a lift up."[1]

Nonetheless, conservatives lost the contemporary culture wars and they lost them badly. As the counterculture mainstreamed, American society continued to drift left. Conservatives lost on tax exemptions for segregation academies. They lost *Bob Jones University v. United States*. They failed to pass constitutional amendments

on either school prayer or abortion. They failed to eliminate the
NEA. They lost on Clinton's impeachment. Today the Vietnam
Veterans Memorial, which conservatives almost uniformly opposed
as un-American, is among the most popular tourist destinations in
the capital. And the ranks of the religiously unaffiliated are rising
dramatically—from 16 percent in 2007 to 23 percent in 2015.[2]

Republicans did well at the ballot box in the 1980s, 1990s, and
2000s, and they trounced the Democrats in the 2014 midterm
elections. Today, conservatives control many evangelical churches,
think tanks, PACs, and talk radio stations. They have power in
Washington, DC, and preach their gospel of loss and revival on their
own culture wars television stations. But it is not the case, as sociologist Todd Gitlin once claimed, that liberals "have lost ground."[3]
Nowadays it is Republicans, not Democrats, who are increasingly
out of touch with ordinary voters on immigration, race, drugs, guns,
women, homosexuality, and the environment. FOX News is rapidly
being reduced to a rickety shrine to white male identity politics—a
wooden bench in front of the town hall where crotchety white men
gather to wax nostalgic about the good old days and complain about
their increasing irrelevance at work, at home, and in church.

Polling data also shows strong leftward shifts on almost every
"family values" issue: 62 percent of Americans now say the ideal
marriage is one in which both spouses work and share housekeep-
ing and child-rearing duties; only 30 percent favor a home with
a male breadwinner and a female homemaker; and 63 percent of
white Catholics say *Roe v. Wade* should not be overturned. These
trends are particularly strong among millennials. In this cohort,
which reached young adulthood in 2000, 68 percent favor same-sex
marriage and 56 percent say abortion should be legal in all or most
cases.[4]

Although pro-lifers have chipped away at *Roe v. Wade*, restrict-
ing the use of government funds for abortions and adding a series of
hoops through which women must jump before ending a pregnancy,

abortion remains legal in every state, and only one in five Americans believe it should be "always illegal."[5] Most Americans now favor marijuana legalization, and as of 2015, recreational marijuana use was legal in four states plus the District of Columbia, with medical use allowed in nineteen more. Four states now allow physician-assisted suicide. Women serve in the army and are training for combat roles. Day care centers are everywhere, and American families are evolving in precisely the direction the Moral Majority had feared, with women working more outside the home and men doing more housework and child care.[6]

The gay rights culture war is not quite over, but it is now plain how it is going to turn out. Those who oppose gay marriage used to be widely lauded as defenders of "traditional values." Today they are widely criticized as bigots. In fact, in a 2015 poll, Americans said they would be more comfortable with a gay president than with an evangelical one.[7]

Thanks to *Obergefell v. Hodges*, gays and lesbians can now marry in all U.S. states. Whereas Pope Benedict denounced homosexuality as an "intrinsic moral evil," his successor, Pope Francis, downplayed homosexuality, asking, "Who am I to judge?"[8] The Southern Baptist Convention did a similar turnabout. During his years at the helm of the SBC's Ethics and Religious Liberty Commission, Richard Land was one of the nation's most outspoken opponents of the "radical homosexual agenda"; in 2013, his successor, Russell Moore, urged Southern Baptists to "love your gay and lesbian neighbors."[9] The demise of Exodus International, an evangelical organization devoted to using "gay lifestyle" therapy to convert homosexuals to heterosexuality, provides a striking example of this cultural rout. As this group closed in August 2013, president Alan Chambers admitted the futility of its therapeutic approach. "I am sorry for the pain and hurt that many of you have experienced," he said to clients and their families. "I am sorry we promoted sexual orientation change."[10]

In almost every arena where the contemporary culture wars have been fought—education, law, media, entertainment, family, and the arts—liberals now control the agenda. In secondary and higher education, the trends decried by 1980s conservatives remain firmly in place. Or, as sociologist Nathan Glazer put it, "We are all multiculturalists now."[11] Most high school students remain religiously and culturally illiterate, and today's college students look very much like the young people Allan Bloom described roughly three decades ago in *The Closing of the American Mind*. Pop culture, especially, has gone over to the liberal side. Movies today make the sort of entertainment decried by the Moral Majority look like *It's a Wonderful Life*. *Modern Family*, a sitcom featuring a gay couple and celebrating the diversity of American families, won five straight Emmy awards for best comedy series. The HBO hit *Girls* is clothing optional. And transgender stars now grace the cover of *Entertainment Weekly*. Reagan may have been a tax revolutionary, but when it comes to cultural politics the Reagan Revolution is a misnomer. "The Left . . . was never in danger of losing the so-called culture wars," writes historian James Livingston. "At the end of the twentieth century . . . the United States was much less conservative than it had been in 1975."[12] And American culture is much less conservative now than it was in 1999.[13]

But liberals are not just defeating conservatives in the contemporary culture wars. All the culture wars explored in this book went the liberals' way. From disputes over Jefferson's heresies to gay marriage, liberals have triumphed. The Federalists lost. The anti-Catholics lost. The anti-Mormons lost. So did the prohibitionists.

With these liberal victories has come an increasingly expansive understanding of religious liberty. It is now difficult to imagine Americans killing one another over which Bible will be read in the public schools or refusing to allow Mormons to serve in the Senate. But we did that. Some of us even claimed that Catholicism and Mormonism were not really religions, so wed were most Americans to a Protestant worldview. Many citizens from the Jefferson wars forward saw religious liberty less as a right and more as a threat—not only to Protestant dominance but also to social order and familial harmony. This history only makes sense if we grant that neither "religion" nor "religious liberty" meant back then what these terms mean today.

In the midst of the "Ground Zero Mosque" controversy, New York City mayor Michael Bloomberg observed that religious freedom has been "hard-won." In the 1650s in New York City (then called New Amsterdam), Bloomberg said, Dutch governor Peter Stuyvesant prohibited Quakers from meeting and denied a petition from Jews to build a synagogue. Not until the 1780s were Catholics able to establish their first parish in New York City. "This nation was founded on the principle that the government must never choose between religions, or favor one over another," Bloomberg said.[14] But for much of American history, the government did just that. Protestantism served as an unofficial religious establishment. Catholics and Mormons were widely seen as deviations from that norm. Religious liberty was afforded infrequently and inconsistently to religious minorities.

This legacy is still with us. Many on the left now see religious liberty not as a protection for religious minorities but as a license for evangelicals and fundamentalists to discriminate against the LGBT community. On the far right, some claim that Islam is not a religion but a cult or a political ideology and is therefore not entitled to First Amendment protections. Still, it is undeniable that Americans' understanding of religious liberty has evolved over time, largely as a result of the culture wars. That evolution has been toward more religious freedom and a more expansive understanding of religion itself. To be sure, Supreme Court justices still read "religion" largely through Christian lenses. And some Americans continue to ape nativists of the past by trying to banish Muslims from the American family. But if history is any guide, they are holding a losing hand.

The history of cultural warfare in the United States is not a

pretty sight. In addition to hateful language and poisonous partisanship, it includes arson, calls for genocide, and the murder of abortion
providers, Catholics, and the founder of America's most successful
new religious movement. But to look at the culture wars over the
long term is to see that Americans, however haltingly, have agreed
to define their nation in increasingly inclusive terms. It is no longer
liberal to view Catholics and Mormons as fellow citizens. That sort
of tolerance is now an *American* value. Soon it will be simply American to welcome gays and lesbians, too.

Why Culture Wars End

AS THESE EXAMPLES suggest, individual culture wars *do* end, for
a variety of interconnected reasons. Sometimes the Right surren-
ders. Sometimes the combatants agree to a truce. Sometimes a new
group to hate emerges and long-boiling antagonisms evaporate into
the ether. Culture wars also end because the political parties that
started and sustained them go out of power. The religious battles
that swirled around the election of 1800 ended in part because the
party that benefited from them—the Federalists—disappeared.
Though Federalists controlled the federal government during the
Washington and Adams administrations, they faded quickly after
the election of 1800, and by the 1820s, they had largely vanished.
The Know-Nothings met this same fate in the 1850s. The Republican Party could be next if it continues to ask "What Would Old
White Men Do?"

Culture wars also end because "outsiders" accommodate themselves to the demands of "insiders." Catholics gained acceptance by
embracing church–state separation and by pledging, as Kennedy did
during his 1960 presidential campaign, to keep their Catholic faith
private. Mormons also made striking concessions. In order to win
statehood for Utah, they gave up on both polygamy and theocracy,
two practices that for decades had all but defined them as Saints.

Demographic shifts also help to explain this waning hostility toward "outsiders." The explosive growth of the Catholic population, which made anti-Catholicism seem imperative to many Protestants as late as Al Smith's 1928 defeat, made anti-Catholicism seem retrograde during the Kennedy–Nixon election. Yes, it was important to include Catholics under the Judeo-Christian sacred canopy as Americans fought the Cold War against "godless communism," but it was also difficult to hate Catholics once "they" had become "us"—our neighbors, our bosses, our employees, our spouses, and our in-laws. A similar dynamic has been at play in recent years with gays and lesbians and the religiously unaffiliated, whose acceptance rose as more and more came out of the closet.

Shifts in public attitudes also helped to end the culture wars of the Roaring Twenties, but here the obvious failure of a particular public policy was key. Conservatives got their way with the ratification of the Eighteenth Amendment, but the unintended consequences that flowed from prohibition (bootlegging, organized crime, disrespect for the rule of law) led surprisingly quickly to its repeal.

In their efforts to purify their symbolic world of every jot of Old World popery and every tittle of New World sin, Puritans transformed America into a land of moralists ever on the lookout for demons in their ranks. By imagining their homeland as a New Zion, they established a precedent for morphing American political projects into religious crusades. So there is a long history here of using government power to impose Protestant values on non-Protestant citizens. But as any American history textbook will tell you, the United States is also the home of the Statue of Liberty, a country forever struggling to live up to its billing as a nation of immigrants (and religions) "yearning to breathe free." In America's many culture wars, this liberty proposition has had the upper hand. In the election of 1800, the Jeffersonians' call for liberty drowned out the Federalists' call for order. In the anti-Catholic and anti-Mormon wars, religious liberty defeated calls for a monoreligious America. The first effort to amend the Constitution in order to restrict liberty—the Eighteenth Amendment—was quickly repealed. And in recent years the freedom of women to have abortions and of gays and lesbians to choose their marriage partners has been vindicated.

Why Culture Wars Persist

IN TELLING THIS story of the lost causes of conservatism, it is important to explain not only why a particular culture war ends but also why culture wars in the plural persist.

Since the 1990s, the culture wars have repeatedly been left for dead. Just months after Pat Buchanan declared a "cultural war" at the 1992 Republican National Convention, neoconservative Irving Kristol remarked, "I regret to inform Pat Buchanan that those wars are over and the left has won."[15] In 1997, reporter Janny Scott observed that the term "culture wars" had become as anachronistic as a "leisure suit." "Not long ago, one could hardly get through a week without stumbling across somebody or other's culture war—outraged fundamentalists or neoconservatives or righteous multiculturalists raving about Hollywood or political correctness or Robert Mapplethorpe or Allan Bloom," she wrote. But now the culture warriors had arrived "at Appomattox."[16] In 2001, in an essay called "Life After Wartime," Andrew Sullivan also smelled surrender:

> It wasn't that long ago that we were all being rushed to the barricades to defend or attack any number of . . . hot-button social topics—abortion rights, gay visibility, pop-culture trash, affirmative action, the war on drugs—and not only as separate political issues but as a contest for the very soul of the country. Almost overnight, though, the energy seems to have seeped out of these conflicts. . . . [T]he crackle of cultural gunfire is now increasingly distant.[17]

More recently, intellectual historian Andrew Hartman argued in 2015 that the culture wars *"are* history. The logic of the culture wars has been exhausted. The metaphor has run its course."[18]

Some evangelicals, angry over how little the Republicans they helped to elect have been able (or willing) to deliver, have retreated from cultural politics. Others, convinced that the fusion of evangelical piety and conservative politics is hurting the cause of Christ, have done the same. But evangelicals who have promised to do cultural war no more remain a minority. Every day new conservative Christians take to the Capitol or to the web to fight the good fight for God and the Good. There they meet up with Tea Party members whose cultural concerns run deep and whose zeal matches that of the most ardent fundamentalists. As a result, there has been no truce in the contemporary culture wars, and no surrender.

In fact, recent years have witnessed an *expansion* of the culture wars, beyond moral and religious questions into bread-and-butter political matters, such as taxing and spending. The modus operandi of the culture wars—the accusations of treason, the rhetoric of good and evil, the character assassinations, and the equation of compromise with surrender—have bled over into politics writ large, infusing government shutdowns and debt-ceiling battles not only with poisonous partisanship but also with the metaphors and mind-set of war. The result is a Culture War of Everything that is rapidly transforming previously bipartisan matters (foreign policy toward Israel, for example) into life-or-death struggles between Democrats and the GOP. Increasingly, we do politics like we have done cultural warfare. We are all culture warriors now.

This persistence and expansion of the culture wars is in some respects evidence of a thriving democracy and a vibrant public square. In a diverse country that welcomes debate, disagreements are inevitable. And in a place where so many different gods mean so much to so many, those differences are going to heat up.

But culture wars are also perennial because of compromises made at the outset of the American experiment, not least the founders' decision to bequeath to their descendants a republic that was "half slave and half free." Say what you want about the Obama presidency and the pitched battles it saw over such matters as whether the highest marginal tax rate should be 35 or 39.6 percent (or whether the debt ceiling should be raised by 2 percent), it simply isn't credible to claim that the polarization that gripped the country in the Obama years had nothing to do with race. Tea Party events are whiter than Utah in winter, and Obama won 95 percent of the African American vote in 2008 and 93 percent in 2012.[19] Despite the pivots of the Moral Majority from race to family and religion, culture wars rhetoric continues to be racially coded and the borders of our culture zones still roughly follow those of the Union and the Confederacy. "Make no mistake," *The Atlantic* columnist Ta-Nehisi Coates wrote in his widely read essay "Fear of a Black President," "today's Republican radicalism, with all of its attendant terrifying brinksmanship, is the grandchild of the white South's devastating defeats in the struggle over racial exclusion."[20]

Regarding the vexed relationship between church and state, the founders rejected the European model of church–state marriage but never finalized a divorce, so this separation remains ambiguous. Is the United States a Christian country? A secular one? It has always been both. The founders signed on to a godless Constitution and did not require presidents to pass any religious test. But the country has never warmed to the French model of a naked public square stripped of religious influence. In fact, whatever wall of separation Americans built in the early republic was short and weak. Many presidents declared national days of fasting and prayer. Congress funded military chaplains and opened its sessions with supplications to the Almighty. This awkward compromise made the culture wars all but inevitable. It also gave Supreme Court justices a lot to try to sort out. Nowadays the nation's highest court seems to be called upon every year to alchemize the murky into the clear—to determine just how many reindeers are required in a municipal Nativity display or what sorts of town-meeting prayers are sufficiently generic to pass constitutional muster.

Culture wars also persist because of the long-standing affinity between white evangelicalism and free-market capitalism. The Election Day victories that culture wars help to produce for Republicans lead to laws that benefit businesses by cutting regulations and securing corporate subsidies. But free-market capitalism does nothing to conserve traditional culture. In fact, it disrupts it. Capitalism's bottom line is the bottom line, so retailers feel no compunction about competing with churches for customers on Sunday mornings or about opening big-box stores that will turn beloved Main Streets into ghost towns. As the economy grows, these losses build, and with them come new anxieties and new culture clashes.[21]

Finally and most basically, culture wars persist because conservatism persists, and because American conservatives from the French Revolution forward have seen cultural warfare as a way to win political power by promising to restore forms of life threatened with extinction. Political scientist Corey Robin is right to see modern conservatism as an effort to maintain hierarchies. Conservatives fight to protect the privileges of superiors—what Edmund Burke called the "chain of subordination" of soldiers to their officers, workers to their employers, tenants to their landlords, and children to their parents.[22] But these political hierarchies are not the only concerns of conservatives, who will also go to the mat to defend cultural, moral, and theological hierarchies. And conservatives fight most fiercely to defend hierarchies that are falling away.

Lost Causes

IN AMERICA'S MANY culture wars, traditionalists have protested the loss of Protestant consensus, the loss of an agricultural economy, the loss of American power overseas, the loss of theological and

moral certainty, the loss of a unified nation, the loss of the hometown, the loss of the traditional family, the loss of a homogeneous
society, and the loss of a simpler way of life threatened by the
complexities of immigration, urbanization, and globalization. So
cultural politics are always a politics of nostalgia, driven by those
who are determined to return to what they remember (rightly or
wrongly) as a better place, where straight, white, Protestant men
ruled the roost and no one dared cluck at their authority.

This is why culture wars are often over before they have begun—
because the fights culture warriors pick are almost always "lost
causes" that are already moving into the liberal column. In fact, to
borrow a term from the financial markets, you can use the culture
wars as "leading indicators." Just as the Dow Jones Transporta-
tion Average is said to forecast the upcoming state of the broader
economy, increasing anger and anxiety about a cultural issue almost
always foretell an impending liberal victory. In this respect, culture
wars are, to borrow a term now from George W. Bush speechwriter
Michael Gerson, a "revolt from reality"—a cry against what is
coming around the next corner. And reality rarely bends to accommodate. This fact more than anything explains why any particular
cultural clash comes to an end.

Today, the fact that the Left is winning the contemporary culture
wars is widely acknowledged by the Right, whose conservative laments over losing the culture wars are commonplace. In an era when
even the pope is saying that too much has been made in recent years
of abortion, contraception, and homosexuality, much of the current
conversation seems to turn on what conservative columnist Ross
Douthat called "the terms of our surrender." "We are not really having
an argument about same-sex marriage anymore," he wrote in 2014.
"Instead, all that's left is the timing of the final victory—and for the
defeated to find out what settlement the victors will impose."[23]

Such concessions do nothing to extinguish the culture wars,
however. In fact, they rekindle them, since conjuring up losses in

cultural politics is a time-honored strategy for securing Election Day victories. The strategy is to speak of losing just enough to keep the base perpetually girded for battle, but not so much to demoralize them. In this way, the culture wars are perpetually rising from the dead. Rather than being killed by any given defeat, conservative culture warriors seem to be revitalized by it. A loss on "man-man marriage," as comedian Stephen Colbert calls it, only underscores the conviction that the nation is going to hell, and stiffens the resolve to fight a new enemy in the name of a new cause.[24] The "religion of the lost cause" is the faith of Southerners who lost the War of Northern Aggression, but Federalists who lost the election of 1800 waxed nostalgic about their own "lost causes." So did anti-Catholics, anti-Mormons, and drys, who lost their crusades for a more homogeneous nation, and members of the Moral Majority who are a majority no more (and, in fact, never were).

Things Out of Place

IN "THE PARANOID Style in American Politics," published in *Harper's* in 1964 as the Cold War was crackling hot and Barry Goldwater was realigning the spine of modern conservatism, historian Richard Hofstadter detected in U.S. history a recurring "sense of heated exaggeration, suspiciousness, and conspiratorial fantasy." Those who are caught up in this "paranoid style," as he put it, see conspiracies at every turn and the apocalypse at the end of every road:

> [The paranoid] does not see social conflict as something to be mediated and compromised, in the manner of the working politician. Since what is at stake is always a conflict between absolute good and absolute evil, what is necessary is not compromise but the will to fight things out to a finish. Since the enemy is thought of as being totally evil and totally unappeas-

able, he must be totally eliminated—if not from the world, at least from the theatre of operations to which the paranoid directs his attention. This demand for total triumph leads to the formulation of hopelessly unrealistic goals, and since these goals are not even remotely attainable, failure constantly heightens the paranoid's sense of frustration.[25]

Hofstadter, "the iconic public intellectual of liberal condescension" according to conservative columnist George Will,[26] has been criticized for finding this irrationality largely on the right—in groups such as the McCarthyites and the John Birch Society—and for reducing American cultural politics to a psychological disorder. (As church historian Philip Jenkins drolly put it: "we are liberal; you are mentally ill."[27]) But Hofstadter was right to home in on psychology as a culture wars catalyst and on the conservative propensity for setting unattainable goals. The psychological style of culture warriors is not paranoia, however. It is anxiety—anxiety about loss, about the passing away of a beloved "way of life." But it is also anxiety about things out of place: Catholics in public schools, women in the workplace, foreigners in communities, gays and lesbians on the street, and a black man in the White House.

In her anthropological classic *Purity and Danger* (1966), Mary Douglas presented an intriguing reading of kosher food prohibitions in the biblical book of Leviticus. Rejecting the popular view that kosher eating began as a form of primitive hygiene—no pork, no trichinosis—Douglas offered a symbolic interpretation. What drove these food restrictions were notions of purity and pollution, and what made things impure and polluted in the symbolic world of the ancient Israelites was their ambiguity—their stubborn refusal to fit existing systems of classification. Animals of the sea are supposed to have fins and scales and swim from place to place. But what about a lobster? What sort of thing is that? It doesn't really swim. It walks on the ocean floor as if it were on land. Obviously, it is confused. Or we are confused about what it is. Either way, it is a disconcerting mongrel, so if we want to stay pure we must avoid it.

This anxiety over ambiguous things—with things out of place—is hyperabundant in American society, which has always been informed by Hebraic as well as Christian values and continues to produce communities eager to return to the purity of original things—to the arrival of the pilgrims or to the spilling of tea in Boston Harbor or to the writing of the Constitution or even to Eden itself, when things were (supposedly) cleaner and less complex, to a time before The Fall.

It makes some sense to classify Senator Helms as a denizen of Hofstadter's "paranoid style." It makes more sense to understand Helms's denunciation of Mapplethorpe's homoerotic photographs in moral and theological terms: Helms is outraged because male homosexuality is condemned in the Bible as an abomination against God and nature. But it is also possible to understand Helms as a man anxious about ambiguity. From this perspective, a man who has sex with another man is akin to a lobster, a disconcerting hybrid at odds with a classificatory scheme in which real men sleep only with their wives and no one even ponders the possibility (until rudely confronted by a disturbing Mapplethorpe photograph) of gay sex.

To attend to Falwell's pro-life rhetoric is to tune in to the thinking of a man deeply troubled by abortion, yes, but also by the ambiguities the 1960s hath wrought. How else to explain his repeated denunciations of long hair on men (banned at Liberty University)? Didn't Jesus have long hair? And Samson? By what logic, then, is long hair to be construed as an offense against holiness? Yet it is clearly an offense against clarity, at least in a system of classification in which short hair is for men and long hair is for women. In such a system, a man with long hair is also a lobster (or, in Falwell's terms, a disturbing portent of a "unisexual society"[28]).

This symbolic perspective highlights the ways in which America's culture wars are truly *cultural* wars—struggles over systems of classification that pit people who value purity against those who glory in impurity; struggles between people who revel in ambiguity, hybridity, and subjectivity (deconstructionists, for example) and those who insist (like Helms) that any book and any photograph must have one plain and simple meaning. It is possible to read the story of prohibition and repeal through moral lenses—as a struggle between the virtue of sobriety and the vice of drunkenness. But the culture wars of the 1920s and 1930s were not just about beer and cocktails, or even temperance and prohibition. They were about speakeasies, where blacks and whites drank, danced, and sweated together and activated, in the process, anxieties about impurity. They were about the "new woman" who cut her hair, smoked cigarettes, and otherwise confused the prevailing category of "woman," much as males who grew their hair long confused for Falwell the category of "man." By practicing polygamy, Mormons confused the categories of "family" just as surely as Catholics confused the category of "Christian." What sort of odd believer was a Catholic or a Mormon anyway? What to make of a "Christian" who reads the wrong Bible (or "another testament" altogether)? Or of an American who pledges her allegiance to a monarch in Utah or Vatican City? Or, for that matter, of a presidential candidate whose religion cannot be clearly understood? What manner of man was Jefferson anyway? A Deist? An infidel? A Muslim?

Interpreters of Serrano's *Piss Christ* clashed over what this photograph meant and whether Serrano designed it to offend Christians. But consider the photograph itself. It literally mixes two categories—the profane ("Piss") and the sacred ("Christ")—which are *supposed* to remain separate. The conservative response is to see this mixing, like the unkosher comingling of meat and milk at a meal, as "unclean." But a pluralistic response glories in mixing these categories. It loves the lobster for its transgressions, for defying what a fish should do, for reminding us that there are always things out of place and that sometimes those things are ourselves.

This angle of approach illustrates how culture wars do cultural work—by surfacing cultural disagreements. But culture wars do more than that. Oddly, ironically, our cultural disagreements typically produce cultural agreements. Even as the culture wars cycle continues, particular conflicts produce consensus. Yes, these conflicts polarize us. But they eventually lead us, kicking and screaming in many cases, to welcome Catholics and Mormons into the American family, and to see families with gays and lesbians as American, too. In other words, culture wars *do* typically end with victories for liberals, but over time conservatives also accept the more inclusive vision of America those victories have secured. In this way, liberal convictions become national norms.

Consider the ongoing battle over immigration. Throughout U.S. history, the federal government has included some newcomers and excluded others. Criminals, stowaways, prostitutes, polygamists, and alcoholics have all been prohibited entry at one time or another. Asian immigration was curbed in the nineteenth century and opened wide in 1965. Today's immigration debate focuses on Hispanics. Obviously, it is in the long-term interests of the Republican Party to welcome this cohort. With a minority-majority nation looming, the GOP needs to broaden its base beyond aging white people. Hispanics, who typically affirm both "family values" and conservative Christianity, are their natural allies. But almost all Republican politicians continue to oppose as "amnesty" any path to citizenship for undocumented immigrants. GOP leaders were embarrassed by businessman Donald Trump, who during his run for the 2016 Republican presidential nomination said of Mexican immigrants, "They're bringing drugs, they're bringing crime, they're rapists."[29] But part of that embarrassment sprang from the fact that his policies did not differ much from those of other Republican candidates (or, for that matter, from Republican Mitt Romney, who earned only 27 percent of the Hispanic vote in 2012 after suggesting that illegal immigrants should follow a policy of "self-deportation"[30]).

Here we see yet another lost cause, which is being fought even as Hispanic clout is growing. If past is prologue, the United States is likely to open up to Hispanics just as it opened up to Chinese and Japanese immigrants. Americans overwhelmingly favor a path to citizenship for undocumented immigrants, and business leaders nationwide rely on inexpensive labor from south of the border. So bashing Hispanics is a losing battle. Once undocumented immigrants are mainstreamed and this culture war fades away, pundits will record yet another victory for liberal inclusion. But soon enough this inclusivism, too, will come to be seen as simply American, freeing up culturally conservative Hispanics to enlist on the "right" side of culture wars to come.

Whither the Culture Wars?

So, WHAT IS next? Where might the culture wars go from here? It is of course possible that the culture wars might fade away. But they have not faded away yet. The United States remains a deeply religious country with a public square still obsessed with sin and righteousness. As long as that remains the case, it is likely that the culture wars cycle will continue to spin out both lost causes and cultural conservatives determined to defend them.

The post-9/11 Islam wars are not over yet. Americans have often fixed their gaze on a religious enemy in their midst, and at least for now that enemy is Islam. Immediately after 9/11, President Bush used his bully pulpit to love-bomb Islam, and for a time it seemed as if the nation's informal religious establishment, which had previously morphed from Protestant to Christian to Judeo-Christian, was about to become Judeo-Christian-Islamic, embracing the "Abrahamic" religions as three branches of a common faith. That did not happen, and every day the Islamic State beheads or burns alive another victim, it seems even less likely to happen.

The rhetoric of the contemporary culture wars could be ratcheted down. One cause of the rise of the "nones" (the religiously unaffili-ated) in recent years has been the widespread linkage of Christianity with political conservatism. There is now good evidence that young people, especially, are leaving Christian churches because they asso-ciate Christianity with bigotry. In a 2014 survey, nearly one-third of millennials who left their families' religious communities said they did so because of "negative teachings" about or "negative treatment" of gays and lesbians, and 70 percent of millennials said they believe religious organizations are "alienating young adults by being too judgmental on gay and lesbian issues."[31]

Another demographic factor at play is the declining power and authority of the old white male demographic. Old white men are the bread and butter of FOX News today, but that cohort is liter-ally dying off. As the country lurches toward a minority-majority population in the 2040s, the population is getting browner by the minute. Meanwhile, women are enjoying a more prominent role in politics. The Republican Party is trying to address this looming fact by cultivating Hispanic and nonwhite leaders, but almost all of these men—from Sen. Marco Rubio of Florida to Louisiana governor Bobby Jindal—are fire-and-brimstone culture warriors.

If part of the furor of today's culture wars has to do with Obama's mixed race, then some of it could subside under future presidents (assuming they are unambiguously white). Structural changes could also dial back the volume on the culture wars. The Tea Party could split off from the Republican Party and lose some of its force. If it does not moderate on issues such as homosexual-ity and immigration, the GOP itself could be weakened. The rapid rise of the religiously unaffiliated could also eliminate for decades any pretense of Christian politicians or ministers to speak for "the American people" as a whole.[32]

Another possibility is that a critical mass of white evangelicals really *will* take their marbles and go home. Meanwhile, a criti-cal mass of Republicans could grow tired of the culture wars for the practical reason that they are hurting their brand among key constituents—blacks, Latinos, young people, women—they desperately need to court.

After all, lost causes only work until they don't. Once they are truly and irrevocably lost, culture warriors will abandon them. That happened in the past with anti-Catholicism and anti-Mormonism, and it is starting to happen with opposition to gay rights. In 2004, ads attacking gay marriage helped to send George W. Bush to the White House; in the 2014 elections, some GOP candidates ran ads in *favor* of same-sex marriage. The LDS Church, which actively fought gay marriage in 2008 by supporting California's Proposition 8, supported an LGBT antidiscrimination law that passed in 2015. Culture wars are about principles more than pragmatic politics, of course. And there will always be true believers who would rather lose an election than compromise on core principles. (In the battle for the 2016 GOP presidential nomination, every candidate expressed his opposition to same-sex marriage, and former Arkansas governor Mike Huckabee called on all Americans to "resist and reject judicial tyranny."[33]) But after the worm turns on any particular issue, these numbers diminish.

Great Tradition of Conciliation

SOME OF MY liberal friends may be tempted to read this book as an argument for pressing for total victory in our culture wars. If liberals typically win these contests, why not demand abject surrender? Why shouldn't gay rights advocates press for the government to force Catholic adoption agencies to place children with LGBT couples? Why shouldn't women's health advocates insist that the government force Catholic colleges to dispense contraception to their students? Why shouldn't nondiscrimination policies at secular universities force evangelical student groups to allow non-Christian officers? To answer these questions you need to decide what sort of country you want to live in—what sort of public space you want to inhabit.

In an extended study of religious liberty and the culture wars, legal scholar Douglas Laycock lays bare the dangers cultural partisanship today poses to both freedom of religion and the American public square. Laycock is worried that America's sexual revolution is going the way of the French Revolution, in which religion and liberty came to be seen as mortal enemies. Today in the United States, pro-choice, gay rights, and women's health care groups increasingly see religious conservatives as bigots who want to impose their beliefs on others, and many on the left are starting to see arguments for religious liberty itself as thin cover for discrimination. Rather than viewing today's culture wars over sex and religion as battles between light and darkness, Laycock sees them as principled disagreements. What one side views as "grave evils," he observes, the other side views as "fundamental human rights." What is needed, if we are to preserve liberty in *both* religion and sexuality, is a grand bargain of sorts in which the Left would agree not to impose secular morality on religious institutions while the Right would agree not to impose its religious rules on society at large. Unfortunately, this grand bargain seems out of reach because "each side is intolerant of the other; each side wants a total win."[34]

Laycock's work challenges combatants on both sides of the sexual revolution to consider what sort of country they want to inhabit. Do we want to live in an increasingly polarized country in which each side hates the other half? Or might we all learn to be satisfied with preserving liberty for ourselves without imposing our ideals on those whose consciences revolt against them?

In a 2013 essay announcing his support for gay marriage, former George W. Bush speechwriter David Frum said that the gay and lesbian couples he knows had prompted his turnabout on this issue. But he had also been "swayed by an intensifying awareness of the harm culture-war politics has done to my party." These politics "have isolated the GOP from the America of the present and future, fastening it to politics of nostalgia for a (mis)remembered past," he wrote. "Worst of all, culture-war politics has taught the GOP to talk to America as if the nation were split into hostile halves, as if more separates Americans than unites them."[35]

Andrew Sullivan has been one of the most outspoken voices for gay rights since the *New Republic* ran his gay marriage cover story in 1989. In 2014, as Americans debated various state bills that would permit discrimination against gays and lesbians on religious liberty grounds, he called on the LGBT community not "to coerce people into tolerance":

> As a gay Christian, I'm particularly horrified by the attempt to force anyone to do anything they really feel violates their conscience, sense of self, or even just comfort. . . . We're living in a time of drastic change with respect to homosexuality. It is perfectly understandable that many traditional-minded people, especially in the older age brackets, are disconcerted, upset and confused. So give them some space; instead of suing them, talk to them. Try seeing things from their point of view.[36]

Frum is Canadian and Sullivan is British, but both speak out of a great tradition of conciliation that since the time of Jefferson's first inaugural has attempted to pull Americans out of the partisan muck. There is Patrick Henry affirming, "I am not a Virginian, but an American."[37] There is Lincoln insisting, in the midst of the Civil War, "We are not enemies, but friends. We must not be enemies."[38] And there is John F. Kennedy observing that "civility is not a sign of weakness."[39]

Defueling the Culture Wars Cycle

AMERICANS TODAY HAVE a choice. We cannot choose to bring our political disagreements to an end. In a country where some eat lobster and some do not, where some cling to the pure and others revel in the mixed, where Christians of all stripes live and work alongside Jews, Buddhists, and the unaffiliated, there are always going to be deep-seated differences about moral, religious, and cultural questions. As Sullivan puts it, there are always going to be gays and bigots. Or, as conservative evangelicals might put it, there are always going to be sodomites and Bible believers. So Americans are not likely to stand united any time soon. Our arguments will continue. They should continue. But we do have a choice about how those arguments will proceed.

The Jewish tradition has long distinguished between two types of arguing: arguing for the sake of ego and arguing for the sake of heaven. On the one hand, there is arguing to win, to prove yourself superior to your opponent, to satisfy vanity and ambition. On the other hand, there is arguing to get closer to the truth. This second approach starts with humility—an awareness that neither side possesses the whole truth (only God has that), so each side stands to learn something by listening to the other. There *is* an American tradition of turning down the volume and tamping down the anger, of arguing on behalf of the nation, especially in wartime. But as this story of America's culture wars demonstrates, much of American public life has been dominated by arguing on behalf of smaller things—the interests of self or social class or political party—with little or no regard for the common good.

Americans are not happy with this state of disunion. Thanks to what George Washington decried as the "mischiefs of the spirit of party,"[40] Congress is now one of the most hated institutions in American life. But "we the people" did this. The DC Republicans who attack liberals as "socialists" and the DC Democrats who call conservatives "terrorists" did not get to the Capitol on their own. We elected them. And if there is no shortage on cable news channels of conservative culture warriors and liberals eager to take them down, we did that too. The question is whether we are going to continue to do more of the same.

As they look back on the story this book has told, liberals can take comfort in the fact that they almost always win our cultural battles—that the arc of American cultural politics bends toward more liberty, not less. Conservatives can take comfort in the fact that they win (politically) by losing (culturally)—that part of the appeal of Republicans who swept to victory in the midterm routs of 1994 and 2014 was the fact that they were willing to stand up and defend "lost causes." But what can *Americans* take away from this story of our many culture wars?

One lesson might be that cultural warfare in the United States is unavoidable. At least from the time of the French Revolution, American politics has been a contest between right and left, with conservatives and liberals fighting fiercely over both economic and moral questions, both politics and religion. So perhaps there is no escaping yet another round of the culture wars cycle. As long as there are people in the United States anxious about the declining power and authority of whites, of men, of Christians, of the patriarchal family, and of America as a world power, there will be people eager to get up a revival dedicated to restoring the old order. As they peruse their towns, states, and country and see the things they hold dear slipping away, they will protest America's moral and spiritual decay and they will blame "liberals" and "radicals" and "socialists" for victimizing them. Then liberals will respond with attacks of their own.

But there is an alternative lesson to be drawn from this story: The culture wars cycle only continues if it is fueled, and the fuel is a populace willing to go along for the ride—to cheer for its heroes and to jeer its political opponents as enemies of God and nation alike. Take away that fuel and the culture wars sputter. From this perspective, cultural warfare, while persistent throughout U.S. history, is not inevitable. It depends on conservatives and liberals playing the roles assigned to them. What if a significant cohort of the Right and the Left stopped playing these roles, stopped enabling politicians and pundits who don't know the difference between a political antagonist and an enemy of the state? What if we refused to vote for them? What if we boycotted the corporations that fund them? What if, to paraphrase Jefferson in his first inaugural, we said, "We are all Republicans. We are all Democrats"?

Americans *can* look back on the culture wars from Jefferson to Obama and sign up for more of the same. Like fundamentalist pastors eager for another holy war against the Islamic world, or Muslim extremists thirsty for holy war against "Zionists" and their American enablers, we can look to the past to justify our belligerence. We can revisit the ugly rhetoric of the election of 1800 and see if we can make it uglier. We can employ the logic we used to justify attacking American Catholics and American Mormons in order to justify attacks on American Muslims. But we can also choose another course. We can refuse to excommunicate our antagonists from the American family. We can turn our culture wars into cultural debates.

A huge first step toward that choice would be to listen a little less to Rush Limbaugh and Bill Maher and a little more to Abraham Lincoln and John Kennedy, to realize that our cultural contests need not be life-or-death battles between patriots and traitors. Our culture wars would not be so enduring or run so deep if each side did not have a legitimate claim on American values. We possess no common creed, and the core texts in our "American Bible" argue against themselves.[41] So when we debate what America means or what it means to be an American, each side typically has some founders on its side, some plausible interpretation of the American story. However hard culture warriors may strain to turn the United States into an either-or nation, Americans have traditionally affirmed *both* the Federalists' beloved order *and* the Jeffersonians' beloved liberty. Their values have included *both* life *and* choice. They have respected *both* the Christianity of the majority *and* the religious liberty of the minority. Like Jefferson himself, they have waxed poetic about liberty as an "inalienable right" yet been unable to put the sordid legacy of slavery and segregation behind them.

Yes, many of our culture wars are prosecuted on behalf of ego and party. They serve to puff up Bill O'Reilly or Donald Trump or to raise money for this PAC or that. But we have in our usable past voices arguing for the sake of heaven as well—voices of Americans struggling against their political opponents not for vainglory or even for an election victory but to make an imperfect nation a little less imperfect. Heed these voices and we all win.

Acknowledgments

F IRST THINGS FIRST: I am grateful to my wife, Meera Subramanian, and my daughters for their understanding and support as I steal away upstairs or downstairs or to some other town or city to do my research and writing.

Friends and colleagues who read and commented on chapters include David Chappell, Seth Dowland, Paul Elie, Kirsten Fischer, Andrew Hartman, Douglas Laycock, Philip Jenkins, Patrick Mason, Mark Massa, Anthony Petro, Molly Prothero, Meera Subramanian, and Daniel Williams. I also received much appreciated assistance from Julie Byrne, Darren Dochuk, Philip Goff, Grace Hale, Susan Harding, Leigh Schmidt, Nancy Lusignan Schultz, Thomas Tweed, Lauren Winner, Molly Worthen, and many others whom I will be embarrassed not to have included here. Current and former graduate students of mine also helped, including Eric Baldwin, Lauren Kerby, and Eva Pascal.

I benefited tremendously from opportunities to discuss specific chapters at colloquia at Boston University; the Walter H. Capps Center for the Study of Ethics, Religion, and Public Life at the University of California, Santa Barbara; and the John C. Danforth Center on Religion and Politics at Washington University in Saint Louis. I also learned a lot from smart and inquisitive undergraduate and graduate students in a seminar I taught at Boston University on the culture wars.

At Boston University, I am grateful (again) for strong support from my department chairs and dean, who have been more than generous in affording me time and resources to devote to my research and writing.

Thanks as well to my editors at *USA Today* (Glen Nishimura), CNN's *Belief Blog* (Dan Gilgoff and Eric Marrapodi), and other magazines and newspapers for giving me a chance to explore the current culture wars in real time.

I also feel lucky to work with such a great team at HarperOne, including my wonderful editors, Roger Freet and Mickey Maudlin, publisher Mark Tauber, and the whole marketing and publicity crew.

Finally, one more deep bow to my indefatigable agent, Sandy Dijkstra, and to her crack staff, including Elise Capron and Andrea Cavallaro.

NOTES

INTRODUCTION: THE CULTURE WARS CYCLE

1. "Kill the Ground Zero Mosque TV Ad," YouTube video, posted by "NRTPac," July 2, 2010, https://www.youtube.com/watch?v=mjGJPPRD3u0.

2. Some have suggested that America's culture wars are a not-so-useful fiction. Are conservatives really from Mars and liberals from Venus? Or are the so-called culture wars an artificial by-product of the machinations of politicians, special interest groups, and cable television networks that stand to benefit from angry partisanship? In *What's the Matter with Kansas?* (New York: Metropolitan Books, 2004), journalist Thomas Frank argued that the contemporary culture wars are economic wars in drag, cynical tactics used by Republican politicians in order to con heartland conservatives into voting against their economic interests. No one is surprised to learn of the existence of cynical politicians, but culture wars should not be reduced to proxies for something else. Human beings *are* motivated by fear and greed, but they are also motivated by moral convictions and theological beliefs. No subterfuge is required, especially in the United States, to create a constituency that frets more about abortion rates than about tax rates. Another strident denial comes from sociologist Alan Wolfe, who insists that most Americans are noncombatants in the culture wars, political and cultural moderates happy to split the difference between liberal Democrats and conservative Republicans. "We are not a nation of zealots determined to make enemies of each other," Wolfe argues. We are "one nation, after all." Echoing Wolfe, political scientist Morris Fiorina writes that "splitting the difference is the American way." Elites may fight over abortion, guns, and the flag, but most Americans, when faced with the polarized positions of politicians and pundits, search for common ground. The culture wars are a "myth," he says. "There is no culture war in the United States—no battle for the soul of America rages." See Wolfe in James Davison Hunter and Alan Wolfe, *Is There a*

Culture War?: A Dialogue on Values and American Public Life (Washington, DC: Brookings Institution Press, 2006), 71; Alan Wolfe, *One Nation, After All* (New York: Viking, 1998); Morris P. Fiorina in *Is There a Culture War?*, by Hunter and Wolfe, 84; and Morris P. Fiorina, Samuel J. Abrams, and Jeremy C. Pope, *Culture War?: The Myth of a Polarized America*, 2nd ed. (New York: Pearson, 2006), 8. Culture war deniers do have a point. Ordinary Americans are not as bitterly divided as talking heads on FOX News and MSNBC. But this does not make the culture wars mythic. It just means that they are more likely to manifest on television sets than over dinner tables. Wolfe and Fiorina concede that partisanship and polarization characterize public debates. And since their books appeared a decade or so ago, political polarization has increased, including in the general population. See Drew DeSilver, "Partisan Polarization, in Congress and Among Public, Is Greater than Ever," Pew Research Center, July 17, 2013, http://www.pewresearch.org/fact-tank/2013/07/17/partisan-polarization-in-congress-and-among-public-is-greater-than-ever/.

3. Pew Research Center, "Political Polarization in the American Public," June 12, 2014, http://www.people-press.org/2014/06/12/political-polarization-in-the-american-public/.
4. Catalina Camia, "Texas GOP Congressman Compares Obama to Hitler," *USA Today*, January 13, 2015, http://onpolitics.usatoday.com/2015/01/13/obama-hitler-randy-weber-twitter/; and Taylor Wofford, "Giuliani, Cruz Criticize Obama Over Islamic Extremism Remarks," *Newsweek*, February 19, 2015, http://www.newsweek.com/giuliani-cruz-criticize-obama-over-islamic-extremism-remarks-308004.
5. Rebecca Riffkin, "Public Faith in Congress Falls Again, Hits Historic Low," Gallup, June 19, 2014, http://www.gallup.com/poll/171710/public-faith-congress-falls-again-hits-historic-low.aspx; Public Policy Polling, "Congress Less Popular than Cockroaches, Traffic Jams," January 8, 2013, http://www.publicpolicypolling.com/main/2013/01/congress-less-popular-than-cockroaches-traffic-jams.html.
6. Rebecca Bratek, "Smartphone App Reveals the Politics in Your Shopping Cart," *Los Angeles Times*, August 25, 2014, http://www.latimes.com/nation/la-na-buy-partisan-20140825-story.html.
7. "Our Cold Civil War Intensifies," *The Dish* (blog), June 12, 2014, http://dish.andrewsullivan.com/2014/06/12/our-cold-civil-war-intensifies.
8. "Mayor Bloomberg Discusses the Landmarks Preservation Commission Vote on 45–47 Park Place," August 3, 2010, City of New York website, http://www1.nyc.gov/office-of-the-mayor/news/337-10/mayor-bloomberg-the-landmarks-preservation-commission-vote-45-47-park-place#/5.
9. *Connecticut Courant*, August 18, 1800, quoted in *Jefferson's Second Revolution: The Election Crisis of 1800 and the Triumph of Republicanism*, by Susan Dunn (Boston: Houghton Mifflin, 2004), 148. Virtually all books on the culture wars trace them to either the 1960s or the 1970s. The 1960s are the key decade in *All in the Family: The Realignment of American Democracy Since the 1960s*, by Robert O. Self (New York: Hill and Wang, 2012); James Livingston, *The World Turned Inside Out: American Thought*

and Culture at the End of the 20th Century (Lanham, MD: Rowman & Littlefield, 2009); and Andrew Hartman, *A War for the Soul of America: A History of the Culture Wars* (Chicago: Univ. of Chicago Press, 2015). David T. Courtwright's political history of the culture wars, *No Right Turn: Conservative Politics in a Liberal Era* (Cambridge, MA: Harvard Univ. Press, 2010), gets going in the late 1960s. The 1970s are emphasized in *Age of Fracture*, by Daniel T. Rodgers (Cambridge, MA: Harvard Univ. Press, 2011). In *God's Own Party: The Making of the Christian Right* (New York: Oxford Univ. Press, 2010), Daniel K. Williams pushes the start of this story back to the 1920s, but even his book focuses almost entirely on events of the last half century.

10. Horace M. Kallen, "Democracy Versus the Melting-Pot," *The Nation*, February 25, 1915, 220.

11. Bruce Chadwick, *George Washington's War: The Forging of a Revolutionary Leader and the American Presidency* (Naperville, IL: Sourcebooks, 2004), 101.

12. James Davison Hunter, *Culture Wars: The Struggle to Define America* (New York: Basic Books, 1991); and "Patrick Joseph Buchanan, 'Culture War Speech: Address to the Republican National Convention,' August 17, 1992," Voices of Democracy, http://voicesofdemocracy.umd.edu /buchanan-culture-war-speech-speech-text/. Before Hunter translated the German term *"Kulturkampf"* into American English, others had found parallels between America's clash of civilizations and the values war that Chancellor Otto von Bismarck waged in 1870s Germany against Jewish and Catholic minorities. In April 1990, amid a controversy over homosexuality, religion, and the arts, Rep. Henry Hyde (R-IL) wrote in a *National Review* cover story that "America is, in truth, involved in a *Kulturkampf*—a culture war, a war between cultures and a war about the very meaning of 'culture.'" He defined this war in moral terms, as a "struggle between those who believe that the norms of 'bourgeois morality' (which is drawn in the main from classic Jewish and Christian morality) should form the ethical basis of our common life, and those who are determined that these norms will be replaced with a radical and thoroughgoing moral relativism" (Henry J. Hyde, "The Culture War," *National Review*, April 30, 1990, 25). Later that year, Rep. Robert Dornan (R-CA) spoke of a "culture war" that extended "from flag burning to abortion to capital punishment to public funding for the arts." He, too, saw this as a moral struggle with obvious good guys and bad guys: "On the one side are the moral relativists, whose philosophy can be summed up with the credo 'If it feels good do it.' On the other side are those who find their moral direction in the Judeo-Christian tradition" (*Culture Wars: Documents from the Recent Controversies in the Arts*, ed. Richard Bolton [New York: New Press, 1992], 268). According to Courtwright's *No Right Turn*, the earliest appearance of this term may well have come in a 1970 memo from Daniel Moynihan to President Nixon, which laments the "collapse of traditional values" and describes a deep-seated conflict between "adversary culture" (6) and the "silent majority" (4).

"Do not doubt," Moynihan wrote, "that there is a struggle going on in this country of the kind the Germans used to call a *Kulturkampf*" (Daniel P. Moynihan, "Memorandum for the President," November 13, 1970, Nixon Presidential Library & Museum, http://nixon.archives.gov/virtuallibrary /releases/jun09/111370_Moynihan.pdf).

13. Ronald Reagan's public letter, "Primary Resources: Alzheimer's Letter," November 5, 1994, *American Experience*, PBS, http://www.pbs.org/wgbh /americanexperience/features/primary-resources/reagan-alzheimers/.

14. See Diana Lobel, *The Quest for God and the Good: World Philosophy as a Living Experience* (New York: Columbia Univ. Press, 2011).

15. In *Culture Wars*, Hunter argued that the key fault line in American public life ran not between competing economic theories, political parties, or religious denominations but between "competing moral visions." On one side were the "orthodox" for whom moral authority was unchanging, transcendent, and external to the self (in scripture or natural law). On the other side were "progressives" for whom moral authority was malleable, earthbound, derived from personal experience, and accountable to scientific advances (43–45). This moral divide may characterize the contemporary culture wars, but moral relativism is a modern invention. Throughout the eighteenth and nineteenth centuries both sides in America's cultural conflicts were advanced by moral absolutists. And though there were challenges to traditional moral norms in the Roaring Twenties, moral relativism itself was still waiting to be born.

16. George M. Marsden, *Understanding Fundamentalism and Evangelicalism* (Grand Rapids, MI: Wm. B. Eerdmans, 1991), 1.

17. Susan Jacoby, *Freethinkers: A History of American Secularism* (New York: Metropolitan, 2004), 185.

18. See Alan Brinkley, "Liberalism's Third Crisis," *American Prospect*, December 19, 2001, http://prospect.org/article/liberalisms-third-crisis.

19. "From Thomas Jefferson to Abigail Adams, 22 February 1787," Founders Online, http://founders.archives.gov/documents/Jefferson/01-11-02 -0182.

20. "Letters to John Taylor (1814)," Federalist Papers Project, http://www .thefederalistpapers.org/founders/john-adams.

21. Hartman, *A War for the Soul of America*, 37.

22. Lars Walker, "Comments on 'Endowed by Their DNA with Certain Inalienable Rights,'" Brandywine Books, June 18, 2012, http://brandy winebooks.net/bloo.discussion.popup.php?post_id=4931. In *The World Turned Inside Out*, Livingston sees left-leaning academics leading an assault on white, male privilege in the Ivory Tower in the eighties and nineties: "They started the skirmishes that became the culture wars" (30). Evangelical blogger Tom Gilson echoes Walker on same-sex marriage: "A legal and social assault has indeed been launched. But we didn't launch it: *they did*. They're the ones attacking historic laws, customs, and morality. They speak as if we're the aggressors, when in reality *they are*. We've had to take up a defensive position, to protect an institution as old as recorded history. We didn't pick this fight, the other side did"

(Tom Gilson, "Gay Rights Distortions and Aggression," Thinking Christian, May 30, 2010, http://www.thinkingchristian.net/posts/2010/05/gay-rights-distortions-and-aggression/).

23. Corey Robin, *The Reactionary Mind* (New York: Oxford Univ. Press, 2011), 21.

24. Robin, *The Reactionary Mind*, 38.

25. I am indebted here to Corey Robin. Conservatism, he argues, is "a meditation on—and theoretical rendition of—the felt experience of having power, seeing it threatened, and trying to win it back" (*The Reactionary Mind*, 4).

26. I am grateful to historian Molly Worthen for allowing me to look at an early draft of her *Apostles of Reason: The Crisis of Authority in American Evangelicalism* (New York: Oxford Univ. Press, 2013), which pushed me to think more deeply about anxiety and the culture wars.

27. Pew Research Center, "The Global Divide on Homosexuality," June 4, 2013, http://www.pewglobal.org/2013/06/04/the-global-divide-on-homosexuality/. Although the United States finished to the right of Canada (80 percent) and Australia (79 percent), it finished far to the left of China (22 percent), Russia (16 percent), and all the African and Middle Eastern countries surveyed.

28. Andrew Sullivan, *The Conservative Soul: How We Lost It, How to Get It Back* (New York: Harper, 2006), 9.

29. William James, *The Principles of Psychology* (New York: Henry Holt, 1890), 1:488.

30. David Brooks, "The Next Culture War," *New York Times*, June 30, 2015, A23, http://www.nytimes.com/2015/06/30/opinion/david-brooks-the-next-culture-war.html. Brooks called the contemporary culture wars a "communications disaster, reducing a rich, complex and beautiful faith into a public obsession with sex."

31. "MSNBC's Toure: Islamophobia Has Become an 'Acceptable Racism' with Some Liberals," Real Clear Politics video, posted by Ian Schwartz on October 13, 2014, http://www.realclearpolitics.com/video/2014/10/13/msnbcs_toure_islamophobia_has_become_an_acceptable_racism_with_some_liberals.html.

CHAPTER 1: THE JEFFERSON WARS

1. Allen West, "Obama Revealed His True Colors at Prayer Breakfast, and True Ignorance of History," AllenBWest.com, February 6, 2015, http://allenbwest.com/2015/02/obama-revealed-true-colors-prayer-breakfast-true-ignorance-history/.

2. James M. Banner Jr., *To the Hartford Convention: The Federalists and the Origins of Party Politics in Massachusetts, 1789–1815* (New York: Knopf, 1970), 4.

3. "To the Public," *Gazette of the United States*, January 10, 1801, reprinted in *Columbian Centinel*, January 21, 1801, in *Jefferson and His Time*, by Dumas Malone (Boston: Little, Brown, and Co., 1970), 5.

4. Bruce Chadwick, *George Washington's War: The Forging of a Revolutionary Leader and the American Presidency* (Naperville, IL: Sourcebooks, 2004), 101.

5. Jefferson to Dr. Jones, March 5, 1810, in *The Writings of Thomas Jefferson*, ed. H. A. Washington (New York: Derby & Jackson, 1859), 5:510.

6. Washington to Jefferson, August 23, 1792, in *The Writings of George Washington*, ed. Worthington Chauncey Ford, vol. 12, 1790–1794 (New York: G. P. Putnam's Sons, 1891), 174.

7. Washington to Hamilton, August 26, 1792, in *The Papers of Alexander Hamilton*, ed. Harold Coffin Syrett (New York: Columbia Univ. Press, 1967), 11:276–77.

8. "First Inaugural Address of George Washington," April 30, 1789, Avalon Project, Yale Law School website, http://avalon.law.yale.edu/18th_century/wash1.asp.

9. John Ferling, *Adams vs. Jefferson: The Tumultuous Election of 1800* (New York: Oxford Univ. Press, 2004), 57.

10. Washington to Burgess Ball, September 25, 1794, in *George Washington: A Collection*, ed. William B. Allen (Indianapolis, IN: Liberty Fund, 1988), 597.

11. "Washington's Farewell Address 1796," Avalon Project, Yale Law School website, http://avalon.law.yale.edu/18th_century/washing.asp.

12. Jefferson to William Duane, March 28, 1811, in *The Writings of Thomas Jefferson*, ed. Albert Ellery Bergh (Washington, DC: Thomas Jefferson Memorial Association, 1907), 13:30. On the Gothic rhetoric, see Rachel Hope Cleves, *The Reign of Terror in America: Visions of Violence from Anti-Jacobinism to Antislavery* (New York: Cambridge Univ. Press, 2009).

13. Susan Dunn, *Jefferson's Second Revolution: The Election Crisis of 1800 and the Triumph of Republicanism* (Boston: Houghton Mifflin, 2004), 103.

14. "An Observer," writing in the *Gazette of the United States*, August 5, 1800, reprinted in *Arthur Mervyn; or, Memoirs of the Year 1793, with Related Texts*, by Charles Brockden Brown, eds. Philip Barnard and Stephen Shapiro (Indianapolis, IN: Hackett, 2008), 415; and "Aurora, Friday, April 27, 1798," in *American Aurora: A Democratic-Republican Returns; The Suppressed History of Our Nation's Beginnings and the Heroic Newspaper That Tried to Report It*, by Richard N. Rosenfeld (New York: St. Martin's Press, 1997), 94.

15. "Mail Routes," *Niles' Weekly Register*, October 6, 1832, 43:83.

16. Jefferson to John Adams, June 27, 1813, in *Memoir, Correspondence, and Miscellanies, from the Papers of Thomas Jefferson*, ed. Thomas Jefferson Randolph (Charlottesville, VA: F. Carr, 1829), 3:202.

17. "'Democrats' and 'Federalists,'" *Niles' Weekly Register*, October 13, 1832, 43:97.

18. *Aurora*, December 23, 1796, quoted in *Scandal and Civility: Journalism and the Birth of American Democracy*, by Marcus Leonard Daniel (New York: Oxford Univ. Press, 2009), 109.

19. *Aurora*, March 6, 1797, quoted in *American Press Opinion*, ed. Allan Nevins (Boston and New York: D. C. Heath, 1928), 21–22.

20. *Porcupine's Gazette*, March 17, 1798, quoted in *Infamous Scribblers: The Founding Fathers and the Rowdy Beginnings of American Journalism*, by Eric Burns (New York: PublicAffairs, 2006), 341–42.

21. *Aurora*, June 27, 1798, quoted in *The Supreme Court in United States History*, by Charles Warren (Boston: Little, Brown, and Co., 1922), 1.434.

22. Jefferson to Abigail Smith Adams, February 22, 1787, in *The Adams-Jefferson Letters*, ed. Lester J. Cappon (Chapel Hill: Univ. of North Carolina Press, 1959), 1:173. According to one historian, "The Federalists may have been the only major party in American history forthrightly to proclaim democracy and freedom dangerous in the hands of ordinary citizens." See Eric Foner, *Give Me Liberty! An American History*, 2nd ed. (New York: W. W. Norton, 2008), 284.

23. Jefferson to Philip Mazzei, April 24, 1796, "The Papers of Thomas Jefferson," Princeton University website, https://jeffersonpapers.princeton.edu/selected-documents/thomas-jefferson-philip-mazzei-0.

24. See John Winthrop, "A Model of Christian Charity," in *The American Bible: How Our Words Unite, Divide, and Define a Nation*, by Stephen Prothero (New York: HarperOne, 2012), 34–51; and Nathan Hatch, *The Sacred Cause of Liberty: Republican Thought and the Millennium in Revolutionary New England* (New Haven, CT: Yale Univ. Press, 1977).

25. Harper to his constituents, January 5, 1797, in "Papers of James A. Bayard, 1796–1815," in *Annual Report of the American Historical Association for the Year 1913*, ed. Elizabeth Donnan (Washington, DC: Government Printing Office, 1915), 2:25.

26. Thomas Paine, *Common Sense, Rights of Man, and Other Essential Writings of Thomas Paine* (New York: New American Library, 2003), 353.

27. "From a Correspondent in Connecticut," "Remarks on the *Aurora*, No. I," in *Minerva & Mercantile Evening Advertiser*, September 3, 1796, quoted in *The Revolution of 1800: Democracy, Race and the New Republic*, eds. James Horn, Jan Ellen Lewis, and Peter S. Onuf (Charlottesville: Univ. of Virginia Press, 2002), 178.

28. Jeffrey L. Pasley, *The First Presidential Contest: 1796 and the Founding of American Democracy* (Lawrence: Univ. Press of Kansas, 2013), 10.

29. Timothy Dwight, *The Duty of Americans, at the Present Crisis* (New Haven, CT: Thomas and Samuel Green, 1798), 20–21.

30. Jefferson to Martha Jefferson Randolph, May 17, 1898, in *The Domestic Life of Thomas Jefferson*, by Sarah N. Randolph (New York: Harper & Brothers, 1871), 249.

31. William Wirt Henry, *Patrick Henry: Life, Correspondence and Speeches* (New York: Charles Scribner's Sons, 1891), 2:610.

32. Edward J. Larson, *A Magnificent Catastrophe: The Tumultuous Election of 1800, America's First Presidential Campaign* (New York: Free Press, 2007), 48.

33. Oliver Wolcott Jr. to "Mrs. Wilcott," in *Memoirs of the Administrations of Washington and John Adams, Edited from the Papers of Oliver Wolcott, Secretary of the Treasury*, ed. George Gibbs (New York: 1846), 2:377–78.

34. Books on this election include Dunn, *Jefferson's Second Revolution*; Fer-
    ling, *Adams vs. Jefferson*; Horn, Lewis, and Onuf, *The Revolution of 1800*,
    178; Edward J. Larson, *A Magnificent Catastrophe*; and Bernard Weis-
    berger, *America Afire: Jefferson, Adams, and the Revolutionary Election of
    1800* (New York: William Morrow, 2000). Articles include Frank Lam-
    bert, " 'God—and a Religious President . . . [or] Thomas Jefferson and No
    God': Campaigning for a Voter-Imposed Religious Test in 1800," *Journal
    of Church and State* 39 (1997): 769–89; Charles O. Lerche Jr., "Thomas
    Jefferson and the Election of 1800: A Case Study in the Political Smear,"
    William and Mary Quarterly 3rd ser., 5, no. 4, (1948): 467–91; Charles
    F. O'Brien, "The Religious Issue in the Presidential Campaign of 1800,"
    Essex Institute Historical Collections 107 (1971): 82–93; and Constance B.
    Schultz, " 'Of Bigotry in Politics and Religion': Thomas Jefferson's Reli-
    gion, the Federalist Press, and the Syllabus," *Virginia Magazine of History
    and Biography* 91 (1983): 73–91.
35. *Gazette of the United States*, November 12, 1798, quoted in *American
    Aurora*, Rosenfeld, 536.
36. George Washington, *The Writings of George Washington*, ed. Jared Sparks
    (Boston: Russell, Shattuck, and Williams, 1836), 11:44.
37. Edward Livingston, "Speech on the Alien Bill," in *American Eloquence:
    A Collection of Speeches and Addresses, by the Most Eminent Orators of
    America*, by Frank Moore (New York: D. Appleton, 1857), 2:224. In
    this speech, delivered in the House of Representatives on June 19, 1798,
    Livingston invoked the biblical story of the binding of Isaac in an effort
    to impel his colleagues to reject this bill: "Our mistaken zeal, like the
    patriarch of old, has bound one victim; it lies at the foot of the altar; a sac-
    rifice of the first born offspring of freedom is proposed by those who gave
    it birth. The hand is already raised to strike, and nothing, I fear, but the
    voice of heaven, can arrest the impious blow." No such voice was heard.
    The bill passed on June 25, 1798.
38. John Ward Fenno, *Desultory Reflections on New Political Aspects of Public
    Affairs in the United States of America, Since the Commencement of the Year
    1799* (New York printed, Philadelphia reprinted: R. T. Rawle, 1800), 6.
39. Fisher Ames, *Works of Fisher Ames* (Boston: T. B. Wait & Co., 1809),
    96–97.
40. *Connecticut Courant*, September 29, 1800, 1, quoted in *Conceived in
    Doubt: Religion and Politics in the New American Nation*, by Amanda Por-
    terfield (Chicago: Univ. of Chicago Press, 2012), 4.
41. Jefferson to Thomas Mann Randolph Jr., February 2, 1800, and Jefferson
    to John Taylor, June 4, 1798, in *The Papers of Thomas Jefferson*, ed. Bar-
    bara B. Oberg (Princeton, NJ: Princeton Univ. Press, 2004), 30:387–90;
    31:357–359.
42. Alexander Hamilton to Theodore Sedgwick, May 4, 1800, in "Creating
    the Bill of Rights: Federalists Fear 'Fangs of Jefferson,' " Library of Con-
    gress   website,   http://www.loc.gov/exhibits/creating-the-united-states
    /election-of-1800.html#obj7; and *Aurora*, December 16, 1800, quoted in
    American Aurora, Rosenfeld, 890.

43. *Daily Advertiser,* April 28, 1800, quoted in *A Magnificent Catastrophe,* Larson, 93.
44. Oliver Wolcott to Alexander Hamilton, October 2, 1800, in *Memoirs of the Administrations of Washington and John Adams, Edited from the Papers of Oliver Wolcott, Secretary of the Treasury,* ed. George Gibbs (New York: 1846), 2:431.
45. *Connecticut Courant,* September 20, 1800, in *The Revolutionary Era Primary Documents on Events from 1776 to 1800,* ed. Carol Sue Humphrey (Westport, CT: Greenwood Press, 2003), 339.
46. Alexander Hamilton, *Letter from Alexander Hamilton, Concerning the Public Conduct and Character of John Adams, Esq., President of the United States, Written in 1800* (Boston: E. G. House, 1809), 10, 18.
47. Adams to Benjamin Rush, January 25, 1806, in *Old Family Letters: Copied from the Originals for Alexander Biddle* (Philadelphia: J. B. Lippincott, 1892), A.92; and Adams quoted in "Enclosure: James McHenry to John Adams, 31 May 1800," Founders Online, http://founders.archives.gov/documents/Hamilton/01-24-02-0469-0003.
48. Callender quoted in *A Magnificent Catastrophe,* Larson, 134; and in *Jefferson's Second Revolution,* Dunn, 169. For such outbursts, Callender was convicted under the Alien and Sedition Acts and sentenced to nine months in jail.
49. Hamilton to James Bayard, December 27, 1800, in *The Papers of Alexander Hamilton,* ed. Harold Coffin Syrett (New York: Columbia Univ. Press, 1977), 25:277.
50. *Independent Chronicle,* June 26–30, 1800, quoted in *A Magnificent Catastrophe,* Larson, 175; and John Wood, *The History of the Administration of John Adams, Esq., Late President of the United States* (New York: 1802), 261.
51. William Linn, *Serious Considerations on the Election of a President: Addressed to the Citizens of the United States* (New York: John Furman, 1800), 32.
52. Lerche, "Thomas Jefferson and the Election of 1800," 487.
53. Robert M. S. McDonald, "Was There a Religious Revolution of 1800?" in *The Revolution of 1800,* Horn, Lewis, and Onuf, 180. On the postelection gossip, see Elise Lemire, *"Miscegenation": Making Race in America* (Philadelphia: Univ. of Pennsylvania Press, 2002), 11–34. For the broader question of the relationship between Jefferson and Hemings, see the extensive bibliography included in "Thomas Jefferson and Sally Hemings: A Brief Account," Monticello.org, http://www.monticello.org/site/plantation-and-slavery/thomas-jefferson-and-sally-hemings-brief-account#bibliography. This story was pursued particularly vigorously by Callender, who first named names in a piece in the *Richmond Recorder* on September 1, 1802. Soon Jefferson was being depicted in political attack ads as "A Philosophic Cock" strutting after a swarthy hen (illustration, Library of Congress website, http://www.loc.gov/exhibits/jefferson/images/vc140.jpg).
54. Encyclopedia Virginia, "Primary Resource: Letter from Thomas Jefferson to Ezra Stiles Ely (June 25, 1819)," Virginia Foundation for the Humanities,

http://www.encyclopediavirginia.org/Letter_from_Thomas_Jefferson_to
_Ezra_Styles_June_25_1819. In an April 21, 1803, letter to Benjamin
Rush, Jefferson wrote, "I am a Christian, in the only sense in which
[Jesus] wished any one to be; sincerely attached to his doctrines, in pref-
erence to all others; ascribing to himself every human excellence; and
believing he never claimed any other" (Thomas Jefferson, *The Writings of
Thomas Jefferson*, ed. Paul Leicester Ford [Washington, DC: Thomas Jef-
ferson Memorial Association, 1903], 10:380).

55. Theophilus Parsons to John Jay, May 5, 1800, in *The Correspondence and
Public Papers of John Jay*, ed. Henry P. Johnson (New York: G. P. Putnam's
Sons, 1893), 4:270.

56. No one seems to know, the *Connecticut Courant* complained on August
18, 1800, "whether Mr. Jefferson believes in the heathen mythology or,
in the alcoran [Quran]; whether he is a Jew or a Christian; whether he
believes in one God, or in many; or in none at all" (quoted in *Jefferson's
Second Revolution*, Dunn, 148).

57. Linn, *Serious Considerations*, 4, 20, 28. The other voices are Mr. Caldwell
and Mr. Lancaster, quoted in *The Debates, Resolutions, and Other Proceedings, in Convention, on the Adoption of the Federal Constitution, as
Recommended by the General Convention at Philadelphia, on the 17th of
September, 1787*, ed. Jonathan Elliot (Washington: Jonathan Elliot, 1830),
3:176, 188. See also "God—and a Religious President," Frank Lambert,
which includes a thoughtful interpretation of the election of 1800 as a
return to this contentious constitutional debate over the religion test.

58. Anonymous, *The Providential Detection*, illustration, Library of Congress
website, http://www.loc.gov/exhibits/jefferson/images/vc136.jpg.

59. Jefferson to Thomas Mann Randolph, February 2, 1800, in *The Works
of Thomas Jefferson*, ed. Paul Leicester Ford (New York: G. P. Putnam's
Sons, 1905), 9:111; Hamilton to John Jay, May 7, 1800, in *The Papers of
Alexander Hamilton*, ed. Harold C. Syrett (New York: Columbia Univ.
Press, 1976), 24:465.

60. Paine to Samuel Adams, January 1, 1803, in his *The Theological Works of
Thomas Paine* (London: R. Carlile, 1824), 307; and John M. Mason, *The
Voice of Warning, to Christians, on the Ensuing Election of a President of the
United States* (New York: John M. Mason, 1800), 8, 27.

61. *Gazette of the United States*, September 10, 1800, quoted in "Was There a
Religious Revolution of 1800?" by Robert M. S. McDonald, in *The Revolution of 1800*, Horn, Lewis, and Onuf, 182.

62. Jedediah Morse, *A Sermon, Exhibiting the Present Dangers, and Consequent
Duties of the Citizens of the United States of America* (Charlestown, MA:
Samuel Etheridge, 1799), 31, 16–17.

63. *Philadelphia Gazette*, September 5, 1800, quoted in "Forgery: A Prop for
Parson Abercrombie," *Aurora*, September 10, 1800, in *American Aurora*,
Rosenfeld, 847.

64. Jefferson's writings on religion include "Syllabus of an Estimate on
the Merit of the Doctrines of Jesus, Compared with Those of Others"
(1803) and two cut-and-paste versions of the New Testament: "The

Philosophy of Jesus of Nazareth" (1804) and "The Life and Morals of Jesus of Nazareth" (1819 or 1820). For thorough discussions of these documents, see Thomas Jefferson, *Jefferson's Extracts from the Gospels: "The Philosophy of Jesus" and "The Life and Morals of Jesus,"* ed. Dickinson W. Adams (Princeton, NJ: Princeton Univ. Press, 1983); and "Thomas Jefferson's Bible" at the National Museum of American History, Smithsonian online, http://americanhistory.si.edu/jeffersonbible/. For an interpretation of Jefferson as someone who loved Jesus but hated the church, see Stephen Prothero, *American Jesus: How the Son of God Became a National Icon* (New York: Farrar, Straus & Giroux, 2004), 19–42.

65. Jefferson to Miles King, September 26, 1814, in *The Writings of Thomas Jefferson*, eds. Andrew A. Lipscomb and Albert Ellery Bergh (Washington, DC: Thomas Jefferson Memorial Association, 1905), 13:198.
66. Anonymous, *The Voice of Warning, to Christians, on the Ensuing Election of a President of the United States* (1800), reprinted in *The Complete Works of John M. Mason*, ed. Ebenezer Mason (New York: Baker and Scribner, 1849), 4:553, 556.
67. Thomas Jefferson, *Notes on the State of Virginia*, ed. David Waldstreicher (New York: Palgrave Macmillan, 2002), 192; and Linn, *Serious Considerations*, 19.
68. *The Augusta Chronicle and Gazette of the State*, July 20, 1799, quoted in "Jefferson's Letter to Philip Mazzei," The Papers of Thomas Jefferson, Princeton University website, https://jeffersonpapers.princeton.edu/selected-documents/jeffersons-letter-philip-mazzei.
69. *Hudson Bee*, September 7, 1800, and *Connecticut Courant*, September 20, 1800, both quoted in "Thomas Jefferson and the Election of 1800," Lerche, 474, 480.
70. A Christian Federalist [pseud.], *A Short Address to the Voters of Delaware* (Kent County: September 21, 1800), 3, Library of Congress website, http://hdl.loc.gov/loc.rbc/rbpe.0130350a.
71. Linn, *Serious Considerations*, 28, 24, 34. For a clergyman's refutation, see Grotius [DeWitt Clinton], *A Vindication of Thomas Jefferson, Against the Charges Contained in a Pamphlet Entitled, "Serious Considerations," &c.* (New York: printed by David Denniston, 1800).
72. Abraham Bishop, *Connecticut Republicanism: An Oration on the Extent and Power of Political Delusion* (Albany, NY: John Barber, 1801), 49–50, 25.
73. John Adams to Thomas Boylston Adams, December 30, 1800, in *Writings of John Quincy Adams*, ed. Worthington Chauncey Ford (New York: Macmillan, 1913), 2:491.
74. Jefferson to Adams, April 15, 1806, in *Memoir, Correspondence, and Miscellanies*, Randolph, 4:522.
75. James Bayard to Richard Bassett, February 17, 1801, in *Papers of James A. Bayard, 1796–1815, Annual Report of the American Historical Association for the Year 1913*, ed. Elizabeth Donnan (Washington, DC: American Historical Association, 1915), 2:127.

76. Jefferson to William Branch Giles, December 31, 1795, in *The Papers of Thomas Jefferson*, ed. John Catanzariti (Princeton, NJ: Princeton Univ. Press, 2000), 28:565–67; Prothero, *American Bible*, 12; Abraham Lincoln, "First Inaugural Address of Abraham Lincoln," March 4, 1861, Avalon Project, Yale Law School website, http://avalon.law.yale.edu/19th_century/lincoln1.asp.

77. "Thomas Jefferson: Thomas Jefferson to Spencer Roane," September 6, 1819, Library of Congress website, http://www.loc.gov/exhibits/jefferson/137.html.

78. *National Intelligencer*, March 6, 1801, quoted in "The Centennial of the First Inauguration of a President at the Permanent Seat of the Government," by Samuel Clagett Busey, *Records of the Columbia Historical Society, Washington, DC* 5 (1902): 98.

79. Margaret Bayard Smith to Miss Susan B. Smith, March 4, 1801, in *The First Forty Years of Washington Society: Portrayed by the Family Letters of Mrs. Samuel Harrison Smith (Margaret Bayard) from the Collection of Her Grandson, J. Henley Smith*, ed. Gaillard S. Hunt (New York: C. Scribner's Sons, 1906), 26.

80. Thomas Jefferson, "Inaugural Address," March 4, 1801, American Presidency Project, http://www.presidency.ucsb.edu/ws/index.php?pid=25803.

81. John Adams, *The Works of John Adams*, ed. Charles Francis Adams (Boston: Little, Brown, 1854), 9:511.

82. Jefferson to Francis Hopkinson, March 13, 1789, in *The Works of Thomas Jefferson*, Ford, 5:456.

83. Jefferson, "Inaugural Address," March 4, 1801, American Presidency Project, http://www.presidency.ucsb.edu/ws/index.php?pid=25803. As Weisberger notes in *America Afire*, "In the printed version, *Federalist* and *Republican* were capitalized, making it sound as if the president was giving his blessing to both parties, a healing if somewhat unrealistic interpretation. But in his hand-written version the labels were not in capitals, and the message was more general. Most Americans, Jefferson was insisting, were moderates" (281).

84. Richard J. Hooker, "John Marshall on the Judiciary, the Republicans, and Jefferson, March 4, 1801," *American Historical Review* 53, no. 3 (April 1948), 519.

85. John Adams to Benjamin Stoddert, March 31, 1801, in *The Works of John Adams*, Charles Francis Adams, 9:582, http://oll.libertyfund.org/titles/2107.

86. King quoted in *One Nation, Under Gods: A New American History*, by Peter Manseau (New York: Little, Brown, 2015), 220–21.

87. Author's correspondence with Lauren Winner, March 2011.

88. Porterfield, *Conceived in Doubt*, 166.

89. Porterfield, *Conceived in Doubt*, 146.

90. Susan Jacoby, *Freethinkers: A History of American Secularism* (New York: Metropolitan, 2004), 67.

91. *National Intelligencer*, November 10, 1800, quoted in "The Presidential Newspaper as an Engine of Early American Political Development: The

Case of Thomas Jefferson and the Election of 1800," by Mel Laracey, *Rhetoric & Public Affairs* 11, no. 1 (Spring 2008): 34.

CHAPTER 2: ANTI-CATHOLICISM

1. Quotes from the banners, the nuns, and the superior appear in "Alvah Kelley's Cow: Household Feuds, Proprietary Rights, and the Charlestown Convent Riot," by Daniel A. Cohen, *New England Quarterly* 74, no. 4 (December 2001): 561, 562, 531. For the shouts of the mob, see United States Catholic Historical Society, "Letter of Sister St. Augustine Relative to 'The Burning of the Convent,'" *Historical Records and Studies* 4 (New York: 1906): 221. Moffatt is described in *The Charlestown Convent; Its Destruction by a Mob, on the Night of August 11, 1834* (Boston: Patrick Donahoe, 1870), 80. Buzzell is quoted in "Burned by a Mob," *Boston Globe*, December 26, 1886, 5. Primary sources for this event include *Ursuline Convent at Charlestown, Trial of John R. Buzzell, Before the Supreme Judicial Court of Massachusetts. . . .* (Boston: Russell, Odiorne, and Metcalf, 1834); and *The Charlestown Convent; Its Destruction by a Mob.* Secondary treatments include Wilfred J. Bisson, *Countdown to Violence: The Charlestown Convent Riot of 1834* (New York: Garland, 1989); and Ray Allen Billington, *The Protestant Crusade, 1800–1860* (New York: Macmillan, 1938), 68–92. The best and most extensive is Nancy Lusignan Schultz, *Fire and Roses: The Burning of the Charlestown Convent, 1834* (New York: Free Press, 2000). The Catholic University of America also maintains an extensive digital archive called "The Ursuline Convent Charlestown, Mass. Collection," http://www.aladin0.wrlc.org/gsdl/collect/ursuline/ursuline.shtml.
2. Paul A. Gilje, *Rioting in America* (Bloomington: Indiana Univ. Press, 1996), 184; David Grimsted, "Rioting in Its Jacksonian Setting," *American Historical Review* 77, no. 2 (April 1972): 364; and Allan Nevins, ed., *The Diary of Philip Hone, 1828–1851* (New York: Dodd, Meade, 1927), 1:134.
3. William Ellery Channing, *Memoir of William Ellery Channing* (Boston: Wm. Crosby and H. P. Nichols, 1848), 3:245.
4. *Niles' Weekly Register*, August 8, 1835, 48:397, quoted in "Rioting in Its Jacksonian Setting," Grimsted, 374.
5. Committee report from Monroe, Oneida, and Onondaga counties, quoted in the New York State Assembly, March 9, 1838, in *Documents of the Assembly of the State of New York, Sixty-First Session, 1838* (Albany, NY: E. Croswell, 1838), 5.241.3. See also Carl E. Prince, "The Great 'Riot Year': Jacksonian Democracy and Patterns of Violence in 1834," *Journal of the Early Republic* 5, no. 1 (Spring 1985). Some blamed this "mobocracy" on President Andrew Jackson, whose 1829 presidential inauguration turned into something of a riot itself, and it was not uncommon for rioters in the 1830s to justify their rioting via Jackson's campaign slogans ("Let the people rule") or other mantras of popular sovereignty ("Resistance to tyrants is obedience to God"). Eventually, this epidemic got so bad that it troubled even Jackson himself. "This spirit of mob-law is becoming too

common and must be checked," he wrote in an 1835 letter, "or ere long it will become as great an evil as servile war, and the innocent will be much exposed" (Jackson to Amos Kendall, August 9, 1835, in *Correspondence of Andrew Jackson*, eds. J. S. Bassett and J. F. Jameson [Washington, DC: Carnegie Institution of Washington, 1926–1935], 5:360). Lincoln later described the mob spirit as an "ill-omen" creeping across America. "Accounts of outrages committed by mobs, form the every-day news of the times," he wrote. "They have pervaded the country, from New England to Louisiana;—they are neither peculiar to the eternal snows of the former, nor the burning suns of the latter;—they are not the creature of climate— neither are they confined to the slaveholding, or the non-slaveholding States. Alike, they spring up among the pleasure hunting masters of Southern slaves, and the order loving citizens of the land of steady habits. Whatever, then, their cause may be, it is common to the whole country" (Abraham Lincoln, "The Perpetuation of Our Political Institutions," address to the Young Men's Lyceum of Springfield, Illinois, January 27, 1838, TeachingAmericanHistory.org, http://teachingamericanhistory .org/library/index.asp?document=157).

6. For a dissenting view of the working-class nature of the mob, see Daniel A. Cohen, "Passing the Torch: Boston Firemen, 'Tea Party' Patriots, and the Burning of the Charlestown Convent," *Journal of the Early Republic* 24, no. 4 (Winter 2004): 527–86. Cohen believes the rioters "represented 'a broad economic cross section' of white Protestant men" (532).

7. Jenny Franchot calls this "chivalric nativism" in her *Roads to Rome: The Antebellum Protestant Encounter with Catholicism* (Berkeley: Univ. of California Press, 1994), 140.

8. Both handbills are quoted in *The Works of the Right Rev. John England*, ed. Ignatius Aloysius Reynolds (Baltimore: John Murphy, 1849), 5:260.

9. Quoted in "'Saving the West from the Pope': Anti-Catholic Propaganda and the Settlement of the Mississippi River Valley," by Bryan Le Beau, *American Studies* 32, no. 1 (Spring 1991): 108.

10. Lyman Beecher, *A Plea for the West* (New York: Leavitt, Lord, 1835), 131, 105.

11. See Nathan O. Hatch, *The Democratization of American Christianity* (New Haven, CT: Yale Univ. Press, 1989).

12. Samuel Adams to John Scollay, December 30, 1780, in *The Writings of Samuel Adams*, ed. Harry Alonzo Cushing (New York: G. P. Putnam's Sons, 1904–8), 4:238.

13. *Public Ledger*, June 8, 1844, quoted in *The Philadelphia Riots of 1844: A Study of Ethnic Conflict*, by Michael Feldberg (Westport, CT: Greenwood, 1975), 95.

14. On convent horror and Indian captivity narratives see Franchot, *Roads to Rome*, xxv and throughout.

15. *Trial of John R. Buzzell*, 21.

16. United States Catholic Historical Society, "Destruction of the Charlestown Convent: Statement by the Leader of the Knownothing Mob," *Historical Records and Studies* 12 (New York: June 1918), 73.

17. Cohen, "Passing the Torch," 548, 541.

18. "Ursuline Convent at Charlestown, Mass.," *Niles' Weekly Register*, August 23, 1834, 46:437.

19. United States Catholic Historical Society, "Destruction of the Charlestown Convent: Stories of the Outrage from Contemporaneous Newspaper Files," *Historical Records and Studies* 13 (New York: May 1919): 115. Fenwick also preached the next Sunday at the Church of the Holy Cross on "Father, forgive them; for they know not what they do" ("Miscellaneous," *Niles' Weekly Register*, August 30, 1834, 46:442).

20. "The Outrage," *Boston Evening Transcript*, August 13, 1834, Gilder Lehrman Center, Yale University, http://www.yale.edu/glc/archive/950.htm.

21. Caleb Stetson, *A Discourse on the Duty of Sustaining the Laws, Occasioned by the Burning of the Ursuline Convent. . . .* (Boston: Hilliard, Gray, 1834), 12, 7. Cleverly, Stetson drew on anti-Catholic stereotypes to oppose anti-Catholic violence. "Do you wish to introduce a Protestant inquisition," he asked, "to establish a religion by law—crush all dissenters from the legal faith, and bring back the age of persecution for opinion?" (14).

22. "The Late Outrage at Charlestown," *Christian Examiner and General Review* 17, no. 1 (September 1834): 131–33.

23. "The Late Outrage at Charlestown," 133.

24. "Great Meeting at Faneuil Hall," *Boston Evening Transcript*, August 12, 1834, Gilder Lehrman Center, Yale University, http://www.yale.edu/glc/archive/951.htm.

25. United States Catholic Historical Society, "Destruction of the Charlestown Convent," 119.

26. Signs quoted in *The Works of the Right Rev. John England*, Reynolds, 5:260.

27. United States Catholic Historical Society, "Destruction of the Charlestown Convent," 71.

28. Franchot, *Roads to Rome*, 140.

29. *Trial of John R. Buzzell*, 32, 33.

30. United States Catholic Historical Society, "Destruction of the Charlestown Convent," 74.

31. "Ursuline Convent at Charlestown: Report of the Committee Relating to the Destruction of the Ursuline Convent, August 11, 1834," in *Niles' Weekly Register*, October 11, 1834, 47:96.

32. Michael Feldberg, *The Turbulent Era: Riot and Disorder in Jacksonian America* (New York: Oxford Univ. Press, 1980).

33. Cohen, "Alvah Kelley's Cow," 558.

34. Arthur Schlesinger Sr. conversation with John Tracy Ellis, recalled in *American Catholicism*, by John Tracy Ellis, 2nd ed. (Chicago: Univ. of Chicago Press, 1969), 151.

35. John Higham, *Send These to Me: Jews and Other Immigrants in Urban America* (New York: Atheneum, 1985), 68. Two books arguing for anti-Catholicism's persistence are Philip Jenkins, *The New Anti-Catholicism: The Last Acceptable Prejudice* (New York: Oxford Univ. Press, 2003); and Mark Massa, *Anti-Catholicism in America: The Last Acceptable Prejudice* (New York: Crossroad, 2003).

36. Luther and the historian quoted in *Protestant Crusade*, Billington, 3.
37. James Davis Knowles, *Memoir of Roger Williams* (Boston: Lincoln, Edmands, 1834), 311. A table of religious restrictions on voting and office holding in colonial America can be found in Ralph E. Pyle and James D. Davidson, "The Origins of Religious Stratification in Colonial America," *Journal for the Scientific Study of Religion* 42, no. 1 (March 2003): 66–68. Ray Billington provides a comprehensive narrative in his *Protestant Crusade*, 1–31.
38. John Winthrop, "A Modell of Christian Charity" (1630), Collections of the Massachusetts Historical Society (Boston: 1838), https://history .hanover.edu/texts/winthmod.html.
39. Pauline Maier, "The Pope at Harvard: The Dudleian Lectures, Anti-Catholicism, and the Politics of Protestantism," *Proceedings of the Massachusetts Historical Society* 97 (1985): 18.
40. Cushing, *The Writings of Samuel Adams*, 1:203.
41. "The Declaration and Resolves of the First Continental Congress: Address to the People of Great Britain, 1774," UShistory.org, http://www.ushistory .org/declaration/related/decres.htm#peoplegb. Citing this letter, some have argued that the Quebec Act was *the* cause of the American Revolution. According to Benedictine historian Cardinal Francis Gasquet, that war "was not a movement for civil and religious liberty; its principal cause was the bigoted rage of the American Puritan and Presbyterian ministers at the concession of full religious liberty and equality to Catholics of French Canada." See Gasquet, "The Price of Catholic Freedom in Canada," in *The Tablet* (London), July 27, 1912.
42. John Adams, *The Works of John Adams*, ed. Charles Francis Adams (Boston: Little, Brown, 1851), 3:450, 453.
43. Jefferson to Alexander von Humboldt, December 6, 1813, and Jefferson to Horatio Spafford, March 17, 1814, in *The Writings of Thomas Jefferson*, eds. Andrew A. Lipscomb and Albert Ellery Bergh (Washington, DC: Thomas Jefferson Memorial Association, 1905), 13:21, 119.
44. Billington, *Protestant Crusade*, 32.
45. On immigration data, see "U.S. Immigrants and Emigrants: 1820–1998" (Table Ad1–2) and "Immigrants, by Country of Last Residence—Europe: 1820–1997" (Table Ad106–120), both in *Historical Statistics of the United States, Earliest Times to the Present: Millennial Edition*, eds. Susan B. Carter et al. (New York: Cambridge Univ. Press, 2006).
46. On Catholic data, see Jay P. Dolan, *The American Catholic Experience: A History from Colonial Times to the Present* (Garden City, NY: Doubleday, 1985), 160–61.
47. Civis [pseud.], *Romanism Incompatible with Republican Institutions* (New York: American Protestant Society, 1845), 11.
48. Susan M. Griffin, "Awful Disclosures: Women's Evidence in the Escaped Nun's Tale," *Publications of the Modern Language Association* 111, no. 1 (January 1996): 93.
49. Billington, *Protestant Crusade*, 53.

50. "American citizens! . . . A Paper Entitled The American Patriot," published by J. E. Farwell, Library of Congress website, http://loc.gov/pictures/resource/cph.3b42500/.

51. W. C. Brownlee, *Popery: An Enemy to Civil and Religious Liberty* (New York: John S. Taylor, 1836), 67; William Hogan, *High and Low Mass in the Roman Catholic Church* (Boston: Jordan and Wiley, 1846), 108; and One of 'Em [pseud.], ed., *The Wide-Awake Gift: A Know-Nothing Token for 1855* (New York: J. C. Derby, 1855), 98. All quoted in *Protestant Crusade*, Billington, 355, 367.

52. Franchot, *Roads to Rome*, xxii.

53. Both books prompted conflicting responses. Mount Benedict's Mary Anne Moffatt wrote *An Answer to Six Months in a Convent, Exposing Its Falsehoods and Manifold Absurdities. . . .* (Boston: J. H. Eastburn, 1835), to which Rebecca Reed responded with *A Supplement to "Six Months in a Convent"* (Boston: Russell, Odiorne, and Metcalf, 1835). Books attempting to capitalize on the popularity of *Awful Disclosures* include Maria Monk (and J. J. Slocum), *Further Disclosures by Maria Monk. . . .* (New York: J. J. Slocum, 1836); and William L. Stone, *Maria Monk's Show-Up!!!; or, The "Awful Disclosures," a Humbug* (New York: Go-Ahead Press, [1836?]).

54. Maria Monk, *Awful Disclosures, by Maria Monk, of the Hotel Dieu Nunnery of Montreal*, 2nd ed. (London: James S. Hodson, 1837), 47.

55. Arthur B. Cross, *Priests' Prisons for Women. . . .* (Baltimore: Sherwood, 1854).

56. Franchot, *Roads to Rome*, 197. See also David Brion Davis, who describes Masons, Catholics, and Mormons as "both frightening and fascinating" in "Some Themes of Counter-Subversion: An Analysis of Anti-Masonic, Anti-Catholic, and Anti-Mormon Literature," *Mississippi Valley Historical Review* 47, no. 2 (September 1960): 208.

57. John Adams to Abigail Adams, October 9, 1774, in *The Letters of John and Abigail Adams*, ed. Frank Shuffelton (New York: Penguin, 2004), 27.

58. David Harry Bennett, *The Party of Fear: From Nativist Movements to the New Right in American History* (Chapel Hill: Univ. of North Carolina Press, 188), 86.

59. Brutus [Samuel F. B. Morse], *Foreign Conspiracy Against the Liberties of the United States* (New York: Leavitt, Lord, 1835), 25, 118.

60. [Morse], *Foreign Conspiracy*, 59, 53, 66; An American [Samuel F. B. Morse], *Imminent Dangers to the Free Institutions of the United States Through Foreign Immigration* (New York: E. B. Clayton, 1835), 12; and [Morse], *Foreign Conspiracy*, 7, 70.

61. [Morse], *Imminent Dangers*, 13, 10, 11.

62. [Morse], *Imminent Dangers*, 12, 13.

63. [Morse], *Imminent Dangers*, 12.

64. In *Rhetorical Campaigns of the Nineteenth Century: Anti-Catholics and Catholics in America* (Lewiston, NY: Edwin Mellen, 1999), Jody M. Roy distinguishes between the "assimilationist" rhetoric of Orestes Brownson and the "confrontational" rhetoric of John Hughes.

65. Orestes A. Brownson, *The Works of Orestes A. Brownson* (Detroit: Thorndike Nourse, 1885), 18:289, 291, 324.

66. John R. G. Hassard, *Life of the Most Reverend John Hughes* (New York: D. Appleton, 1866), 105, 107.

67. *Freeman's Journal*, January 21, 1843, and Hughes, quoted in *Protestant Crusade*, Billington, 158, 231. Hughes was referring to the burning of Moscow by Russians in the face of an advancing Napoleon in 1812.

68. American Protestant Association poster quoted in "For the Honor and Glory of God: The Philadelphia Bible Riots of 1840," by Vincent P. Lannie and Bernard C. Diethorn, *History of Education Quarterly* 8, no. 1 (Spring 1968): 62.

69. Bishop Kenrick to the board of controllers of the public schools, November 14, 1842, in *United States Catholic Magazine* 2 (February 1843): 125–26.

70. Rev. Walter Colton, "The Bible in Public Schools," *Quarterly Review of the American Protestant Association* 1 (January 1844): 22.

71. January 10, 1843, resolution, in *Twenty-Sixth Annual Report of the Controllers of the Public Schools of the City and County of Philadelphia* (Philadelphia: Board of Controllers, 1844), 6.

72. L. Giustiniani, *Intrigues of Jesuitism in the United States of America*, 7th ed. (New York: printed for the author by R. Craighead, 1846), 168.

73. American Protestant Association, *Address of the Board of Managers of the American Protestant Association; with the Constitution and Organization of the Association* (Philadelphia: American Protestant Association, 1843), 7.

74. Giustiniani, *Intrigues of Jesuitism*, 169.

75. *New York Observer*, March 16, 1844, quoted in *Protestant Crusade*, Billington, 222.

76. *Presbyterian*, March 16, 1844, quoted in "For the Honor and Glory of God," Lannie and Diethorn, 66.

77. *Native American*, May 6, 1844, quoted in "For the Honor and Glory of God," Lannie and Diethorn, 73.

78. Billington, *Protestant Crusade*, 224.

79. "George Shiffler," song sheet, printed by G. S. Harris, Philadelphia, 1844, Library of Congress website, http://www.loc.gov/item/amss000431/.

80. *Native American*, May 7, 1844, quoted in *Protestant Crusade*, Billington, 225.

81. "Foreign News: America," in *Gentleman's Magazine* 177 (July 1844): 80.

82. *Native American*, May 9, 1844, quoted in *Protestant Crusade*, Billington, 226.

83. Giustiniani, *Intrigues of Jesuitism*, 170.

84. *Spirit of the Times*, May 9, 1844, and *Pennsylvania Freeman*, May 9, 1844, quoted in "For the Honor and Glory of God," Lannie and Diethorn, 78.

85. *Public Ledger*, July 19, 1844, quoted in "Violence in Philadelphia in the 1840s and 1850s," by Elizabeth M. Geffen, *Pennsylvania History* 36, no. 4 (October 1969): 403–4.

86. "The Philadelphia Anti-Catholic Riots," *United States Catholic Magazine and Monthly Review* 3 (June 1844): 379.

87. *North American*, May 21, 1844, in "For the Honor and Glory of God," Lannie and Diethorn, 79.
88. Feldberg, *The Turbulent Era*, 3.
89. Gilje, *Rioting in America*, 10.
90. "Design of the American Protestant," *American Protestant Magazine* 1, no. 1 (June 1845): 2. "We rather pity than censure the great mass of these deluded men," the magazine wrote of the "Romanists."
91. Lawrence Kehoe, ed., *Complete Works of the Most Rev. John Hughes, D.D., Archbishop of New York* (New York: Catholic Publication House, 1864), 2:101.
92. Samuel Irenaeus Prime, *Memoirs of the Rev. Nicholas Murray, D.D. (Kirwan.)* (New York: Harper & Brothers, 1863), 310.
93. Prime, *Memoirs of the Rev. Nicholas Murray*, 309–10.
94. Harriet Beecher Stowe, "What Will the American People Do?" *New-York Evangelist* 17 (January 29 and February 5, 1846), quoted in *Mightier than the Sword: "Uncle Tom's Cabin" and the Battle for America*, by David S. Reynolds (New York: W. W. Norton, 2011), 32.
95. Bennett, *The Party of Fear*, 90, 118.
96. Anti-convent tales of the 1850s include Charles W. Frothingham, *The Convent's Doom: A Tale of Charlestown in 1834* (Boston: Graves & Weston, 1854); and Josephine M. Bunkley, *The Testimony of an Escaped Novice from the Sisterhood of St. Joseph, Emmitsburg, Maryland* (New York: Harper & Brothers, 1855).
97. A Native Protestant [pseud.], "Violence the Natural Consequence of the Know Nothing Organization and Doctrines," in *Washington Union*, reprinted in *A Biographical Sketch of Henry A. Wise*, by James P. Hambleton (Richmond, VA: J. W. Randolph, 1856), 328.
98. Alessandro Gavazzi et al., *Father Gavazzi's Lectures in New York*, 3rd ed. (New York: De Witt and Davenport, 1853), 77. In culture wars style, Gavazzi described himself as a "soldier" who "came here to excite the Americans for war" (79).
99. Gavazzi quoted in "Know-Nothings, Nationhood, and the Nuncio: Reassessing the Visit of Archbishop Bedini," by David J. Endres, *U.S. Catholic Historian* 21, no. 4 (Fall 2003): 7; and Bedini quoted in *Protestant Crusade*, Billington, 303.
100. Billington, *Protestant Crusade*, 345.
101. Billington, *Protestant Crusade*, 386.
102. The Know-Nothing "Ritual" quoted in *A Biographical Sketch of Henry A. Wise*, Hambleton, 51.
103. Witte quoted in *Journal of the House of Representatives of the United States* 50 (February 5, 1855): 313–14.
104. Seward and other New York legislators quoted in *The Party of Fear*, Bennett, 121.
105. A Native Protestant [pseud.], "Violence the Natural Consequence," in *A Biographical Sketch of Henry A. Wise*, Hambleton, 329–30. Ralph Waldo Emerson's critique was pithier. The Know-Nothings are "an immense joke," he said, and to vote for them was to put your head in a bag (Em-

erson antislavery lecture, January 26, 1855, quoted in "A Know-Nothing Legislature," by George H. Haynes, *New England Magazine* 2, no. 1 [March 1897]: 27).

106. Hambleton, *A Biographical Sketch of Henry A. Wise*, 8, 14.

107. Hambleton, *A Biographical Sketch of Henry A. Wise*, 9, 12, 25.

108. Hambleton, *A Biographical Sketch of Henry A. Wise*, 26, 354, 20.

109. Hambleton, *A Biographical Sketch of Henry A. Wise*, 112.

110. Hambleton, *A Biographical Sketch of Henry A. Wise*, 24, 12. Wise also confessed to being a proud Virginian, a proud Protestant, and a proud American who saw "the freedom of opinion and the liberty of conscience" as the "essence in Americanism" (13). And all this from a slaveholder and future Confederate general who served as the governor of Virginia during the raid of abolitionist John Brown on Harper's Ferry in 1859.

111. *Fremont's Romanism Established. Acknowledged by Archbishop Hughes.* . . . [1856], 11, 4, Internet Archive, http://www.archive.org/stream /fremontsromanism00slsnrich#page/n1/mode/2.

112. *Col. Fremont Not a Roman Catholic* [1856?], Schoenberg Center for Electronic Text and Image, http://sceti.library.upenn.edu/sceti/printedbooks New/index.cfm?TextID=73540_O&PagePosition=1.

113. On this episode, see Elizabeth Fenton, *Religious Liberties: Anti-Catholicism and Liberal Democracy in Nineteenth-Century U.S. Literature and Culture* (New York: Oxford Univ. Press, 2011), 96–101.

114. *New-York Mirror* quoted in *Washington Evening Star*, November 3, 1856, quoted in *The Origins of the Republican Party, 1852–1856*, by William E. Gienapp (New York: Oxford Univ. Press, 1987), 371.

115. Gilje, *Rioting in America*, 67.

116. *The Pope's Dream—A Roman Catholic America*, illustration, *Puck*, July 24, 1889, Library of Congress website, http://www.loc.gov/pictures /resource/cph.3b01146/.

117. Will Herberg, *Protestant-Catholic-Jew: An Essay in American Religious Sociology* (New York: Doubleday, 1955), 98, 101, 90.

118. Abraham Lincoln, "Inaugural Address," March 4, 1865, American Presidency Project, http://www.presidency.ucsb.edu/ws/index.php?pid=25819.

CHAPTER 3: THE MORMON QUESTION

1. Joseph Smith, *General Smith's Views of the Powers and Policy of the Government of the United States* (Nauvoo, IL: printed by John Taylor, 1844), 9.

2. "Resolutions," *Nauvoo Expositor*, June 7, 1844, 2, Special Collections, SolomonSpalding.com, http://www.solomonspalding.com/docs/exposit1 .htm.

3. On the history of anti-Mormonism, see Patrick Q. Mason, *The Mormon Menace: Violence and Anti-Mormonism in the Postbellum South* (New York: Oxford Univ. Press, 2011); J. Spencer Fluhman, *"A Peculiar People": Anti-Mormonism and the Making of Religion in Nineteenth-Century America* (Chapel Hill: Univ. of North Carolina Press, 2012); J. B. Haws, *The Mormon Image in the American Mind: Fifty Years of Public Perception* (New

York: Oxford Univ. Press, 2013); Christine Talbot, *A Foreign Kingdom: Mormons and Polygamy in American Political Culture, 1852–1890* (Urbana: Univ. of Illinois Press, 2013); Sarah B. Gordon, *The Mormon Question: Polygamy and Constitutional Conflict in Nineteenth-Century America* (Chapel Hill: Univ. of North Carolina Press, 2001); and Terryl L. Givens, *The Viper on the Hearth: Mormons, Myths, and the Construction of Heresy* (New York: Oxford Univ. Press, 1997).

4. "Golden Bible," *Palmyra Freeman*, August 11, 1829, Rev. Sidney Rigdon Memorial Web-Site, http://www.sidneyrigdon.com/dbroadhu/NY/wayn1830.htm#081129.

5. "Blasphemy—'The Book of Mormon,' Alias The Golden Bible," *Rochester Daily Advertiser and Telegraph*, April 2, 1830, Rev. Sidney Rigdon Memorial Web-Site, http://www.sidneyrigdon.com/dbroadhu/NY/miscNYSf.htm#040230.

6. "The Book of Pukei—Chap. 1," *The Reflector*, June 12, 1830, 36–37, Rev. Sidney Rigdon Memorial Web-Site, http://www.sidneyrigdon.com/dbroadhu/NY/wayn1830.htm#061230; and *The Reflector*, January 1, 1831, Rev. Sidney Rigdon Memorial Web-Site, http://www.sidneyrigdon.com/dbroadhu/NY/wayn1830.htm#010131a.

7. "Mormon Emigration," *The Telegraph* (Painesville, OH), May 17, 1831, Rev. Sidney Rigdon Memorial Web-Site, http://www.sidneyrigdon.com/dbroadhu/OH/paintel2.htm#051731.

8. For an early use of the term "Mormonites," see Alexander Campbell, "An Analysis of the Book of Mormon. . . . ," *Millennial Harbinger*, February 7, 1831, LDS-Mormon.com, http://www.lds-mormon.com/campbell.shtml. Before the end of the year this coinage would find its way into an encyclopedia. See Francis Lieber, ed., *Encyclopaedia Americana* (Philadelphia: Carey and Lea, 1831), 8:492.

9. Willard Richards journal, February 16, 1847, Church History Library, Church of Jesus Christ of Latter-day Saints, Salt Lake City, UT, quoted in *Brigham Young: Pioneer Prophet*, John G. Turner (Cambridge, MA: Harvard Univ. Press, 2012), 161.

10. Joseph Smith—History, 1:18, Church of Jesus Christ of Latter-day Saints website, https://www.lds.org/scriptures/pgp/js-h/1.18,19?lang=eng.

11. "The Articles of Faith," Church of Jesus Christ of Latter-day Saints website, https://www.lds.org/scriptures/pgp/a-of-f/1.8?lang=eng.

12. "Kentucky Mob Cuts Down Mormon Church," *Atlanta Constitution*, August 5, 1899, quoted in *The Mormon Menace*, Mason, 138.

13. "From Rev. B. F. Morris, Warsaw, Illinois," in *Home Missionary* 14, no. 7 (November 1841): 149.

14. *Sparta Ishmaelite*, reprinted in "Mormonism and the Remedy," *Atlanta Constitution*, August 23, 1879, quoted in *The Mormon Menace*, Mason, 30.

15. Edje Jeter, "Graphical Images of Horned Mormons," *Juvenile Instructor*, November 10, 2013, http://www.juvenileinstructor.org/graphical-images-of-horned-mormons/.

16. James A. Garfield, "Inaugural Address," March 4, 1881, American Presidency Project, www.presidency.ucsb.edu/ws/index.php?pid=25823.

17. Orson Pratt, "Farewell Message of Orson Pratt," November 8, 1845, *Times and Seasons* (Nauvoo, IL: John Taylor, 1845), 6:1042; Brigham Young in *Salt Lake City Herald*, April 10, 1869, quoted in *The Lion of the Lord: A Biography of Brigham Young*, by Stanley P. Hirshson (New York: Knopf, 1969), 278–79; and Wilford Woodruff, "Epistle of Elder Wilford Woodruff," *Millennial Star*, April 21, 1879, 243. In 1858, Brigham Young opined that both President Polk and President Taylor were "weltering in hell" ("Remarks by President Brigham Young," *Millennial Star*, January 16, 1858, 33).

18. Mason, *The Mormon Menace*, 44.

19. Jesse Townsend letter, August 16, 1834, reprinted in "Mormonism," *Sackets Harbor Courier*, August 1834, Rev. Sidney Rigdon Memorial Web-Site, http://www.sidneyrigdon.com/dbroadhu/NY/miscNYSb.htm#080034.

20. Alexander Campbell, *Delusions: An Analysis of the Book of Mormon* (Boston: Benjamin H. Greene, 1832), 15, 11, 13.

21. E. D. Howe, *Mormonism Unvailed* (Painesville, OH: E. D. Howe, 1834), 145.

22. John C. Bennett, *The History of the Saints; or, An Exposé of Joe Smith and Mormonism* (Boston: Leland & Whiting, 1842), 5–6. Later in his *History*, Bennett calls Smith "the Pontifical Head of the Mormon Harem" (254).

23. Thomas Nast, *Religious Liberty Is Guaranteed but Can We Allow Foreign Reptiles to Crawl All Over Us?* illustration, Library of Congress website, http://www.loc.gov/pictures/resource/cai.2a14002.

24. "The American Nation and Tribes Are Not Jews," *Atlantic Journal and Friend of Knowledge* 1, no. 1 (Spring 1832): 98; and "The Yankee Mahomet," *American Whig Review* 13, no. 78 (June 1851): 554–64.

25. Reverend S. G. Wright quoted in "Correspondence of the A.H.M.S.," *Home Missionary* 14, no. 4 (August 1841): 81.

26. John C. Bennett to General James Gordon Bennett, August 27, 1842, in *The History of the Saints*, Bennett, 151.

27. "Affidavit of Thomas B. Marsh," Richmond, Missouri, October 24, 1838, *Document Containing the Correspondence, Orders, &C. in Relation to the Disturbances with the Mormons. . . .* (Fayette, MO: Boon's Lick Democrat, 1841), 58. Also in *Document*, John Corrill (another disaffected Mormon) attributes a similar quote to Smith: "If the people would let us alone, we would preach the gospel to them in peace; but, if they came on us to molest us, we would establish our religion by the sword; and that he would become to this generation a second Mahomet" (111).

28. Quoted in "Mormonism," *Western Monitor*, August 2, 1833, reprinted in *The History of Jackson County, Missouri* (Kansas City: Union Historical Company, 1881), 254. Marvin S. Hill observes that the causes of anti-Mormonism differed by locale. See his *Quest for Refuge: The Mormon Flight from American Pluralism* (Salt Lake City: Signature Books, 1989). Some historians are convinced that hostility to the Mormons was largely religious. See Fluhman, *"A Peculiar People."* Others agree with Kenneth H. Winn, who argues in *Exiles in a Land of Liberty: Mormons in America, 1830–1846* (Chapel Hill: Univ. of North Carolina Press, 1989) that "the

majority of those who opposed the Mormon Church did so for nonreligious reasons" (64).

29. Alphonso Wetmore, comp., *Gazetteer of the State of Missouri* (St. Louis: C. Keemle, 1837), 94.

30. Sidney Rigdon, *Oration Delivered by Mr. S. Rigdon on the 4th of July at Far West, Caldwell County, Missouri* (Far West, MO: Journal Office, 1838), 12.

31. "Mormon Extermination Order," October 27, 1838, Quaqua Society website, http://www.quaqua.org/extermination.htm. This order was rescinded in 1976 by Missouri governor Christopher Bond.

32. The "sinned against" article was widely reprinted in venues such as *New York Gazette and General Advertiser* (November 22, 1838); *American Sentinel* (Philadelphia: November 22, 1838); *The New-Yorker* (November 24, 1838); *Niagara Courier* (Lockport, NY: November 28, 1838); *Constitutionalist* (Bath, NY: November 28, 1838); and *Northampton Courier* (Northampton, MA: November 28, 1838). A similar sentiment appears in an account of a "state convention" held in Boston in support of Smith's run for the presidency. See "Mormon War in Boston," *New York Herald*, July 4, 1844, http://wiki.nycldshistory.com/w/1844-07-04 -New_York_Herald-Mormon_War_in_Boston.

33. William Henry Channing, "Outrages of Missouri Mobs on Mormons," *Western Messenger* 7, no. 3 (1839): 209–14.

34. R. Laurence Moore, *Religious Outsiders and the Making of Americans* (New York: Oxford Univ. Press, 1986), 31. Objecting to Moore's claim that Smith self-consciously employed a "rhetoric of deviance" (33), Givens claims that "Mormons engaged in a quite conscientious 'campaign of superior virtue,' by which they intended to persuade their compatriots that they were *not* social deviants, but rather more American than apple pie" (*Viper on the Hearth*, 17). I side here with Moore.

35. Brigham Young, April 9, 1844, speech in *Wilford Woodruff's Journal, 1833–1898: Typescript*, ed. Scott G. Kenney (Midvale, UT: Signature Books, 1983–84), 2:390, quoted in *Brigham Young*, Turner, 106.

36. Doctrine and Covenants, 130:22, Church of Jesus Christ of Latter-day Saints website, https://www.lds.org/scriptures/dc-testament/dc/130.22.

37. Joseph Smith, "The Globe," *Nauvoo Neighbor*, April 17, 1844, 2, http://boap.org/LDS/Nauvoo-Neighbor/1844/4-17-1844.pdf. On Smith's multiple marriages, see "Plural Marriage in Kirtland and Nauvoo," Church of Jesus Christ of Latter-day Saints website, https://www.lds.org/topics /plural-marriage-in-kirtland-and-nauvoo?lang=eng. This essay first appeared on the official LDS website in 2014.

38. Eliza R. Snow, "Let Us Go," in her *Poems, Religious, Historical, and Political* (London: Latter-day Saints' Book Depot, 1856), 1:147.

39. Harold Bloom, *The American Religion: The Emergence of the Post-Christian Nation* (New York: Simon & Schuster, 1992), 108.

40. Cong. Globe, 32d Cong., 1st Sess. 354 (January 24, 1852) ("Election of the Delegate from Utah," statement of Rep. David Cartter).

41. *Deseret News—Extra*, September 14, 1852, 14, 19.

42. *Deseret News—Extra*, September 14, 1852, 25–28.
43. Brigham Young, "Mormon History, Nov 16, 1847: Minutes, Quorum of Twelve," Mormon Church History, http://mormon-church-history.blogspot.com/2013/09/mormon-history-nov-16-1847_7903.html.
44. "From Utah: A Personal Interview with Brigham Young," *New York Times*, July 31, 1858, 1.
45. Edgar E. Folk, *The Mormon Monster; or, The Story of Mormonism* (Chicago: Fleming H. Revell, 1900), 273.
46. Robert Baird, *Religion in America. . . .* (New York: Harper & Brothers, 1844), 288.
47. Mason, *The Mormon Menace*, 155.
48. Cong. Globe (Appendix), 33d Cong., 1st Sess. 593 (May 4, 1854) ("Polygamy Hostile to Republican Institutions," statement of Rep. Hiram Walbridge).
49. "The Mormon Question: Shall We Admit into the Union an Anti-Christian and Barbarous State?" *Christian Advocate and Journal*, July 19, 1855, 114.
50. Cong. Globe, 36th Cong., 1st Sess. 1500 (April 2, 1860) (statement of Rep. Emerson Etheridge).
51. Barbee quoted in *The Mormon Menace*, Mason, 75.
52. Rabbi Louis Weiss letter to *Chattanooga Times*, August 3, 1899, quoted in "'Let Truth Stand If Heavens Fall': The 1899 Weiss-Rich Correspondence," by JB [pseud.], January 30, 2014, *Study and Faith* (blog), http://study-and-faith.blogspot.com/2014/01/let-truth-stand-if-heavens-fall-1899.html.
53. *Bangor Daily Whig and Courier*, April 18, 1857, 2.
54. Brigham Young, August 17, 1856, sermon, in *Journal of Discourses*, 4:32, Mormon Research Ministry, http://jod.mrm.org/4/20.
55. Robert Tyler to James Buchanan, April 27, 1857, reprinted in "President Buchanan Receives a Proposal for an Anti-Mormon Crusade, 1857," by David A. Williams, *BYU Studies* 14, no. 1 (1974): 103–5.
56. James Buchanan, "First Annual Message to Congress on the State of the Union," December 8, 1857, American Presidency Project, http://www.presidency.ucsb.edu/ws/index.php?pid=29498.
57. Brigham Young, "Remarks by President Brigham Young," *Millennial Star*, January 16, 1858, 33–34.
58. Brigham Young, *Proclamation by the Governor* (broadside), August 5, 1857, Internet Archive, http://archive.org/stream/proclamationbygo00youn#page/n0/mode/2up.
59. Brigham Young, *Proclamation by the Governor* (broadside), August 5, 1857, Internet Archive, http://archive.org/stream/proclamationbygo00youn#page/n0/mode/2up.
60. Patrick Mason, correspondence with author, April 10, 2014.
61. Cong. Globe, 33d Cong., 1st Sess. 1098, 1095, 1097 (May 4, 1854) (statements of Rep. John Goodrich, Rep. George Simmons, and Rep. Samuel Benson).

62. Cong. Globe, 36th Cong., 1st Sess. 1410 (March 28, 1860) (statement of Lawrence Branch).

63. Cong. Globe, 36th Cong., 1st Sess. 1500 (April 2, 1860) (statement of Emerson Etheridge).

64. Cong. Globe, 36th Cong., 1st Sess. 1099–100 (May 4, 1854) (statement of Rep. Laurence Keitt).

65. Cong. Globe, 33d Cong., 1st Sess. 1110, 1094 (May 4, 1854) (statement of Rep. William Boyce).

66. Cong. Globe, 33d Cong., 1st Sess. 1110, 1094 (May 4, 1854) (statement of Rep. Alexander Stephens).

67. Cong. Globe, 34th Cong., 3d Sess. 288–89 (February 2, 1857) (statement of Rep. Justin Morrill).

68. Lincoln quoted in *The "Americanization" of Utah for Statehood*, by Gustave O. Larson (San Marino, CA: Huntington Library, 1971), 60.

69. Abraham Lincoln, "The Emancipation Proclamation," January 1, 1863, U.S. National Archives and Records Administration, http://www .archives.gov/exhibits/featured_documents/emancipation_proclamation /transcript.html.

70. *Christian Index*, August 3, 1882, quoted in *The Mormon Menace*, Mason, 61; A. Conan Doyle, "A Study in Scarlet," in *Beetons Christmas Annual 1887* (London: Ward, Locke, 1887), 1–95; and Pope Leo XIII, "Arcanum," February 10, 1880, Libreria Editrice Vaticana, http://w2.vatican .va/content/leo-xiii/en/encyclicals/documents/hf_l-xiii_enc_10021880 _arcanum.html.

71. Historian Jan Shipps, who has charted American attitudes toward Mormons, describes 1881–1885 as the "lowest point in negative attitudes for the entire century." In his study of Southern anti-Mormonism, historian Patrick Mason sees violence against Mormons spiking in the South in the mid-1880s. See Jan Shipps, *Sojourner in the Promised Land: Forty Years Among the Mormons* (Urbana: Univ. of Illinois Press, 2000), 64; and Mason, *The Mormon Menace*, 130–32.

72. Mason, *The Mormon Menace*, 100.

73. Chester A. Arthur, "First Annual Message," December 6, 1881, American Presidency Project, http://www.presidency.ucsb.edu/ws/index .php?pid=29522.

74. "Mormonism," *Tennessee Baptist*, October 4, 1884, quoted in *The Mormon Menace*, Mason, 62.

75. John C. Bennett, *The History of the Saints; or, An Exposé of Joe Smith and Mormonism* (Boston: Leland & Whiting, 1842), 257. One scholar gives Bennett's exposé "the prize as the most entertaining and comprehensive nineteenth-century condemnation of Mormonism." See Stephen Eliot Smith, "Barbarians Within the Gates: Congressional Debates on Mormon Polygamy, 1850–1879," *Journal of Church and State* 51, no. 4 (Autumn 2009): 594.

76. Cong. Globe, 36th Cong., 1st Sess. 1514 (April 3, 1860) (statement of Rep. John McClernand).

77. Benjamin G. Ferris, *Utah and the Mormons: The History, Government, Doctrines, Customs, and Prospects of the Latterday Saints, from Personal Observations During a Six Months' Residence at Great Salt Lake City* (New York: Harper & Brothers, 1854), 247.
78. Eric A. Eliason, "Curious Gentiles and Representational Authority in the City of the Saints," *Religion and American Culture: A Journal of Interpretation* 11, no. 2 (Summer 2001): 159.
79. "The Mormon Problem Must Be Solved," *San Francisco Daily Evening Bulletin*, June 18, 1857.
80. Gregory Pingree, "'The Biggest Whorehouse in the World': Representations of Plural Marriage in Nineteenth-Century America," *Western Humanities Review* 50, no. 3 (Fall 1996): 213–32.
81. Jennie Fowler Willing, *On American Soil; or, Mormonism the Mohammedanism of the West* (Louisville, KY: Pickett, 1906), 15.
82. Mary W. Hudson, *Esther the Gentile* (Topeka, KS: G. W. Crane, 1888), 166.
83. "Is a Community Safe When Mormon Elders Are Allowed to Inhabit It?" *Alabama Baptist*, November 17, 1887, quoted in *The Mormon Menace*, Mason, 65; and Hudson, *Esther the Gentile*, 166.
84. *News and Observer* (Raleigh, NC), July 20, 1881, quoted in *The Mormon Menace*, Mason, 72.
85. "The Mormons," *Harper's Weekly*, April 25, 1857, 1.
86. Ann Eliza Young, *Wife No. 19* (Hartford, CT: Dustin, Gillman, 1875), 321.
87. Maria Ward, *Female Life Among the Mormons: A Narrative of Many Years' Personal Experience* (New York: J. C. Derby, 1855), 429. In a clear nod to Maria Monk's *Awful Disclosures*, later editions of this book included on the title page the phrase "Maria Ward's Disclosures."
88. Willing, *On American Soil*, 21–22.
89. Alfreda Eva Bell, *Boadicea: The Mormon Wife* (Baltimore: Arthur R. Orton, 1855), 54.
90. Young, *Wife No. 19*, 7, 32.
91. Harriet Beecher Stowe, preface to *"Tell It All": The Story of a Life's Experience in Mormonism*, by Mrs. T. B. H. Stenhouse (Hartford, CT: A. D. Worthington, 1874). Stowe concluded this preface by sending a prayer up to God the Liberator: "May He who came to break every yoke hasten this deliverance" (vi).
92. Harriet Beecher Stowe, "Women of America," *Anti-Polygamy Standard*, April 1880, 1.
93. Nancy Bentley, "Marriage as Treason: Polygamy, Nation, and the Novel," in *The Futures of American Studies*, eds. Donald Pease and Robyn Wiegman (Durham, NC: Duke Univ. Press, 2002), 347.
94. Barbara Welter, "The Cult of True Womanhood, 1820–1860," *American Quarterly* 18, no. 2 (Summer 1996): 151–74.
95. Bentley, "Marriage as Treason," 347.
96. "Consent is an obsessive theme of antipolygamy fiction," writes Nancy Bentley in "Marriage as Treason," 347.

97. Associate Judge W. W. Drummond quoted in "Dreadful State of Affairs in Utah," *New York Herald*, March 20, 1857.

98. William Harris, *Mormonism Portrayed* (Warsaw, IL: Sharp & Gamble, 1841), 15.

99. *Nauvoo Expositor*, June 7, 1844, 1–2, SolomonSpalding.com Special Collections, http://www.solomonspalding.com/docs/exposit1.htm. Smith's decision to destroy the *Nauvoo Expositor* printing press confirmed to many that he was intent on consolidating ecclesiastical and political power in a manner wholly incompatible with republicanism. To Thomas Sharp, this action by "Mormon Mobocrats" was a "most diabolical outrage" designed "to ROB men of their property and RIGHTS." "War and extermination" were now "inevitable," he said. "Let it be made WITH POWDER AND BALL!" ("Unparralled Outrage at Nauvoo," *Warsaw Signal*, June 12, 1844, Rev. Sidney Rigdon Memorial Web-Site, http://www.sidneyrigdon.com/dbroadhu/IL/sign1844.htm#0612).

100. Minutes of July 23, 1851, Box 2, Folder 31, General Church Minutes, CR 100 318, Church History Library, Church of Jesus Christ of Latter-day Saints, Salt Lake City, UT, quoted in *Brigham Young*, Turner, 201.

101. Cong. Globe (Appendix), 34th Cong., 2d Sess. 285 (February 23, 1857) ("Utah Territory and Its Laws—Polygamy and Its License," statement of Rep. Justin Morrill).

102. "Highly Interesting from Utah. . . ." *New York Times*, May 19, 1857, 1; and "The Mormon War," *New York Times*, November 19, 1857, 4.

103. Cong. Globe (Appendix), 34th Cong., 2d Sess. 289 (February 23, 1857) ("Utah Territory and Its Laws—Polygamy and Its License," statement of Rep. Justin Morrill).

104. Josiah Strong, *Our Country: Its Possible Future and Its Present Crisis* (New York: American Home Missionary Society, 1885), 60, 61, 66, 61, 64.

105. "The Mormon War," *New York Times*, November 19, 1857, 4.

106. Robert A. Wilson, *Mexico and Its Religion* (New York: Harper & Brothers, 1855), 291.

107. W. J. Scott, "Mormonism," *Quarterly Review of the Methodist Episcopal Church, South* 6, no. 3 (July 1884): 434.

108. Willing, *On American Soil*, 4, 30, 83–84.

109. E. W. Tullidge, "Views of 'Mormonism' and the 'Mormons,'" *Millennial Star*, February 2, 1861, 66–68. For an extended discussion of Mormonism and Islam, see Fluhman, *"A Peculiar People,"* 31–39.

110. Matilda Joslyn Gage, *Woman, Church and State* (Chicago: Charles H. Kerr, 1893), 408–9, 411.

111. Kate Field quoted in "Crimes Committed in Utah: Miss Kate Field Favors a National Marriage Law," *New York Times*, November 22, 1885, 7, and "Kate Field in the West," *Chicago Tribune*, February 25, 1887, 9.

112. Willing, *On American Soil*, 53.

113. "House Joint Memorial No. 1," House Committee on the Territories, Admission of Utah: Report of the Committee on Territories on the Admission of Utah as a State, to the House of Representatives, 50th Cong., 2d Sess., H.R. Rep. 4156, at 179 (1889).

114. Smith, "Barbarians Within the Gates," 595.
115. "Meddling with the Mormons," *Daily Graphic*, December 9, 1873, quoted in *Solemn Covenant: The Mormon Polygamous Passage*, by C. Carmon Hardy (Urbana: Univ. of Illinois, 1992), 59.
116. Metta Victoria Fuller, *Mormon Wives* (New York: Derby & Jackson, 1856), xi; Howe, *Mormonism Unvailed*, 74; Allen G. Campbell, "Has Utah a Republican Form of Government?" *Century Magazine*, March 1882, 716; and "Separate Report of John A. McClernand," *Report of the Secretary of the Interior for the Fiscal Year Ending June 30, 1889* (Washington, DC: Government Printing Office, 1890), 3:207.
117. "Kansas—The Mormons—Slavery: Speech of Senator Douglas," *New York Times*, June 23, 1857, 2.
118. See David J. Whittaker "Early Mormon Polygamy Defenses," *Journal of Mormon History* 11 (1984): 43–63; and David J. Whittaker, "The Bone in the Throat: Orson Pratt and the Public Announcement of Plural Marriage," *Western Historical Quarterly* 18 (July 1987): 293–314.
119. July 12, 1843, revelation, Doctrine and Covenants 132:6, Church of Jesus Christ of Latter-day Saints website, https://www.lds.org/scriptures/dc-testament/dc/132.
120. Annie Musser Sheets, "Mormonism Is Not Malevolence," *Deseret News*, June 10, 1885, 7.
121. "The Mormon Question," *New York Herald*, May 3, 1857.
122. Robert G. Ingersoll, *The Works of Robert G. Ingersoll*, ed. and comp. by David Widger (New York: Dresden, 1902), 8:260.
123. The Book of Mormon does allow for polygamy when it is commanded by God (Jacob 2:30).
124. Parley P. Pratt, *Marriages and Morals in Utah* (Liverpool, England: Orson Pratt, 1856), 8.
125. Belinda Marden Pratt, *Defence of Polygamy, by a Lady of Utah. . . .* (Salt Lake City: 1854), 5. This letter, originally dated January 12, 1854, was later reprinted in full in Richard Burton's *City of the Saints* (New York: Harper & Brothers, 1862).
126. Peggy Pascoe, *Relations of Rescue: The Search for Female Moral Authority in the American West, 1874–1939* (New York: Oxford Univ. Press, 1990), 67.
127. Woman speaker quoted in "Special Correspondence: Utah," by J. M. Coyner, *New England Journal of Education* 9, no. 6 (February 6, 1879): 90.
128. Cong. Globe (Appendix), 41st Cong., 2d Sess. 173–79 (March 23, 1870) ("Polygamy in Utah," statement of Rep. William Hooper).
129. Cong. Globe, 33d Cong., 1st Sess. 1112 (May 5, 1854) (statement of Rep. John Letcher).
130. A. S. Bailey, "Anti-American Influences in India," in *Christian Progress in Utah: The Discussions of the Christian Convention* (Salt Lake City: Frank H. Nelden, 1888), 19.
131. "Among the Mormons," *St. Louis Christian Advocate*, November 8, 1876, quoted in *The Mormon Menace*, Mason, 98–99.
132. Rev. William H. Strickland, "Mormonism," *Daily American*, August 25, 1884, quoted in *The Mormon Menace*, Mason, 47.

133. Joseph Belcher, *The Religious Denominations in the United States* (Philadelphia: J. E. Potter, 1854), 850, 862.

134. Schuyler Colfax, *The Mormon Question*. . . . (Salt Lake City: printed by Deseret News Office, 1870), 4, 7. Though no friend of religion, Mark Twain thought Colfax's argument was a joke. "Considering our complacent cant about this country of ours being the home of liberty of conscience, it seems to me that the attitude of our Congress and people toward the Mormon Church is matter for limitless laughter and derision," he wrote in an 1886 letter. "The Mormon religion *is* a religion . . . and so I shall probably always go on thinking that the attitude of our Congress and nation toward it is merely good trivial stuff to make fun of" (S. L. Clemens to Kate Field, March 8, 1886, in *Kate Field: A Record*, by Lilian Whiting [Boston: Little, Brown, 1900], 449).

135. Gordon, *The Mormon Question*, 13. See also Philip Hamburger, *Separation of Church and State* (Cambridge, MA: Harvard Univ. Press, 2002).

136. "The Mormon Question: Shall We Admit into the Union an Anti-Christian and Barbarous State?," 114.

137. Cong. Globe (Appendix), 34th Cong., 2d Sess. 288–89 (February 23, 1857) ("Utah Territory and Its Laws—Polygamy and Its License," statement of Rep. Justin S. Morrill).

138. Cong. Globe (Appendix), 34th Cong., 2d Sess. 288–89 (February 23, 1857) ("Utah Territory and Its Laws—Polygamy and Its License," statement of Rep. Justin Morrill).

139. Gordon, *The Mormon Question*, 157–58, 275.

140. John Taylor, August 20, 1882, Journal of Discourses 23:240–41, Mormon Research Ministry, http://jod.mrm.org/23/235.

141. "Official Declaration 1," Doctrine and Covenants, Church of Jesus Christ of Latter-day Saints website, https://www.lds.org/scriptures/dc-testament/od/1?lang=eng.

142. See D. Michael Quinn, "LDS Church Authority and New Plural Marriages, 1890–1904," *Dialogue: A Journal of Mormon Thought* 18, no. 1 (Spring 1985): 9–105.

143. See Cristine Hutchison-Jones, "Reviling and Revering the Mormons: Defining American Values, 1890–2008" (Ph.D. thesis, Boston University, 2011).

144. Jan Shipps, "From Satyr to Saint: American Perceptions of the Mormons, 1860–1960," in her *Sojourner in the Promised Land*, 51–97.

145. "The Mormons," *Harper's Weekly*, April 25, 1857, 1.

146. George F. Will, "The Mormons Have a Different Reality," *Boston Globe*, January 22, 1979, 10.

CHAPTER 4: PROHIBITION AND PLURALISM

1. "John Barleycorn's 'Wake' Very Wet," *Boston Globe*, January 16, 1920, 1.

2. *New York Herald*, January 15, 1920, quoted in *The Dry Decade*, by Charles Merz (Seattle: Univ. of Washington Press, 1969), 51.

3. "Bury John Barleycorn," *Los Angeles Times*, January 19, 1920, 2:5.

4. "Churches Hold J.B.'s Funeral; Cremate Effigy," *Chicago Daily Tribune*, January 19, 1920, 10.
5. William T. Ellis, *"Billy" Sunday: The Man and His Message* (Lima, OH: Webb Book and Bible, 1914), 87–88, 89, 91, 101–102.
6. "Billy Sunday Speeds Barleycorn to Grave: Preaches at Mock Obsequies, with Devil as Mourner, in Norfolk Tabernacle," *New York Times*, January 17, 1920, 3.
7. Ellis, *"Billy" Sunday*, 99. Hoover never called prohibition a "noble experiment." However, in an August 11, 1928, speech accepting the Republican Party nomination, he called it "a great social and economic experiment, noble in motive and far-reaching in purpose" (quoted in *Public Papers of the Presidents of the United States: Herbert Hoover, 1929* [Washington, DC: Office of the Federal Register, 1974], 511).
8. Norman H. Clark, *Deliver Us from Evil: An Interpretation of American Prohibition* (New York: W. W. Norton, 1976), 144.
9. "Southern Baptists," *Time*, May 26, 1930, 47.
10. Barbara Welter, "The Cult of True Womanhood: 1820–1860," *American Quarterly* 18, no. 2 (Summer 1966): 151–74. According to Lawrence Levine, the 1920s exemplified "the central paradox of American history": "a belief in progress coupled with a dread of change; an urge towards the inevitable future combined with a longing for the irretrievable past" (Lawrence W. Levine, *The Unpredictable Past: Explorations in American Cultural History* [New York: Oxford Univ. Press, 1993], 191). This "paradox" is not particularly paradoxical, however. It is yet another expression of the nation's liberal–conservative split.
11. Richard Hofstadter, *The Age of Reform* (New York: Vintage, 1960), 289–90.
12. Tim Stafford, "Gender Prohibition," *Books & Culture: A Christian Review*, May/June 2000, http://www.booksandculture.com/articles/2000/mayjun/8.26.html.
13. William J. Bryan, "The Case Against Alcohol," *The Commoner*, May 1915, reprinted in *Selected Articles on Prohibition of the Liquor Traffic*, ed. Lamar T. Beman (White Plains, NY: H. W. Wilson, 1917), 65–72; and Clarence Darrow, "The Ordeal of Prohibition," *American Mercury* 2 (August 1924): 419–27.
14. Virginius Dabney, *Dry Messiah: The Life of Bishop Cannon* (New York: Knopf, 1949), 181, 183; and *The Sun* (Baltimore), October 19, 1928, quoted in *Prohibition and Politics: The Life of Bishop James Cannon, Jr.*, by Robert A. Hohner (Columbia: Univ. of South Carolina Press, 1999), 227.
15. Michael Monahan, *Dry America* (New York: Nicholas L. Brown, 1921), 9.
16. Ellis, *"Billy" Sunday*, 90.
17. Alfred E. Smith, *Campaign Addresses of Governor Alfred E. Smith, Democratic Candidate for President* (Washington, DC: Democratic National Committee, 1929), 108, 216, 246, 247, 299.
18. Alfred E. Smith, "Catholic and Patriot," *The Atlantic*, May 1927, http://www.theatlantic.com/magazine/archive/1927/05/catholic-and-patriot/306522/.

19. "Ben M. Bogard's Speech in City Park, Little Rock," *Baptist and Commoner*, August 1, 1928, 5, quoted in *American Apocalypse: A History of Modern Evangelicalism*, by Matthew Avery Sutton (Cambridge, MA: Harvard Univ. Press, 2014), 204.

20. Fellowship Forum quoted in *God's Rascal: J. Frank Norris and the Beginnings of Southern Fundamentalism*, by Barry Hankins (Lexington: Univ. Press of Kentucky, 1996), 59.

21. Henry S. Clubb, *The Maine Liquor Law: Its Origin, History, and Results* (New York: Fowler and Wells, 1856), 5–6; and Clark, *Deliver Us from Evil*, 17. The data on *Arbella* alcohol is from Mark Edward Lender and James Kirby Martin, *Drinking in America: A History* (New York: Free Press, 1987), 2.

22. Martin Luther to Jerome Weller, July 1530, in *The Life and Letters of Martin Luther*, by Preserved Smith (Boston: Houghton Mifflin, 1911), 324.

23. Increase Mather, *Wo to Drunkards.* . . . (Cambridge, MA: printed by Marmaduke Johnson, 1673), 3–4.

24. Jessica Kross, *American Eras: The Colonial Era, 1600–1754* (Detroit: Gale Research, 1998), 300.

25. Clark, *Deliver Us from Evil*, 16.

26. Ian R. Tyrrell, *Sobering Up: From Temperance to Prohibition in Antebellum America, 1800–1860* (Westport, CT: Greenwood, 1979), 18; and W. J. Rorabaugh, *The Alcoholic Republic: An American Tradition* (New York: Oxford Univ. Press, 1979), 151.

27. Frederick Marryat's *A Diary in America* (Paris: Baudry's European Library, 1839), 45–47. See also Rorabaugh in *The Alcoholic Republic:* "Alcohol was pervasive in American society; it crossed regional, sexual, racial, and class lines. Americans drank at home and abroad, alone and together, at work and at play, in fun and in earnest. They drank from the crack of dawn to the crack of dawn. . . . From sophisticated Andover to frontier Illinois, from Ohio to Georgia, in lumbercamps and on satin settees, in log taverns and at fashionable New York hotels, the American greeting was, 'Come, Sir, take a dram first.'" (21).

28. Anthony Benezet, *The Mighty Destroyer Displayed.* . . . (Philadelphia: printed by Joseph Crukshank, 1774), 17, 8. Benezet also gave voice to American Indian opposition to strong drink, quoting Chief Scarrooyady as saying, "The rum ruins us: we beg you would prevent its coming in such quantities, by regulating the traders. We never understood the trade was for whiskey. We desire it may be forbidden . . . in the Indian country" (11–12).

29. Benjamin Rush, *An Inquiry into the Effects of Spirituous Liquors on the Human Body.* . . . (Boston: Thomas and Andrews, 1790), 12.

30. "On Intemperance," in *Tracts Published by the New England Tract Society* (Andover, MA: Flagg and Gould, 1814), 1:1–2.

31. John Ware, address to the Massachusetts Society for the Suppression of Intemperance, May 1825, in "Extracts from Dr. Ware's Address," in *Hopkinsian Magazine* 2, no. 4 (April 1826): 86–87.

32. Lyman Beecher, *Six Sermons on the Nature, Occasions, Signs, Evils, and Remedy of Intemperance* (New York: American Tract Society, 1827), 7–8, 52–53.

33. Abraham Lincoln, "Temperance Address: An Address, Delivered Before the Springfield Washington Temperance Society, on the 22d February 1842," in *The Collected Works of Abraham Lincoln*, ed. Roy P. Basler (New Brunswick, NJ: Rutgers Univ. Press, 1953), 1:271–79.

34. "Song of the Cold Water Army," in *Journal of the American Temperance Union* 8, no. 7 (July 1844): 104. This journal's motto was "Total Abstinence from All That Intoxicates."

35. J. W. Goodrich, *A Second Declaration of Independence; or, The Manifesto of all the Washington Total Abstinence Societies of the United States of America* (Worcester: printed by Spooner & Howland, 1841), 3.

36. L. M. Sargent, *Address, Delivered at the Beneficent Congregational Meeting House, July 4, 1838; Being the First Temperance Celebration of American Independence, in Providence* (Providence: B. Cranston, 1838), 4; and A. L. Stone, *Mr. Stone's Oration Before the Sons of Temperance, at Charlestown, N.H., July 4, 1850* (Boston: John P. Jewett, 1850), 9.

37. John W. Frick, *Theatre, Culture and Temperance Reform in Nineteenth-Century America* (New York: Cambridge Univ. Press, 2003), 73.

38. "Temperance Address," in *The Collected Works of Abraham Lincoln*, Basler, 1:279.

39. Rorabaugh, *The Alcoholic Republic*, 214.

40. Heman Humphrey, *Parallel Between Intemperance and the Slave-Trade* (New York: John P. Haven, 1828), 10, 12, 3, 2, 3, 11.

41. Frederick Douglass, *My Bondage and My Freedom* (New York: Miller, Orton & Mulligan, 1855), 256.

42. Mrs. F. E. W. Harper, "Symposium-Temperance," *African Methodist Episcopal Church Review* 7, no. 4 (April 1891): 373.

43. William Whipper, "Address Delivered Before the Colored Temperance Society of Philadelphia, January 8, 1834," in *The Liberator*, June 21, 1834, 100; June 28, 1834, 104; and July 5, 1834, 108, http://fair-use.org/the-liberator/.

44. "On Intemperance," in *Tracts Published by the New England Tract Society*, 1:29.

45. T. S. Arthur, *Ten Nights in a Bar-Room, and What I Saw There* (Boston: L. P. Crown; and Philadelphia: J. W. Bradley, 1854), 239.

46. *Laws for the Suppression of Drinking Houses and Tippling Shops* (Augusta, GA: William T. Johnson, 1853), 8.

47. "Ingersoll's Denunciation of Alcohol," *The Commoner*, July 11, 1913, 13, Chronicling America, Library of Congress website, http://chroniclingamerica.loc.gov/lccn/46032385/1913-07-11/ed-1/seq-13/.

48. Edward Huntington Williams, "What Shall We Do About It?" speech at the National Conference on Race Betterment, Battle Creek, Michigan, January 10, 1914, reprinted in *Selected Articles on Prohibition of the Liquor Traffic*, ed. Lamar T. Beman, 2nd ed. (New York: H. W. Wilson, 1917), 111.

49. 52 Cong. Rec. (63d Cong., 3d Sess.) H526 (December 22, 1914) (statement of Rep. Daniel Garrett).

50. Frick, *Theatre, Culture and Temperance Reform*, 74.

51. Nation quoted in *Carry Nation*, by Herbert Asbury (New York: Knopf, 1929), xvii; and in *Vessel of Wrath: The Life and Times of Carry Nation*, by Robert Lewis Taylor (New York: New American Library, 1966), 4.

52. "Mrs. Nation Angers a Coney Island Audience," *New York Times*, September 9, 1901, 1.

53. "The New Kansas 'Twister,'" *Los Angeles Times*, January 25, 1901, 8.

54. Nation quoted in "People and Events: Carrie Nation," American Experience website, www.pbs.org/wgbh/amex/1900/peopleevents/pande4.html.

55. H. L. Mencken, *A Mencken Chrestomathy* (New York: Knopf, 1949), 624.

56. Ronald G. Walters, *American Reformers: 1815–1860*, rev. ed. (New York: Hill and Wang, 1997), 143.

57. 52 Cong. Rec. (63d Cong., 3d Sess.) H569, 513, 594 (December 22, 1914) (statements of Rep. Percy Quin, Rep. Willis Hulings, and Rep. Hubert Stephens). See, too, these words on alcohol from Atlanta journalist Henry Grady, quoted repeatedly on the House floor: "It is the mortal enemy of peace and order. The despoiler of men, the terror of women, the cloud that shadows the face of children, the demon that has dug more graves and sent more souls unshrived to judgment than all the pestilences that have wasted life since God sent the plagues to Egypt, and all the wars that have been fought since Joshua stood beyond Jericho" (Henry W. Grady, "A Plea for Prohibition," in *The Complete Orations and Speeches of Henry W. Grady*, ed. Edwin DuBois Shurter [New York: Hinds, Noble & Eldredge, 1910], 128).

58. 52 Cong. Rec. (63d Cong., 3d Sess.) H607 (December 22, 1914) (statement of Rep. Richmond Hobson).

59. 52 Cong. Rec. (63d Cong., 3d Sess.) H497 (December 22, 1914) (statement of Rep. Philip Campbell).

60. 52 Cong. Rec. (63d Cong., 3d Sess.) H605 (December 22, 1914) (statement of Rep. Richmond Hobson).

61. 52 Cong. Rec. (63d Cong., 3d Sess.) H513, 514, 503 (December 22, 1914) (statements of Rep. Willis Hulings, Rep. Richmond Hobson, and Rep. M. Clyde Kelly).

62. 52 Cong. Rec. (63d Cong., 3d Sess.) H514, 536 (December 22, 1914) (statements of Rep. Richmond Hobson and Rep. Andrew Volstead).

63. *Proceedings, Fifteenth National Convention of the Anti-Saloon League of America* (Westerville, OH: American Issue, 1913), 89.

64. 52 Cong. Rec. (63d Cong., 3d Sess.) H504, 572, 569 (December 22, 1914) (statements of Rep. M. Clyde Kelly, Rep. James Bryan, and Rep. Percy Quin).

65. 52 Cong. Rec. (63d Cong., 3d Sess.) H526 (December 22, 1914) (statement of Rep. Daniel Garrett).

66. 52 Cong. Rec. (63d Cong., 3d Sess.) H497, 520, 555 (December 22, 1914) (statements of Rep. J. Campbell Cantrill, Rep. Oscar Underwood, and Rep. Andrew Barchfeld).
67. 52 Cong. Rec. (63d Cong., 3d Sess.) H542 (December 22, 1914) (statement of Rep. Robert Henry).
68. 52 Cong. Rec. (63d Cong., 3d Sess.) H544–45, 509 (December 22, 1914) (statements of Rep. Robert Henry and Rep. Charles Coady).
69. 52 Cong. Rec. (63d Cong., 3d Sess.) H588, 554 (December 22, 1914) (statements of Rep. Martin Morrison and Rep. Andrew Barchfeld).
70. 52 Cong. Rec. (63d Cong., 3d Sess.) H508 (December 22, 1914) (statement of Rep. Edward Pou).
71. 52 Cong. Rec. (63d Cong., 3d Sess.) H534, 535 (December 22, 1914) (statements of Julius Kahn and Rep. J. Hampton Moore).
72. 52 Cong. Rec. (63d Cong., 3d Sess.) H582, 535, 558 (December 22, 1914) (statements of Rep. James Gallivan, Rep. J. Hampton Moore, and Rep. Henry Vollmer).
73. 52 Cong. Rec. (63d Cong., 3d Sess.) H548, 506, 582 (December 22, 1914) (statements of Rep. Richard Bartholdt and Rep. Edward Pou; and a rereading of a portion of 1887 speech by Rep. Roger Q. Mills).
74. 52 Cong. Rec. (63d Cong., 3d Sess.) H562, 548 (December 22, 1914) (statements of Rep. James Buchanan and Rep. Richard Bartholdt).
75. 52 Cong. Rec. (63d Cong., 3d Sess.) H595, 539, 513 (December 22, 1914) (statements of Rep. John McKenzie, Rep. Caleb Powers, and Rep. Richmond Hobson).
76. 52 Cong. Rec. (63d Cong., 3d Sess.) H502 (December 22, 1914) (statement of Rep. Clyde Kelly).
77. 52 Cong. Rec. (63d Cong., 3d Sess.) H513 (December 22, 1914) (statement of Rep. Willis Hulings).
78. 52 Cong. Rec. (63d Cong., 3d Sess.) H536, 513, 529 (December 22, 1914) (statements of Rep. Francis Lindquist, Rep. Willis Hulings, and Rep. Edwin Webb).
79. John Strange quoted in *The Pabst Brewing Company: The History of an American Business*, by Thomas C. Cochran (New York: New York Univ. Press, 1948), 320.
80. *Baptist Observer*, May 1, 1924, quoted in *Citizen Klansmen: The Ku Klux Klan in Indiana, 1921–1928*, by Leonard J. Moore (Chapel Hill: Univ. of North Carolina, 1997), 35.
81. Merz, *The Dry Decade*, 211.
82. Mark Matthews quoted in *Deliver Us from Evil*, Clark, 199; and "Calls Prohibition a Complete Success," *New York Times*, November 26, 1925, 25.
83. "Find Sober Men Critical," *New York Times*, April 13, 1922, 11.
84. Warren G. Harding, "Second Annual Message," December 8, 1922, American Presidency Project, http://www.presidency.ucsb.edu/ws/?pid =29563.
85. H. L. Mencken, "The Perihelion of Prohibition," *Sydney Bulletin* (Australia), July 20, 1922, in his *A Mencken Chrestomathy*, 411–12.

86. H. L. Mencken, "Five Years of Prohibition," *American Mercury* 3, no. 4 (December 1924): 420.
87. Clarence Darrow, "The Ordeal of Prohibition," *American Mercury* 2, no. 8 (August 1924): 419–27.
88. Matthews quoted in *The Dry Years: Prohibition and Social Change in Washington*, by Norman H. Clark (Seattle: Univ. of Washington Press, 1988), 66, 208, 111.
89. Michael A. Lerner, *Dry Manhattan: Prohibition in New York City* (Cambridge, MA: Harvard Univ. Press, 2008), 113, 122, 177.
90. Percy Andreae, *The Prohibition Movement in Its Broader Bearings upon our Social, Commercial and Religious Liberties* (Chicago: Felix Mendelsohn, 1915), 10, 12, 10, 13.
91. Ralph Waldo Emerson, "The Conservative," lecture delivered at the Masonic Temple, Boston, December 9, 1841, Ralph Waldo Emerson Texts website, http://www.emersoncentral.com/conservative.htm.
92. Jefferson to John Adams, August 1, 1816, in *The Writings of Thomas Jefferson*, ed. H. A. Washington (Washington, DC: Taylor & Maury, 1854), 7:27.
93. Chandler Owen, "The Cabaret—A Useful Social Institution," *The Messenger*, August 1922, 461.
94. Horace M. Kallen, "Democracy Versus the Melting-Pot," *The Nation*, February 18 and 25, 1915, 190–94, 217–20.
95. Nicholas Murray Butler to "Fritz," September 4, 1928, quoted in *Dry Manhattan*, Lerner, 235; and Stephen S. Wise, "Ku Klux Klanism," *Reform Advocate*, October 22, 1921, 303.
96. Jones quoted in "Smith Overcoming Alabama Enemies," *New York Times*, October 7, 1928, E2.
97. Mencken, *A Mencken Chrestomathy*, 412.
98. Martha Bensley Bruère, *Does Prohibition Work?* (New York: Harper & Brothers, 1927), 282.
99. Clark, *Deliver Us from Evil*, 224.
100. Clark, *Deliver Us from Evil*, 176–78.
101. Merz, *The Dry Decade*, 220.
102. Rev. S. Parkes Cadman and Rev. Charles S. Macfarland quoted in *The Politics of Moral Behavior: Prohibition and Drug Abuse*, ed. K. Austin Kerr (Reading, MA: Addison-Wesley, 1973), 131.
103. "This *Is* Armageddon," *Christian Century*, March 1, 1933, 281.
104. Sabin quoted in "Four Women Lead Attack on Dry Law," *New York Times*, February 14, 1930, 18.
105. "Telegram from W. R. Hearst to E. J. Clapp," January 2, 1929, in *Brooklyn Standard Union*, January 30, 1929, 6. John D. Rockefeller Jr., a lifelong teetotaler who had previously contributed generously to the Anti-Saloon League, also turned against the Eighteenth Amendment. See "Text of Rockefeller's Letter to Dr. Butler," *New York Times*, June 7, 1932, 12.
106. Merz, *The Dry Decade*, 224.
107. Raskob quoted in "National Affairs: Raskob et Al.," *Time*, July 23, 1928, 9.

108. 52 Cong. Rec. (63d Cong., 3d Sess.) H548 (December 22, 1914) (statement of Rep. Richard Bartholdt).

109. Franklin D. Roosevelt, "187—Proclamation 2065—Repeal of the Eighteenth Amendment," December 5, 1933, American Presidency Project, http://www.presidency.ucsb.edu/ws/?pid=14570.

110. Mencken quoted in *Drink: A Cultural History of Alcohol*, by Iain Gately (New York: Penguin, 2008), 399.

111. "Harding Appeals for Party Unity and Rebukes Bloc," *New York Times*, February 12, 1922, 2.

112. Harding quoted in *New World Coming: The 1920s and the Making of Modern America*, by Nathan Miller (New York: Scribner, 2003), 65.

113. Fitzgerald quoted in *Sometimes Madness Is Wisdom: Zelda and Scott Fitzgerald: A Marriage*, by Kendall Taylor (New York: Ballantine Books, 2003), 62.

114. F. Scott Fitzgerald, *The Great Gatsby* (London: Urban Romantics, 2012), 18, 34.

115. Walter Lippmann, *Men of Destiny* (New York: Macmillan, 1927), 28.

116. Walter Lippmann, *A Preface to Morals* (New York: Macmillan, 1929), 51, 3.

117. Theodore Roosevelt, "On American Motherhood," March 13, 1905, National Center for Public Policy Research, http://www.nationalcenter.org /TRooseveltMotherhood.html.

118. Roosevelt to Richard M. Hurd, January 3, 1919, in *The Letters of Theodore Roosevelt*, ed. Elting E. Morison (Cambridge, MA: Harvard Univ. Press, 1951–54), 8:1422.

119. "Milestones: 1921–1936: The Immigration Act of 1924 (The Johnson-Reed Act)," U.S. Department of State, Office of the Historian, http:// history.state.gov/milestones/1921-1936/immigration-act.

120. Randolph S. Bourne, "Trans-national America," *The Atlantic*, July 1916, 86–97, http://www.theatlantic.com/magazine/archive/1916/07 /trans-national-america/304838/.

121. Wise, "Ku Klux Klanism," 303.

122. Kallen, "Democracy Versus the Melting-Pot," *The Nation*, February 25, 1915, 220.

123. Horace M. Kallen, "The Meaning of Americanism," *Immigrants in America Review* 1 (January 1916): 12–19.

124. Calvin Coolidge, "Address Before the American Legion Convention at Omaha, Nebraska," October 6, 1925, American Presidency Project, http://www.presidency.ucsb.edu/ws/?pid=438.

125. James A. Morone, *Hellfire Nation: The Politics of Sin in American History* (New Haven, CT: Yale Univ. Press, 2003), 311.

126. 52 Cong. Rec. (63d Cong., 3d Sess.) H555 (December 22, 1914) (statement of Rep. Andrew Barchfeld).

127. Anti-Saloon League and *New York World* quoted in *Last Call: The Rise and Fall of Prohibition*, by Daniel Okrent (New York: Scribner, 2010), 3.

128. Robert H. Wiebe, *The Search for Order, 1877–1920* (New York: Hill and Wang, 1967), 4.

CHAPTER 5: THE CONTEMPORARY CULTURE WARS

1. Patrick J. Buchanan, "The Aggressors in the Culture Wars," March 8, 2004, American Cause, http://www.theamericancause.org/patculturewars.htm.
2. On the "bad sixties," see Bernard von Bothmer, *Framing the Sixties: The Use and Abuse of a Decade from Ronald Reagan to George W. Bush* (Amherst: Univ. of Massachusetts Press, 2010).
3. Andrews quoted in Anthony Lewis, "Supreme Court Outlaws Official School Prayers in Regents Case Decision," *New York Times*, June 27, 1962, 16; Alexander Burnham, "Edict Is Called a Setback by Christian Clerics—Rabbis Praise It," *New York Times*, June 27, 1962, 17.
4. Carl McIntire, "Supreme Court on School Prayer," *Christian Beacon*, September 13, 1962, 1, 8, quoted in *God's Own Party: The Making of the Christian Right*, by Daniel K. Williams (New York: Oxford Univ. Press, 2010), 63.
5. W. Barry Garrett, "High Court Holds Abortion to Be 'A Right of Privacy,'" *Baptist Press Initial Reporting on Roe v. Wade*, January 31, 1973, http://thegospelcoalition.org/blogs/trevinwax/2010/05/06/baptist-press-initial-reporting-on-roe-v-wade; *Moody Monthly* quoted in Jonathan Dudley, *Broken Words: The Abuse of Science and Faith in American Politics* (New York: Crown, 2011), 45.
6. On "plain-folk" evangelicals in the Sunbelt, see Darren Dochuk, *From Bible Belt to Sunbelt: Plain-Folk Religion, Grassroots Politics, and the Rise of Evangelical Conservatism* (New York: W. W. Norton, 2010). For the prior consensus, see David O. Moberg, *The Great Reversal: Evangelism Versus Social Concern* (Philadelphia: J. B. Lippincott, 1972); and Joel Carpenter, *Revive Us Again: The Reawakening of American Fundamentalism* (New York: Oxford Univ. Press, 1997). The new consensus largely rejects this "great reversal" thesis, arguing that evangelical politicking was far more robust between the Scopes Trial and the 1970s. See, for example, Matthew Avery Sutton: *American Apocalypse: A History of Modern Evangelicalism* (Cambridge, MA: Harvard Univ. Press, 2014), xii–xiv. "Theirs was a politics of apocalypse," Sutton writes, and at its heart was this paradox: "the call to exercise influence in politics and culture as aggressively as possible while preparing the world for the oncoming apocalypse" (6, 39).
7. David Nevin and Robert E. Bills, *The Schools That Fear Built: Segregationist Academies in the South* (Washington, DC: Acropolis: 1976); Jerome C. Hafter and Peter M. Hoffman, "Segregation Academies and State Action," *Yale Law Journal* 82, no. 7 (June 1973): 1453. Between 1964 and 1969, private schools in the South saw a tenfold jump in enrollment. See James E. Ryan, "Brown, School Choice, and the Suburban Veto," *Virginia Law Review* 90, no. 6 (October 2004): 1637.
8. *Green v. Connally*, 309 F. Supp 1150 (1971).
9. "Slaps IRS for Aiding Biased Dixie Schools," *Chicago Defender*, February 8, 1971, 5.
10. "The Judicial Role in Attacking Racial Discrimination in Tax-Exempt Private Schools," *Harvard Law Review* 93, no. 2 (December 1979): 381.

11. National Election Statistics of the Center for Political Studies at the University of Michigan, cited in *God's Name in Vain: The Wrongs and Rights of Religion in Politics*, by Stephen L. Carter (New York: Basic, 2000), 46–47.
12. Weyrich quoted in *The Jesus Machine: How James Dobson, Focus on the Family, and Evangelical America Are Winning the Culture War*, by Dan Gilgoff (New York: St. Martin's Griffin, 2008), 79.
13. Grace Elizabeth Hale, *A Nation of Outsiders: How the White Middle Class Fell in Love with Rebellion in Postwar America* (New York: Oxford Univ. Press, 2011), 268.
14. Ralph Reed, *Active Faith: How Christians Are Changing the Soul of American Politics* (New York: Free Press, 1996), 105.
15. Ronald Reagan, "Private Schools" radio address drafted November 28, 1978, quoted in *Reagan, in His Own Hand*, eds. Kiron K. Skinner, Annelise Anderson, and Martin Anderson (New York: Free Press, 2001), 355.
16. Republican National Convention, "Political Party Platforms: Republican Party Platform of 1980," July 15, 1980, American Presidency Project, http://www.presidency.ucsb.edu/ws/?pid=25844.
17. Hale, *A Nation of Outsiders*, 237–76.
18. Billings quoted in "Christian Lobbyist at the Congress," *Journal-Champion*, March 23, 1979, 1.
19. Jerry Falwell, *Ministers and Marches* (Lynchburg, VA: Thomas Road Baptist Church, 1965), 2, 14, 7. "As far as the relationship of the church to the world," Falwell explained, "it can be expressed as simply as the three words which Paul gave Timothy—'preach the Word.' We have a message of redeeming grace through a crucified and risen Lord. This message is designed to go right to the heart of man and there meet his deep spiritual need. Nowhere are we commissioned to reform the externals. We are not told to wage wars against bootleggers, liquor stores, gamblers, murderers, prostitutes, racketeers, prejudiced persons or institutions, or any other existing evil as such. . . . I feel that we need to get off the streets and back into the pulpits and into our prayer rooms" (3, 17). Thanks to Matthew Sutton for providing me with a copy of this oddly hard-to-find document. See also "Advancing Through Prayer," in which Falwell criticized civil rights leaders for turning their back on the Bible: "The church has not been called to a political ministry of lobbying in Washington for any kind of legislation" (Falwell, "Advancing Through Prayer" [1964], unpublished sermon quoted in "Defending Manhood: Gender, Social Order and the Rise of the Christian Right in the South, 1965–1995," by Seth Dowland [Ph.D. thesis, Duke University, 2007], 132).
20. Jerry Falwell, "America—Back to God," quoted in *The Book of Jerry Falwell: Fundamentalist Language and Politics*, by Susan Friend Harding (Princeton, NJ: Princeton Univ. Press, 2001), 22; Jerry Falwell, *Listen, America!* (New York: Doubleday, 1980), 259; Falwell quoted in "A Disciplined, Charging Army," by Frances Fitzgerald, *New Yorker*, May 18, 1981, http://www.newyorker.com/magazine/1981/05/18/a-disciplined-charging-army; Falwell on *ABC Evening News*, July 7, 1980; and Falwell quoted in *All in the Family: The Realignment of American Democracy Since the 1960s*, by Robert O. Self (New York: Hill and Wang, 2012), 340.

21. Falwell, *Listen, America!*, 244, 19, 13.
22. Ronald Reagan, "Inaugural Address," January 20, 1981, American Presidency Project, http://www.presidency.ucsb.edu/ws/?pid=43130; Robertson quoted in Self, *All in the Family*, 346.
23. Concerned Women for America, "Mission Statement," 2015, http://www.cwfa.org/about/.
24. Howell Raines, "Reagan Backs Evangelicals in Their Political Activities," *New York Times*, August 23, 1980, 8.
25. "A Tide of Born-Again Politics," *Newsweek*, September 15, 1980, 36.
26. Francis Schaeffer, *The Complete Works of Francis Schaeffer* (Westchester, IL: Crossway, 1982), 5:142.
27. Falwell quoted in Craig Unger, *The Fall of the House of Bush* (New York: Scribner, 2007), 69.
28. Randall Balmer, *Thy Kingdom Come: How the Religious Right Distorts the Faith and Threatens America* (New York: Basic Books, 2007), 11. Here is how Balmer characterizes this "abortion myth": "These selfless, courageous leaders of the Religious Right, inspired by the opponents of slavery in the nineteenth century, trudged dutifully into battle in order to defend those innocent unborn children, newly endangered by the Supreme Court's misguided *Roe* decision" (12).
29. See Hale, *A Nation of Outsiders*, 270; and Southern Baptist Convention, "Resolution on Abortion," 1980, http://www.sbc.net/resolutions/amResolution.asp?ID=19. The SBC passed pro-choice resolutions in 1971 and 1974. This 1980 resolution called for legislation "prohibiting abortion except to save the life of the mother."
30. Balmer, *Thy Kingdom Come*, 16.
31. William C. Martin, *With God on Our Side: The Rise of the Religious Right in America* (New York: Broadway, 1996), 173.
32. Viguerie quoted in *Chain Reaction: The Impact of Race, Rights, and Taxes on American Politics*, by Thomas Byrne Edsall, with Mary D. Edsall (New York: W. W. Norton, 1992), 132. See also Grover Norquist: "The religious right did not get started in 1962 with prayer in school. And it didn't get started in '73 with *Roe v. Wade*. It started in '77 or '78 with the Carter administration's attack on Christian schools and radio stations. That's where all of the organization flowed out of. It was complete self-defense" (Dan Gilgoff, "Exclusive: Grover Norquist Gives Religious Conservatives Tough Love," *U.S. News & World Report*, June 11, 2009, http://www.usnews.com/news/blogs/god-and-country/2009/06/11/exclusive-grover-norquist-gives-religious-conservatives-tough-love). Scholarly discussions of the roots of the Religious Right in this "segregation academy" fight include Matthew D. Lassiter, "Inventing Family Values," and Joseph Crespino, "Civil Rights and the Religious Right," both in *Rightward Bound: Making America Conservative in the 1970s*, eds. Bruce Schulman and Julian E. Zelizer (Cambridge, MA: Harvard Univ. Press, 2008), 13–28, 90–105.
33. Robert Billings quoted in "Mobilizing the Moral Majority," *Conservative Digest*, August 1979, 14.

34. In a 1958 sermon, "Segregation or Integration—Which?" Falwell had promised to answer that question by recourse to "the Bible alone." The "Curse of Ham" had fallen upon his Ethiopian, Egyptian, and African descendants, he claimed. And "God's plan for the races" indicated that African Americans belong in Africa. In the activities of desegregationists, Falwell saw "the hand of Moscow" and the machinations of "the Devil himself." He affirmed separate but equal schools on the ground that "when God has drawn a line of distinction, we should not attempt to cross that line": "If Chief Justice Warren and his associates had known God's Word and had desired to do the Lord's will, I am quite confident that the 1954 [*Brown*] decision would never have been made." In a telling 1964 interview with the *Lynchburg News*, Falwell blasted the Civil Rights Act. "It is a terrible violation of human and property rights. It should be considered civil wrongs rather than civil rights," he said. Falwell also hosted on his *Old-Time Gospel Hour* such unrepentant segregationists as Alabama governor George Wallace and Georgia governor Lester Maddox. "We are trying to make everybody equal," he complained in a sermon in the late 1970s, but "God did not create us all equal. We are very unequal. God loves us equally, but every one of us is created unequal." See Jerry Falwell, "Segregation or Integration—Which?" *Word of Life* 1, no. 1 (October 1958): 1, 4; Jerry Falwell, *Strength for the Journey: An Autobiography* (New York: Pocket, 1988), 277; and Falwell quoted in *A Nation of Outsiders*, Hale, 264.
35. James Dobson quoted in "The Empire Built on Family Faith," by Laura Sessions Stepp, *Washington Post*, August 8, 1990, C3.
36. Self, *All in the Family*, 351.
37. Ronald Reagan, "A Time for Choosing," October 27, 1964, Ronald Reagan Presidential Library and Museum, http://www.reagan.utexas.edu/archives /reference/timechoosing.html.
38. Ron Reagan, *My Father at 100: A Memoir* (New York: Viking, 2011), 8.
39. *Bob Jones University v. United States*, 461 U.S. 574 (1983).
40. Ronald Reagan, "Interview with Managing Editors on Domestic Issues," December 3, 1981, American Presidency Project, http://www.presidency. ucsb.edu/ws/index.php?pid=43315; and Robert G. Kaiser, "On Welfare: Democrat Bullish, Republican Bearish (but Less Now)," *Washington Post*, October 23, 1980, A2.
41. Reagan quoted in *Washington Post*, February 14, 1977, A3.
42. Corey Robin, *The Reactionary Mind* (New York: Oxford Univ. Press, 2011), 107.
43. Richard John Neuhaus, *The Naked Public Square: Religion and Democracy in America* (Grand Rapids, MI: Eerdmans, 1984).
44. Robin, *The Reactionary Mind*, 104.
45. Ronald Reagan, "Remarks at the Annual Convention of the National Religious Broadcasters," January 31, 1983, American Presidency Project, http://www.presidency.ucsb.edu/ws/?pid=40550.
46. On this pivot, see Daniel T. Rodgers, *Age of Fracture* (Cambridge, MA: Harvard Univ. Press, 2011); Robert D. Putnam and David E. Campbell,

American Grace: How Religion Divides and Unites Us (New York: Simon & Schuster, 2010); Self, *All in the Family;* and Dowland, "Defending Manhood." All four read the contemporary culture wars as a fight over what Putnam and Campbell refer to as "sex and family issues" (387).

47. Paul VI, *Humanae Vitae,* July 25, 1968, Libreria Editrice Vaticana, http://www.vatican.va/holy_father/paul_vi/encyclicals/documents/hf _p-vi_enc_25071968_humanae-vitae_en.html.

48. Dowland, "Defending Manhood," 119.

49. Self, *All in the Family,* 357.

50. Abzug quoted in *All in the Family,* Self, 320.

51. Charles Reagan Wilson, *Baptized in Blood: The Religion of the Lost Cause, 1865–1920* (Athens: Univ. of Georgia Press, 1980).

52. Henry Steele Commager, "Religion and Politics in American History," in *Religion and Politics,* eds. James E. Wood Jr. (Waco, TX: Baylor Univ. Press, 1983), 52–54.

53. A. Bartlett Giametti, "A Liberal Education and the New Coercion," in his *A Free and Ordered Space: The Real World of the University* (New York: W. W. Norton, 1990), 109–17.

54. Giametti, "A Liberal Education and the New Coercion," 115.

55. Frederick Douglass, "Composite Nation," lecture, delivered in the Parker Fraternity Course, Boston, 1867, Library of Congress website, http://www.loc.gov/resource/mfd.22017/#seq-1.

56. In 1973, a review of women in popular U.S. history textbooks (most of them published in the 1960s) found far more absence than presence, though it did note some attention to the Seneca Falls Convention on women's rights of 1848, to the role played by Carry Nation and other women in the temperance movement, and to such notables as Harriet Beecher Stowe, Jane Addams, Dorothea Dix, and Frances Perkins. In 1982, a follow-up study found "a decade's progress" amid lingering stereotypes and continued neglect. By 1986, however, another study concluded that "the extent to which these textbooks have included the contributions of notable American women is nothing short of remarkable." Eleanor Roosevelt, for example, "appears in all the texts" and is depicted not only as "a full partner in her husband's political ambitions" but also "as a person in her own right, concerned for the unfortunate of the world, particularly minorities and women" (218, 220). See Janice Law Trecker, "Women in US History High School Textbooks," *International Review of Education* 19, no. 1 (1973): 133–39; Mary Kay Thompson Tetreault, "The Treatment of Women in U.S. History High School Textbooks: A Decade's Progress," *Women's Studies Quarterly* 10, no. 3 (Fall 1982): 40–44; and Mary Kay Thompson Tetreault, "Integrating Women's History: The Case of United States History High School Textbooks," *History Teacher* 19, no. 2 (February 1986): 211–62.

57. William J. Bennett, *To Reclaim a Legacy: A Report on the Humanities in Higher Education* (Washington, DC: National Endowment for the Humanities, 1984), 2, 1, 3, 4, 16, 29.

58. Bennett, *To Reclaim a Legacy,* 7, 9.

59. Bennett, *To Reclaim a Legacy,* 29, 7, 30, 29, 9.

60. Bennett, *To Reclaim a Legacy*, 30.
61. E. D. Hirsch Jr., *Cultural Literacy: What Every American Needs to Know* (Boston: Houghton Mifflin, 1987), 19.
62. Hirsch, *Cultural Literacy*, 1, xii, xvii, 2, 25, 23.
63. Allan Bloom, *The Closing of the American Mind* (New York: Simon & Schuster, 1987), 179.
64. Camille Paglia, "Ask Camille," *Salon*, July 1997, http://archive.today /s48CK.
65. Bloom, *The Closing of the American Mind*, 347, 25.
66. Albert O. Hirschman, *The Rhetoric of Reaction: Perversity, Futility, Jeopardy* (Cambridge, MA: Harvard Univ. Press, 1991), paraphrased in *The First Presidential Contest: 1796 and the Founding of American Democracy*, by Jeffrey L. Pasley (Lawrence: Univ. Press of Kansas, 2013), 240.
67. Bloom, *The Closing of the American Mind*, 239, 250.
68. Bloom, *The Closing of the American Mind*, 320, 322.
69. Bloom, *The Closing of the American Mind*, 344, 372.
70. Jonathan Z. Smith, "Jonathan Z. Smith on William J. Bennett's *To Reclaim a Legacy: A Report on the Humanities in Higher Education*," *American Journal of Education* 93, no. 4 (August 1985): 541–46.
71. Henry Louis Gates Jr., *Loose Canons: Notes on the Culture Wars* (New York: Oxford Univ. Press, 1993), 17, 35.
72. Robert Scholes, "Three Views of Education: Nostalgia, History, and Voodoo," *College English* 50, no. 3 (March 1988): 327.
73. *Multi-Cultural Literacy: Opening the American Mind*, eds. Rick Simonson and Scott Walker (St. Paul, MN: Graywolf, 1988), 191.
74. Norman Podhoretz, "How Can an Indictment of Liberalism Be a Best-Seller?" *Washington Post*, July 2, 1987, A21.
75. David Rieff, "The Colonel and the Professor," *Times Literary Supplement*, September 4, 1987, 950.
76. Robert Paul Wolff, review of *The Closing of the American Mind*, by Allan Bloom, *Academe* (September/October 1997): 64.
77. Benjamin R. Barber, "The Philosopher Despot: Allan Bloom's Elitism Agenda," *Harper's*, January 1988, 61–62.
78. Bloom, *The Closing of the American Mind*, 271.
79. Hirsch, *Cultural Literacy*, 18, 93.
80. Bloom, *The Closing of the American Mind*, 239.
81. Allan Bloom, *Giants and Dwarfs: Essays, 1960–1990* (New York: Simon & Schuster, 1990), 17.
82. The next flurry of "canon wars" books was even more partisan and polarizing. In *Tenured Radicals: How Politics Has Corrupted Our Higher Education* (New York: Harper & Row, 1990), *New Criterion* editor Roger Kimball reported from the front on "the assault on the canon" (1). What he found at academic conferences were "blatantly political" professors disseminating work that was "needlessly obscure, hopelessly trivial, or frankly at odds with the traditional purposes of humanistic study" (143). In *Illiberal Education: The Politics of Race and Sex on Campus* (New York: Free Press, 1991), Dinesh D'Souza reported from six college campuses,

speaking to students and professors and attending classes. Where others lauded curricular diversity, he found "a relentless, even fanatical, conformity of thought" (214). But his complaint about the "victim's revolution on campus" extended far beyond curricular matters, to the injustices of affirmative action in admissions and hiring, and the "bigotry, intolerance, and balkanization of campus life" (230).

83. Richard Bernstein, "In Dispute on Bias, Stanford Is Likely to Alter Western Culture Program," *New York Times*, January 19, 1988, A12.
84. Stanford University Committee on Undergraduate Studies, *Proposal Concerning the Area One Requirement: Cultures, Ideas and Values* (Stanford, CA: Stanford University, 1988).
85. William J. Bennett, "Why the West?" lecture at Stanford University, April 18, 1988, in Gilbert T. Sewall, *The Eighties: A Reader* (New York: Perseus, 1998), 276, 274, 279–80.
86. Colman McCarthy, "How the West Was Lost," *Washington Post*, May 1, 1988, 92.
87. George Will, "Stanford's Regression," *Washington Post*, May 1, 1988, 53.
88. Charles Krauthammer, "A Battle Lost at Stanford," *Washington Post*, April 22, 1988, A23.
89. Gertrude Himmelfarb, "Stanford and Duke Undercut Classical Values," *New York Times*, May 5, 1988, A31.
90. Ronald Takaki quoted in *Student Movements for Multiculturalism: Challenging the Curricular Color Line in Higher Education*, by David Yamane (Baltimore: Johns Hopkins Univ. Press, 2001), 93.
91. John Wallace quoted in "Huck Is Given a Reprieve in Fairfax Schools," by Mike Sager and Molly Moore, *Washington Post*, April 13, 1982, A1; Justin Kaplan, *Born to Trouble: One Hundred Years of Huckleberry Finn* (Washington, DC: Library of Congress, 1985), 19.
92. Arthur M. Schlesinger Jr., *The Disuniting of America: Reflections on a Multicultural Society* (New York: W. W. Norton, 1998), 107, 20, 147, 23.
93. Ronald Reagan, "Remarks at Memorial Day Ceremonies Honoring an Unknown Serviceman of the Vietnam Conflict," May 28, 1984, American Presidency Project, www.presidency.ucsb.edu/ws/?pid=39975.
94. "Vietnam Veterans Memorial," in *The American Bible: How Our Words Unite, Divide, and Define a Nation*, by Stephen Prothero (New York: HarperOne, 2012), 346–56.
95. Donald Wildmon, "Letter Concerning Serrano's *Piss Christ*," April 5, 1989, in *Culture Wars: Documents from the Recent Controversies in the Arts*, ed. Richard Bolton (New York: New Press, 1992), 27. Wildmon learned of this matter via a letter to the editor blasting the Virginia Museum of Fine Arts, which displayed *Piss Christ*, for "promoting and subsidizing hatred and intolerance." See Philip L. Smith, "'Appalled' by Photography on Display at Museum," *Richmond Times-Dispatch*, March 19, 1989, D6.
96. William H. Honan, "Artist Who Outraged Congress Lives amid Christian Symbols," *New York Times*, August 16, 1989, C20.
97. Patrick Buchanan, "Losing the War for America's Culture?" *Washington Times*, May 22, 1989.

98. D'Amato and Helms quoted in *Culture Wars*, Bolton, 28, 31–33, 30.
99. Armey quoted in *Art Matters: How the Culture Wars Changed America*, eds. Brian Wallis, Marianne Weems, and Philip Yenawine (New York: New York Univ. Press, 1999), 223.
100. Damien Casey, "Sacrifice, *Piss Christ*, and Liberal Excess," *Law, Text, Culture* 5, no. 1 (2000–2001): 20.
101. D'Amato, Helms, and the Helms amendment quoted in *Culture Wars*, Bolton, 28, 31, 73–74.
102. *Washington Times*, Henry Hyde, and Dan Coates quoted in *Culture Wars*, Bolton, 40, 192, 79.
103. Grenier, Jesse Helms, and Pat Buchanan quoted in *Culture Wars*, Bolton, 44–45, 78, 86.
104. Samuel Lipman, "Can We Save Culture?" *National Review*, August 26, 1991, 53.
105. Samuel Lipman, *Culture and Its Contents* (Washington, DC: Heritage Foundation, 1991), 3–4; and Lipman quoted in *Culture Wars*, Bolton, 217.
106. Lipman quoted in *Culture Wars*, Bolton, 218.
107. Rodgers, *Age of Fracture*; Lipman quoted in *Culture Wars*, Bolton, 219.
108. Gorton, Helms, and the American Family Association press release (July 25, 1989) quoted in *Culture Wars*, Bolton, 36, 101, 72.
109. Arthur Levitt Jr., "Top-Line Thinking at the NEA," *Wall Street Journal*, June 28, 1990, A14.
110. Kennedy, Allen Ginsberg, and Brustein quoted in *Culture Wars*, Bolton, 80, 92, 43.
111. "Background Information on Issues Related to the Reauthorization of the National Endowment for the Arts," September 1990, Digital Collections, Carnegie Mellon University Libraries, http://digitalcollections.library.cmu.edu/awweb/awarchive?type=file&item=414079.
112. Danforth quoted in *Culture Wars*, Bolton, 105. Art critic Robert Hughes made a similar point: "A grant for an exhibition of Gothic ivories could be pulled on the grounds that the material was offensive to Jews (much medieval art is anti-Semitic), to Muslims (what about those scenes of false prophets in hell with Muhammad?) or, for that matter, to atheists offended by the intrusion of religious propaganda into a museum" (Robert Hughes, "A Loony Parody of Cultural Democracy," *Time*, August 14, 1989, 82).
113. Brustein quoted in *Culture Wars*, Bolton, 90.
114. Moynihan quoted in *Culture Wars*, Bolton, 85.
115. Durland, Williams, and Sullivan quoted in *Culture Wars*, Bolton, 117, 266, 212.
116. Hale, *A Nation of Outsiders*.
117. William Dannemayer, "Christianity Under Attack by 'New Bigotry,'" *AFA Journal* (May 1990) in *Culture Wars*, Bolton, 229.
118. Andres Serrano, "Letter to the National Endowment for the Arts," July 8, 1989, in *Theories and Documents of Contemporary Art: A Sourcebook of Artists' Writings*, eds. Kristine Stiles and Peter Selz (Berkeley: Univ. of California Press, 1996), 280.

119. William H. Honan, "Congressional Anger Threatens Arts Endowment's Budget," *New York Times*, June 20, 1989, C15.

120. Andres Serrano to Hugh Southern, acting NEH chairman, July 8, 1989, in *Theories and Documents of Contemporary Art*, Stiles and Selz, 280. *Piss Christ* was part of a broader exploration by Serrano of bodily fluids and religious iconography. Earlier, he produced *Blood Cross* (1985), which depicted cow's blood in a Plexiglas cross, and *Milk Cross* (1987), a cruciform tank of milk floating in a sea of blood.

121. Frank Schaeffer article in *Rutherford Institute Journal* (January 1992), 9, quoted in "Position Paper on Blasphemy," by Gary North, March 1992, GaryNorth.com, http://www.garynorth.com/freebooks/docs/a_pdfs/newslet/position/9203.pdf.

122. Buchanan quoted in *Culture Wars*, Bolton, 186.

123. Jonathan Jones, "Andres Serrano's *Piss Christ* Is the Original Shock Art," *Guardian*, April 18, 2011, http://www.theguardian.com/artanddesign/2011/apr/18/andres-serrano-piss-christ-shock.

124. Lucy Lippard quoted in *Culture Wars*, Bolton, 201. See also Australian theologian Damien Casey, who calls *Piss Christ* "a profoundly religious work" (Casey, "Sacrifice, *Piss Christ*, and Liberal Excess," orig. date June 2000, Australian Catholic University website, http://dlibrary.acu.edu.au/staffhome/dacasey/Serrano.htm).

125. The Helms amendment quoted in "Supporters Vow to Save Compromise on Arts Endowment," by Martin Tolchin, *New York Times*, October 18, 1990, C17.

126. Wojnarowicz quoted in *Art Matters*, Wallis, Weems, and Yenawine, 76.

127. Barbara Gamarekian, "Ad Campaigns Join Battle over Arts Aid," *New York Times*, June 21, 1990, C22.

128. "Loudon Wainwright III and Philip Glass on NBC—1989," YouTube video, recorded from *Night Music* TV show, aired October 15, 1989, posted by "Goaitsen van der Vliet," August 15, 2007, https://www.youtube.com/watch?v=QcOpa4aHcSY.

129. Pat Robertson, Christian Coalition direct mail, October 25, 1989, in *Culture Wars*, Bolton, 124.

130. Gamarekian, "Ad Campaigns Join Battle over Arts Aid," C22.

131. Buchanan quoted in "Buchanan Turns to Quotas, Morality for Push in South," by Michael Ross, *Los Angeles Times*, February 28, 1992, http://articles.latimes.com/1992-02-28/news/mn-2958_1_buchanan-campaign. Marlon Riggs, the filmmaker behind *Tongues Untied*, saw in protests against his documentary "a brazen display of anti-gay bigotry," adding that "the persecution of racial and sexual difference is fast becoming the litmus test of true Republican leadership" (Marlon T. Riggs, "Meet the New Willie Horton," *New York Times*, March 6, 1992, A33).

132. Patrick J. Buchanan, "1992 Republican National Convention Speech," August 17, 1992, Patrick J. Buchanan website, http://buchanan.org/blog/1992-republican-national-convention-speech-148.

133. Ivins quoted in "Molly Ivins Is Dead at 62; Writer Skewered Politicians," by Katharine Q. Seelye, *New York Times*, February 1, 2007, B7.

134. Buchanan, "1992 Republican National Convention Speech."
135. Robison quoted in "Reagan Backs Evangelicals in Their Political Activities," by Howell Raines, *New York Times*, August 23, 1980, 8.
136. Legislation quoted in "The Mapplethorpe Censorship Controversy," by Margaret Quigley, n.d., Political Research Associates, http://www.publiceye.org/theocrat/Mapplethorpe_Chrono.html.
137. Patrick Buchanan, "Where a Wall Is Needed," *Washington Times*, November 22, 1989, in *Culture Wars*, Bolton, 138.
138. E. J. Dionne Jr., "Is Buchanan Courting Bias?" *Washington Post*, February 29, 1992, A12; and Susan Yoachum, "Buchanan Calls AIDS 'Retribution;' Gays Angered by His Bid to Win Bible Belt Votes," *San Francisco Chronicle*, February 28, 1992, 1.
139. Robertson quoted in *Culture Wars*, Bolton, 183.
140. 135 Cong. Rec. (101st Cong., 1st Sess.) S12967 (October 7, 1989) ("Amendment No. 153 in Disagreement," statement of Sen. Jesse Helms).
141. George H. W. Bush, "Address Accepting the Presidential Nomination at the Republican National Convention in New Orleans," August 18, 1988, American Presidency Project, http://www.presidency.ucsb.edu/ws/?pid=25955.
142. William J. Clinton, "Address Before a Joint Session of the Congress on the State of the Union," January 23, 1996, American Presidency Project, http://www.presidency.ucsb.edu/ws/?pid=53091; and William J. Clinton, "The President's Radio Address," December 18, 1999, American Presidency Project, http://www.presidency.ucsb.edu/ws/?pid=57098.
143. Terry quoted in "Religion Notes," by Ari L. Goldman, *New York Times*, October 24, 1992, 7.
144. Charles Colson, "Intimations of Insurrection," May 8, 1996, Breakpoint website, http://www.breakpoint.org/commentaries/5196-intimations-of-insurrection.
145. Various, "The End of Democracy? The Judicial Usurpation of Politics," *First Things*, November 1996, http://www.firstthings.com/article/1996/11/001-the-end-of-democracy-the-judicial-usurpation-of-politics. Many conservatives thought that the special issue in which these remarks ran was ill considered. "The extremist hysteria of the old counterculture of the '60s is back, this time under a conservative banner," wrote Norman Podhoretz, while David Brooks asked, "Is the Right about to go anti-American?" See Podhoretz's letter to Neuhaus, quoted in Podhoretz's contribution to "On the Future of Conservatism: A Symposium," *Commentary*, February 1997, reprinted in *The End of Democracy?: The Judicial Usurpation of Politics*, ed. Mitchell S. Muncy (Dallas: Spence Publishing, 1997), 101–2; and David Brooks, "The Right's Anti-American Temptation," *Weekly Standard*, November 10, 1996, http://www.weeklystandard.com/Content/Protected/Articles/000/000/007/934zgpid.asp?page=3.
146. Falwell fund-raising letter, December 1998, quoted in "Clinton, Conspiracism, and the Continuing Culture War," by Chip Berlet, *Public Eye* 13, no. 1 (Spring 1999): 15.

147. William J. Bennett, *The Death of Outrage: Bill Clinton and the Assault on American Ideals* (New York: Free Press, 1998), 10.

148. Alan M. Dershowitz, *Sexual McCarthyism: Clinton, Starr, and the Emerging Constitutional Crisis* (New York: Basic Books, 1998).

149. Gallup, "Presidential Approval Ratings—Bill Clinton," http://www.gallup.com/poll/116584/presidential-approval-ratings-bill-clinton.aspx.

150. "Letter to Conservatives by Paul M. Weyrich," February 16, 1999, National Center for Public Policy Research website, http://www.nationalcenter.org/Weyrich299.html.

151. Randall Terry, "Treachery in Our Midst?" *WND Commentary*, May 31, 1999, WorldNetDaily, http://mobile.wnd.com/1999/05/2776/.

152. Cal Thomas and Ed Dobson, *Blinded by Might: Can the Religious Right Save America?* (Grand Rapids, MI: Zondervan: 1999).

153. "Letter to Conservatives by Paul M. Weyrich," http://www.nationalcenter.org/Weyrich299.html.

154. Bush quoted in Frank Bruni, "Bush Tangles with McCain over Campaign Financing," *New York Times*, December 14, 1999, A24.

155. Ron Suskind, "Faith, Certainty and the Presidency of George W. Bush," *New York Times Magazine*, October 17, 2004, http://www.nytimes.com/2004/10/17/magazine/17BUSH.html?_r=0.

156. Bob Woodward, *Plan of Attack* (New York: Simon & Schuster, 2004), 421.

157. CNN, "Transcripts: Special Event: Gov. Bush: 'I'm a Uniter, Not a Divider,'" aired February 29, 2000, http://transcripts.cnn.com/TRANSCRIPTS/0002/29/se.01.html.

158. George W. Bush, "Remarks Prior to Discussions with Muslim Community Leaders and an Exchange with Reporters," September 26, 2001, American Presidency Project, http://www.presidency.ucsb.edu/ws/?pid=64877.

159. "'You Helped This Happen,'" partial transcript of comments from the Thursday, September 13, 2001, edition of the *700 Club*, Beliefnet, http://www.beliefnet.com/Faiths/Christianity/2001/09/You-Helped-This-Happen.aspx.

160. Gustav Niebuhr, "Muslim Group Seeks to Meet Billy Graham's Son," *New York Times*, November 20, 2001, B5.

161. Gayle White, "Pastors Back Vines' Comments on Islam," *Atlanta Journal-Constitution*, June 12, 2002, 3A.

162. "Lawmaker Tries to Explain Remark," *Washington Post*, November 21, 2001, A2.

163. Ann Coulter, "This Is War," *National Review Online*, September 13, 2001. *National Review* fired Coulter shortly after this column appeared and it is no longer available on its website.

164. Nick Natalicchio, "Robertson: 'Islam Is Not a Religion. It Is a Worldwide Political Movement Meant on Domination,'" Media Matters for America, June 12, 2007, http://mediamatters.org/research/2007/06/12/robertson-islam-is-not-a-religion-it-is-a-world/139073.

165. Rachel L. Swarns, "Congressman Criticizes Election of Muslim," *New York Times*, December 21, 2006, A31.

166. Rob Morlino, "Hannity Suggested Use of Quran in Representative's Swearing-In Same as Using 'Nazi Bible' *Mein Kampf*," Media Matters for America, December 1, 2006, http://mediamatters.org/research/2006 /12/01/hannity-suggested-use-of-quran-in-representativ/137441.

167. Ronald Reagan, "Inaugural Address," January 20, 1981, American Presidency Project, http://www.presidency.ucsb.edu/ws/?pid=43130; and Ronald Reagan "Remarks at the Annual Convention of the National Association of Evangelicals in Orlando, Florida," March 8, 1983, American Presidency Project, http://www.presidency.ucsb.edu/ws/?pid=41023.

168. Viguerie quoted in *God's Own Party*, Williams, 197.

169. Self, *All in the Family*, 369.

170. Cizik quoted in "Explaining McCain's Success Among Evangelicals," by Lester Feder, *Huffington Post*, January 20, 2008, http://www.huffingtonpost .com/lester-feder/explaining-mccains-succes_b_82378.html?.

171. Barack Obama, "Remarks at the National Prayer Breakfast," February 3, 2011, American Presidency Project, http://www.presidency.ucsb.edu/ws /?pid=88960.

172. Nugent quoted in "Nugent: Obama a 'Subhuman Mongrel,'" by Justin Sink, *The Hill*, January 22, 2014, http://thehill.com/video /administration/196156-nugent-obama-a-subhuman-mongrel; and "Pastor Steve Anderson Prays for Obama to Die," YouTube video, posted by "Imr892," August 22, 2009, https://www.youtube.com/watch ?v=a-qr6gxIHhQ.

173. According to a 2010 Pew Forum poll, the Tea Party is a religious party that shares with the Religious Right conservative policies on both economic and social issues. See Pew Research Center, "The Tea Party and Religion," February 23, 2011, http://www.pewforum.org/2011/02/23 /tea-party-and-religion/.

174. "Rep. Pittenger: President Obama Is Still 'Enemy Number One,'" *Charlotte Observer*, March 7, 2014, http://www.charlotteobserver.com/news /politics-government/article9102563.html.

175. "Klayman Calls for Non-Violent Revolution—World War II Memorial, Sunday, October 13, 2013," YouTube video, posted by "Freedom Watch, Inc.," October 17, 2013, https://www.youtube.com/watch ?v=OPNmf0RcFgc.

176. "Glenn Beck: 'Obama Has a Deep-Seated Hatred for White People,'" YouTube video, posted by "Greg Hengler," July 28, 2009, https://www .youtube.com/watch?v=MIZDnpPafaA.

177. Christopher S. Parker and Matt A. Barreto, *Change They Can't Believe In: The Tea Party and Reactionary Politics in America* (Princeton, NJ: Princeton Univ. Press, 2013), 51; and Pew Research Center, "Little Voter Discomfort with Romney's Mormon Religion," July 26, 2012, http://www .pewforum.org/2012/07/26/2012-romney-mormonism-obamas-religion/.

178. Waters quoted in "Moore Award Nominee," *The Dish* (blog), February 17, 2012, http://dish.andrewsullivan.com/2012/02/17/moo-2/; Weber quoted in "Malkin Award Nominee," *The Dish* (blog), January 28, 2014, http://dish.andrewsullivan.com/2014/01/28/malkin-award

-nominee-83/; and Fatima Najiy, "Allen West to Liberals, President Obama: 'Get the Hell Out of the United States of America,'" Think Progress, January 30, 2012, http://thinkprogress.org/politics/2012/01/30/414425 /allen-west-get-the-hell-out/.

179. Dan Balz and Jon Cohen, "Within Parties, Partisan Divides Are Deeper, Wider," *Washington Post*, August 19, 2012, A1. See also Pew Research Center, "Political Polarization in the American Public," June 12, 2014, http://www.people-press.org/2014/06/12/political-polarization-in-the -american-public/.

180. Michael Gerson, "Obama's Radical Power Grab on Health Care," *Washington Post*, January 30, 2012, http://www.washingtonpost.com/opinions /obamas-radical-power-grab-on-health-care/2012/01/30/gIQANB7XdQ _story.html; and Rebecca Shabad, "Republican Blasts Dem 'War on Whites,'" *The Hill*, August 4, 2014, http://thehill.com/blogs/blog-briefing -room/news/214245-republican-accuses-dems-of-launching-war-on -whites-in-border.

181. Brad Wilmouth, "Olbermann: Bin Laden's Driver Is 'Victim' of Bush Admin 'Urinating' on Constitution," Mission Research Center NewsBusters, August 8, 2008, http://newsbusters.org/blogs/brad -wilmouth/2008/08/08/olbermann-bin-laden-s-driver-victim-bush -admin-urinating-constitution; and Keith Olbermann, "Olbermann: If the Tea Party Wins, America Loses," NBCNews.com, October 27, 2010, http://www.nbcnews.com/id/39875964/ns/msnbc-countdown _with_keith_olbermann/t/olbermann-if-tea-party-wins-america-loses/# .UxydCfSwLhs.

182. Keith Olbermann, "Olbermann: Scott Brown Is a Racist, Teabagging, Ex-Nude Model," Real Clear Politics, January 19, 2010, http://www .realclearpolitics.com/video/2010/01/19/olbermann_scott_brown_is_a _racist_teabagging_ex-nude_model.html.

183. Thomas Frank, *What's the Matter with Kansas? How Conservatives Won the Heart of America* (New York: Metropolitan, 2004), 7.

184. Andrew Sullivan, "Here Comes the Groom: A (Conservative) Case for Gay Marriage," *New Republic*, August 28, 1989, http://www.newrepublic .com/article/79054/here-comes-the-groom.

185. *Boy Scouts of America v. Dale*, 530 U.S. 640 (2000).

186. James C. Dobson, "Marriage on the Ropes," Focus on the Family newsletter, September 2003, quoted in *God's Own Party*, Williams, 257.

187. Matt Sigl, "#82—Same Sex Marriage," *You Aught to Remember* (blog), October 11, 2009, http://youaughttoremember.blogspot.com/2009/10/82 -same-sex-marriage.html.

188. @NateSilver538, tweet, October 9, 2014, 4:31 p.m.

189. *Obergefell v. Hodges*, 576 U.S. (2015). Also in 2005, a Gallup poll found that 60 percent of Americans favored legalizing same-sex marriage, with 37 percent opposed. See Justin McCarthy, "Record-High 60% of Americans Support Same-Sex Marriage," Gallup, May 19, 2015, http://www .gallup.com/poll/183272/record-high-americans-support-sex-marriage .aspx.

CONCLUSION: WILL THE CULTURE WARS EVER END?

1. Robert O. Self, *All in the Family: The Realignment of American Democracy Since the 1960s* (New York: Hill and Wang, 2012), 398.
2. Pew Research Center, "America's Changing Religious Landscape," May 12, 2015, http://www.pewforum.org/2015/05/12/americas-changing-religious-landscape/.
3. Todd Gitlin, *The Twilight of Common Dreams: Why America Is Wracked by Culture Wars* (New York: Metropolitan, 1995), 235.
4. Wendy Wang, "For Young Adults, the Ideal Marriage Meets Reality," Pew Research Center, June 10, 2013, http://www.pewresearch.org/fact-tank/2013/07/10/for-young-adults-the-ideal-marriage-meets-reality/; Pew Research Center, "Roe v. Wade at 40: Most Oppose Overturning Abortion Decision," January 16, 2013, http://www.pewforum.org/2013/01/16/roe-v-wade-at-40/; and Pew Research Center, "Millennials in Adulthood," March 7, 2014, http://www.pewsocialtrends.org/files/2014/03/2014-03-07_generations-report-version-for-web.pdf.
5. "CNN Poll: Wide Divide over Abortion," *Political Ticker* (blog), March 6, 2014, http://politicalticker.blogs.cnn.com/2014/03/06/cnn-poll-wide-divide-over-abortion.
6. Pew Research Center, "Majority Now Supports Legalizing Marijuana," April 4, 2013, http://www.people-press.org/2013/04/04/majority-now-supports-legalizing-marijuana/.
7. MSNBC, "NBC News/Wall Street Journal Survey," April 26–30, 2015, http://msnbcmedia.msn.com/i/MSNBC/Sections/A_Politics/SECTION_More_Politics/V215179%20NBC-WSJ%20APRIL%20Poll%20(2).pdf.
8. Congregation for the Doctrine of the Faith, "Letter to the Bishops of the Catholic Church on the Pastoral Care of Homosexual Persons," October 1, 1986, http://www.vatican.va/roman_curia/congregations/cfaith/documents/rc_con_cfaith_doc_19861001_homosexual-persons_en.html; and John L. Allen Jr., "Pope on Homosexuals: 'Who Am I to Judge?'" *National Catholic Reporter*, July 29, 2013, http://ncronline.org/blogs/ncr-today/pope-homosexuals-who-am-i-judge.
9. Land and Moore quoted in "Evangelical Leader Preaches Pullback from Politics, Culture Wars," by Neil King Jr., *Wall Street Journal*, October 21, 2013, A1.
10. Ian Lovett, "After 37 Years of Trying to Change People's Sexual Orientation, Group Is to Disband," *New York Times*, June 20, 2013, http://www.nytimes.com/2013/06/21/us/group-that-promoted-curing-gays-ceases-operations.html.
11. Nathan Glazer, *We Are All Multiculturalists Now* (Cambridge, MA: Harvard Univ. Press, 1997).
12. James Livingston, *The World Turned Inside Out: American Thought and Culture at the End of the 20th Century* (Lanham, MD: Rowman & Littlefield, 2010), xv.
13. A 2008 Stanford study provides striking evidence of the multiculturalists' victory in secondary education. Researchers asked U.S. public high school

students to list the most "famous Americans" (excluding presidents). Their top-ten list included three white men (Benjamin Franklin, Thomas Edison, and Albert Einstein), but it began with three African Americans: Martin Luther King Jr., Rosa Parks, and Harriet Tubman. Rounding out the top ten were Susan B. Anthony, Amelia Earhart, Oprah Winfrey, and Marilyn Monroe. These results represent a total reversal from the 1950s, when textbooks "virtually ignored black Americans except in their faceless guise as slaves." See Sam Wineburg and Chauncey Monte-Sano, "'Famous Americans': The Changing Pantheon of American Heroes," *Journal of American History* 94, no. 4 (March 2008): 1186.

14. "Mayor Bloomberg Discusses the Landmarks Preservation Commission Vote on 45–47 Park Place," August 3, 2010, City of New York website, http://www1.nyc.gov/office-of-the-mayor/news/337-10/mayor-bloomberg-the-landmarks-preservation-commission-vote-45-47-park-place#/5.

15. Irving Kristol, "'Family Values'—Not a Political Issue," *Wall Street Journal*, December 7, 1992, A14.

16. Janny Scott, "At Appomattox in the Culture Wars," *New York Times*, May 25, 1997, http://www.nytimes.com/1997/05/25/weekinreview/at-appomattox-in-the-culture-wars.html.

17. Andrew Sullivan, "The Way We Live Now: 3-18-01; Life After Wartime," *New York Times Magazine*, March 18, 2001, SM15, http://www.nytimes.com/2001/03/18/magazine/the-way-we-live-now-3-18-01-life-after-wartime.html.

18. Andrew Hartman, *A War for the Soul of America: A History of the Culture Wars* (Chicago: Univ. of Chicago Press, 2015), 285.

19. Data on black voters appear in "Changing Face of America Helps Assure Obama Victory," Pew Research Center, November 7, 2012, http://www.people-press.org/2012/11/07/changing-face-of-america-helps-assure-obama-victory/.

20. Ta-Nehisi Coates, "Fear of a Black President," *The Atlantic*, August 22, 2012, http://www.theatlantic.com/magazine/archive/2012/09/fear-of-a-black-president/309064/.

21. One classic formulation is Daniel Bell, *The Cultural Contradictions of Capitalism* (New York: Basic Books, 1976).

22. Burke quoted in *The Reactionary Mind*, by Corey Robin (New York: Oxford Univ. Press, 2011), 13.

23. Ross Douthat, "The Terms of Our Surrender," *New York Times*, March 1, 2014, http://www.nytimes.com/2014/03/02/opinion/sunday/the-terms-of-our-surrender.html?. See also Matt K. Lewis, "The Culture War Is Over, and Conservatives Lost," *The Week*, January 3, 2013, http://theweek.com/article/index/238329/the-culture-war-is-over-and-conservatives-lost.

24. "John Boehner vs. America's Anti-Gay Marriage Crusaders," Narr. Stephen Colbert, *The Colbert Report*, aired October 8, 2014, Comedy Central, http://thecolbertreport.cc.com/videos/khi8w0/john-boehner-vs-america-s-anti-gay-marriage-crusaders.

25. Richard Hofstadter, "The Paranoid Style in American Politics," *Harper's*, November 1964, 82, 85.

26. George Will, "Candidate on a High Horse," *Washington Post*, April 15, 2008, A15.

27. Philip Jenkins, "The Paranoid Style in Liberal Politics," *American Conservative*, November 6, 2013, http://www.theamericanconservative.com /the-paranoid-style-in-liberal-politics/.

28. Falwell quoted in *A Nation of Outsiders: How the White Middle Class Fell in Love with Rebellion in Postwar America*, by Grace Elizabeth Hale (New York: Oxford Univ. Press, 2011), 268.

29. "Donald Trump Announces U.S. Presidential Run with Eccentric Speech," *The Guardian*, June 16, 2015, http://www.theguardian.com /us-news/2015/jun/16/donald-trump-announces-run-president.

30. Jeff Zeleny and Jim Rutenberg, "Romney Unleashes Attack with Gingrich Sole Target," *New York Times*, January 24, 2012, 1.

31. Public Religion Research Institute, "Survey: A Shifting Landscape: A Decade of Change in American Attitudes About Same-Sex Marriage and LGBT Issues," February 26, 2014, http://publicreligion.org /research/2014/02/2014-lgbt-survey/.

32. Pew Research Center, "'Nones' on the Rise," October 9, 2012, http:// www.pewforum.org/2012/10/09/nones-on-the-rise/.

33. Huckabee quoted in Tom LoBianco, "GOP 2016 Hopefuls Seek Footing on Marriage Ruling," CNN, June 26, 2015, www.cnn.com/2015/06/26 /politics/2016-candidates-gay-marriage-supreme-court/.

34. Douglas Laycock, "Religious Liberty and the Culture Wars," *University of Illinois Law Review* (June 4, 2014): 839, 879.

35. David Frum, "Why I Signed the Republican Brief Supporting Gay Marriage," *Daily Beast*, February 27, 2013, http://www.thedailybeast .com/articles/2013/02/27/david-frum-why-i-signed-the-republican-brief -supporting-gay-marriage.html.

36. Andrew Sullivan, "The Morning After in Arizona," *The Dish* (blog), February 27, 2014, http://dish.andrewsullivan.com/2014/02/27/the-morning -after-in-arizona/.

37. Patrick Henry, *Patrick Henry: Life, Correspondence and Speeches*, ed. William Wirt Henry (New York: Charles Scribner's Sons, 1891), 1:222.

38. Abraham Lincoln, "Inaugural Address," March 4, 1861, American Presidency Project, http://www.presidency.ucsb.edu/ws/?pid=25818.

39. John F. Kennedy, "1—Inaugural Address," January 20, 1961, American Presidency Project, http://www.presidency.ucsb.edu/ws/?pid=8032.

40. "Washington's Farewell Address 1796," Avalon Project, Yale Law School website, http://avalon.law.yale.edu/18th_century/washing.asp.

41. See Stephen Prothero, *The American Bible: How Our Words Unite, Divide, and Define a Nation* (New York: HarperOne, 2012).

INDEX